The Trials of Jeremiah Brandreth, William Turner, Isaac Ludlum, George Weightman, and Others, for High Treason: Under a Special Commission at Derby, On Thursday the 16Th, Friday the 17Th, Saturday the 18Th, Monday the 20Th, Tuesday the 21St, Wednesday the

William Brodie Gurney, Isaac Ludlum

Nabu Public Domain Reprints:

You are holding a reproduction of an original work published before 1923 that is in the public domain in the United States of America, and possibly other countries. You may freely copy and distribute this work as no entity (individual or corporate) has a copyright on the body of the work. This book may contain prior copyright references, and library stamps (as most of these works were scanned from library copies). These have been scanned and retained as part of the historical artifact.

This book may have occasional imperfections such as missing or blurred pages, poor pictures, errant marks, etc. that were either part of the original artifact, or were introduced by the scanning process. We believe this work is culturally important, and despite the imperfections, have elected to bring it back into print as part of our continuing commitment to the preservation of printed works worldwide. We appreciate your understanding of the imperfections in the preservation process, and hope you enjoy this valuable book.

[Entered at Stationers Hall.]

Printed by Luke Hansard & Sons,
near Lincoln's-Inn Fields, London.

THE TRIAL

OF

WILLIAM TURNER,

FOR

High Treason.

SPECIAL ASSIZE, DERBY,

Tuesday, 21st October 1817—(continued.)

REPLY.

Mr. ATTORNEY GENERAL.

May it please your Lordship,
Gentlemen of the Jury,

IT becomes now my duty to address to you, some observations in answer to those which have been made by my learned friends who are Counsel for the Prisoner; and also to make some observations upon the case as it has been proved on the part of the Crown, and remains totally and entirely unanswered by anything in the shape of evidence on the part of the Prisoner at the bar. Whether the observations that have been made to you; the ingenious observations that have been made by both my learned friends, shall do away a body of evidence, the truth of each and every part of which, I will venture to say, can upon no ground of solid reason be disputed, remains to be seen by the verdict that you shall hereafter give: a verdict which you are called upon to give by the common and ordinary duties imposed upon you as honest men—a verdict which you are called upon to give by the sacred and solemn obligation of that solemn appeal which you have made to your Maker, in the oath which you have taken—a verdict which you are called upon to give by that oath, not according to the observations which shall be made by my friends on the one side, or which shall be made by me on the other, but according to the evidence, so help you God.

Gentlemen, I should not occupy much of your time in commenting upon this case, but for some observations that have been made by my learned friends on the other side; no matter what my impressions may be upon the subject, for according to my impressions, you are not to decide; yet my impression being that the case is so strongly proved as almost to make it a waste of time to make many observations upon that which has been proved, I should take up very little of your time, but that I think it incumbent upon me for the sake of the Public, for the sake of the administration of the justice of the country, for the sake (if I may use the phrase) of the learned Judges who are sitting here, and least of all, which is of much less importance, than the other considerations, for my own sake as well as of my learned friends exercising our duty, (God knows as far as relates to myself, with little enough of talent to enable me to exercise it; but I hope I may say, with as much desire to do it with integrity, as any man who ever stood in the situation in which I am placed;) in justice to that character, am I called upon to make some observations in answer to what has fallen from my learned friend. Gentlemen, no man can very well answer for his wisdom; every man either can or ought to be able to answer for his integrity.

Gentlemen, my learned friends have addressed to you an observation upon the subject of the nature of the Court and of the Tribunal in which this Prisoner at the bar is tried; they have told you, that the Attorney and Solicitor General, with an array of Counsel, come down here, I think the phrase was, as it were to make or levy war upon these Prisoners, under a special commission, and that this is not conducted at the common and ordinary tribunal of the assizes, which are holden twice a year in this county;

why gentlemen, let it be recollected, and my learned friends should have recollected, that unless the proceeding were under a special commission, the trial of these men must have been postponed from the last assizes till the next; for that statute which has given the Prisoner the benefit and the right to the two Counsel who have been heard on his behalf by you, actually prevented, from its rules and regulations in favour of prisoners, these trials from being decided at the last assizes.

Gentlemen, a law which was passed immediately upon the glorious revolution in 1688, gives rights to a prisoner, which I thank God he has, however sometimes it may create inconvenience, personal inconvenience to persons who have to decide upon such cases. When a bill of indictment is found against a Prisoner, before he can be arraigned and desired to answer that indictment, he must have a copy of that indictment delivered to him above ten days previous to that arraignment; he must have an opportunity of having counsel assigned to him during the same period of time, to advise him as to the nature of his defence, and not merely to address the Jury in court, when he shall come to be tried; he must have a list of all and every witness it may peradventure be necessary to call against him, or any of those indicted with him, for the same period of time; he must have a list, with proper description of every gentleman of the jury, who may chance in the allotment of jurymen, after either side have exercised their right of objecting either with, (or without cause as far as relates to the Prisoner,) to come there. All these things must be done, and ought to be done for the benefit of the prisoner; let it be recollected, for it is for his benefit that that statute was passed; and these things make it absolutely impossible, without interfering with the ordinary justice and mode of proceeding in the country, to try the prisoner at the assizes, at which the bill of indictment is found, unless those assizes shall be adjourned over till after all the rest of the circuit is passed through. But gentlemen, that is not all; did ever man hear this sort of objection made before to the constitution of a court;

been proved upon his trial, and not by any thing which has been proved or said or done upon another trial. Gentlemen, my learned friends have said, that there has been management in the cause, in trying Brandreth first; and they suppose that we tried that man first, because in the course of the transaction an unfortunate event took place from the circumstance of its being committed by his, I mean Brandreth's hand, and that therefore we managed to bring that man first to trial who had been guilty of causing the death of one of his fellow subjects, in order that the jury who were to try him for treason, might be influenced by that act; and that then, if in consequence of that, the jury should find him guilty of that act, it might afford some prejudice in the minds of those other Gentlemen of the Jury, who might try other people as charged with the same crime of treason that he was charged with; Gentlemen, I beg leave utterly and absolutely to disclaim any such motive, intention, or purpose, or management. Brandreth was brought to trial first, because Brandreth was elected by those who were his co-conspirators and actors, the leader of the insurrection on that night; William Turner has been brought to trial second, because, I say, from the evidence, as it will appear to you he was, I might say, the next in command and leading to Brandreth; that however does not make the one man guilty of high treason more than the other, if all were conspiring together; do not you misunderstand me, when I am saying that as the separate challenges by the counsel, which they had a right to make, made it necessary for us to begin singly, and go on one by one, some selection was to be made, and I say, that the selection was the most right, the most correct, and the most proper, of bringing those first to trial who stood most prominent in the acting of the scene.

Gentlemen, I have made this observation to you, that Brandreth or William Turner, as the leaders and most prominent, are therefore not the most guilty of treason, if all conspired together, because as to those who act together in all bodies, some one or some certain number must necessarily take, as it were, the lead. Now, Gentlemen, I agree with my learned friends, that it does not follow that there may not be cases where men may be doing the same acts, and yet certainly may not have the same guilt; one may be perfectly innocent and the others completely guilty, doing the same acts. One of my friends put a case as to officers and soldiers, in the year 1745, and he asks, if any two officers or three officers of any of the King's regiments, or a whole body of officers of the King's regiments, had intended to go over to the side of the Pretender, to the Rebels, had done so, had led the men of their regiments to join the Pretender, when they, the men, thought they were obeying the commands of their officers for the purpose of supporting the cause of the King, though the leaders, he says, would be rebels and traitors, would the men? Oh no, God forbid; and why? because the men would not be acting with one common purpose that their leaders had; the men would be acting under the impression of loyalty to their King and Country; the officers would be acting, or at least those concerned together, in the common purpose of betraying their men into resistance to their King; one set would be completely guilty as traitors, and the other completely innocent, as men who had nothing to do with the purpose the officers themselves were intending; perhaps I am premature in making that observation, but it struck me at the moment, and I did not lose the opportunity of making it.

Now, Gentlemen, having said thus much upon the subject of the tribunal here constituted, and upon the subject of the selection and management, I will beg leave to state to you a few observations upon the law of this case. Gentlemen, my learned friends have put their case in this view, as it seems to me, that though here was outrage and riot and robbery (I do not use these expressions for the purpose of prejudicing the case, and I beg leave to be so understood) yet there was not high treason committed. One of my learned friends has said, it is difficult to say where riot ends, and where treason shall be said to begin; and, says he, I cannot tell you where the line is to be drawn. Now it may in some particular cases be difficult to draw the line upon the particular and immediate facts; but what is riot and what is treason, is, as a general proposition, as clearly defined by the law and by the construction that has been laid down by all the judges up to the present time, as a distinction between any two crimes can be: treason begins and exists when there is a conspiracy or common mind and intent to effectuate a general purpose, not of a particular and private and individual nature, by assembling together with force and arms for the purpose, by hostile force of effecting that general purpose; there treason begins and continues; that is, levying war against the King. One of my learned friends has said, that levying war, which is a phrase used by this statute, " if any one shall levy war against our Lord the King," is a mere question of fact; but before we come to the fact, surely we must ask this question, when we are told that if a man do levy war against the King, he is guilty of treason. What is levying war against the King? Some one must answer that question, and when it is answered, it should be answered by a general rule or rules of construction, settled and understood, handed down from time to time, to which as an authority all men may refer for the purpose of regulating their actions and their conduct. Now, Gentlemen, I beg leave to state, that there is no man in England or in the world, who more highly respects, venerates, and loves the constitution of the trial by jury than myself; but this I take leave to state, that if questions of serious law were to be a subject matter to be decided by gentlemen of the jury, the law would have no rules of certainty by which to regulate men's conduct, but must fluctuate according either to the wisdom or talent or notions of the different classes of His Majesty's subjects, who at different times may happen to be placed in the jury box. You twelve might think that the law was so and so; another twelve might think that the law was otherwise; a third twelve might be of a different opinion from you two; and instead of there being any rule, which is most important, by which men should regulate their actions, by which men should hereafter be judged, in case they have misconducted themselves in any way; instead of having any rule for the guide of all and each man's conduct, we should be in one chaos of confusion and uncertainty, and be reduced to that uncertain state from which this statute of Edward III. was meant to redeem us, by laying down as far as a statute can lay down a general rule; instead of leaving treason open to construction on this sort of conduct or the other sort of conduct, and confining it to those which are offences against the King.

Now what do I mean by offences against the King? not as it has been almost put to day, offences of hostility against the person of the King, for that statute which declares the levying war against the King to be treason; in a subsequent part takes the distinction, making treason both the offences which are against the King, meaning his person, and those which are against His Royal Majesty; for those very words are in the statute. In those days, as my learned friends know, the term Majesty was not applied to the King, I mean as to his person; the King of those days was not called His Majesty; "the Royal Majesty of the King" as used in the statute as distinct from his person, means his state, his dignity, his functions, as a component and essential part of the government and the constitution of the country.

Mr. Denman. Mr. Attorney, that is not so in my edition, there is nothing about the King's Royal Majesty in Lord Coke's transcript.

Mr. Attorney General. Then, Gentlemen, I will read it to you.—" When a man doth compass and imagine the death of the King, or of our Lady his Queen;" then " if a man do violate the King's companion," and so on, " or if a man do levy war against our Lord the King in his realm, or be adherent to the King's enemies in his realm, giving to them aid and comfort; if a man conterfeit the King's great or privy seal, or his money;" if a man do certain other things, such as kill the chancellor, and so on, in his place; " and it is to be understood, that in the cases above rehearsed (which includes them all) that ought to be judged treason which extends to our Lord the King and His Royal Majesty."

Mr. Denman. I beg your pardon, I thought you stated levying war against His Royal Majesty.

Mr. Attorney General. Gentlemen, my observation was this, that when the statute has stated the different treasons, such as compassing the death of the King; such as levying war against the King; such as slaying the King's chancellor, the King's privy councillors, or his judges, being in their office; it is declared to be the intention that all things above rehearsed, which do extend to our Lord the King and His Royal Majesty, which is the Royal Majesty of our Lord the King, shall be adjudged treason. Will any man tell me, that when men assemble with a hostile force to levy war, that war must be declared to be against the King's person, or that I need resort to that, which would be natural reasoning enough, that if it be intended against the King, it must be against his person. Now I say it is declared, that if the war be levied against the constitutional quality of the King in this country, as the King is the representative of the country, and the guardian of the laws, that being one of the main integral parts of the constitution and government of the country, it is as much war against our Lord the King, as if they published when they marched together, that they had an object to take the King's person to put him to death.

Gentlemen, what is the Government and Constitution? I do not mean the word government, as it is used in speaking in common parlance of the King's Ministers of the day; I use it, and always will, as the old sound legal discription of the constitution of the country; when our old proceedings were in Latin, "*gubernationem,*" was the constant term; and much as I love the constitution of my country, there are such vague, indefinite, strange constructions put upon that word, that I like to stick to the old word known to the common law, the government of the country as constituted by law. What is it, what has it been, with all its variations and imperfections, from the earliest times, so far as we can trace it; composed of the

King, the Lords Spiritual and Temporal, and Commons, in Parliament assembled; that is the Government of England, that became the Government of Great Britain upon the union of the two countries of Scotland and England; that has become, and still remains, the Government of the United Kingdom of Great Britain and Ireland upon the union of the two Parliaments; and God Almighty grant that it may ever continue so.

Gentlemen, as an integral part of that Government has the King always existed from the earliest period of the common law; and in the year 1688, let it be recollected, when the present Government and Constitution perhaps received its final polish (that is hardly the term), final perfection (as far as Government can be made perfect), the great and the wise men of that day still continued that blessed Constitution, though *they* made declarations wisely of certain rights which had not been properly ascertained or attended to. But the King, and the Lords Spiritual and Temporal and Commons in Parliament assembled, were the Government of England: now, I take the liberty to state this, that no man can levy war or conspire to levy war against any part of that Government without levying war against the King, who is a necessary integral component part, who is considered by the law and constitution of the kingdom, as in some degree pervading the whole.

Then, Gentlemen, if levying war is so used in the statute as that general term, that we must ask what is a levying war, who is to expound that, and how has it been expounded from the earliest times; perhaps I ought, indeed to make another observation upon the statute of Edward III, for my learned Friends know perfectly well one of the objects of that statute of Edward III was this; to take care to distinguish between offences against the Government and of a general nature; and the wars and quarrels, and riots and tumults, that in those early days took place between powerful individuals. Every man who knows the history of that statute, knows that in those and former days there were great Barons and persons in great power; the Lords Marchers for instance of Wales; the

Earls of Gloucester, and several others, whose names are mentioned in the books, who waged, what in common parlance may be called war, as far as giving battle went, as much as any war between two hostile states; and that though they had nothing but private quarrels amongst themselves, yet that still in those days, from the nature and extent of their proceedings, constructions had been put upon those acts, and they had been constituted, or at least decided to be, high treason. The statute therefore was passed to make nothing treason but acts of levying war against the King, and not war, to whatever extent of outrage it might be carried; that was only between two individuals.

Gentlemen, in conformity to that principle, whenever a question has arisen, as to whether acts that have been done amount to a levying war, not merely in times that have been spoken of by my learned Friends, the reigns of Charles the first and of Charles the second, but immediately after that glorious Revolution, which had in part of its contemplation the law of treason, and when was framed the statute which has given the Prisoner the advantage of my learned Friend's assistance by one of the greatest judges that ever lived (I speak of Lord Chief Justice Holt); by one who was himself an active cause of that Revolution, for I think he was a party to that Revolution; by one under whose eye that statute of the 7th King William was constructed, framed and passed. That learned judge, assisted by other judges certainly not more eminent, and, in the eye of mankind, not so eminent, though very likely equally wise as lawyers; that learned judge thus lays down the law:—" There may be a war levied without any design upon the King's person, or endangering of it, which, if actually levied, is high treason; as for example, if persons do assemble themselves, and act with force in opposition to some law which they think inconvenient, and hope thereby to get it repealed, this is a levying war and treason, though purposing and designing it is not so; so when they endeavour in great numbers, with force, to make some reformation of their own heads, without pursuing the methods of the law, that is a levying of war and treason; but the purposing and designing it is not so." In the 9th year of Queen Anne, little more than a year after the 7th of Queen Anne was past, further to regulate trials for treason, Lord Chief Justice Parker, to whom were associated Lord Chief Baron Ward and two other learned judges, in trying persons who were accused of high treason for assembling themselves with an armed force to pull down all meeting-houses, pronounced that the object being a general one to pull down *all* meeting-houses, that was a levying war against our Lord the King; and under his judgment, and under his statement to the jury, which never afterwards was gainsaid, were those men convicted and executed.

Mr. Denman. No, not executed.

Mr. Attorney General. They were convicted; true they were not executed; but that arose from no objection in point of law, but from the political reasons given by Sir Michael Foster. Gentlemen, from that period of time I defy my learned Friends to shew an instance in which that law has been ever disputed by any learned judge who has been called upon to pronounce an opinion.

Gentlemen, let us come to later times. You have heard the name of Sir Michael Foster mentioned to you, who was one of the greatest and the wisest judges, and as much a friend to liberty as any man in this country; he, anxious and desirous that the law of treason should be well understood, has certainly written and stated one of the ablest discourses upon that crime that ever was penned by man. It was said the other day, it was only the production of a man in his closet; it *was* the production of a man in his closet; and if it had not been adopted by subsequent judges, or had ever been quarrelled with by subsequent judges, I would not have stated it, for this reason; that however wise a man may be in his closet, the law is to be taken from the judges acting in their judicial character; but his doctrine on this subject having been repeated by every judge who has ever presided on a charge of treason since, I say, it is not to be undervalued because it was the production of a man in his closet, but on the contrary, coming from such a man, and sanctioned by the judicial opinion of men sitting in their places in judgment; it does, in my mind, derive additional force from that circumstance. It was the wise composition of a wise man exercising a judicial function himself, who had formed his opinions from a long course of study and of wisdom, and who gave to the world this discourse. He perhaps might be too modest a man to think so, but I take leave to state, gave to the world this discourse as one of the most beneficial gifts that he could bestow upon them on such a subject. He states as the law, that all risings, all insurrections with a hostile force, for any general object, such as the pulling down all inclosures, the pulling down all meeting-houses, and so on, is a levying of war against the King.

Gentlemen, there is another case which I met with in a book, compiled by a learned gentleman, whose authority I do not cite, but as giving you the case from the manuscript notes of Mr. Justice Yates, as great a judge as ever lived. Mr. East has mentioned a case decided on the northern circuit, in page 76 of his book on criminal law, in which, before Mr. Justice Bathurst, and another learned judge, an armed assembly, for the purpose of resisting the general militia laws by force and arms, was holden to be high treason, in levying war against the King, and under that authority the persons accused, were convicted and executed in two of the northern counties; and why? because the assembling in hostile array, and with hostile force, against any general body of laws, is an insurrection against the Government of the country: and that Government being composed as an integral part of our Soverign Lord the King, it is a levying war under the statute of Edward III against the King.

Gentlemen, since that time the law has been laid down in the same manner by all the Judges; and I will venture to say without dispute. My Lord George Gordon was tried for high treason; he was charged with levying war—what was it? the way it was to be made out, was by shewing that he had assembled a large number of persons together; for what purpose? for the purpose by the extent of their numbers, of going down and overawing the Parliament; for that was the way it was attempted to be made out. Lord George Gordon was acquitted; why? not because if that was the intent and object with which he assembled them together, and he heading them and regulating their proceedings had that in view, he had not been guilty of high treason; no, but that it was not made out to the satisfaction of the jury, that he did intend that those persons whose petitions he presented, should by force and by numbers overawe the Parliament. No person disputed, that if those persons did go down for the purpose of overawing the Parliament, and obliging them to repeal a particular bill, it was levying war against the King.

Gentlemen, I will not occupy more of your time by stating my opinions of the law, only concluding my observations upon that subject, with this particular request; my learned friends have stated their notions, I have been bound to state mine; we differ in our statements; trust neither of us: not because you do not believe our integrity, but because you may think our understandings upon the subject may be incorrect; take the law from whence, by the constitution of this country, the law in point of direction ought to come; hear it from the learned judges who in stating the law to you, are not only enlightened by reading and by wisdom upon the subject; but if it were possible to suppose they could want any additional sanction or motive, to the sound and solid integrity of their own minds, you will recollect are acting under the sacred obligation of an oath, to deliver you the law, just as much as you are acting under the sacred obligation of an oath, to find your verdict according to the law and to the evidence.

Now Gentlemen, having stated that, let me come to the particular facts of this case: Gentlemen, if a number of persons assemble themselves together, arming themselves and intending by armed force to effectuate a general object, much more when that general object is to destroy the Government and Constitution of the country, that is high treason; every man who acts with them for the purpose, (always recollect) in the effecting that common object and intent, is guilty of high treason, whether he was party to the original conspiracy when first laid; whether he comes in at one period of the time or at another, if he is cognizant of their intention; if his intention is the same with theirs; if he acts with them in furtherance of the design, more or less, each performing the different parts which fall to men in any general transaction, he is guilty of treason.

Now let us see these facts; facts uncontradicted, and facts that might have been contradicted, if they had been capable of contradiction; and when I come to state them to you shortly, which I will do, for the narrative of these proceedings consists only certainly in two days; let me ask, whether any human being can doubt that the case is made out on the part of the Crown. Here is a meeting on the 8th of June, at the White Horse at Pentridge; the persons who are there, from that which passed amongst them, could not have met by accident; how came the map there; was that by accident? I am speaking now of Brandreth, sitting with a map at that meeting. William Turner makes his appearance there; was he there by accident? was it by accident he asked for a return of arms from the different parishes and places to which he did not himself belong? was it by accident, and only by accident, that he produced a return of arms from Southwingfield, the parish to which he did belong?—was it by accident, and accident alone, that he reproached the others for not being so forward as the Southwingfield men were? or was it not that he brought himself there in consequence of something understood between them, that there they were to meet at that time for the purpose of arranging the order of their march, and the disposition of their proceedings on the following night when the insurrection was to take place; then there they were with the purpose of having arms—was that by accident? I would ask another question, as to those pikes which he spoke of, that were to be found in a stone quarry; were all these things by accident at an inadvertent meeting; or do they not mark a settled previously concerted plan which was soon to come into action, and the particular details of which were to be made at that time to the different persons who were there?

My learned Friends have made some reflections on the different witnesses who have proved these facts, Martin and Asbury, they say they are accomplices and not to be believed on their oaths. I beg leave to say they were not accomplices. If you ask me whether, if I had been at that meeting, or if they ask whether you, Gentlemen, would not have gone immediately to magistrates, if you had been at such a meeting; you or I would have gone immediately and given notice; but you are not to say, that men of that class in life are not to be believed, because they do not act with the same firmness and the same decision upon such an occasion as we should act; that is not the fair way of trying the conduct of mankind. These men, too, heard what was said upon the subject of what was to be done with those who should go and disclose any thing that passed at that meeting, at the White Horse; and give me leave to say, that though perhaps it ought not to operate upon men's minds, yet we are not to say they are accomplices, and not to be believed, because upon an impression of fear, they did not go immediately and disclose what they knew.

But here is another observation made upon these men: they were special constables; they had been sworn in by Mr. Goodwin to be special constables a day or two before; they did not then know it was their duty, as special constables, immediately to inform a magistrate. Now, I think that man gave an extremely sensible answer upon that; it is not the answer I should have given, because I have read the law books upon the subject of the duties of constables. I do not apprehend these men had ever read such treatises; but they had got a general impression which I will venture to say is an impression with much more enlightened men than themselves, that a special constable is only sworn in for the purpose of assisting, in case there should be any riot or tumult. Why, Gentlemen, they were right in supposing that to be the general object of swearing in special constables; and therefore, say the men, I did not know, that as special constable, I had any duty but to act in case of riot or tumult. But I would ask, was there no meeting at the White Horse; was the company not changed from time to time; was it so, or was it not? I will tell you whom we could have in one moment, if it was not so; Mrs. Weightman, the mother of one of the persons indicted, could tell you if it was a fabrication. They cannot say, that upon this trial they did not know what was to be proved; for they heard these facts proved in the trial of Brandreth, and knew who the witnesses were to be, if Mrs. Weightman did not say that which has been stated when these men were in the kitchen, to the men in the parlour; for you recollect what Asbury said was this, that, when he went there with Elsden, they went into the kitchen; Mrs. Weightman went to the parlour, and said, there were two Butterley men, might they come in; and that the answer was, "Yes; the two Butterley men may come in;" there is no contradiction to this. Then they go there, and they have told you that which might have been contradicted by God knows how many people, if not true. What was the declaration, what was the conversation, what was the conduct, when they were there? Now, did William Turner know what the object was when he brought the returns of the arms he had collected at Southwingfield; when he reproached the others that they were not equally forward; when the conversation was stated from time to time as the company varied, that the object was a revolution, that the object was to act against the Government of the country?

Gentlemen, there is another observation not unimportant with respect to those verses; I do not mean to say that they are very poetical; but we must not treat with indifference the writings of men because they are not learned. These lines are written not merely under the impression of distress for bread. I know the constitution of human nature, that when there are to be risings or insurrections, couplets and songs, and poetry, good or bad, always have been used for the purpose of infusing the general notions into the minds of others, and keeping them in a sort of harmony together: the Marsellois Hymn and the Caira tune were powerful auxiliaries towards the destruction and demolition of the French government Gentlemen, what are these lines:—

" Every man his skill must try,
He must turn out and not deny."

Mark how these words, and the lesson which is read by these lines, was verified by the acts that took place on the night of the 9th of June :—

" Every man his skill must try,
He must turn out and not deny.
No bloody soldiers must he dread;
He must turn out and fight for bread.
The time is come you plainly see,
When government opposed must be."

" No bloody soldier must he dread;"—he must have no fears, when this government is to be overturned, of any of those forces, whether they happen to be of the King's forces or of the yeomanry, or any other in the shape of military; he must have no fear of those called out to oppose him: no; the time is come when every man must try his skill—when every man must exert his courage, and try his skill and his courage, when the government and constitution of the country must be opposed. I say, no man of common sense can put any other sense upon any line or any word of that paper. Does that, or does it not, mark an intention to make war against the government of the country?

Gentlemen, it is extremely important to consider how that which was then stated to be the plan to be adopted the next night, was acted upon the next night; because, if they attack the evidence of Martin and Asbury, the acting on the plan the next night is proved by witnesses upon whose credit I defy them to throw the slightest degree of aspersion. The map was marked; they were to assemble at Hunt's Barn; some of them (the Southwingfield people) were to be in readiness; and that which is extremely important to be considered, there was one function that they intended to perform; I thank God they did not; which was to " kill their own vermin;" " each parish to kill their own vermin;" what that vermin was, they have left us in no doubt about; certainly it was, that there were certain persons who were to be taken off, because those persons were supposed to be in hostility to them; and being of an higher order of people, were the most likely to act with vigour against their plans.

Gentlemen, then Brandreth pointed out upon the map or plan, which way they were to march, and so on, on the 9th of June. William Turner is found at Hunt's Barn; William Turner, armed with a gun; William Turner marches with Brandreth, and with that particular party from Hunt's Barn to Mr. Hardwick's, to Topham's Close, to Mr. Walker's, to Samuel Hunt's, to Mary Hepworth's, I shall make an observation upon that presently—to Samuel Fletcher's, and last of all, let it be recollected, in that line of march, to John Storer's. Gentlemen, if he sets out with them with a gun, and marches with them with a gun, whether he may be, as Thomas Turner said, and I dare say that young man truly said; whether he might be within three yards or six yards of one man at one time, or another man at another time no matter, every man cannot be at the same time in the different places; but whatever his relative position in the body, if he acted with the whole body, it matters not; he is with them there all the time; and there is one important observation which I will make now, though rather out of order, lest I should forget it, that William Turner is proved to have marched by the side of the ranks more in the quality of an officer than of a common man in the ranks, for a reason which I did not know, till a witness whom they called had proved it. Recollect, this Brandreth at one period of the transaction, desires to know who had been soldiers, or who had been in the militia, that they may turn out and help to form the men; from that period, William Turner, though I do not mean to say he answered as a soldier, acted as an officer by marching at the side of the ranks, and sometimes at the head of them with Brandreth; why the witness they have called to give him a character, has proved that he had been *a soldier.*

Gentlemen, when they went to Mrs. Hepworth's, there took place that unfortunate event of which you have heard. Now, Gentlemen, I beg leave to state to you what I have stated before, and what was stated by my learned friend the Solicitor General, that except so far as it marks their intention, you are to try this case, whether high treason or not, precisely the same as if no human being had fallen in consequence of that gun having been fired; you are not to convict this man of high treason because his companions were guilty of murder, nor ought you to convict him of high treason even if he committed that act himself; but there he was at the time this act was done; he knew it had been done, and I mention that circumstance for this reason, that he holds out that act—uses it, not as was put by Mr. Denman, as a warning to others, that is to say, as a warning for them not to come into mischief; he does put it as a warning, but a warning in the shape of a mighty threat, " The captain has shot one man at Mrs. Hepworth's, and you will be shot if you do not go." Is that warning a man from mischief, or is it not warning a man, Mark me, Sir, I call upon you to do such and such an act, and I warn you if it is not done, you will be shot; and that my learned Friend calls a friendly warning, arising from the charity of the prisoner's disposition. I say no; it was a ferocious threat, instead of a friendly warning; and it was, as was put by my learned friend the Solicitor General, not a lamentation but an adoption of the act done by Brandreth, for the purpose of forwarding, through the medium of the terror of that act, the object they had in view.

Gentlemen, the object they had in view, which was opposing and levying war against the Government, was to be effected by another means, which I take leave to state, marks the common design; was it merely that a certain number of persons, ready to make a riot for bread, or anything else, were to go on in that intention? no, but that all the persons who had no such intention, who were easy in their circumstances, who had families to attach them to their homes, who had an interest in the stability of their country; all those persons who were willing and contented to live under the laws of their country, were to be forced; were to be made rebels also, by force of arms; they were to be obliged to commit acts, subjecting them to the laws of their country, in order to enable these men to effectuate their abominable and wicked purpose. Good God, can any man describe this as a mere ebullition of a riotous disposition of deluded people; oh no; it shews a deep and serious purpose, (whether they had means to effectuate it or not,) to levy war; to raise men for the purpose of levying war against the King; aye, and to force into their ranks even those who were unwilling to join in any such purpose; Gentlemen, let it not be forgotten, that where they could not get the father to go, there they got the son: never let it be forgotten that their object was not merely to have a gun, but a gun and a man from every house; in some places they did not take the man. In my opinion, your countrymen did themselves infinite honour in resisting the sort of attack made upon them; it does them infinite honour, not only as courageous men, but infinitely more honour in point of goodness, and adhesion to the laws and constitution of their country.

Gentlemen, here again I cannot help making an observation, when I speak of Elijah Hall, the very case to illustrate the observation of my learned friend, as to the rebellion in 1745, and his question, " would you say that all who were acting were guilty?" No, certainly not. I will put the case of Elijah Hall, and of Mr. Hole and others, they had guns on their shoulders, but were they guilty? no certainly not; because they had not the same intent and purpose; their bodies were carried along with the traitors, but their minds were abhorent of that which they were about, and they made their escape as soon as they could.

Then Gentlemen, after having gone through a great many places, and I merely mention a great many places, as shewing the deliberate plan and line of march and course intended to be pursued, of taking guns from the persons in Southwingfield, and that there was hardly a house they missed in their line of march; for this reason, that they were extremely correct there in their account of arms: who had made them so? William Turner, who produced a return of all the arms in Southwingfield, on Sunday the 8th, in order that they might be taken on Monday the 9th, in their march.

Now, Gentlemen, we come to Mr. Storer's. Let us see who came to Mr. Storer's, William Turner; he was the man who headed that party at first at Mr. Storer's, whilst Brandreth and some part of the party were doing something at one house, other parties were doing something at another house. Who headed them at Mr. Storer's? William Turner, who was one of the persons who addressed Mr. Storer; William Turner, who was the person who talked about the revolution, and about the regaining liberty and the destruction of tyranny; I am not sure whether those words came from the mouth of William Turner; but it was in his presence, while acting as the captain of that particular party, that those expressions were used; it was, at Mr. Storer's, that they were told they should be shot if they did not comply, and he acquainted Brandreth that Mr. Storer would not go. Why then, do my learned friends mean to say, that William Turner was in the situation of a soldier in the rebel army misled by his officer? No, he was acting in equally a prominent situation with Brandreth, only with this difference, some one must take the lead, and he, from the evidence, was acting as one of the seconds in the command upon that occasion.

But, Gentlemen, let us come to an important conversation, namely, what passed at Mr. Raynor's; but before that, you will recollect, that they went to the premises of Mr. Sterland, and marched into the barn, and found three men, whom they forced to join them. Who was one of the persons who went to this barn? William Turner is one of the most active partizans throughout the whole course of the transaction.

Then, Gentlemen, we come to Mr. Raynor's. At Mr. Raynor's house, William Turner was the first man who entered the house; he had a gun in his hand; he presented his gun at him, and said, what? a friendly warning? you had better go, because we have shot one man; no, this was his friendly warning, " damn your eyes, turn out;" he cocked his gun; the prisoner says, and he should have the benefit of all he says, the gun was not cocked. Now, Gentlemen, whether Mr. Raynor may or may not be mistaken in the fact of the prisoner's cocking his gun; but supposing that he did not cock it, whether he did or not makes no difference upon earth in the question we are trying; for if he was there and said, damn your eyes turn out, and insisted upon his turning out and joining their party; If as Mr. Raynor says, he told him to remember they had shot one, and he should be the other, what signifies whether he cocked his gun or not, or pretended to do it. " I told him I should not go; he jobbed me several times in the side with his gun," says Mr. Raynor; and then Mr. Raynor's gun was handed down from the joists of the room where it was; and then the prisoner, William Turner, charged that gun of Mr. Raynor's, and several other guns were charged at that time, then it was, that in the presence of William Turner, and I think by him the declaration was made, that they were going to wipe of the national debt and begin again; that they were marching upon Nottingham, they said. Now, Gentlemen, here is an important fact, they had half-an-hour to spare, and they would halt at his house; Gentlemen, you observe in the outset of the proceeding they were to have got to Nottingham forest by two in the morning; before they got to Nottingham forest that hour had expired, and you will naturally ask how came they to have time to halt. They had sent George Weightman to Nottingham for intelligence. George Weightman was to meet them at Langley

Mill. Mr. Raynor's house was shortly before they came to Langley Mill. George Weightman had not had time to come back to Langley Mill. Mr. Raynor's house was the last house before they got to Langley Mill, and therefore they had half-an-hour to wait; then Mr. Raynor says, that four or five pitch forks were taken from his house; fifty men came into his house, and his servant James Raynor, went with them, being compelled to go.

Gentlemen, I will now allude shortly to that which passed at Nottingham. You will be pleased to recollect that declarations were made by different persons in the course of the transaction to different people, that they had better go, for if they did not, there would a cloud from the north come down next day; they expected a general rising in the country; Nottingham was to be the head point, and this party were marching to Nottingham, expecting to be joined there. What was going on on that very night at Nottingham? it has been proved by Captain Philips that there was much agitation at Nottingham. Mr. Roper has proved to you, that on Nottingham Forest at twelve o'clock at night there was an assembly of a hundred men with poles, whether with pikes I care not; and those hundred men, at the only house at which we can trace them, namely, at Mr. Roper's, which is a lone house, came for the express purpose of demanding arms, in the same way as the men at Pentridge and at South-wingfield had done. Then, Gentlemen, I say, every thing stated by Martin and by Asbury is confirmed by witnesses against whom I defy them to cast the least imputation. Martin and Asbury have told you in a most natural way, the delineation and the detail of the plan at the White Horse at Pentridge: and every witness I have called has proved that every thing which the conspirators said they intended to do, they did do, nay, that there were preparations by persons in Nottingham Forest ready to receive these people when they should get to Nottingham Forest.

Gentlemen, I really ought to apologize to you for having taken up so much of your time, but it is my duty not to omit any observations that occur to me in the course of the progress of the statement I have made to you. Gentlemen, I agree with my learned friends that it is a most important consideration for the Public and for the Prisoner at the bar. No jurymen can ever, upon any occasion, be put into a jury-box to decide upon a crime punishable with loss of life, without feeling that he is put into a situation in which he is called upon by the duties he has to perform in society, which if he could exercise his will upon the subject he would willingly avoid; but it is a duty cast upon every man in his turn, and each man must perform it, and each man must and ought, and I am sure you will perform it, by considering calmly, deliberately, temperately, dispassionately, and yet firmly, what the case has been as proved before you. If I am correct in the statement I have made of the law, have you any doubt of the truth of the facts which have been proved? If you have not, what verdict, according to the evidence, can you give? You must either disbelieve the evidence, or the evidence proves the case; and I do really think (but what I think matters not, as I have said before, unless it is sanctioned by your judgment,) that so far from this case leaving any doubt upon the mind of any one, that there is not a hinge or loop on which to hang one single doubt. If I am right in that, why then the necessary consequence must be that this Prisoner must be found guilty; but having said that, let me again request you only to attend to the statement of the law as it shall come from the mouth of the learned judges, and to recollect that it is of the utmost importance for the welfare of this country that justice should be correctly and impartially administered; that this never can be done if it is done from caprice and bias; it can only be impartially and justly administered when it is administered according to law.

SUMMING UP.

Mr. Justice DALLAS.

Gentlemen of the jury,

THE Case being now closed in point of evidence and observation, it becomes my duty to draw your attention to the nature of this charge, to state the evidence given in support of it, and the law as it applies to the facts which have been proved. And you have been truly told that the charge itself is of High Treason, being the greatest crime which it is possible for a subject to commit. The indictment is founded upon two statutes on which the different Counts are framed; the first being on the ancient statute of the 25 Edward III, cap. 3, and the two others upon an Act which passed in the 36th year of the present reign. The first Count, in substance, charges levying war against the King, by assembling with others in great numbers, armed in a warlike manner, parading and marching, endeavouring by force and arms, to destroy the government and constitution of this realm as by law established. The second Count, and the third, which are founded upon the latter statute, in substance, charge the assembling, the arming, the parading, the marching, the attacking the houses of many of the King's subjects, intending to destroy if opposed, the soldiers of the King, and others of His Majesty's subjects; and finally, to destroy and overturn the constitution and government of the realm as by law established. This is the substance of the second Count; and the third, with a very little variation, charges the same sort of acts. But it has been stated by the Attorney General, and properly so, because the more unity and simplicity we give to subjects of this sort the better, that, in effect, the case in substance and result is levying war against the King in his realm, with the specific intent charged.

Having thus pointed out the nature of the charge, I shall next state to you briefly what the law is, as applicable to a case of this description, reserving myself to enter more particularly into the subject hereafter. In consequence of observations which I have heard this day made by the counsel for the prisoner, and the law, as it relates generally to the present case, is this: " If there be an insurrection, that is a large rising of people, in order by force and violence to accomplish or avenge not any private objects of their own, or private quarrels of their own, but to effectuate any general public purpose, that is considered by the law as a levying of war against the King; there must be an insurrection; force must accompany that insurrection, and it must be for an object of a general nature; but if all these circumstances concur, that is sufficient to constitute the offence of levying war against the King." Gentlemen, I will only add, that this point has been under the consideration of learned judges at different periods of time, and has received from all the same determination. If therefore in this case there has been an insurrection, force and violence made use of, and the intent not to effect a private but a general and public purpose, being the purpose charged in the indictment, then most undoubtedly war has been levied, the charge against the prisoner is made out, if such were his intent, and he was engaged in thus raising an insurrection, and upon this, as the law of the land applying to the fact, there can be no judicial doubt.

The next point that arises for consideration is, whether the facts, which are in proof, bring the conduct of the prisoner, compared with the charge, within the law which I have stated. This must depend upon the facts, and the facts themselves, upon the evidence; and therefore I shall now proceed to state to you, as accurately as I have been able to take it, all the evidence given, and which during so many hours has occupied so much of your attention.

Gentlemen, the first witness who was called, is Anthony

Martin, who has told you that he lived in the service of Messrs. Outram, Jessop and company, at Butterley works, in June last. He says, " I know the prisoner; on the 8th of June in the morning, I went to Pentridge with John Cope; we went from Butterley; we arrived about ten, and went immediately to the White Horse public house; first we went into the house part, and afterwards into the parlour. There were five or six people there at first; the people kept coming in, and Brandreth was one, George Weightman, Thomas and Joseph Weightman were also there. Nanny Weightman kept the house, and the persons whom I have last-mentioned, are her sons. There is also another Weightman, Joseph, who lives in another part of the town. John Bacon and Ormond Booth, were also there. This was after dinner, between one and two, when I went in. Brandreth and others were there. There might be a score, Isaac Ludlam, Edward Moore, John Moore, Mac Kesswick, Elsden, Shirley Asbury, and Bramley, were all there, and they were all talking about the revolution, when Turner, the prisoner at the bar, came in. The conversation was about pikes, arms, pistols, and swords. He wanted to know of John Cope, if the Pentridge people were ready; where their arms were, and a list of them. Cope said, they had not got a list, they had got a few guns but no pikes. The Prisoner said, he thought their parish," meaning Wingfield, " was the most forward of the country, for that they had turned out in the day time to get pike shafts. They were talking about drawing the badger. Cope said he had heard there was a plan to draw the badger, and he wanted to know what it was. The Prisoner said, they would lay down some straw, and set it on fire; the badger would come out, and they would shoot him. It was not explained who this was. The Prisoner said, they had got vermin in their own parish, and meant to kill it. Turner produced a list or paper, and Ludlam read it. It contained an account of the arms in Southwingfield; and it was stated therein that they had got a quantity of pikes made, and that those pikes were ready, and deposited in a stone quarry. The conversation was public in the room; the room was open, and the houses were mentioned which were supposed to contain the arms, specifying each where the different arms were to be had. They mentioned George Godber's, Colonel Halton's; and there was an account of the different houses; I do not recollect the particular names, but the paper stated where all the houses were to which they were to go, and they were all in Wingfield parish. The prisoner Brandreth," the person last tried, "had been there all the time. They addressed him as captain. He was sitting near the door; he had a map open before him, and was pointing out the different places where they were to assemble and go to, as I suppose. He pointed out where they were to meet on the map with a pin, and then he pricked it through with a pin; all this was openly discussed, and not a secret; and they said that nothing could be done without the overthrow of the present government. Turner took no part in this conversation about the government, but was present. Brandreth was the person who said that; and said it more than once;" and then he adds from recollection, "I cannot recollect that it was in the presence of Turner; but all the conversation was about a revolution, and how they were to get their arms. They were to go to Nottingham. Brandreth was the person who mentioned this. They were to go there in order to take the town; and when that was taken, they were to return and go to the barracks. He did not say in my hearing, or any one, what was to be done at the barracks, except that they were to go to the barracks till the next day, when a large party was to come. All the northern parts were to furnish people. I do not recollect the names of the particular places mentioned. They were to make barracks of Butterley works, where they were to return, and they were to take a part of the men at those works with them; they said they would make all go that would go, and those that would not go, they would shoot them. They said the tide could as soon be stopped as they. I cannot recollect what was said, as to success or failure of the enterprize; but they said they thought they should have a good succeeding. Then some verses were recited by Brandreth; and they were these,

"Every man his skill must try,
He must turn out and not deny;
No bloody soldier must he dread,
He must turn out and fight for bread;
The time is come you plainly see,
That government opposed must be."

"I do not know that that was spoken while the prisoner was there. The prisoner wanted to know where the Ripley arms were; and wanted them to assist in drawing the badger, and killing the vermin in his parish. Cope said he thought they should have enough to do in their own parish without assisting them. Turner said he thought they could get through themselves, but they would rather have a little assistance. Then the prisoner talked about shooting the badger, and gathered money; each subscribed to send Joseph Weightman off to Nottingham, to know if the Nottingham people were ready; this was before Turner came into the room. I do not remember his saying any thing about any party that was to come from Nottingham. Mac Kesswick afterwards came in; he looked round, and he said he thought there were too many there for such a business. I do not recollect any particular conversation being had. When he came in, he asked the captain (Brandreth) how he was; the other looked at him as if at a stranger, and said he did not know him; upon which the other said, do not you remember my coming part of the road with you from Nottingham? and then he recollected him, and said he did. About three on Tuesday morning, I was disturbed at the Butterley works; I cannot remember whether the prisoner was there; two parties came; I saw the last party, in which was the prisoner's brother. I do not know who the leader of the second party was. They thundered at the door, and took some men along with them. Joseph Onion and John Walker were there. I do not know whether beyond taking the men, they took any arms from this place."

On his cross examination, he says, " I went there," that is, to the public house, " originally between nine and ten in the morning, with a friend of mine. I believe Cope was a person who was connected with this business, and he went there on it;" that is, as the witness states, he knew something about it. " I was a constable, but though such, I went with Cope, not knowing that he was going on that business when I went with him. I staid from nine till three or four in the afternoon there, about six hours. Cope," he again says, " had something to do with these matters; he objected to some part of what they said; he entered into deliberation with the rest, and in some part of what was proposed he concurred. I took no part; I was drinking a pint of ale, and we were all conversing together in the parlour, and the room was always open; no secret was made of what was passing, and no endeavour was exerted to prevent my going away: but I waited in the room in order to go away with Cope, with whom I had come; and when Cope had finished his business we went home. The nearest residence of any justice of the peace was at the distance of two miles. I was frightened from going before a justice, as they threatened to take my life; they threatened that if any person told, he should be shot. I did not know any thing of telling a justice of the peace. I told them to mind what they said; and I told them this many times. Though I had been sworn in a special constable, I did not understand that it was my duty to go before a justice of the peace. I had only been sworn in on the Saturday night before; and I conceived I was sworn in only to act in a case of riotous disturbance. I do not know what became of Cope on the Monday. I did not on our way home take Cope before any justice. I did not spend the evening with him, but I went home; we went along the road together; I had nothing to do with him afterwards; and on the road, and on going along, nothing was said by me to him about what had passed in this room; nor did any thing on this subject pass between us after we left the public house." When he is asked why he did not go before a magistrate, he says, "I did not know what to think of this business; I did not understand it clearly. They had all had some little liquor, no great deal; I saw no arms in the room. I left between three and four. Part was over before the prisoner came to the room, but not the greatest part; though I cannot distinguish clearly what was said or what was done before the prisoner came into the room from what passed after. I cannot recollect whether the prisoner was there at the time we were talking about overthrowing the government. I did not learn the verses there, but part only. I saw them on paper the next day, and I saw the paper handed about on the Sunday." And then he mentions Asbury, Cope and Weightman, as persons to whom copies of those verses had been delivered; and by one or all of whom they had been shown to him. He says, " I recollected the lines, which I could not repeat when I was last before the Court," having been an evidence against Brandreth, " I had forgotten them at the moment of my examination, but I recollected the whole just after I went out of Court; nobody has reminded me; the people were asking what the lines were, and I recollected them; I got them by heart in order that I might keep them secret; I did not mind much about keeping the secret, for they were spoken openly; and this was all I heard. I cannot say that I saw the prisoner on the Monday at Butterley."

Then on his re-examination, he says, " the stone quarry was mentioned as the place in which the arms were deposited. I do not recollect what directions I myself received as special constable."

Then Shirley Asbury is next called. He says, " I live in the parish of Ripley, and worked at the time in question at the Butterley works; John Elsden was also a workman there in June last. On Sunday morning I took a walk with him, and I called at the White Horse public house about twelve o'clock; I went into the kitchen first, and called for something to drink, not knowing there was any body in the house at the time. Mrs. Weightman, who kept the house then, went into the parlour, in which many people were assembled; and she told them there were some Butterley lads in the kitchen, and asked whether they might come in. I was a stranger; I knew none of them except the person with whom I went. They told her we might come in, for what they were doing there was no secret. She came and asked us if we would go into the parlour; I said I had no objection. We went in; and there were about twenty there. There were John Cope, Brandreth, Ormond Booth, Mac Kesswick, the prisoner Turner, Ludlam, the three Weightmans, Anthony Martin," the first witness, whose evidence I have read to you, " and some others; they were talking about the revolution that was to commence the next night. Brandreth was the person who mentioned this; he took out a map, and pointed out different places as those where they were to assemble; I saw marks pricked with a pin upon the map. They were to overthrow the government; and they thought there would be no good done till this was effected. The prisoner was the person who said this; he came in about one o'clock: I did not hear what was to be done precisely in order to overturn the government; they were to go to Pentridge, to Wingfield, and to Nottingham Forest. The prisoner wanted Cope to go to Wingfield to join them. Cope said he would have nothing to do with them in their preparations, he had enough to do at home. They were, it was stated, to go and take Nottingham, and then to go to Newark; they said it would be like a journey of pleasure, to go down by the Trent boats. Brandreth was the person who said this; then the poetry was repeated," which I have already read to you, and need not therefore repeat again. " I remember Mac Kesswick coming in; he said there were too many for that sort of business. Ludlam came in with Turner at one o'clock. The old man, I cannot tell his christian name, when Turner produced the paper having the list upon it, he gave it to Ludlam, and he read it. What he read, consisted of a specification of the arms that they had; the pistols and the spikes; and the prisoner said they had forty spikes in a stone quarry for any men that volunteered; he said they would come from Wakefield and Chesterfield and Sheffield to meet them. They were talking of drawing the badger; they said they would put straw before the door, the badger would come out, and they would shoot him: William Turner said this. Turner wanted to know where the list was belonging to the Butterley people. They told him they had none: Cope said this. Turner seemed to make game of them because they were not so forward as they were at Wingfield, for that they went out to get pike shafts in the day time." It was to Colonel Halton's they were to go to do what they called draw the badger; " in their own parish every man was to kill their own vermin; Turner was the person who said this; and he then asked Cope to go and help them at Wingfield; Cope said he should not go, he had enough to do at home. Turner, the prisoner, said that when at Nottingham, they were to get plenty of rum and roast beef, and one hundred guineas each; they seemed to be in good spirits, and said there would be no good till the government was overthrown; they said there was no doubt they should succeed in what they were going to undertake. Edward Moore was there; he took no part in the conversation, except that generally he was talking among the rest; I do not recollect particularly what he said. Money was gathered for Joseph Weightman to go to Nottingham; he was to go there to bring information how they were going on. Brandreth was to be the captain; he wanted a barrel of gunpowder to be produced, that he might tell them how to make cartridges; and as to lead, he said, there would be plenty of that on the road from the churches."

Then, on his cross-examination, he says, " I came this morning from the Old Flower Pot, in this town. Since I was last here, I have talked with Martin about this; but I did not teach him the verses. Turner was not there when I first went. I might say, when examined before, that Turner was there when I first came, but I do not know that I did say so; but if I did, I was wrong in saying so." Now, the question put to him before was equivocal in itself; he being desired to mention the persons who were there, mentioned all the names, amongst which was Turner's. He says, "I do not recollect having had any conversation with Martin since the time till I was examined before, as to when Turner came into the room; but if I did say Turner was there, I said that which was not correct. Both Brandreth and Turner said there would be no good till the government was overturned: both said it, the one after the other. Turner continued there after this conversation till they broke up. William Turner was the person who mentioned it first:" that is, that no good would be done till the government was overturned. " Brandreth repeated it afterwards, and said the same thing. The first witness, Martin, was all the time in the room;" and Martin not having mentioned any part of this conversation, this witness is asked whether Martin must not have heard it? to which he says, that Martin was out occasionally, once, twice, or thrice; that he was backwards and forwards, and might not have heard every part of the conversation; but the witness swears that he did. He says, " I was not taken up on this business; but I first told it when I was called upon. This was not in the course of the same week, or of the same month. I did not volunteer in giving any information; I did not know it was my duty to tell; I was sworn in as a constable, and I said, there are constables in the room. They said, if we said any thing, they would put us up the chimney. I was sworn in to protect my master's place; I ate his bread; and though I heard all this, I did not disclose it; but I swear I did not do it because I did not know it was my duty so to do; and I was only sworn in the night before. Both Brandreth and the prisoners said the same as to going to Nottingham, and having one hundred guineas. They said it in the room where I was; and besides this, it was said generally; not to me only, but to me as well as the rest, and not so soon as they came in. Cope is here—not at the Flower Pot. Since Thursday I cannot say that I have spoken to Martin about the evidence in this cause; but I have said something to him. I gave money for Joseph Weightman to go to Nottingham. I did not receive any. Brandreth subscribed, and I gave sixpence. I did not know what I was giving it for. They asked me for sixpence, and did not tell me what it was for till afterwards. Turner did not tell me what it was for; but it was mentioned in the room to send Joseph Weightman to Nottingham to know what was going on. I staid in this room from one or two till four. I was not prevented from going away, and I did not ask for my sixpence back. At length I went home, and to Jessop's—the next day to Butterley works; there I saw Mr. Goodwin, but I did not tell him what had passed, nor Mr. Wragg, nor any magistrate; because I did not know it was my duty so to do."

The next witness who is called is Thomas Turner, who describes himself as a frame-work knitter. He says, "In June last I lived with my father, at or near South-wingfield. I have been taken up upon this business, and in custody for some time past. On the evening of the 9th of June, I left my father's house; it was nearly nine; and I was in company with Samuel Ludlam and John Walker. We went to facing the meeting-house in South-wingfield, opposite nearly to Colonel Halton's gate, and there I saw the prisoner at the bar. I have known him long; he was with George Weightman and Brandreth; and each of them had a gun. They were two or three hundred yards from Balguybrook, and from Colonel Halton's gate, and" he says, "the prisoner was loading his gun with bullets; I was very near when he was doing this. George Weightman said, come lads I expect an engagement very soon at Butterley furnace with Jessop's men, but I do not expect it will last long; the prisoner told us where we were to meet, that was at Hunt's Barn; I did not know Brandreth before. I asked the prisoner who Brandreth was, and the prisoner said he is our captain from Nottingham; they all three went to the barn, and I and the others followed; the other three went first; there were men assembled at the barn, perhaps a score or better; they were armed; they had pikes, guns and swords; those arms were in their hands, and beyond those there were a few spikes by the road side; William Barker was there, he had a spike; John Hill had a spike, Ludlam the same; Robert Turner I think had a sword: I cannot recollect whether he had a sword then; but I saw him with a sword afterwards. Manchester Turner, the man who had lost an eye, had also a sword, and Charles Swaine had a spike. I cannot recollect that I heard Brandreth say where we were to go to, but I heard Weightman say we must go to Topham's; captain Brandreth said we must go to Nottingham Forest, and when there there would be a great many come to meet us; we went away; we were formed before we went away in order by the prisoner at the bar and by Brandreth, into rank like soldiers. I received a bag of bullets from George Bramley to carry; we marched to Topham's ground, better than a score; and Brandreth commanded us on the march; we went to Mr. Hardwick's, I saw nothing taken there; the party went next to Tomlinson's, I did not go there; I delivered the bullets to Samuel Ludlam, and went the nearest way to meet them at Topham's Close, where I expected the Pentridge people were to have met us, which I learned from George Weightman, but none joined us till we got to Topham's Close, when Isaac Ludlam and his two sons, Isaac and William, did; they had each a spike; the Pentridge people did not come; it was agreed George Weightman was to take the bag of bullets, and if he met them to turn them back to Pentridge-lane End. Weightman took the bag of bullets and went that way, accompanied by Brandreth and the prisoner, to Elijah Hall's; when they got there, Hall was on the outside of the door, dressed; he had a son, and at this place a gun and the son were taken; he did not give them up willingly, they were taken by force, and for this purpose Brandreth went into the house; I saw the prisoner at the door, I cannot say that I saw him in the house. We next went to Mr. Walker's, and there I saw a pistol taken; Brandreth had it, and put it into his apron, which went round his waist like a belt, and it appeared to me to be a brass-barrelled pistol. I cannot say whether William Turner was there. Barker was at Hall's; he told Mr. Hall he had waited long for that day to come, but that it had come at last. We went to Mr. Bestwick's, there the windows were broken; I heard the sound, but did not see it done. We went to Samuel Hunt's next; he gave us bread and cheese and beer; he dressed, and when his man dressed, they came with us; the prisoner was with us, and was actually in Hunt's house. We went next to Mrs. Hepworth's, and there a gun was taken; Brandreth was the first person who demanded admission, others of the party seconded him in so doing, but admission was not given; they were asked what they wanted; they said they wanted a gun out of the house; it was refused; they attempted to break in; and the windows I think were broken, not the fastenings, but the windows; large stones were thrown at the door by Samuel Hunt; Brandreth shot through the window and killed Robert Walters; I saw him lying dying or dead upon the floor afterwards. I told Brandreth, he should not have shot that innocent young man; he said it was his duty to do so, and he would do it, and if I said any thing more he would blow my brains out; I was three or four yards from him; Elijah Hall was near, and William Ludlam. I saw the prisoner in the yard a minute or two before Robert Walters was killed; and after Walters had fallen by the shot discharged by Brandreth, the gun was delivered. We went next to Pentridge Lane End, and met with a party from different places of about a score. About this time the size of our party altogether amounted to forty or fifty; most of those who joined were armed like ourselves; some had guns, some had spikes. While at Pentridge Lane End, I heard a noise of the same kind as I had heard at other houses; there was a great disturbance at Butterley, and then I heard other noises, and at last they got men from Butterley; I do not know whether they got arms; and then they afterwards marched towards Pentridge: in marching to Pentridge, Brandreth asked whether any had been in the militia and knew discipline, because they must turn out and keep the men in order; Charles Swaine turned out, he said he had been in the militia, and they were formed into ranks by Brandreth, by the prisoner, and by Charles Swaine; those who had guns were placed in the first rank, those who had spikes, in the rear; we were two and two, and marched in this way to Pentridge, under the command of Brandreth, and the prisoner at the bar appeared to be the second in command; at Pentridge, Edward Turner and Joseph Turner, and several others joined; Edward had a gun; of the remainder, some had guns some not, the rest had spikes; at Pentridge I did not see the arms taken, but that they were taken, I believe, from the noise which I heard from the people being called up; George Weightman rejoined us a little before we got to Pentridge; we went to William Booth's, his poney was taken, and I saw George Weightman with it; a person of the name of Storer was placed upon the poney, he pretended to be ill, which was the reason for putting him upon it; we then marched to Butterley; when we were near the office, Mr. Goodwin came out, and something passed which I did not hear, and therefore do not know what it was; we were then marched by Brandreth, to Ripley, and the prisoner continued to accompany us all the time; when we arrived at Ripley, we were ordered to halt and give three cheers; I did not hear it said for what purpose; we then went to Codnor, to a public house called the Glass-house, we got some ale there; the landlord was knocked up, and the prisoner and Brandreth ordered the bill; it amounted to about eight and twenty shillings: then we went to a farm yard near Codnor; the prisoner, with his brother and others, were present during all this time; we brought three men out of the barn, we were not then in rank, they were placed in our body, they went not very willingly; we then went to Langley Mill, and met in our way George Weightman on Booth's poney; he had been to Nottingham, as I understood; he said that Nottingham had risen and was taken, and that the soldiers would not come out of the barracks, and we must march on; we did; I went two or three miles with them towards Eastwood, and then with some others I quitted them there; at this time, the rest were going towards Nottingham, but there were few left; when

I left them, Brandreth and the prisoner at the bar, were consulting together; William Turner was never in the line, and appeared throughout the whole of these proceedings, to be the second in command."

On cross-examination, he says, " I had a weapon; I threw it down when I escaped, by one side of the road by some nettles; and I afterwards pointed it out to some soldiers. I am a frame-work knitter; I was at this time in full employ. I saw Brandreth fire; I blamed him for it. The man appeared to be killed as he was lying on the floor. I did not hear several others blame him for it. I do not believe the prisoner was in sight or near him when he shot. I might quit them between nine and ten, the following morning. The men dropped off fast, and there were very few left at last. They were going off scattering in different directions. I should think there might be a dozen or a score, when I quitted."

On his re-examination, he says, " There were more parties than one; some were forwards, some were backwards, some elsewhere; there were few remained with Brandreth and the prisoner at the bar."

Gentlemen, as far as I have hitherto proceeded, I have stated to you, I fear but a very inconsiderable part of the evidence; the remainder will occupy probably a very considerable portion of time; and therefore I beg you will be seated.

Henry Tomlinson is next called, who tells you that he is a farmer at Wingfield Park; he says, " on the 9th of June, I saw John Machin at my house, at about a quarter before ten; I got information from him, and in consequence of that information, my wife and I locked the door and went into the yard; as we stood at one end of it, a quantity of people came in at the other end, they went up to the house door and began to rattle at it; I went up to them and asked them what they wanted; their number appeared to be between thirty and forty; they were armed, some with spikes, some with guns, and they said if I would not open the door they would break it, and search my house for my gun. I knew the prisoner, I saw him and I spoke to him; I opened the door, and the captain and another man followed me in; at this time I did not know precisely all those that went in; they insisted upon taking my gun and upon searching my house; and I fetched them the gun from the tester of my bed and delivered it to them; they then went out, and I went out and stood just within the door; they said to me, come you must go; upon which I said I would not; they said you had better go now than wait till the morning, for that there was a great gang coming from Sheffield, and a great cloud from the north, which would sweep all before them; I told them I would not go, but stop till the morning; then the captain Brandreth levelled his gun, and swore he would shoot me; the crowd said damn his eyes strike his head off; some said bring him, others said leave him, others said never mind; the captain said they were going to Nottingham, that he should be there by half past eight or nine in the morning; that London would be taken by the time they got to Nottingham, and then they need go no further; I locked the door and went into the yard, and George Weightman was there, whom I knew; there were three others there whom I knew; they gave me a spike, but I asked to have my own gun; they said I should not have it, I must have a spike; I went with them about three hundred yards; George Weightman took the spike and bade me turn again; in my own yard I had said to him it was a very hard case to offer to take me away, and to leave my wife without protection in a solitary place; he said it was, and then he gave me a nudge; I spoke to the prisoner in the yard, and said, William is that you, and the Prisoner answered, yes."

Then upon being cross-examined he says, " I went with them because they forced me to it. I do not recollect Wakefield or Huddersfield being mentioned; the captain talked about Sheffield and a cloud from the north."

Elijah Hall senior is next called, who tells you that he is a farmer and miller, and that he lives at Southwingfield Park. He says, "I had closed my doors and fastened them on Monday about eleven o'clock at night; a part of my family was gone to bed. I heard the footsteps of two men approaching the door, and then when they had approached it, they asked me whether any men had been at my house that night for guns; I told them there had; they said, have they taken any away; I told them they had; they then went away. I opened the door, and went out to see whether anybody was without with an intent to take away the fire-arms, and I saw a number of men coming into my yard, advancing towards my door; this was a few minutes after the two men had gone away; they were armed with pikes and guns, and one of them had a sword. I asked them what they were doing there at that time of the night; some of them said they wanted a bigger loaf, and the times altering. I told them it was not in my power to give them a bigger loaf, or to alter the times; they said, they did not suppose it was, but they wanted my fire-arms. I told them I had none for them; they said they knew positively that I had; and I had better deliver them up to prevent further mischief, that was to prevent the house from being fired; they then advanced towards the door, and demanded entrance; I told them it was not in my power to open the door, I being at this time on the outside of the door as well as themselves; they then endeavoured to force the door with pikes and other weapons; a gun was then given through one of the windows; they then required me to go along with them; I told them I should not; some then said he has sons, we will take them; the captain said, if he has sons, we will take the young, and not the old man; the captain said, we must force the door," this was in answer to a question by the others, " how must it be ?" he ordered them to blow the door in pieces; a little time before this I had heard a gun go off at a village at about the distance of half a mile; they then tried to force the door open, and when the captain was ordering the men to blow it in pieces, somebody from within opened the door; and the door being opened, the captain and several others went in, and I did the same; there were twelve or more went in. I had not heard of the general purpose; when I got into the house I heard of it; when I got in, they demanded my sons, and they told me to fetch them; I told them I should not; the captain gave me two pushes with the muzzle of his gun, presented it at me, and told me he would blow my brains out if I did not immediately light a candle, and fetch my sons to go along with them. I told him I should not; he took a candle from some one of the family, lighted it at the fire, and then went up stairs, and several others followed him; I heard them threaten my sons to hash them in pieces, or to hash them up if they would not go with them; they brought my son Elijah down; I have several children and several sons, but of those, two only are grown up; they brought Elijah down, part dressed, and they compelled him to finish dressing, all but tying his shoes. They were hunting about for more fire arms. I asked the captain where he was going; he said to Nottingham, and that he believed Nottingham was taken at that time; he said they should proceed from Nottingham to London, wipe off the national debt, and begin afresh; when out of the house I saw that they had taken my son. I followed them, and desired them not to take him, but they said they would; they said I need be under no apprehension, they would bring him back and the gun; he had better go with his neighbours whom he knew, than go the next day with those he did not know, for he believed there were thousands coming who would be there the next day; the captain and Ludlam, senior and junior, had been there, and William Ludlam, William Barker, Thomas Turner and Robert Turner; I cannot positively say I saw the prisoner that night, but I suppose I heard his voice."

Then Elijah Hall, the son of the last witness, is called, and he tells you, he lives with his father; he says, " the family was disturbed on the 9th of June, after they had gone to bed, by a great quantity of people; several people came into my bed-room between eleven and twelve, or thereabouts, some with guns and some with swords, requiring me to get out of my bed, and go along with them; I went with them, because I was compelled to do it; when I went down there were many others below; they were standing close together, I dressed and went with them; I saw several I knew, the Nottingham captain was there. I did not observe any other persons I knew in the house, but in the road I saw Ludlam the father, and the two sons, and Manchester Turner, whom I knew by sight. I did not see the prisoner within thirty or forty yards of the house, but there I did, and he had a gun with him, and he joined the rest of the party; we went first to Isaac Walker's, there we demanded arms; a gun was asked for. I knew the prisoner before; I have no reason to recollect whether I was nearer to him than thirty or forty yards, nor do I believe him to have been nearer to this spot; we got a gun and a pistol; Mr. Isaac Walker gave them not willingly, but because they threatened to shoot him if he did not give them. From thence they went to Bestwick's, into his house, and brought out a gun; they made a noise first; they did not get a man there, and they carried the gun away with them; the prisoner was with us; we went next to Samuel Hunt's, three or four closes off, went into the house, and most of the party got bread and cheese and beer. Hunt dressed and came along with them and his man, a gun being got from this place the man carried the gun; from thence we went to Mary Hepworth's, which is several closes from Hunt's; the prisoner continued with us; he was very near; there was a great disturbance at the door, and they demanded men and arms, but they got none; when they demanded men and arms, and the answer was they had got none, the window was broken; I do not know by which of the party: then a gun went off from the hand of the Nottingham captain, and shot Mrs. Hepworth's man, Robert Walters. I did not see the prisoner at that time; I saw him before I left the house not far off, in the yard, and near the house, but I cannot say that I saw him near Brandreth; Manchester Turner, William Turner, Isaac Ludlam, and William Ludlam, were also there; the rest of the party were about the place; after this we got one gun at Mrs. Hepworth's, and from thence we went to Pentridge Lane End, where they got several men by force, most of them whom they got were in bed when they went up to the houses; I heard a great noise at several doors; I do not know whether they got arms as well as men; they then went to Pentridge, broke into several houses for men and arms; I do not know whether they got any there, for here I left them; they were breaking into some house, and I got away, and went home as soon and as fast as I could."

The next witness who is called is Isaac Walker; he tells you he is a farmer at Southwingfield Park; he says, " I was disturbed on the 9th of June, by persons coming to my house; about half past eleven, having retired with my family to bed; on being disturbed, and looking out, I saw about forty persons coming up the yard to the front of the house, armed with pikes and guns; they demanded a gun, a brace of pistols, and a servant man; I told them I had a gun, but no pistols; they said they were determined to have my gun and pistols too: I was at this time at the bed-room window; they were speaking from the yard below, and pointed a gun at me; the captain did (the man who appeared to be captain,) and said, if I did not deliver up my arms they would fire; he ordered them to break the door open; with that I went down and opened the back door, not the front door; they were then there, and afterwards went round to meet me at the back door; I took the gun down from where it hung, and delivered it them; they then demanded my servant; I told them I had none; they went away, and I fastened the door, and was going up to bed, but they knocked again; I then asked them what they were coming back for, and where they were going to; they said they were going to Nottingham, and that they were come back, for that they knew I had a pistol, and were determined to have it; if I had not two I had one; I told them I had one, but I begged they would let me keep it; they said they had orders to take all I had, and then I was forced to give it them; I gave it to the captain; he asked me if it was loaded; I told him it was, and he fired it off at the door.; I did not see where he put it, but he had it in his hand when he fired it off;

knew Isaac Ludlam, William Barker, and Thomas Maslam or Masden, but I did not know any of the others."

Then, upon being cross-examined, he says, " I have lived at Wingfield for five and twenty years; I have not known William Turner long; during all this time, I have known nothing one way or the other as to his general character."

Mary Hepworth is next called, who says, " I occupy a farm in Southwingfield, and did so in June last; I was disturbed between eleven and twelve, being then in bed, by a loud knocking at the door and windows; I got up and came down stairs, and found William Hepworth my son, and my two servant men, Fox and Robert Walters, in the kitchen; the men on the outside called out for guns and men; I told them they should have neither guns nor men; they then moved to the front part of the house; some broke the kitchen window; the shutter was on the inside, and that was broken and forced into the room, and they continued to demand the guns and men; a gun or pistol, I do not know which, was then immediately fired into the kitchen, and Robert Walters was shot and killed by it, at least he died in perhaps ten minutes; he was stooping down, when the firing took place, in the act of putting his boots on, and the ball entered his neck; I was then obliged to give them the gun; they still continued to call out for a gun and a man, and a gun was given to them out of the window; they did not take any men; I told them they should have none; they told me they would serve me the same if I did not retire from the window; I told them that they had shot one man, and said was not that sufficient; they said they would serve me the same if I was not silent; after they were gone away I went out; I saw a pike that was found, and there were a great many stones at the door; the pike found is like that little one (referring to one you saw displayed upon the table,) but it had a shorter stick and a longer iron."

Joseph Wilkinson was next called; he says, " I lived with my father at Southwingfield on Sunday the 8th and Monday the 9th of June, before the rising took place; in the afternoon of Monday I was at the house of a person of the name of Farndley, about half a mile from Thorpe Hill Wood; I saw some persons go by; Isaac Ludlam, James Taylor, Joseph Taylor and Benjamin Taylor; I saw them afterwards returning from the wood; they had with them poles about three yards long; they were carrying them on their shoulders; the bark was not then off them, and they had two or three each; on that evening I happened to go to James Taylor's, at about seven o'clock; there I saw George Weightman, William Ludlam, James Taylor, Isaac Ludlam; the bark was now off the poles; I did not see any thing put upon them, nor did I afterwards see them when armed with any iron that night; about twenty people came to my father's house; some unarmed and some armed with spikes and the poles; the poles were about the size of the poles I have seen here; James Taylor, Abraham James, Miles Bacon, and George Weightman were there, but did not come up to the door; one of James Taylor's brothers was there, but I do not know his christian name; a pike was put into my hand by James Taylor; I went with them to Frickley's; they there got nothing; they went next to Mr. Marriott's wire mill; there they got a gun; James Taylor was there; George Weightman demanded it, and I afterwards joined a large party at Mr. Fletcher's; Brandreth was the captain, and the prisoner was of the party; he had a gun; Edward Turner was in it; Thomas Turner was in it, they both had guns; another Turner was also in it, that is Manchester Turner, and he had a sword; Samuel Hunt had a pike; I cannot say whether Samuel Ludlam was there, but William Ludlam was, and had a pike; the captain had a pistol and a gun; I went with the party beyond Eastwood; I do not know whether the captain went all the way; I did not see him when I left the party; I do not know whether the prisoner did, but I saw him at the land end with a gun; I cannot recollect seeing him any where else; I went through Pentridge with them and to Codnor, and thence to Eastwood."

Then Samuel Fletcher was next called; he says, "On the 9th of June last I lived at Pentridge Lane End; I went to bed with my family about eleven o'clock; about twelve I heard a very great noise at the door, as if persons were breaking in; I got up out of bed, and ran towards the window and opened it; I saw thirty persons and more, five or six of them with guns, which they levelled at my head, all standing round the window; the others appeared to have large sticks or poles; they cried out, 'Your arms, your arms, damn you, we want your arms.' I said, 'What arms?' they said, 'Your fire arms; bring them down and open the door, or we will blow your brains out;' I said I had got but one; they kept on swearing that they would blow my brains out; I ran to the other side of the house to get away; there appeared nearly as many there as on the other side; finding I could not escape I stood where I was, and they kept on beating at that door, and swearing very hard; I ordered my servant Shipman, to fetch the gun down; he fetched it, and it was handed out of the window; the person who took it desired to have the but end towards himself; they said, 'get you dressed, or we will blow your brains out;' and then they called out for Shipman to go with them, saying that if he did not they would blow his brains out, and I desired him, he going with them, to take notice who they were. I said, 'thou knowest them, they are all Pentridge and Wingfield people: escape as soon as you can, and come back to me; while you are with them, observe them and what they do."

William Shipman is a servant to Mr. Fletcher. He says, " I was disturbed on the night of the 9th of June last, about twelve o'clock, by a knocking at the door, which aroused me; I rose and looked out at the window, and saw Joseph Topham and several other persons, who told me I must come and go with them; they said, they had a man and a gun from every house, and they must have one from this. The captain bade me come down, or that he would blow my brains out; he said he had shot one man already, and he would shoot me if I did not come down; I afterwards came down and joined them under compulsion; I went with them as far as Kimberley, beyond Eastwood, on the road to Nottingham; then we went to Pentridge-lane-end, through Pentridge; in the way there, I saw James Weightman near the meeting-house; he had in his hand a hat full of bullets; I took three or four out; he said, 'do not take any, for we shall be short enough;' Thomas Weightman was there; this was ten yards after I had seen the bullets; he said, James and he had orders to make the bullets, and to make cartridges; I saw George Weightman at this time there; one Tapleton of Heage told him there were two barrels of gunpowder at a place he mentioned; but that they had not strength enough to get it out. Heage is about two miles from Pentridge. They knocked at many houses at Pentridge while I was with them, calling for arms. I heard the conversation about the barrel of gunpowder. Young Weightman went off, and I afterwards saw him on a poney riding towards Nottingham. We went to Butterley, then to Codnor, then to Langley Mill, and there we met George Weightman. We stopped at Raynor's, on the side of the road to Langley Mill. We met George Weightman on his return from Nottingham. The poney was sweating very bad. At Nottingham he said they were going on well; that the soldiers were in the barracks, and if we marched forwards, we should have nothing to do when we got there. The prisoner was with this party. I saw him at Pentridge-lane-end, and I saw him at Codnor. He had a gun there. They formed us in ranks opposite Mr. Storer's. The captain picked out a serjeant who was to be over us. The prisoner marched by the side of the men, and the captain, Brandreth, did the same. I saw him (the prisoner) at Langley Mill, I saw him at Raynor's, and the last I saw of him was at Eastwood, and there they formed us into ranks. I cannot say whether the prisoner assisted, but he was by the side. At Kimberley I got away, and returned to my master. I went with them a little distance beyond Eastwood; as far as Kimberley."

On his cross-examination he says, " I did not see William Turner, the prisoner, take any part in forming us into ranks, nor at my master's house; but I saw him about a quarter of a mile from it. I did not see him when

I left the party; but I saw him as far as Eastwood. I cannot say how long he was with the party. I saw him at Codnor and at Raynor's."

On his re-examination he says, " I saw him at Storer's, which is four miles from Codnor. I saw him at Eastwood, which is three miles further. I do not recollect seeing him after that;" so that he had seen him for seven miles, or thereabouts.

Henry Hole lives at Pentridge-lane-end. He says, " On the 8th of June I saw before George Turner's door Samuel Hunt, and eight or ten others. I had gone for a jug of milk to a neighbour's house, and I met Samuel Hunt on the turnpike road. He said, ' thou art fetching that for the men to-night.' I said, ' What men?' He said, ' those revolutioners who will come to-night or to-morrow night.' I said, ' No, I believe not;' and he offered to lay me a wager of five shillings that they would come that night or the Monday night, the next night. About twelve o'clock on the Monday night, my wife and I were awoke by a violent knocking at the door. I got up to the window, and cried out, ' Who is there? what do you want?' They said, ' We want you to volunteer yourself to go with us, or else we will break the door down, and murder you.' I went down and opened the door, and I saw four men, two of whom I knew, Joseph Weightman and Joseph Topham, the two others I did not know. They had pikes similar to those on the table. I asked where they were going? They said, ' to Nottingham.' I said, ' I could not pretend to go with them; that I had no money to carry me there, nor any body to take care of my family while I was gone.' They said they would keep me on roast beef and ale, and that people were fixed (who would come in two days) to take care of every man's family. I went out: a pike was forced upon me. They said, I had better go that night, than stop till morning; that they would come in a cloud out of Yorkshire the next morning, and sweep all before them; and those who refused to go would all be shot. I told them, if they were going to Nottingham, I should not be able to carry the pike, it was so heavy. I threw it down, and one picked it up. I had gone about twenty or thirty yards along the turnpike-road, when I saw twenty or thirty men armed with guns and other weapons. I went to Fletcher's. I saw the captain there, but I did not know him particularly. I saw the prisoner there, and Manchester Turner. I saw Ludlam senior, William Ludlam, William Turner, by whom I mean the prisoner. I had known him eight or nine years. The party in which the prisoner was came up as I was going into Fletcher's yard. I heard a gun fired about Mrs. Hepworth's, and the party seemed to come from that direction. Brandreth was among them, and had a pistol and a gun. The prisoner, when I first saw him, had a gun in his hand; the Ludlam's had pikes. They were all armed, and took William Shipman from Fletcher's. Brandreth gave the word of command, and the prisoner marched as a sort of officer—sometimes by the side, sometimes in the front, with Brandreth. We formed into line at Pentridge-lane-end, and the prisoner assisted. We divided there into two parties. This was before they were put into ranks. After they were formed into ranks, the party I was with went to Samuel Booth's. The prisoner was with the other party. We took Mr. Booth's son Hugh, and from Buckland Hollow three men. I saw George Weightman upon William Booth's poney. I had some conversation about the shooting with William Ludlam. I asked who it was? he said Robert Walters. I afterwards went to Butterley works; the prisoner and Brandreth walked together in front of the party, and knocked at the door with the but ends of their guns. George Goodwin came to the door, and said, 'what do you want?' and the Prisoner said, 'your men;' he said, 'you have a great deal too many already, without it were a better object;' and then they marched off towards Ripley; we went by the turnpike road to Ripley; there we halted, and Brandreth said we must give three cheers at Ripley, to let them know how we were going on. When we left Ripley, we were marched on towards Codnor, and halted at the glass-house, and there we had some ale. While we were there I saw John Bacon, whom I saw before we got to Butterley; he marched as well as us. I heard him make a speech; he said that Government had robbed them and plundered them of all they ever had; this was the last shift they could ever make, they must either fight or starve. Before we left the glass-house we were joined by a party that came up to us, headed by Manchester Turner; he was not with us before. The landlord then gave Bacon and Brandreth the bill at the glass-house, and they said they would pay in a fortnight, when the job was over. We were next joined by a party that came from Swanwick; we then went along the road for Langley mill, and halted again at Raynor's; and I stood in the ranks. I could hear part of what passed, but not all. I heard the prisoner order the men to go in and take his man and his gun; this was at Raynor's. Young Raynor said he would not go; the prisoner said if he would not go he would shoot him; he said he would rather suffer than go; the prisoner went out and called Brandreth to his assistance, who came and said, 'If you do not turn out, I will blow a bullet through you.' A great deal of bad language was used by the prisoner and Brandreth to Raynor. They took away Raynor's man and gun, and a pitch fork. We then proceeded on the road towards Langley Mill, and in our way we met a man with five cows; we took him away with us by compulsion; we met George Weightman at Langley Mill upon a poney; he said, being asked the question, 'All is right; they have bombarded Nottingham at two o'clock this morning, and it is given up to them, only keep marching on;' and they kept marching on. The captain Brandreth, and the prisoner William Turner, had some private conversation, and then we marched on to Eastwood. I saw James Barnes; he had a gun in his hand; he came from Swanwick with the party, and joined at Codnor; I said to him, 'art thou one of them;' and he said, 'yes.' I asked him what they were going to do at Nottingham; he said they had fixed up a fresh Government at Nottingham; and they were going there to defend it until the other counties came into their terms; he said that by a letter he had yesterday seen from London, the keys of the Tower would be given up to the Hampden club party, if they were not already; he said he had never been seated since four o'clock yesterday morning five minutes together. I asked him what he had been doing; he said he had been providing guns, spikes, and ammunition at Eastwood. The companies seemed quite disordered, and Brandreth ordered them into the ranks. I went into rank again; I staid a few minutes, and then I turned out of the rank. Brandreth came and ordered me into the rank; I said I would not go in again for him or any of his men. I was armed with a stack paring knife; when I said I would not go in again, I saw him cock his gun; the knife with which I was armed was pu into a stick about a yard long; when he cocked his gun, I stepped up to him, and said if he offered to level his gun I would hack his head off; he stood a little while, and then he turned off from me. I marched back towards Langley Mill; I went about fifty or sixty yards, and then I heard a cry of ' do not shoot.' I turned round, and I saw Brandreth with his gun up to his shoulder, and pointed towards me; I saw Thomas Turner take hold of him and pull the gun off; marching a little further Savage followed me; he had a short pistol, and said if I did not turn back he would blow a bullet through me. At Codnor we were about two hundred strong; on my return I saw a party of about fifty apparently, some of them were armed; but the biggest part had no arms. I saw a party afterwards which appeared to be about sixty; in short, I think altogether there might be better than three hundred men in these several transactions of which I have spoken. The prisoner appeared to be a sort of captain or commander under Brandreth, under whom we all were."

Then, upon his cross-examination, he says, " Nobody heard what Barnes said but myself; Turner was not in the room when Bacon said what he did."

William Booth tells you, that in June last he lived at Pentridge-lane end. He says, " on Monday, the 9th of June, I was disturbed between twelve at night and one in the morning, by a parcel of men, who came with pikes and guns, rapping at the door. I got up and went to the window, and I observed a quantity of men standing round the door, some with spikes and some with guns; they called loudly, and I went to the window, saying, 'what do you want';—'you, and your guns, was the answer.' I said, 'I have no guns;' and they replied, 'then we must have you.' I said, 'I cannot go, I am ballotted for the militia, and must go to Derby to-day.' They said, 'come down and open the door; we will free you from the militia; or if you do not come down, I will blow your brains out.' This was said all by one person. I went down stairs, they were breaking the door; there was a large iron bolt to the door, and as I was drawing the bolt, part fell into my hand. I observed many people when the door was opened, some had guns, some had spikes; six or eight rushed into the house. The captain said, 'where are your clothes?' I said, 'they are up stairs,' and he told me to put them on immediately. I went up stairs, nobody went up with me; the captain and some others lighted a candle and followed me up. The prisoner was one who followed me up stairs. Above, the captain ordered me to dress as fast as I could. I said, 'I would make what haste I could.' The captain said, 'make haste; look sharp or I will blow your brains out.' The prisoner was one up stairs at this time. The captain told me to look sharp; and said, 'you seem to wish me to shoot you.' I said, 'I had rather you would not.' He said, 'If you do not look sharp I shall.' They took me down stairs into the house place. I was going to set down on the squab to put my boots on, and to lace them; and he said, 'if I staid to lace my boots, he would blow me through.' They drove me out of the house before them. One called me by my sirname, and said, 'have not you a gun;' and I said, 'no.' They said, 'you must take a fork.' I told them I could not find one; I took nothing with me at all. They took me to the end of the lane, out of the yard into the high road, and there I saw a number of men standing in ranks, two deep; some had arms, some had not; some had pikes, and some had guns. The captain took me along the ranks, until he came to a man with a gun, and he said to him, 'take this man as a prisoner, if he offers to get away, shoot him.' When in Pentridge-lane, I heard men over the road; they were knocking at the door, and calling to them to get up. They went to Mr. Storer's, where they halted; he was taken. Some other men came up while we stood there; the captain said, ' if there be any of you that have been in the volunteers or in the local militia, step forwards three paces;' none did. The men were placed at this time three deep. We went to Pentridge-lane-end; a gun was fired to give a signal near Butterley. I saw George Weightman with Mr. Booth's poney. Brandreth said to him, ' take this poney and ride to Nottingham Forest, to see what is going on there, and come back and meet us at Langley Mill to bring tidings.' The captain said, ' I thought Pentridge would have been all ready. It is the worst place we have been at. We should have been at Nottingham by three o'clock.' And then we went to Butterley after that. We there saw Mr. Goodwin, from the foundry; we went over the coke croft to Ripley and Codnor, thence to the glass-house; old Isaac Ludlam was there. He was one. He said, ' captain, some man must stop out in the road, or the biggest part of the men will get away.' He staid at the door all the time. I asked the prisoner, ' when did you begin last night, and where.' He said, ' at ten o'clock at Wingfield.' I asked him whether he had called at Pearce's; he said, 'no; we mean to call on that beggar when we come back.' When we went from Codnor, we went by the house of Mr. Sterland; the party was halted there. Some men went to Mr. Sterland's yard, and brought out some men and some forks. William Turner and Samuel Hunt were among those that went. From thence they went to Mr. Raynor's, and stopped there. I saw the first man go in; Turner was among them, he had a gun. Turner came out in about a quarter of an hour, and called for the captain, and said, ' he is not willing to go.' The captain said, ' shoot him then; we will either have him dead or alive.' The prisoner returned into the house again, and in about five or six minutes he came out again, and called to the captain to come to him; the captain did; they talked together about five minutes, and he then went in again. We went next to Langley Mill; George Weightman was there. Some of the men went round the road, or crossed over by the mill a shorter way. We met again at the toll bar. I do not know whether George Weightman had been at Nottingham, but one of the men asked him how they were going on; he said, 'very well; the soldiers are in the barracks; march on as fast as you can.' I saw Hole there; and when he was going away, he told the prisoner he would not stop any longer; that he would go back. The prisoner said, 'if you go back you will be shot.'—'Well,' he said, 'I do not mind, I will not go any further.' The prisoner immediately called out to the captain, and said, 'that a man was going back;' and the captain came immediately to Hole;" and then in other respects, he confirms the account which Hole had given himself.

Upon his cross examination he says, "the prisoner warned Hole that if he went away he would be shot; he was neither shot nor fired at, notwithstanding the threats used; the captain was the person who levelled the gun at him, and was prevented by some of the party from firing it off. I joined them at Pentridge-lane End; we went from thence to Pentridge, then to Butterley, Ripley and Codnor. I did not hear Bacon make a speech; I saw him go into the house; the prisoner was where I was, which was the parlour, and Bacon in the kitchen; I did not hear a word. I went from Codnor as far as Langley Mill, and I left the party beyond Eastwood; there were not so many when I came away as when I went to the party; when I left them I think there were nearly one hundred."

John Storer is next called, who tells you he is a farmer at Pentridge; he says, "On the 9th of June, about one o'clock in the morning, I was disturbed by a party of persons who came to my house, they appeared to be in number twelve or fifteen; I was awakened by a dog's barking first, and I went to the window, and there were a number of guns and pikes pointed directly at me; they said ' damn your eyes you must go with us instantly,' this was said by the prisoner, William Turner; I asked, was there no excuse, and the prisoner answered, ' no;' he said there were several at our house liable to go, and he said, if I did not go and take a gun instantly, they would break into the house immediately and shoot me and all that were in it; the captain had just shot Mrs. Hepworth's man, and all must go or be shot; I was undressed at this time, and I went from the window to dress myself; I told him if he would give me a little time I would go; my inducement was, that I thought I should be shot; while I was dressing myself they called to me, and told me to make haste or they would make me so that I could not go; I dressed myself, took my gun and went out immediately; somebody asked me, I do not know who, whether my gun was loaded; I told them it was not; they asked me if I had got any shot and powder; I told them I had got a little shot but no powder; they said it did not matter, they should have plenty of powder in a short time; when I got to the gate leading to the lane, I told them I had been very unwell the day before, and was not fit to go; I said I could not carry the gun any further, they said then it must go with the baggage; I asked them where the baggage was; they said they had not any at that time, but that they should have; they expressed great impatience for the arrival of the captain and their party from the lane end; in about twenty minutes they came up; I asked where they were going to; they said they were going to Nottingham; they were going immediately there, that it was to be a general rising, and people were coming in all directions; that twenty-five or thirty thousand men were coming from Sheffield; that there would be ten thousand assemble that day; that liberty would be proclaimed, and there would be an end of tyranny; they stood all in a body, the prisoner was one of that body; he had a gun; Isaac Ludlam senior, and William Barker was there; they said the captain was at Pentridge-lane end, and would soon come up; he did with the other body; and when they were all together there were about a hundred; the greatest number armed with guns and pikes; the captain ordered them to fall in three deep; those with guns in front; then he held a consultation with the prisoner and with Manchester Turner, and the principal men, and then he said it would be best to appoint non-commissioned officers; he then asked, if there were any men who knew their duty, or had been in the Local Militia; that they wanted non-commissioned officers, and those who knew their duty, or had been in the Local Militia, would be so appointed, and would have the command of a number of men each. I have no doubt some turned out; the men were formed three deep; they were ordered to march by the captain, who was in advance, and then I saw Isaac Ludlam senior, who commanded the rear-guard; we then marched; the prisoner was out of the ranks; I do not know who marched at the head; we marched up the lane towards Pentridge, and there a great many houses were attacked, and guns were taken by them, and men also; while at Pentridge I feigned myself ill, and when I got to the bottom of it, I told them I could not go any further; the captain came up, and said I must go, that they would all do in that way; some said 'damn him, shoot him;' some said, 'run a pike through him;' they then appointed two men to take hold of each arm and lead me up Pentridge; in the midst of the body I pretended illness, and the two men held me up. I went with them all the way up Pentridge, and then a poney of Booth's was fetched out, and I was put on it. I did not continue long, and then I pretended to fall off the poney; I was not put on again, this brought the captain up, and he said, 'damn him put a pike through him.' I said, 'you had better shoot me,' and he or some person said, 'damn him, leave him, we can do without one;' he ordered the men to face about to the right, and march, which they did, and left me: I did not go with them more than three quarters of a mile altogether. I saw the prisoner frequently; he was actively employed in Pentridge going to different houses, the doors of which they were breaking open. After I had quitted them, I went to William Booth's, and we went to the house of William Weightman; he came in while we were at William Booth's; the party was but just gone; I did not see William Weightman in the party; at his house I saw a bag of bullets; I went with Booth to the constables' and gave information, and we went back to Weightman's house to get the bullets; his wife held the door, but I could neither find Weightman nor the bullets; we did not go into the house; Thomas Weightman was of the party, armed with a pike, Joseph Weightman senior, had a pike, Manchester Turner had a sword, William Ludlam had a pike, Hunt had a pike, Topham had a pike, Johnson had a pike, James Taylor a pike, Joseph Taylor a gun, William Barker had a pike; they were altogether about a hundred; when I left them there appeared to be a great many less, a great many had quitted.

On his cross-examination, he says, " I had known the prisoner before, and I have not the least doubt about his person; I saw him last Thursday or Friday; I was not examined upon the former trial."

George Goodwin is called, he tells you, that he is one of the clerks at the Butterley works; that there are about six or seven hundred people in the employ of the Butterley Company; then he says, " under an apprehension of some disturbance, special constables were sworn in on Saturday the 7th of June; I was sworn in as one; in consequence of information received, we armed some of our men on the 9th, and I took the command of them myself. I was at Ripley, and remained there on the alert till day light in the morning of the 10th; our men had guns, and they were to defend the works; while at Ripley I heard a noise of guns firing, which appeared to be at Pentridge and Pentridge-lane-end; at break of day I returned to the works; at a little after three o'clock, I saw George Weightman on horseback, he was going on the road from Pentridge to Nottingham; I called to him to stop; he did not, and soon after this I saw an hundred men in a body, marching like a body of soldiers, two abreast, in column; they marched up in front of the house; the doors of the iron works were closed; the captain looked at the gates, and I saw him knock; he cried out to the men, 'halt, to the right face, front;' they fronted the office, which was before to the right. I asked him, 'what is your object here?' he said, 'we want your men;' I told him he should not have one, that there were too many already, unless they were going for a better purpose. I told them to disperse, the law was too strong for them; they were going with halters about their necks, and would be hanged. Isaac Ludlam the elder, James Taylor, and Isaac Moore, were there; I spoke to Ludlam, and said, 'go home, you have got a halter about your neck, you will be hanged;' he said, 'I cannot go back, I am as bad as I can be, I must go on.' I had men in the office at this time, armed; when I saw the rebels approaching, I ordered them to retire into the office, and defend themselves there. I took Ludlam by the shoulders, and pushed him towards the office; I did the same to the other men whose names I have mentioned, but neither of the three went into the office; others went in, and remained there sheltered and secure; after a short pause, in which the two parties stood looking at each other, the captain gave the word, 'march,' and took the men away; and they proceeded towards Nottingham; another body came shortly afterwards, perhaps about forty, but they did not come near to us; they were armed with pikes and guns; they came about a quarter of an hour after the first party, and proceeded on towards Nottingham. I saw also other stragglers going in the same direction; about half an hour after I saw William Weightman on horseback; Taylor was with him; I laid hold of his bridle, and stopped him; I took a bag of bullets from him," which he produces, "it weighed about eighty-four pounds; they were for guns of different bores, and in number they might amount to from 1,500 to 2,000; in the bag there were moulds for cartridges, and there was paper also to make them."

Then in his cross-examination, he says, " I was sworn in a special constable, and Martin and Shirley Asbury were sworn in at the same time. I am not aware that they had any particular directions as to their duty. They were sworn in upon the spur of the moment."

Then George Raynor is called. He says he is a farmer, and that he lives with his father. " Early in the morning of the 10th of June last, some persons came to our house, which is situate near the turnpike-road from Codnor to Nottingham. There were about four hundred armed with guns and pikes. I know the prisoner, and he was the first that entered; when I first saw him, I stood in my father's doorstead. He had a gun in his hand; he presented it at me, and said, ' damn your eyes, turn out.' I said, ' no, I will not turn out.' He followed me, and said, ' Then you will not turn out?' I said, ' no, I will not.' After speaking to me twice, he then cocked a gun, and insisted upon my turning out and joining their party. He desired me to remember that they had shot one man, and that I should share the same fate for my stupidity, if I did not immediately turn out. I told him I should not go. I kept retiring towards the house. He pushed the gun into my side several times, and insisted upon my turning out. When I got about the middle of my house door, this was again repeated; that is, ' damn your eyes, if you stir one step, I will blow it at you.' I had a gun on one of the joists at the top of the house. The prisoner took it down, and said, ' You have got a gun, I see; I must have this.' He charged it, with several other pieces which were charged at the same time. He next came to me, and said, ' You must go along with us.' I told him I should not go; before I left my own house, I must know on what business they were going. The prisoner told me they were going to wipe off the national debt, and begin again:—that they were marching upon Nottingham. The prisoner said, they had half an hour to spare, and would halt at our house. They remained more than half an hour. There were about fifty persons in the house place, parlour, and kitchen. There was a servant of the name of James Raynor, whom they took along with them."

On his cross-examination, he says, " I said I had rather lose my life than go along with them. They did me no harm. They killed a dog; and some pitchforks were taken. I am quite sure," he says, " that the prisoner took the gun down from his shoulder, and cocked it. I saw him cock it; to the best of my belief it was cocked when he jobbed it into my side. It never was uncocked. I saw it cocked immediately before he jobbed against my side. I think the number of the party altogether might be four hundred; fifty came into my house. The rest remained outside, searching for forks and other things. I did not know the prisoner before. James Raynor, the servant, was away about two hours and a half, to the best of my remembrance. The party were at our house about six, and James Raynor might return about nine."

On his re-examination, he says, " They took three or four hayforks, and a pitching fork."

William Roper lives at the race stand upon Nottingham Forest. He says, " I was at Nottingham on the evening of Monday the 9th of June. At about half past eleven I set out to return home. On coming on the race-course, I met two people, and afterwards others. I should think I saw altogether about a hundred, more or less, in a line, one behind another, two deep; and there were several in the centre speaking to the others. I passed by them, Mr. Percival being with me, in the front of them. When we had passed them about twenty yards, there were eight or ten came after us. The men in the line were armed with poles, about a dozen of them. The men that came after us had long poles. They stopped us, and brought down the poles to a charge on Percival and me. I could not see what was at the end of the poles. We afterwards had conversation upon the subject, and I passed on, and went to my own house. It began to rain. I again came out. There is a shed near my house. Some of them came up while I stood under the piazzas. I remained there some time. They came up, drawn up as before, two deep. I left them, and went into the house, and about one o'clock they knocked at the door. I asked what they wanted. They asked whether I had not got some arms. I told them, ' Yes.' They said, ' You must deliver up your arms.' I told them I would not. They said if I did not, they must break my door open, and take them by force. I said, that if they did, I should blow the first man's brains out that came in. They said, ' Will you ?' I answered, ' Yes.' They said, ' Bring the men up with the fire-arms.' They did not finally succeed in getting the arms. They asked what arms I had. I told them I had a fusee and a rifle-piece, which I would not deliver up, and they went away without them about two o'clock. Some were left behind; but I heard the greater part of them go. After they were gone, I went out about three in the morning, and picked a pole up, not so good as those here."

Upon his cross-examination, he says, " It was a wet night and dark. I saw about a hundred men, and about a dozen of them had poles."

On being re-examined, he says, " If the others had had any poles, I should have seen them."

Captain Phillips of the 15th hussars, was next called. He was at that time an officer, stationed in the barracks within half a mile of the town of Nottingham. He says, that on the 9th of June there was a good deal of bustle and confusion in the town; but he was not in the town himself, and therefore cannot speak to it from any local observation. He says, the military were sent for in consequence of what had happened, he supposes, in the town. They remained about a quarter of an hour, and then returned. Then he says, " The next morning, about half past six, I was called out; and I went with Mr. Rolleston and Mr. Mundy, with twenty men, in the direction of Pentridge. About half a mile before we got to Eastwood, I saw some men armed with pikes flying over fields in different directions, on both sides of the road. They were so far off we could not overtake them. We proceeded on through Eastwood, and between Eastwood and Langley Mill we came up with a party of about sixty men. One man attempted to rally the others, and to make them stand, as if he had been the chief of them. Most of the men were armed with pikes and guns. They paid no attention to him; they fled over the hedges, and dispersed in all directions. We took about six-and-thirty of them prisoners. We found a considerable number of guns and pikes, which had been thrown away. Five or six of the men were found and taken with the arms in their hands."

On his cross-examination, he says, " I was about sixty yards from them when I saw this person attempt to form them; I have been stationed at Nottingham about a month, and I am not quartered there at this time."

The last witness who is called is the High Sheriff of this county, who, in the ready and vigorous execution of the high duties with which he is intrusted, on receiving information of this, whatever it is to be termed, went in pursuit of the party; he saw what Captain Phillips has stated; and his evidence concludes with stating, that he saw the prisoner in a ditch, and took him into custody.

This, Gentlemen, is the whole of the evidence given in support of the prosecution. After the counsel for the prisoner, and his witnesses had been heard, as it was my duty to do, I called upon the prisoner to know if he had any thing to urge in his own defence; but all he has said consists in denying that the gun was cocked at the time that it was driven against the side of the witness, whose evidence I have read to this point. In effect, therefore, he has left his defence to the powerful observations so ably made by the learned counsel who have addressed you on his behalf.

Some witnesses were then called for the prisoner, who speak not to the facts of the case, for no testimony has been given to controvert or vary that of any of the witnesses in support of the prosecution, so that as far as these witnesses are deserving of credit, of which it is for you to judge, the evidence is all in one scale; but witnesses have been led to speak to the character of the prisoner, during a long course of time, as to sobriety, loyalty, and humanity in the exercise of the different duties of life, in the various situations in which he has been placed.

The first witness called is William Taylor, who tells you that he is a farmer living at Southwingfield; that he has known the prisoner three and thirty years, and that he never knew anything of him but a true and loyal man, of humane disposition, till this affair happened. He says, " I know of his having been a soldier, and when he came back from being a soldier he was particularly loyal, and disagreed with any man who said anything against the government."

John Burton was next called, who said he has known the prisoner ten or twelve years, during which time he never behaved otherwise than as a loyal subject, for anything that ever he knew or heard, till this happened.

Then John Armstrong was called; he says that he is a framework-knitter in Southwingfield; that he has known the prisoner from a child, and that he has always borne a good character as a loyal, peaceable and humane man.

Such, Gentlemen, is the whole of the evidence on the one side and on the other, and in the result of which you are called upon in the discharge of a duty not incurred by choice, but cast upon you by the law, truly to pronounce upon the guilt or innocence of the prisoner at the bar.

And now, Gentlemen, I shall beg leave to call once more your attention to what the law is, and having briefly stated it in the outset, I will only again say, that there is no legal doubt or difficulty belonging to this part of the case. The learned judges with whom I act upon this occasion, being of opinion with all their predecessors, whose doctrine and decisions have been referred to, " that if there be an insurrection, by which is meant a large rising of the people, in order by force and violence to accomplish and avenge not any private objects of their own, not any private quarrels of their own, but to effectuate any general purpose, that is considered by the law as a levying of war;" and this you may take to be clearly the law of the land; nor is it the law of the land, as depending upon the authority of any single judge; it pervades every page of the criminal law of England, as applicable to the case of high treason; it may be traced back to antiquity, more or less remote; has been delivered down and is acted upon at the present day; but drawn as much into controversy as it has been on this occasion, I think it necessary, not in my own words, for I will not trust myself to any looseness of expression, when a rule of law is to be given affecting the life of man; but once more I will state, and more at length, the law as delivered by the greatest authorities; looking therefore, at what has been said by every one of the great authorities referred to, Mr. Justice Foster says, " Every insurrection which in judgment of law," not every insurrection which in point of fact, but " every insurrection which in judgment of law is intended against the person of the King, be it to dethrone or imprison him, or to oblige him to alter his measures of government, or to remove evil counsellers from about him, these risings all amount to levying war within the statute, whether attended with the pomp and circumstances of open war or not." That great and venerable judge, as eminent in his public as he was estimable in his private character, Sir Matthew Hale, as on this day, the subject and so justly of brilliant panegyric, by the counsel for the prisoner, who has laboured so much to draw this doctrine into destruction, lays down the law in different terms, but to the same effect; he says, " If divers persons levy a force of multitude of men, to pull down a particular inclosure, this is not a levying of war within the statute, but a great riot; but if they levy war to pull down all inclosures," speaking of a general intention, " or to expulse strangers, or to remove counsellors, or against any statute, as namely the statute of labourers, or for enhancing salaries and wages, this is a levying war against the King; and why? " because it is generally against the King's laws, and the offenders take upon them the reformation which subjects by gathering power, ought not to do;" and therefore, Gentlemen, the question for you will be, whether this be or be not an attempt to make a change in the government, by the gathering of power either with or without arms, which Lord Hale says, which Mr. Justice Foster repeats, and which all judges agree with them, in stating, is a levying of war against the King in his realm.

Gentlemen, having now stated to you what is the law upon this subject, the first question for your consideration will be, was there or was there not any insurrection or rising for any purpose whatever? In point of form, I state this to you as the question; but in point of substance, it can be no question whatever. The fact of a rising, of an insurrection, is not disputed, nor was it possible it should be. The previous meeting; the map produced; the returns called for; the assembling in different places; the firing of signals; the formation of pikes; the parading and proceeding in large bodies from different places to one point of union; the going from house to house; the breaking into the dwellings of many of the King's subjects, in the dead hour of night, forcibly taking their arms, dragging their servants and children from their beds, forcing them into the ranks; all these circumstances form such proof of insurrection and rising, that upon this part of the case there can be no possibility whatever of doubt.

What then, Gentlemen, is the next question? and which is equally for your consideration. With what intent did this rising take place? was it for a private or for a public purpose? Of private purpose, no trace appears upon the evidence, nor am I aware that any has been even pointed at in observation. The question therefore being, whether this was not a rising for a general and public purpose, I know only of two ways, by one or both of which intention and purpose can be ascertained; the one is, by the declarations of the parties concerned, for what is passing within their own breasts, must be best known to themselves. If, therefore, you find many of those assembled in the hearing of the prisoner, and the prisoner himself to different persons, declaring and avowing that those measures were taken for the purpose and with the view of bringing about a general change in the government of the country, as far as declarations are proof of intention, the evidence is decisive in this respect, and not encountered by any contradiction.

But there is yet another way of ascertaining purpose and intention; and this is, by the test of conduct.—Declarations may be obscure in themselves—imperfectly remembered—witnesses may speak without a strict and due regard to truth—but there are facts of a description which cannot possibly deceive. The assembling in military array—the long line of march—breaking into different houses—taking away arms—men forced out—formed into line—pikes, swords, muskets—the word of command given and obeyed—the advance towards Nottingham, till in sight of, and almost in conflict with the King's troops—putting aside all the declarations proved;—say, Gentlemen, upon these facts singly, was all this for a private, or a public purpose?

If you are satisfied that there was an insurrection—that it was for a purpose of a general nature, and that the purpose charged in the indictment, then the only remaining question will be, whether the prisoner by his conduct is involved. As to that, I have recapitulated the evidence which you had before heard, and I shall content myself now with merely directing your attention to the leading facts. And here you will recollect that many of the witnesses have been commended even by the counsel for the prisoner; and with the exception of two, not one is impeached; and the two are attacked only by observation. But unfortunately even the declaration of purpose does not stand upon the testimony of those two witnesses alone You have had other persons called, who have sworn to declarations by the prisoner himself, so far confirming the witnesses in question. When you find therefore the prisoner in person at a meeting previous to the rising, calling for the returns of arms from the different parishes; if you find him afterwards by the testimony of all, acting as second in command, parading, marching, drilling the men—at all the different houses—continuing with the assembled multitude from the beginning to the conclusion of the scene—then seen to come out of a ditch, and taken into custody after his companions had fled;—attending to all these facts, it will be for you to say whether, there being an insurrection, and for a general purpose, the prisoner was or was not concerned in it.

On the whole of the case you have been truly told, that if you have any doubt, you ought to give the prisoner the benefit of that doubt, and acquit him; and to this I agree. But it must be a fair, and notwithstanding the observation made, it must be a reasonable doubt—an honest doubt—such as you can reconcile with your consciences, and with the solemn obligation under which you are bound to deliver your verdict. You have been reminded that when this day shall have passed never to return, and this scene shall have closed never again to open, it may happen to you at some future time to look back upon what your conduct has been upon the present occasion; and you have been earnestly pressed to consider when in the chamber of sickness, on the bed of death, in the hour of approaching judgment, what reflections from that review and retrospect may arise. This appeal was fairly and properly made in favour of life; I do not wish to weaken it, nor would it become me, placed where I am, to follow further on this ground. I will therefore only say, that here and elsewhere—now and hereafter—in health and in sickness—throughout life and in death—and in that state which is to follow; your best support and consolation here, looking back upon the result of the present enquiry—your own justification hereafter, will be a faithful discharge of the duty cast upon you this day, by acting up to the sacred obligation under which you have become bound truly to decide according to the evidence to the best of your judgment and belief. Finally therefore, Gentlemen, looking to the charge, to the evidence, to the observations made from every quarter, to the law as stated and explained, you will say whether you deem the prisoner guilty or not guilty. If you really think that notwithstanding the declarations proved, the acts done, the purpose was not that which the indictment imputes; if of this even you entertain doubt, give the prisoner the benefit of that doubt, applying to it the character he has received. But if unfortunately the case be too clear to admit of any doubt, you will discharge your duty without consideration of the consequences that may follow; confining your attention to what your own duty is, and declaring the prisoner to be guilty, if you are satisfied that he is proved to be so. Consider and decide.

The jury retired at a quarter past three, and returned into Court in a quarter of an hour, with a Verdict, finding the prisoner GUILTY; *and that he had no lands, &c. to their knowledge at the time of the offence committed.*

Lord Chief Baron Richards. — The Court is very anxious to use all the expedition consistent with justice; whether it will be more convenient to proceed now, or to adjourn until to-morrow morning, must be pretty well left to you, Gentlemen.

Mr. Attorney General.—My Lord, I am sure I am as anxious to save your Lordships time, and to expedite the proceedings, as your Lordships can possibly be. I do not know that your Lordships will save a great deal of time by proceeding on one of the trials now; a portion of time to be sure will be saved, namely, that of selecting the gentlemen of the jury; but only to do that, as your Lordships know, would be in fact confining the gentlemen of the jury without any thing to exercise their judgment upon, so far as the trial had gone. I doubt, myself, whether your Lordships would very much expedite the proceeding.

Lord Chief Baron Richards.—I feel great doubt whether we should expedite.

Mr. Attorney General.—When I say that I am quite in your Lordships judgment.

Lord Chief Baron Richards.—Does any thing occur to you, Mr. Cross.

Mr. Cross.—My Lord, we are so sensible of the attention of your Lordships, that we would wish to leave the matter entirely in the discretion of the Court, as that in which we feel no interest.

Mr. Justice Dallas.—The great objection will be, that the jury sworn will be locked up all night, with nothing upon which to exercise their judgment. One is only anxious that there should be no idea that time is wasted for a moment.

Mr. Justice Abbott.—If we impanel a jury now, the consequence may be, that the jury will be impanelled two nights; whereas, if we adjourn till to-morrow morning, in all probability the trial will be over next day, and then again we shall come to confining the jury two nights again; we should be sorry to confine the jury more than is absolutely necessary.

Lord Chief Baron Richards.—It would come to our confining a jury during the Sunday; perhaps we may as well adjourn to to-morrow morning.

Adjourned to eight o'clock to-morrow morning.

THE TRIAL

OF

ISAAC LUDLAM, the Elder.

SPECIAL ASSIZE, DERBY.
Wednesday, 22d October, 1817.

*L*ORD *Chief Baron Richards.*—Mr. Solicitor General and Mr. Denman, is there any objection to the jury being called from No. 84, to which the call has already proceeded.

Mr. Denman.—I have none at all, my Lord.

The Jurors returned by the Sheriff were called over.

Francis Agard, merchant, not a freeholder of the county of Derby to the amount of 10*l.* a year.

Mark Porter the younger, roper, challenged by the prisoner.

Joseph Garner, farmer, excused on account of illness.

George Poyser, farmer, challenged by the prisoner.

Abraham Harding Beale, woolstapler, challenged by the crown.

James Sutton, gentleman, challenged by the prisoner.

James Soresby, gentleman, challenged by the crown.

Thomas Moore, farmer, challenged by the prisoner.

Philip Waterfield, gentleman, sworn.

James Osborne, farmer, challenged by the prisoner.

John Edensor, farmer, challenged by the prisoner.

William Hayward, farmer, challenged by the prisoner.

Benjamin Stone, the elder, farmer, not properly described in the panel.

Anthony Allsopp, bar master, sworn.

William Dunn, farmer, sworn.

James Northage James, gentleman, challenged by the prisoner.

John Blackwall, esq. excused on account of illness.

Robert Blackwall, mercer, challenged by the prisoner.

Thomas Lomas, baker, challenged by the prisoner.

Joseph Willshaw, builder, challenged by the prisoner.

David Gregory, farmer, challenged by the prisoner.

Daniel Wilson, miner, challenged by the prisoner.

Samuel Hartley, plumber, challenged by the prisoner.

William Nuttall, farmer, challenged by the prisoner.

Thomas Hall, farmer, challenged by the prisoner.

John Wright (of Wirksworth) grocer, challenged by the crown.

Edward Mather, grocer, challenged by the prisoner.

Edward Haslam, cooper, challenged by the prisoner.

John Wilson, wheelwright, challenged by the prisoner.

John Harlow, mason, challenged by the crown.

John Hemsworth, maltster, sworn.

William Sutton, draper, challenged by the prisoner.

Thomas Motterham, grocer, challenged by the prisoner.

John Whitham, druggist, challenged by the crown.

John Downes, innkeeper, challenged by the crown.

John Barnes, grocer, challenged by the crown.

Robert Blore, vintner, challenged by the prisoner.

William Campion, farmer, sworn.

Thomas Leedham, farmer, challenged by the prisoner.

Thomas Freer, farmer, sworn.

Thomas Brown Dumelow, farmer, sworn.

John Hunt, brickmaker, challenged by the prisoner.

Thomas Cooper, farmer, sworn.

John Lea, gentleman, challenged by the crown.

Thomas Hassall, gentleman, excused, having been sent for home on particular business.

Thomas Brown, farmer, challenged by the prisoner.

John Smith, farmer, challenged by the crown.

John Needham, farmer, not summoned, residing out of the county.

William Burton, farmer, challenged by the crown.

John Cox, farmer, challenged by the crown.

Edward Stevenson, grazier, sworn.
Robert Creswell, gentleman, sworn.
Hemsworth Newton, farmer, challenged by the prisoner.
John Clarke Ward, maltster, challenged by the prisoner.
William Wayte, farmer, challenged by the prisoner.
Richard Marbrow, farmer, challenged by the prisoner.
Henry Wayte, farmer, sworn.
John Somers, miller, challenged by the prisoner.
Thomas Hawksworth, farmer, challenged by the prisoner.
Thomas Whittingham, farmer, challenged by the prisoner.
Humphrey Trafford Nadin, gentleman, challenged by the crown.
William Bodill, farmer, not a freeholder, &c.
John Garner, farmer, challenged by the prisoner.
Francis Hamp, farmer, challenged by the crown.
Isaac Twiggs, the younger, miner, challenged by the crown.
Daniel Sellors, cooper, challenged by the crown.
John Wright (of Bradborne) farmer, sworn.

THE JURY.

Philip Waterfield.	Thomas Brown Dumelow.
Anthony Allsopp.	Thomas Cooper.
William Dunn.	Edward Stevenson.
John Hemsworth.	Robert Creswell.
William Campion.	Henry Wayte.
Thomas Freer.	John Wright.

The Jury were charged with the prisoner in the usual form.

The Indictment was opened by Mr. Balguy.

Mr. ATTORNEY GENERAL.

May it please your Lordship,
Gentlemen of the Jury,

GENTLEMEN, you have heard from my friend, Mr. Lowndes, who read this indictment to you, and from my learned friend who has also stated its contents to you, that the charge against the prisoner at the bar is that of having been guilty of high treason; and that the species of treason with which he is charged is that of having levied war against the King, as charged in the first count of the indictment; and as charged in the two others, of having conspired to levy war against the King; in one of them for the purpose of deposing the King, and in the others, for the purpose of compelling the King to change his measures. The first charge in this indictment, that of levying war, is the one to which I wish principally to direct your attention; because it appears to me, that if the facts I am about to state to you shall be made out by evidence, and if they are not made out by evidence, of course my statement will go for nothing; for you are to decide this cause according to the evidence that you shall hear upon oath: I say, if I shall make out by evidence the facts that I shall state to you, the prisoner at the bar, in common with other persons, has been guilty of the offence of levying war.

Gentlemen, after what has passed in this court, and the law having been laid down by the learned judges, perhaps it might be considered a waste of time in me to be entering at length into the discussion of the law in this case; but I will shortly state to you my notions of the law, knowing that if I am mistaken in the statement, it will be corrected by the learned judges who are presiding upon this trial; and you will recollect, that I do not desire you to adopt any one principle that I shall lay down in the short address I have to make to you, unless that principle is sanctioned and recommended by the opinion of the learned judges: for in all cases, whether they be in the trial of the civil rights of our fellow-subjects, or whether they be in those more important trials, deciding whether our fellow-subjects, or any of them, have been guilty of criminal offences against the laws, it is from the constitutional judges of the land, from those who are placed in office for the purpose of executing the high and sacred function, from those who have passed their lives in the consideration and in the investigation and in the decision of matters of law, it is from them that juries are to receive directions in point of law, and not from the counsel discussing the civil rights of parties, or conducting prosecutions, or from those who are counsel for prisoners; it is only for the purpose of elucidating and applying the facts more directly to your consideration, that I take the liberty of stating to you my humble conceptions of the law.

The statute upon which the first charge in this indictment is made, was an Act of Parliament passed in the reign of King Edward the third; by the recital of which statute it appears that there had been different statements and opinions of judges and of others, what species of conduct did or did not amount to high treason. For the purpose of doing that which is most important for the safety of the community and of each individual belonging to it, for the purpose of reducing as far as by any general enactment you can reduce any species of crime to a definite description, and to certainty, this statute stated what should be high treason; it begins, and I merely mention that as introductory to the others, it begins by enacting as high treason, or declaring rather I should say as high treason (for the greater part of this statute has always struck me as rather declaratory of what was, the principle of the common law, than any new enactment of the law upon the subject,) it begins; " that to compass and imagine, that is to intend the death of the King, is high treason;" that is not the species of treason about which you are inquiring now. It then goes on to mention certain other acts, such as compassing the death of the Heir Apparent, and violating the companion, that is, the wife of the King. Then it comes to this, " or to levy war against our Lord the King in his realm; that is the general position and description of the statute, but what does or does not amount to levying war must necessarily be a question of law; whether the facts that have taken place in the particular case, into which you or any other gentlemen upon other occasions placed in your situation are enquiring, have been committed, so as to bring the parties accused within that, which by the rule of law is a levying of war, is a question of fact for the consideration of gentlemen sitting upon the jury; but what does constitute a levying of war, is a question of law which must depend upon a general rule; for if it does not, so far from our having any rule of conduct by which the subjects of this country can square their actions, we are left in the most perfect state of uncertainty, and that statute of Edward the third might as well not have been passed. You twelve gentlemen, in case you are to lay down the rule of law, and to put a construction upon this statute, may be of one opinion, another twelve gentlemen may upon that subject be of another opinion, a third set of twelve gentlemen who are sworn in the box to try any man upon this species of crime, differing from the other two according to their notions, according to the extent of information possessed by each, according as any of them may or may not have applied your minds to the consideration of this important subject, which does require the application of the human mind to its consideration, whatever may be, its natural ability and talent, may be of a different opinion; and thus will the rule of law vary; and instead of having one rule and standard to which we can look by which to regulate our conduct, we may get in the most important actions of our lives, or at least in those which are most important to the conduct of our lives, into chaos, uncertainty and confusion.

Where then, Gentlemen, are we to look for what is the rule of law. We are to look at what has been the constant, unvaried, uniform course of decision and opinion not merely by judges in those times, upon which reflections may be thrown by those who stand as counsel for the prisoners, but by that which has been uniformly laid down and invariably acted upon by the judges of all and of the best times, without one deviation from that rule by any judgment given by any judge, without one deviation from that rule by any man competent to write that which should be read as a rule, in his closet, upon due, weighty and mature consideration. When I take the liberty of stating the law upon the subject, I feel a degree of confidence in stating it, and why, because I find the same thing to have been stated not by counsel at the bar, but I find the same thing to have been stated by the greatest, the most intelligent, the wisest, and what is better than all, the best men that ever blessed this country sitting in the seat of judicature. I have wisdom, I have that which is better, virtue, for my foundation in the statement.

Gentlemen, to levy war against the King, is not merely to levy war against the person of the King, but if war be levied against what I will call (because the term is used in that very statute) the royal majesty of the King, that is, against the state and government of which he is the great and prominent member, and in this respect, I may say the representative in his executive character, it is high treason.

To begin (for I will go no further back for the present purpose) with that which was laid down at a time when it was peculiarly the subject of consideration by the great men of this country, who had but a very short time before stood forward for the purpose of maintaining its liberties against encroachments that had been made. Almost immediately after, or at least within seven years after that revolution which was effected in the year 1688, the law of high treason was peculiarly the subject of consideration by the great and wise men of the land, for it was in the 7th year of King William that an Act of Parliament was passed for the purpose of regulating the trials for high treason, in order to give peculiar privileges and just advantages to those persons who might be charged with that crime. My Lord Chief Justice Holt (and when I mention his name it is a name that no lawyer, that no free man who loves the liberty of his country, ever mentions without veneration, or ever thinks of without love and affection,) my Lord Chief Justice Holt, within a short year after that statute of the 7th of King William was passed, laid down the law of treason, as far as relates to levying war, in the very words that I am about to read to you.

Gentlemen, in a trial which came on before Lord Chief Justice Holt, in the eighth year of the reign of King William the Third, the trial of Sir John Friend, a question arose, whether conspiring to levy war, where no war was in fact levied, was a species of treason within another branch of the statute; and my Lord Chief Justice Holt, in deciding that question, found it necessary to state what is the actual levying of war. My Lord Chief Justice Holt was not at that time sitting alone. I should have thought indeed, that the authority of my Lord Chief Justice Holt, even though his opinion had not been delivered in the presence of others judges who sat with him at the time, would of itself have been quite sufficient; and particularly when I recollect, and know that that opinion has, from that hour to the present time, been adopted, laid down, and acted upon, by all subsequent judges. But my Lord Chief Justice Holt was sitting at that time, associated with my Lord Chief Justice Treby, a great and learned lawyer of his day; and with two other learned judges, Mr. Justice Neville, and Mr. Justice Rokeby, and with those learned judges assisting him in his statement of the law, states, as far as relates to the levying war, in these terms: "There may be a war levied without any design upon the King's person, or endangering it;" that is the King's person; "which, if actually levied, is high treason and designing," says he, "to levy war without more would not be treason;" nor was it. The subsequent counts in this indictment are founded upon an Act of Parliament made since, which constituted the designing to levy war a treason, as designing to levy war. But I read to you, for the purpose of stating to you, what Lord Chief Justice Holt says, as to the levying war: "There may be a war levied without any design upon the King's person, or endangering of it, which if actually levied is high treason; as for example, if persons do assemble themselves, and act with force in opposition to some law which they think inconvenient, and hope thereby to get it repealed;" with force, you will please to remember; "this is a levying war, and treason, though purposing and designing it is not so;" that is purposing to assemble that force, is not. "So when they endeavour, in great numbers, with force to make some reformation of their own heads, without pursuing the method of the law, that is a levying of war, and treason; but the purposing and designing it, is not so." Now, Gentlemen, there is the opinion of my Lord Chief Justice Holt, sanctioned by the presence of three other most learned and wise and honourable judges of the land, sitting in conjunction with him at that time.

Gentlemen; Mr. Justice Foster, who was one of the greatest judges that ever lived, has laid down the law precisely in the same manner, in a discourse upon the subject of high treason, which has been considered of authority ever since it was published to the world, and has been considered of authority for this reason; not merely because it was written by Mr. Justice Foster, though that adds great sanction to it; but because the doctrines contained in it had been sanctioned by all his predecessors, and have been found to be replete with wisdom, by all those who have succeeded him. I take the liberty therefore to state to you, without going through the variety of cases in which that has been laid down, that the assembling of a number of persons together, arming themselves for the purpose by means of force, of producing any general object upon which their own particular and peculiar interests are not merely and immediately concerned, is a levying war against our Lord the King in his realm, and is by law high treason; the persons charged with it must have the purpose of effecting some general object, through the medium of the force that they have assembled together; whether the means which they have adopted, were sufficient and competent to effect the end, can make no difference. If the means are competent to effect the end, and the end is effected, those persons who have been guilty of treason, never afterwards can be adjudged to be so; for if men assemble themselves together with an armed force, to effect a revolution, and it be by competent means, the revolution must necessarily be effected; and they becoming successful in their revolution, of course there can be no government left who can ever charge them with high treason; so that, when you talk of the means being competent to the end, and the offence depending upon the consequences which follow this absurdity, arises that, if war were levied through the realm, and it ever came to hostile battle in the field, day after day; if the treason were defeated, the means would not be competent to the end, and according to that argument no treason would ever be committed. Gentlemen, if they use the means, competent or incompetent, by which they intend to effect their purpose, and begin to endeavour to effect it, the treason is complete, because the war is levied.

Now, Gentlemen, having stated that, I will state to you shortly, what are the particulars of this case, begging leave to preface that which I am about to state with respect to the facts, with another observation, which is this, that when persons act together or assemble together with common intent and object, they cannot act for one common object, without one man doing one thing and another another; each cannot be at the same moment doing the same thing, but they each take several parts, and do several acts in the course of the transaction, and all working towards one effect. The law says, because common sense says, that when men are acting together, with one common intent and purpose, the act of one is the act of the other, that is to say, each is responsible for the acts that the others are committing, all acting with one common intent, and therefore, whether in the levying war, one man is at one place endeavouring to collect his forces and his arms, and another man at another place, and so on, each performing his functions, and what he conceives at the moment his duties for that purpose, that which the one does the other is responsible for, because they have a common mind, and are acting for one common object.

Gentlemen, the case that I shall present to you, is this:—On the 8th of June, at a place called the White Horse, at Pentridge, a number of persons were in the course of the day assembled and congregated together; we may judge upon many occasions, from what is doing at one given time, whether anything and what had been done before; if we find men assembled together, and some of those persons who have assembled together are doing acts and making declarations, which it is impossible could have suggested themselves at the moment in which they are so got together, what is the inference?—that something must have taken place in common between them, or some of them at least, previous to that period of time, and I ought to state to you here, a proposition of law, as clear and as undisputed as any can be, which is this, that if men act together with a common intent and object, those who come into the transaction after it has been originally planned, and begin to act from the time in which they so come, in furtherance of the common purpose and design, are equally guilty with those who originally planned and contrived it; they are combined with them in the guilty purpose which they have; it makes no difference in the eye of common sense, whether a man joins in the war, or joins the party who are about to levy war at this or that hour, or at a subsequent period, if he joins them in their acts with his mind intending to effect the same purpose they do; at whatever period of the transaction he becomes combined with them, no matter, he is equally guilty with them. Gentlemen, common sense points this out, and the rules of law, as far as they affect the conduct of mankind in these respects, are founded upon the principles of common sense and common justice; in such points as these, the rules of law are not technical; the rules of law are founded upon the great principles of moral justice, sanctioned by the great principles of common sense.

On the 8th of June a number of persons were together at the White Horse, at Pentridge, a man was there, who was seated in the room, with a map before him, for the purpose of receiving and of talking to all those who should there come; a number of persons came there, and he pointed out to them, from that map, what was to be the course and operations of their proceedings on the next day, which was the intended period of their rising, or the intended period at which they were to commence the levying of war; and this is not an unimportant part of the consideration, that it was not merely a certain number of specific persons who had got together at one particular time of the day, but that he was sitting, during the greater part of the day, to receive those that should come from time to time, for the purpose of being actually informed what they should do the next day, in the course of their design of levying war; he shewed them the line of march they were to take, the course they were to pursue the next day towards Nottingham; and let it not be forgotten, that he pointed out how they were to march, and to where they were to march. As the persons who were thus to be concerned together, were the inhabitants of different places in that part of the country, of Pentridge, of Southwingfield, of Swanwick, and of other places, which were all mentioned; it was intended that all those coming from the different villages, should at a certain place (as far as they could) join together for the purpose of then proceeding on their march to Nottingham, and I think the Southwingfield people were to collect themselves at a place they call Hunt's Barn, in Southwingfield, they were to proceed on a certain line of march till they got to the close or land of a Mr. Topham, Topham's close, in Southwingfield, where it was projected that the people from Pentridge were to join the Southwingfield men; from thence they were to proceed all together, in order to be joined at the subsequent points by the persons who were to come from Swanwick, and other places from which they expected bodies of men. When they had concentrated the forces to come from those different places, they were then to march to Nottingham Forest, where they expected to be joined by a considerable body of insurgents, in order to take, to possess themselves, by force, of the town of Nottingham; and it was stated by the person who was there sitting, that the people in other parts of the kingdom would rise at the same time on that day, at Sheffield, at Chesterfield, and at other places pointed out by this man, upon the map; in short, to use one of their own phrases, though I believe used at a subsequent time, there would be a cloud from the North, which would come and sweep all before them.

Of course this proceeding could not be effected without the tumultuous multitude thus to be assembled being furnished with some sort of arms: to a certain extent they, had previously furnished themselves, I say they had previously furnished themselves, because the peculiar sort of arms of one sort which they had, are not such arms as men in this country keep in their houses, or are possessed of generally, and they had been made or manufactured some where or somehow by the persons who were to put them into the hands of those who should so assemble. Every Englishman, or most of us, perhaps, have a gun, but we have not a pike; that is not the common and ordinary arms which the subjects of this country possess for their defence.

Gentlemen; another thing which I say manifestly shews previous conspiracy and consultation, was this, that on the 8th of June, at this White Horse at Peutridge, one of the persons who was there, called for a return, an account of the arms that were possessed in the different villages that were to rise; not a return of the arms that were possessed by the persons who were rising, but a return of the arms that belonged to the other inhabitants of those villages who had no intention so to rise, but which it was declared that these insurgents were to seize and possess themselves of in the line of their march. Gentlemen, when I allude to the conduct of other persons, I beg you will have the goodness to understand me upon that subject; the only person now upon his trial is the prisoner at the bar, and I would not allude to the conduct of any other person, except that it is necessary so to do, because, he being charged with a conspiracy with others, the conduct of the others with whom he was a party becomes necessarily a part of his own conduct, and explains his transactions, and the motives which operated upon his mind, when in his presence, and with his sanction, they did what they did, and said what they said. At this meeting, on the 8th of June, the prisoner, Isaac Ludlam, was present; he heard that which passed at the different periods of the day at that meeting, and you will judge from that which he did when this actual insurrection took place, whether he was or was not joining with them in the common intent to do that which at different times was professed, sometimes by one man and sometimes by another, to be their object, namely, to overturn the government of the country, to wipe off, as they stated, the national debt, to begin afresh; in fact, to effect a revolution.

I will come now to the evening of the 9th. I have told you that it was settled on the 8th, that on the evening of the 9th the rising was to take place. Gentlemen, the rising began, or at least certain persons assembled themselves together near Hunt's Barn; two persons who were concerned in this business, a man of the name of William Turner, and a man of the name of George Weighman, went to Hunt's Barn, at Hunt's Barn the prisoner was not at first, but that which passed there is just as much, and as competent evidence against the prisoner, as if he had been himself there, for the reason I have stated, that when persons effect a general rising, some must be doing one thing and some another at the same time; and the question must be, whether they were not acting simultaneously for the same purpose.

Gentlemen; about ten o'clock at night, and before the prisoner joined the party who assembled at Hunt's Barn, and proceeded from thence, he living at a place near the Coburn quarry, was seen with several others, he the prisoner armed with a pike; after he had been so seen he joined the party who came from Hunt's Barn down to Topham's close, that is, a piece of land belonging to a Mr. Topham, in the line of march that had been pointed out to them the day before, he came and joined that party, and carried a pike; he marched with them; he was present with them at the different houses that were attacked for the purpose of seizing arms, and not only for the purpose of seizing arms, but attacked for the purpose also of forcing others to join them, under the most imperious threats and menaces, in order to swell their numbers, and in order to compel others to do that which they themselves were about to do, and which they did do, to compel others to put themselves in hostile array against the laws and the constitution of their country.

Without going through the detail in my statement of that which they did at different houses, and the outrageous acts that were committed to collect arms as they proceeded, their numbers were increased by some who were to join them as volunteers, by others whom they obliged to march with them; their ranks were to be formed, the men were to be kept together; there were many persons who were with them that were anxious and desirous, though they had been compelled to join, to get away; the prisoner at the bar was one of those who was watching the conduct of those persons, and when he perceived that any person was attempting to quit them, he kept them in their ranks, and prevented their escaping from the party. Gentlemen, this will be proved to you by several of the witnesses. Another thing, not unimportant to manifest that this man was a party with the others, and had a common mind and intent with them, is this, they formed this body of men at different times to preserve something like order; those that were the principal leaders marched in front; the person placed in the rear to keep them up was Isaac Ludlam, the prisoner, placed in an effective and important situation, in order to keep together those forces which they were assembling for the purpose of marching upon Nottingham forest, in order to join those whom they expected to be there, and to do that, which they stated at different times in the course of the transaction was their object.

Gentlemen, they went to Mr. Hall's, to Mrs. Hepworth's, to Mr. Storer's, and a great many other houses, till at last, when they had assembled a very considerable number, and I think had been joined by a party coming from Swanwick, they arrived at a place called Codnor. But before I state to you what passed at Codnor, I would beg leave to state to you one most important fact, as it affects the prisoner at the bar. In the course of this line of march, there are some most important works called the Butterley Iron Works, and it appears to have been a considerable object of this party, to get the Butterley men to join them, and if they could have done it, to get possession of the Butterley works; to these works they proceeded; however, Mr. Goodwin, a person who is one of the managers under Messrs. Jessop and Outram, the proprietors of these works, met the insurgents at the door of the office, and refused to let any of them come in, refused to let them have any men from those works, and entered into an expostulation with them; there were several persons who took that opportunity, as Mr. Goodwin was determined to defend his works, of escaping into the works from, this party, which they had been forced to join; Mr. Goodwin particularly addressed himself to the prisoner at the bar, and expostulated with him; he had the opportunity, if he pleased, of escaping with others, and when Mr. Goodwin told him, in plain language, what would probably be the consequence of his conduct, his answer was, "I am as bad as I can be, I must go on." Gentlemen, I wish the prisoner had recollected that there is no period of a man's life till the hour comes when it closes, that he is as bad as he can be; there is time at all periods, for something like repentance, though perhaps the time may be gone by when a man is capable of making restitution; but he, though remonstrated with, determined to proceed, and it is obvious from that declaration of his, that he was a volunteer upon the subject with the rest, that he was acting in conjunction with the rest, that he was determined to persevere with those who did persevere, and that he was completely guilty of this treason.

From Butterley they proceeded on to Codnor; when they got to Codnor, they went to a place called the Glass-House Inn, a public house; a great many of them went into that house; a few of them went into a house called the French Horn, being in too large numbers to get into this house, where they stopped to get some refreshment; it rained very hard; it was suggested, that while they were in the house, in all probability some of the persons who had been forced to join them would escape; the prisoner at the bar was the person who made the proposal that a guard should be placed at the door, to prevent that; nay more, so fully was he persuaded of the necessity of doing it, that it was he, together with another, who performed the office of standing guard at that door, to prevent any of those persons who had been forced to join them, from escaping, or to prevent any of those persons who had joined voluntarily, and who might have repented, who peradventure might have overheard the salutary advice that man had received from Mr. Goodwin, and might have been willing to take advantage of that admonition; but he who had gone on to be as bad as he could be, and was determined to go on to the end, was determined also, that as far as in him lay, others should go on also, and at the door of this house he stood as a guard, to prevent any of the persons from leaving the party, who might have been inclined so to do.

Gentlemen, other witnesses will state to you the different periods of time on the march, and while they were at Codnor, at which he was conducting himself as a man who was keeping together their ranks, and in fact acting, I might almost say, as an officer in the service. Gentlemen, it will be proved to you also, by other witnesses, that he said " we were to have been at Nottingham by two o'clock this morning, and we shall be too late;" and other expressions of the same sort; it will also be proved to you, as manifesting his intention and his mind, that in speaking of the rising, he said, " it is brought to a head at last." What is brought to a head at last? why our rising; the revolution is brought into effect at last. " We are going to Nottingham; there is a parliament formed at Nottingham, we are going to guard it, and the business will be done before we get there." Gentlemen, I will not weary you, because you must hear it from the witnesses, by stating the different expressions this man used; but from the beginning to the end of this transaction, you will find him a party and partizan, as much engaged by his acts, and in his demeanor, and in his declarations, as any man could possibly be in such a transaction.

Gentlemen, I have addressed myself rather to stating to you the evidence, as it affects the prisoner particularly, because really it would be almost wasting your time to be be stating the acts generally that took place, to prove that this was a treasonable insurrection, and levying of war. I have stated to you that the parties stated that it was their object to be at Nottingham by two o'clock in the morning; now, Gentlemen, what was doing at Nottingham? acts not to the extent this man hoped and expected, thank God! but on that night, on Nottingham forest, which they declared to be the place at which they were to join the Nottingham insurgents, there was a body of men assembled together at twelve o'clock at night, continuing there till two in the morning, which was the time when this man hoped to reach Nottingham from Pentridge, though they were from various causes delayed after that time; there was that simultaneous rising, which confirms the object and intention of these persons who declared that it was their intention to march to Nottingham, where they expected to be joined by other persons.

Gentlemen, in the course of their line of march, some of them began to doubt whether they should find all things at Nottingham quite so ripe as they expected; and this accounts for some of the delay in their march, and therefore it was agreed that a person of the name of George Weightman should take a horse, which they had taken out of the stable of a Mr. Booth, that he should ride on to Nottingham as fast as he could, that he should come back when he had got intelligence, and meet them at a place called Langley mill, which is in a place beyond Codnor, of which I have spoken. Weightman went. Whilst Weightman was gone towards Nottingham they attacked the house of a Mr. Raynor, which is in the road before you come to Langley mill, at which Langley mill Weightman was to come back from Nottingham to meet them. I will not detail to you the particular and specific facts myself, because Mr. Raynor will state them to you; that they insisted upon his going, telling him they had shot one man, and that they would shoot him too if he did not go, and compelling him to bring his son and his servant to go with them; but there they said they would halt to rest themselves, for that they had half-an-hour to spare. Gentlemen, George Weightman was not come back. Mr. Raynor's house was just before they got to Langley mill; and calculating the time, they had half-an-hour before he could get back to Langley mill; they did stop there; they then proceeded to Langley mill; just before they got there they were met by George Weightman. George Weightman had some conversation with the leader of this party; what that was I know not; but in consequence of a short conference with the leader of the party, George Weightman rode up to them, saying to them, " push on, my lads, all is right at Nottingham, the soldiers will not come out of their barracks, and Nottingham is taken." Now, that George Weightman told them what was untrue there is no doubt, but that is not material; it shows their object and intention; they had embarked in this design, and George Weightman who had been one of their leaders, having been thus sent to Nottingham, those who were leading them having gone on so far as they had, were by imposition at last encouraging and inducing the others still to go on, in hopes that by proceeding they should collect other forces, in the desperate expectation that they should succeed in the object they had in view.

Now, Gentlemen, from what I have stated to you, was the prisoner or was he not acting with the common mind? I am about to state to you a circumstance as to the prisoner which pains me much, which manifests that he was so acting, because he was not satisfied with joining those persons himself; whom he joined without any force or any persuasions used towards him, or at least that sort of force and persuasion which compelled some persons whom I shall call to you as witnesses, namely, Mr. Hall and others, who could not help joining them, but escaped as soon as they could; but he brought his sons with him into that traitorous field; he saw them acting at the time he was with them. Why, Gentlemen, a man who was an unwilling attendant upon such a party as this, when he received that admonition from Mr. Goodwin, and when he had an opportunity of escaping into these Butterley works, if he had pleased to make an effort so to have done, if he had been an unwilling joiner of such a party as this, if he had not intended to further that which was the common object; if he had felt any repugnance, would he not in the course of this transaction, whatever had become of himself, would he not with the injunction of a parent have dismissed his sons at least, and have endeavoured to have persuaded them not to continue in the transaction? Oh, Gentlemen, well may treason be called the highest offence in the law; for when men are once determined to commit it, there is hardly any crime either legal or moral in which they may not in the progress of their evil course be involved.

Gentlemen, I have stated to you very much in the outline, and only in the outline, the transactions of this case. If the facts that I have stated are proved, it appears to me impossible that human understanding can doubt of the guilt of the prisoner. You have a most important duty to perform; aye, and you have also a most anxious duty to perform; for whatever be the offence with which a fellow-subject may be charged, if it involves any thing like capital punishment, beyond all doubt the duty of the jury is an anxious and a painful duty; but I know, and I am persuaded, you will recollect that to pronounce a fair, honest, and impartial verdict according to the evidence, is your duty as men and as jurymen; and I am sure you will recollect (indeed you do not want to be put in mind of it) that to perform that duty well, and to perform it truly, you are bound to pronounce your verdict according to the evidence; to do this, you are under the sacred and solemn obligation of an oath. It is not, that capricious doubts are to be entertained; where there are any fair and reasonable and honest doubts created in the case, certainly the prisoner should have the benefit of them; but it must not be that species of doubt which amounts only to this,—Why the thing is not so proved as if we had seen it with our own eyes. If, according to the common principles of common sense and common reason, the prisoner appears to have been guilty of that which I have charged upon him, you, I know, however painful it may be, will exercise your duty in pronouncing that verdict which the law and which your oaths call upon you to pronounce.

EVIDENCE FOR THE CROWN.

Anthony Martin sworn.

Examined by Mr. Solicitor General.

Q. I believe you are in the employ of Messrs. Outram and Jessop, at the Butterley works?

A. Yes.

Q. And were so in June last?

A. Yes.

Q. Did you on Sunday, the 8th of June, go from Butterley to Pentridge?

A. Yes.

Q. About what hour in the morning was it?

A. Between nine and ten o'clock in the morning.

Q. Who went with you?

A. John Cope.

Q. Was he also a person employed at the Butterley works?

A. Yes.

Q. Did you go with him to the White Horse, at Pentridge?

A. Yes; we went to the Croft below the White Horse first?

Q. What induced you to go into the White Horse?

A. A little girl came from the White Horse to John Cope.

Q. And you went in with him?

A. Yes.

Q. Who keeps that house,—the White Horse?

A. Nanny Weightman.

Q. Into what part of the house did you go?

A. Into the house part first; then they asked John Cope to go into the parlour, and I went in with him.

Q. Whom did you find in the parlour when first you went in?

A. There was Brandreth there.

Q. Was that the person they called the captain?
A. Yes.
Q. Who else, when first you went in?
A. George Weightman.
Q. Any of the other Weightmans?
A. Joseph Weightman.
Q. John Weightman?
A. There was another, Joseph Weightman.
Q. Was John Bacon there?
A. Yes.
Q. Were there other persons there when you went in?
A. Yes, there was Thomas Weightman.
Q. Do you recollect any other when first you went in?
A. Ormond Booth was in.
Q. Whilst you were there, did other persons come in from time to time?
A. Yes, they kept coming in.
Q. How many were occasionally in the room at once?
A. About twenty.
Q. Was Brandreth sitting?
A. He was sitting in the centre of the room by the table.
Q. Do you know the prisoner, Isaac Ludlam?
A. Yes.
Q. Did you see him there?
A. Yes.
Q. What time did he come in?
A. Between one and two o'clock.
Q. Did any one come with him?
A. Yes.
Q. Who?
A. Turner.
Q. Was that William Turner?
A. Yes.
Q. Where does Ludlam live?
A. At Wingfield, in the parish.
Q. The parish of Southwingfield?
A. Yes.
Q. Does Turner live there also?
A. Yes.

Q. How far is Wingfield from Pentridge?
A. A mile.
Q. Do you know the prisoner's house?
A. No.
Q. What was the subject of the conversation?
A. It was about overturning the present government.
Q. Was that stated after Ludlam the prisoner came into the room?
A. I do not remember that it was.
Q. Had it been mentioned before?
A. Yes.
Q. By whom?
A. By the captain.
Q. Was anything said about arms?
A. Yes.
Q. After the prisoner came in?
A. Yes.
Q. What was said about arms?
A. Turner pulled a list out of his pocket, which Ludlam read.
Q. Is that William Turner?
A. Yes.
Q. Do you mean the prisoner Ludlam?
A. Yes.
Q. What was said by Turner when he pulled out the list?
A. He said he had got a list of all the guns and pikes and swords that they had in their parish.
Q. What else did he say?
A. He wanted to know where the guns and pikes were that belonged to the Pentridge and Ripley people?
Q. Did you say the prisoner Ludlam read it?
A. Yes.
Q. Did he read it so that people might hear it?
A. Yes, they might hear it.
Q. He read it to the persons in the room?
A. Yes, he did.
Q. What did you hear him say when he was reading?
A. I heard him say that there was a quantity of pikes in a stone quarry.

Q. Who said that?

A. The Prisoner, Ludlam.

Q. Was that what he read from the paper, or what he said after he read the paper?

A. They were talking of that after he read the paper.

Q. What did he read from the paper?

A. There was an account of the arms, what people's houses they were at, and where they had to fetch them from.

Q. After that had been read, there was a conversation about pikes, and the Prisoner said there were pikes in a stone quarry?

A. Yes.

Q. Was that said by Turner as well, or by Ludlam only?

A. It was said by Turner as well.

Q. They both said that?

A. Yes.

Mr. Justice Abbott. Did they mention the number?

A. That they had about forty pikes in a stone quarry.

Mr. Solicitor General. Do you know what the Prisoner is by business?

A. He is a stone getter.

Q. After they had talked about the arms, what was the conversation then?

A. I did not hear what Ludlam said.

Q. What where they talking about whilst he was there?

A. They were talking about the present revolution, and how they were to proceed on it.

Q. Did they state how they were to proceed on it?

A. Yes; they were talking about going to Nottingham.

Q. When were they to go to Nottingham?

A. They were to go to Nottingham on the Monday night; they were to start first on Monday night at ten o'clock.

Q. Had Brandreth, the captain, any thing before him?

A. Yes, he had got a map before him.

Q. What was upon that map, or what did he say about it?

A. He had got some dots and some pricks, where they were to meet, and where they were to proceed to.

Q. Was that map before him when Ludlam and Turner came in?

A. No.

Q. Where was it then?

A. It was in Brandreth's pocket.

Mr. Justice Abbott. Was it produced after they came in?

A. I do not recollect that it was.

Mr. Solicitor General. Was any thing said as to what was to be done when they got to Nottingham?

A. Yes, that they were to take the town.

Q. What else?

A. That they were to return back then to Butterley works, and to make barracks of that?

Q. You say they talked about arms, was any thing said about men?

A. Yes, they said they would make all go that they met with, and them that would not go they would shoot.

Q. Do you recollect whether any verses were repeated by Brandreth?

A. Yes.

Q. Was that before or after the prisoner came in?

A. That was before the Prisoner came in; it was not repeated after he came in that I heard, I believe it was not.

Q. What were those verses?

A. " Every man his skill must try."——

Mr. Cross. I submit to your lordships, as it is now distinctly in evidence that the prisoner at the bar was not present when those verses were read, and had not come upon the premises before they were read, that they cannot, in the present stage of the examination at least, be received in evidence against him; there is no sort of act at present proved against the prisoner to connect him with what we know to be the contents of those verses. I submit that at present we should not hear what they were, as they were not spoken in the prisoner's presence.

Mr. Denman. I submit my learned friend's objection must be sustained, at least for the present, for there is not at present any evidence to go the jury of conspiracy for the

H 2

purpose supposed to be alluded to by those verses; those verses were recited behind the back of this prisoner, and I submit therefore we cannot yet hear what these parties might be saying in a public house.

Lord Chief Baron Richards. They were talking about the revolution, and the proceeding to Nottingham, and taking Nottingham, after he was there.

Mr. Cross. That remains yet to be enquired into; I have not collected from this witness whether any of the conversation respecting going to Nottingham or about the revolution was or was not in the presence of the prisoner.

Mr. Justice Abbott. I have taken it, that while the prisoner was there they were talking about the revolution and how they were to proceed; that they talked of proceeding to Nottingham and taking the barracks; the effect of it is one thing; but it is impossible that all the evidence can be given together.

Mr. Denman. Certainly, my lord.

Mr. Cross. I do not insist upon the objection my lord.

Mr. Justice Abbott. Even as the evidence now stands it is certainly admissible.

Mr. Solicitor General. State if you can what those verses were which Brandreth repeated?

A. " Every man his skill must try,
He must turn out and not deny;
No bloody soldiers must he dread,
He must turn out and fight for bread;
The time is come you plainly see.
That government opposed must be,"——that was not stated while he was in.

Q. So we understand; did Brandreth during the whole time you were there, act and appear as the leader of the party?

A. Yes, he did.

Q. Do you remember after Ludlam came in any thing being said about a badger?

A. Yes, Turner was talking about it.

Q. William Turner who came with Ludlam?

A. Yes.

Q. What was said?

A. They were talking about the plan about drawing the badger.

Q. Who talked?

A. Turner.

Q. Who else?

A. John Cope said he had heard they had a plan about drawing the badger, and asked what it was; and Turner told him what it was, to lay a bundle of straw before the door and the badger would come out, and as he came out they would shoot him.

Q. How long did you stay there; what time did you leave?

A. Between three and four o'clock.

Q. Was any thing more said about the Wingfield people?

A. Yes.

Q. What?

A. They were talking about the pikes.

Q. Who was talking about the pikes?

A. Turner; and about how they were to assemble together, and what time of the night, and where to start, and where the pikes lay.

Q. Whilst you were there during those several hours, did several persons come in and go out?

A. Many did from time to time.

Q. When they came in from time to time, was the subject you have been talking of mentioned?

A. Yes, it was mentioned to some of them.

Q. You went away between three and four?

A. Yes.

Q. When you went away was the party broken up, or did you leave any persons there?

A. I left the prisoner there and Turner as well.

Q. And Brandreth?

A. Yes.

Q. Who else do you recollect?

A. I do not recollect who there were left.

Q. Do you recollect a person of the name of Mac Kesswick coming in?

A. Yes.

Q. What time did he come in, do you recollect?

A. I do not recollect exactly.

Q. Did he say anything on coming in?

A. Yes; he asked the captain how he was; he said he did not know him; he asked him if he did not recollect his coming a little way along the road with him.

Q. Did he then recollect him?

A. Yes, he recollected him then; and asked how he was then.

Q. Did Mac Kesswick say anything?

A. Yes, he turned himself round, and said, he thought there were too many in the room for that business.

Q. Was anything said upon that?

A. No.

Q. Was this conversation public in the room during all the time you were there?

A. Yes.

Q. There was no secret made of it?

A. No.

Q. Had you been sworn in as a special constable before?

A. Yes.

Q. When?

A. On the Saturday night, the night before.

Q. What was the purpose of your being sworn in as a special constable?

A. To protect our master's property in case of any riot, or any disturbance; that was what I understood.

Cross-examined by Mr. Cross.

Q. You were sworn in you say?

A. Yes.

Q. What was the oath you took upon that occasion?

A. I do not recollect; we were to keep the peace on our master's premises; to keep the peace at Buttetley works, in case of there being any disturbance, that we were to be ordered out in case of any disturbance.

Q. Who swore you?

A. The magistrate's clerk.

Q. You cannot remember the words of your oath?

A. No.

Q. You seem to have a very ready memory for sedition, but you cannot remember your oath?

A. No.

Q. Was any thing said at the public-house about your masters?

A. They were talking about making barracks in the works; that was all that was said about our masters.

Q. Was any mischief to be done to your masters?

A. Not that I recollect.

Q. You stayed there about six hours?

A. Yes.

Q. Where did you go to after you left that place?

A. Home.

Q. Was that near Mr. Goodwin's.

A. Yes.

Q. Did you attend at the works the next day?

A. Yes.

Q. Did you tell Mr. Goodwin, you had heard it publicly announced at the ale-house, that the works you were sworn to defend, were to be made barracks?

A. No; it was narrated about the place before, and I thought I had no need.

Q. You heard it talked of?

A. Yes, by many, before that Sunday.

Q. Did you see Mr. Goodwin the next day?

A. No.

Q. How many of you were sworn into this office?

A. I cannot say how many there were.

Q. Was Cope one?

A. I am sure I do not know whether he was or not.

Q. What has become of Cope?

A. I am sure I do not know where he is.

Q. Is he following his business with you as usual?

A. Yes, he has been following his business at Butterley works.

Q. Since?
A. Yes.
Q. And is now?
A. I do not know whether he is now.
Q. Has he been in custody?
A. He was taken up in custody, but he was liberated again.
Q. You say that the prisoner came to the public-house with Turner?
A. Yes, and Barker.
Q. Do you mean to say, you saw the prisoner enter the house with Turner?
A. He came into the house; they were all in at the same time.
Q. That is not what I am asking you about; but did you see the prisoner come into that house in the company of Turner?
A. Yes,
Q. That you swear?
A. They all came in to a minute, one with another, or more; there were three of them all came in together.
Q. Within a minute or two of each other?
A. Yes, within a small trifle of each other.
Q. Then you mean to say they did not come together; you did not see them come in together?
A. They all came in together.
Q. Then there was no trifle of time between them if they all came in together?
A. They came in at the door as fast as they could.
Q. Do you recollect particularly?
A. Yes.
Q. Where were you sitting at the time?
A. I was sitting in the room.
Q. There were more rooms than one?
A. I was sitting in the parlour.
Q. Did you go through the house into the parlour?
A. Yes.
Q. You staid there all the time, did not you?
A. No, I was in and out two or three times.

Q. You told us before, you were there only for amusement?

A. I had no business with them.

Q. Only for the sake of amusement?

A. And of getting a pint of ale.

Q. You admonished them of the danger of their proceedings, did not you?

A. I told them about it, but they threatened to cram me up the chimney.

Q. That did not intimidate you at all from staying?

A. No; I did ask Cope to go, but he did not chuse to go, and I stopped till he went, and Asbury and Elsden, and we all went together.

Q. You told them you were a constable?

A. Yes.

Q. That they had better take care what they said?

A. Yes.

Q. And they only threatened to put you up the chimney?

A. Yes.

Q. Were you afraid of that?

A. I was afraid if I said any more that they would.

Q. You did all that you thought it prudent to do to put a stop to the mischief?

A. We thought it was not right.

Q. What do you mean by we?

A. Me and Shirley Asbury.

Q. And Cope?

A. I did not say anything to Cope about it, whether it was right or not.

Q. But you attended with Cope?

A. Yes, I went there with Cope; but I did not know what business he was going on.

Q. You did not take any part in this business?

A. He did say something, but I cannot recollect what it was.

Q. It is extraordinary that you did not take notice what was said by your friend who was there?

A There were many people there that I did not know.

Q. But cannot you recollect what your friend said?

A. I know he said something about those matters, but I do not recollect what it was.

Q. That you swear?

A. I shall not swear anything about it.

Q. But you shall swear something about it; do you or not recollect what he said?

A. I do not recollect what he did say.

Q. Do you mean to swear that you do not recollect what he said?

A. I do not recollect what he said in that place.

Q. Before he went to that place?

A. He did not say anything to me before he went to that place.

Q. Do you mean to swear, that neither before you went to that place, nor there, you heard him say anything about that business?

A. He said nothing to me about the business; he asked me to go to Pentridge; that he had a little business, and to take a pint of ale.

Q. Did not you hear Cope say something about the business of which you have been telling the jury before you went there?

A. No.

Q. Nor while you were there?

A. He was talking amongst them, but I cannot recollect what he did say.

Q. Not one word that he said?

A. Not exactly.

Q. Tell us as nearly as you can recollect?

A. I cannot recollect anything about it.

Q. Then what do you mean by exactly, you cannot recollect at all?

A. No.

Q. You recollect what Turner, Brandreth, and Ludlam said?

A. Ludlam was not taking any active part that I heard, further than reading the paper.

Q. You heard what Turner said, and Brandreth said, and

Ludlam said; you recollect what they said, but you do not recollect what Cope said, though Cope was the man whom you accompanied to the scene, and with whom you left?

A. I did not sit exactly along-side him while I staid there.

Q. Were not you waiting for Cope till he had finished his business, that you might go away?

A. Yes, I was waiting for Cope, and Asbury and Elsden.

Q. And Cope you state had business to transact at this meeting?

A. I do not know whether he had or had not.

Q. That you swear?

A. Yes.

Q. Nor you did not perceive, though you sat six hours in the room?

A. He said he had a little business to do at Pentridge, but he did not say whether it was in that room.

Q. You mean to swear in the face of the jury, that though you sat six hours in the room, you cannot tell whether Cope had any business to do there or not?

A. He was talking amongst them; I cannot recollect what he was saying, or what a great many others said.

Q. You were six hours in the room?

A. Yes.

Q. Chiefly in that room?

A. Yes.

Q. You went with Cope, because he had some business to transact?

A. Yes.

Q. You waited till he had finished his business at least for six hours, and yet you mean to swear you do not know what Cope's business was?

A. It was not my business to ask him what business he was going on, or what he did there.

Q. That is not my question——

Mr. Justice Abbott. That is hardly a question; perhaps he may not understand all that is comprehended in your question.

Mr. Cross. Do you mean to state, that though you waited six hours till his business was over, you do not know at all what his business was about?

A. No, I do not.

Q. Then what do you mean by saying that you waited for him all that time, till he had finished his business?

A. I do not know what his business was.

Q. What was he doing?

A. He was sitting amongst people in the room, and I was sitting amongst the people in the room.

Q. Did he or not take any part in what was going on in the room?

A. I did not see him take any active part.

Q. You say the prisoner read the paper that was produced by Turner?

A. Yes.

Q. He read there of some pikes in a stone quarry out of that paper?

A. I did not say that he did.

Q. I ask you whether he did or not——

Mr. Justice Abbott. That is not a question, it is a very common thing; I do not find any fault with it, but you must not be angry with the witness, if what he says is not an answer to a question, when it really is not a question which is put.

Mr. Cross. I stated the matter interrogatively; it is very often done.

Mr. Justice Abbott. Yes, I know it is very often done.

Mr. Cross. Then we are to understand he did not read it from the paper, but stated it from his own knowledge?

A. He and Turner were reading it.

Q. Was he reading it to Turner, or Turner to him?

A. Turner to him.

Q. There was a collection to send Weightman to Nottingham?

A. Yes.

Q. How much did Cope contribute?

A. I do not know.

Q. Did he contribute anything?
A. I do not know.
Q. You swear you do not know that?
A. Yes.
Q. Did you contribute anything?
A. No.
Q. Did anybody ask you?
A. No.
Q. The prisoner, I think you stated, was not in the room?
A. He was not in the room when the money was gathered.
Q. The prisoner was not?
A. No.
Q. You were of course there when the money was gathered?
A. Yes.
Q. The prisoner was not there, of course, when they talked about taking Nottingham?
A. I cannot recollect whether he was or not.
Q. Nor when those verses you have repeated were mentioned?
A. No.
Q. Was there anything else besides those you have already recited?
A. No.
Q. Was anything else connected with those verses?
A. No.
Q. That was the whole was it?
A. Yes.

Re-examined by Mr. Solicitor General.

Q. You have been asked about a person of the name of Weightman being sent to Nottingham, what was he to be sent to Nottingham for?
A. He was to go to Nottingham to see whether the people of Nottingham were ready to join them, and to bring back a particular account that night.
Q. The money was collected to enabled him to go?
A. Yes.

Mr. Justice Abbott. Were any threats made use of against persons who should tell?

A. Yes.

Q. What was said about that?

A. That any man that should tell anything about them, they would call on him another day.

Mr. Solicitor General. I did not ask whether Asbury was there, it did come out on cross examination that he was there.

Mr. Justice Abbott. Yes, he stated that he came in.

Shirley Asbury sworn.

Examined by Mr. Serjeant Vaughan.

Q. I believe you are an engine-fitter at Pentridge?

A. At Butterley.

Q. You belong to the parish of Pentridge?

A. No, Ripley.

Q. You are in the service of Messrs. Jessop and Company, at Butterley works?

A. Yes.

Q. Did you on the morning of the 8th of June, go to the White Horse at Pentridge?

A. Yes.

Q. About what time, and with whom?

A. About twelve o'clock, with John Elsden.

Q. About mid-day?

A. Yes.

Q. Whom did you find there?

A. There were Cope, Anthony Martin, Brandeth, Mac Kesswick, John Moore, Edward Moore, William Smith, and several others in the room; I did not know all of them.

Q. How many might there be at the time when you first went there?

A. About twenty.

Q. In the room at one time?

A. Yes.

Q. Tell me whether in the course of that morning, after

you had been there some time, you saw anything of the prisoner at the bar, Isaac Ludlam?

A. Yes.

Q. Do you remember who he came in with?

A. William Turner.

Q. Were the prisoner and William Turner both Wingfield men?

A. Yes.

Q. Upon his coming into the room, had he any conversation, or did Turner produce anything in his presence?

A. Yes.

Q. What was it?

A. He produced a paper consisting of what guns they had.

Q. Of what guns they had where, in what parish or place?

A. He did not say in what parish; what guns such and such people had.

Q. Were the people's names mentioned, were they read from this paper?

A. Yes.

Q. Can you tell us the names of any of those people?

A. No, I cannot.

Q. But there were people mentioned who had guns?

A. Yes.

Q. And what number of guns?

A. Yes.

Q. Was it stated from this paper where those people lived, who had the guns?

A. I cannot recollect that it was.

Q. Turner produced the paper?

A. Yes.

Q. Having produced the paper, to whom did he deliver it?

A. He produced it to that man there.

Q. To the prisoner?

A. Yes.

Q. Having delivered it to the prisoner, what did the prisoner do with it?

A. He read it over to the company.

Q. Was it read more than once?
A. No.

Q. What remarks were made upon this paper by the prisoner, or anybody in his presence?
A. I do not recollect anything more than its being mentioned what guns there were.

Q. Was there anything said about the Wingfield men being more or less forward than their neighbours?
A. William Turner seemed to say that the Wingfield people were more forward than the Butterley, for they went out to get pike shafts in the day time.

Q. What was said about those pikes, where were they?
A. There were some pikes that were in a stone quarry.

Q. Who said that?
A. William Turner said that; about forty that were for the men that volunteered.

Q. Was the place mentioned where those pikes were lying?
A. He did not say; he said they were in a stone quarry.

Q. Was anything said as to what was to be done with those pikes?
A. Yes.

Q. What?
A. He said, in the first place, they were to go to Wingfield.

Q. Ludlam came in with Turner?
A. Yes.

Q. Was Ludlam present when the paper was read, and this conversation passed?
A. Yes.

Q. William Turner said they were to go first to Wingfield.
A. Yes.

Q. What were they to do at Wingfield?
A. They were going to draw the badger in the first place.

Q. How was the badger to be drawn?
A. They were to take a bundle of straw and set it on fire, and as soon as it was set on fire, he would come out, and then they were to shoot him.

Q. Was it explained who this badger was?

A. Yes, Mr. Halton.

Q. Colonel Halton, the magistrate?

A. Yes.

Q. Was any thing said about vermin?

A. Yes, William Turner said that they had vermin to kill, and every one was to kill their own vermin.

Q. Did you hear the prisoner Ludlam say any thing?

A. No, I cannot recollect that I heard him say anything more than reading the paper over.

Q. Was Nottingham talked of?

A. Yes.

Q. Did you hear Ludlam say any thing about Nottingham?

A. No, I cannot recollect that I did further.

Q. What was said about Nottingham, and by whom?

A. Brandreth mentioned Nottingham; he said they were to go to take Nottingham, and every one was to have plenty of rum, and a hundred guineas when they got there.

Q. You say Brandreth said that?

A. Yes.

Q. Did you hear any body but Brandreth use words of that sort?

A. Yes, William Turner mentioned it too.

Q. Did you hear anybody but Brandreth and Turner use those expressions?

A. No, I cannot recollect that I did.

Q. You have no recollection of that?

A. Not of anybody else mentioning it.

Q. Was the government talked of?

A. Yes; they said there would be no good done till such time as the government was overthrown.

Q. Who said that?

A. William Turner.

Q. Did you hear anybody besides William Turner use those expressions?

A. No, I do not recollect that I did; I do not recollect anybody else mentioning them.

Q. Was it said how this was to be done?

A. That they were to go to Nottingham in the first place?

Q. What was to be done when they got to Nottingham?

A. They were to take Nottingham; and then they were to go down the Trent by the Trent boats to Newark, and to take Newark.

Q. What was to be done then?

A. Then they were to go from thence to London; to make the best of their way to London.

Q. What were they to do when they got to London?

A. They were to go to overturn the government; that there would be no good done till they had overturned the government.

Q. How long might this conversation last about the government, and Nottingham and London, and the pikes?

A. It was talked from the time I went until I came away; they said they had no doubt they should succeed in what they were going to undertake.

Q. At what time did you come away?

A. About four o'clock.

Q. Then you were there about four hours?

A. Yes.

Q. In what way was this mentioned and talked of, privately?

A. Yes, privately.

Q. What do you mean by privately?

A. They spoke up to every one that was in the room, not privately.

Q. Do you mean to each individually, or to all together in the room?

A. To all together.

Q. Was it spoken loud enough for all in the room to hear?

A. Yes.

Q. Was anything said as to the time of their setting out; when this was to take place?

A. At ten o'clock the next night they were to set out.

Q. Did you see anything there of a man of the name of Joseph Weightman?

A. Yes.

Q. He was there?

A. Yes he was.

Q. Was he directed to do anything while you were there, or was it proposed that he should do anything?

A. Yes, he was to go to Nottingham, and see how they were going on, and money was collected.

Q. At whose expence was he to go there?

A. There was a subscription made for him to go.

Q. Do you mean in your presence?

A. Yes.

Q. To pay his expences?

A. Yes.

Q. When was he to set out?

A. He was to set out as that night.

Q. Where was he to come to, or what was to be done after he had been at Nottingham?

A. He was to come home again.

Q. You say money was collected for that purpose?

A. Yes there was.

Q. Did you see any map in the room whilst you were there?

A. Yes, Brandreth produced a map.

Q. What was done with that map?

A. He was pointing out and pricking out the places where they were to go to, which they were to take.

Q. Was anything said about ammunition?

A. Yes.

Q. What was said about that?

A. Brandreth wanted a barrel of gunpowder produced, so that he might learn them how to make cartridges.

Q. What barrel of gunpowder was this that he wanted produced?

A. Some barrel that they had by them.

Q. Was it mentioned that they had a barrel by them?

A. Yes.

Q. Was there more than one barrel of gunpowder spoken of?

A. No.

Q. What other sort of ammunition were they to have besides gunpowder?

A. They had no more ammunition but gunpowder, but he said they could get plenty of lead upon the road, there were plenty of churches upon the road, that they could get lead from.

Q. Brandreth said that?

A. Yes.

Q. You have spoken of Nottingham, was any thing said as to who were to be met at Nottingham, or what was to be done there?

A. That they were to take Nottingham.

Q. Was there anybody to be there?

A. Yes, there was to be a party there to meet them?

Q. Was it said where those were to come from that were to meet them at Nottingham?

A. Yes, it was said that Sheffield and Chesterfield were to meet them.

Q. At Nottingham?

A. No; that they were to go from Wingfield, and that Sheffield and Chesterfield were to meet them and join them, and go to Butterley.

Q. Was it said when they were to meet?

A. No, but they were to meet that night; the Monday night.

Q. Was any thing said about the North?

A. I cannot recollect.

Cross-examined by Mr. Denman.

Q. Was it mentioned that they expected a party to join them at Nottingham before they sent Weightman, before they collected the money?

A. It was not mentioned then; when they started they were to meet a quantity of men at Nottingham.

Q. Had that been mentioned, that when they started they should meet a quantity of men at Nottingham, before the money was raised for Weightman to go there.

A. I do not recollect that it was mentioned before that time, it was mentioned after.

Q. Are you sure it was not mentioned before?

A. Yes I am.

Q. Had any thing been said before about the overturn of the government before the money was collected?

A. I cannot recollect that there was any thing said before, but there was something said after.

Q Had any thing been mentioned about the stone quarry before the money was collected, or did that come after?

A. I do not know whether that came before or after, it came after I think; at least I am sure it did.

Q. Was the prisoner in the room when the money was collected?

A. I do not know, I am sure, whether he was or was not.

Q. You cannot tell whether he gave any thing, or what he gave?

A. No; I cannot tell whether he gave any thing.

Q. Did you give sixpence to send Weightman to Nottingham?

A. Yes, I did; but I did not know what it was for.

Q. Did you give it him out of charity?

A. I put it upon the table; I did not know what it was for.

Q. Who required you to pay sixpence?

A. I saw the rest of them giving sixpence.

Q. And so seeing the rest of them giving sixpence, you gave sixpence too?

A. Yes.

Q. You did not know at all what was to be done with that?

A. No; I did not.

Q. You had not an idea that it was to take Weightman to Nottingham, till afterwards?

A. Yes.

Q. That is as true as all the rest you have told us?

A. I have said nothing but the truth.

Q. That is as true as the rest you have said?

A. Yes.

Q. Did they all give?
A. I cannot say.
Q. You gave without knowing whether all the rest did or not?
A. Yes.
Q. What did Cope give?
A. Sixpence, I believe.
Q. What did Martin give?
A. I do not know that Martin gave any thing; I do not recollect; he might.
Q. Can you state any body in the room, that did not give any thing?
A. No; I cannot state who did give and who did not.
Q. There was no dispute, all gave their money very freely?
A. Yes.
Q. I think you say that the prisoner Ludlam, was not in the room at that time?
A. When the money was gathered, I cannot recollect whether he was in the room at that time or not.
Q. Can you tell whether before the money was gathered, any thing at all had been said about revolution, or overturning the government, or any thing of the kind?
A. I do not recollect that.
Q. You mean to swear, you do not know whether when the money was collected, any thing had been said about overturning the government?
A. Yes.
Q. Had the verses been recited before that time?
A. I do not know whether it was before or after, but it was mentioned.
Q. You do not know whether the verses had been recited before or after?
A. No.
Q. Had the map been produced before that time?
A. No; I do not think it had.
Q. Will you swear it had not?
A. Yes.
Q. Had any thing then been said about a cloud from the North?
A. I do not recollect any thing about a cloud from the North.

Q. Had any thing been said about Sheffield, Chesterfield, Huddersfield, Wakefield?

A. I can remember Chesterfield and Sheffield.

Q. Had they been mentioned before the money was collected?

A. I cannot recollect whether it was mentioned before or after.

Q. Had the name of Oliver then been mentioned?

A. I never heard Oliver's name mentioned at all.

Q. Never, till I mentioned it now?

A. Oh yes; I have heard his name mentioned since, but not at that time.

Q. Then you have heard it since?

A. Yes, I have heard it since.

Q. How soon after that meeting, did you first hear it?

A. It was a long time after that.

Q. Were the names of Jessop and Goodwin and Wragg, mentioned at this meeting?

A. Yes, they were.

Q. They were your masters?

A. Yes.

Q. What was said about them?

A. Sheffield and Chesterfield were to meet the Wingfield men at Butterley, and they were to take the place, and to kill Mr. Wragg and Mr. Jessop.

Q. That was mentioned in your hearing?

A. Yes.

Q. In Cope's hearing?

A. I do not know whether Cope might hear it; I heard it.

Q. Was he present when it was mentioned?

A. Yes; he was.

Q. Was Martin present when that was mentioned?

A. Yes.

Q. Was Elsden present when that was mentioned?

A. I cannot tell whether Elsden was or not.

Q. Had you seen him go out before that time?

A. He went out to make water, several times.

Q. But you heard that?

A. I heard it.

Q. Did you tell Mr. Jessop?
A. No.
Q. Did you tell Mr. Goodwin?
A. No.
Q. Did you tell Mr. Wragg?
A. No.
Q. Did you leave them to be shot, without any warning?
A. There was talk before that, that this was to commence.
Q. Did you leave them to be shot, without any warning?
A. I did not tell them.
Q. What had been mentioned before?
A. I said, I did not tell Jessop, nor Goodwin, nor Wragg, they were to be shot.
Q. What do you mean by saying, this had been mentioned before?
A. This revolution was talked of before.
Q. Before you went to this meeting at the White Horse, you knew there was something of the kind talked of?
A. No, not before I went to the White Horse, it was talked of afterwards.
Q. When did you know it had been talked of?
A. I did not know when it was talked of exactly.
Q. Why did not you tell Mr. Goodwin, Mr. Jessop, and Mr. Wragg, they were in such imminent danger?
A. I do not know that I had any right to tell, for they mentioned that if we mentioned any thing, they should cram us up the chimney; we told them there were constables in the room: and they said, that if we mentioned any thing, they should cram us up the chimney.
Q. You did not know that you had a right to tell your masters, because this party said, they would ram you up the chimney if you told?
A. Yes, we were to be murdered too.
Q. Why did you not mention that when you were examined before; you were twice examined before, why did not you mention that you were to be murdered too?
A. I did mention that.
Q. Do you mean that there was any threat against you?
A. If we mentioned anything about what was said there.

Q. Do you mean that there was any threat against you if you mentioned what passed, or only that those who mentioned should be attacked?

A. They said, that if we mentioned anything, we should be rammed up the chimney, and likewise that we should be murdered.

Q. Do you mean to swear your fear of being rammed up the chimney, or being murdered, prevented your telling those gentlemen what you had heard about them?

A. Yes.

Q. You saw them the next day; Mr. Goodwin, Mr. Jessop, and Mr. Wragg?

A. Yes.

Q. You had an opportunity of telling them?

A. Yes, I might have told them, if I had thought of it.

Q. Oh, you did not think of it?

A. I did not trouble my head, because I was sworn in the night before to protect my master's place.

Q. You were sworn in the night before to protect your master's place, and therefore when you saw him the next day, after you had heard he was to be murdered, you did not think to tell him?

A. I did not think *nothing* about him; but they said if we did, we should be murdered.

Q. When were the Chesterfield and Sheffield people to come?

A. They were to come the very next night.

Q. You had been sworn in a special constable for the express purpose of protecting their property, not their lives?

A. I did not mention anything about their lives, but to protect our master's place.

Q. You never said a word about it to them?

A. No.

Q. Did Cope tell them, do you know; perhaps you left it to him to tell them?

A. I do not know that he told them.

Q. Have you any reason to think that he did?

A. No, I have not.

Q. Did Martin tell them?

A. I cannot say that he did; I never heard him say that he did?

Q. How came you to go to this public house?

A. I did not know that I was going to this public house.

Q. How came you to go?

A. I was taking a walk towards Butterley, and was talking to some young men, and John Elsden asked me whether I would take a walk? I said I had no objection; we went to Swanwick, and had two pints of ale, and he asked me whether I would take another walk? I said I had never been at Pentridge, and should have no objection to go there.

Q. You went to Pentridge out of curiosity on this Sunday?

A. Yes.

Q. Who then proposed to go to the White Horse; did you happen to propose to go to the White Horse, or was it Elsden?

A. I do not know; it could not be me, for I never had been there before; I did not know anything of the White Horse.

Q. But you might see it flying in the street?

A. Yes; I asked him whether he would have a pint of ale? and he said, yes.

Q. And it was in consequence of that you went there?
A. Yes.

Q. By the merest accident in the world?
A. Yes.

Q. Being at the White Horse?
A. Yes, it was in my road home?

Q. Then you found those people talking about this matter of overturning the government, and as it might happen, murdering your master?

A. Not when I first went in.

Q. But soon afterwards?

A. Yes; they did not make it any secret at all; they said that every man would be obliged to go; and they did not keep it any secret at all.

Q. How soon after you first went did they begin to talk in this way?

A. Very soon after; I did not go into the parlour for some time after I went in.

Q. How long had you been in the house before you went into the parlour?

A. Perhaps it might be half an hour.

Q. What time did you first go to the house?

A. Twelve o'clock.

Q. About half after twelve you might go into the parlour?

A. Yes.

Q. And they began talking about this very soon after you got into the room?

A. Yes.

Q. I suppose you desired your friend Elsden to get out of this bad company as soon as you could?

A. I did not like it myself.

Q. Did you try to get away?

A. If I had tried, I might have come away; but I did not like to come away without him.

Q. You stayed to hear all that passed?

A. No, I did not; there was a good deal passed after I came away, as I heard; I left at half past three or four o'clock.

Q. You stayed from twelve to half past three or four, and they were talking of this all the time you were there?

A. Yes.

Q. You told them you were a constable?

A. Yes.

Q. They did not mind that?

A. No.

Q. Can you tell me the constable's oath?

A. When I was sworn in?—no, I cannot.

Q. How soon after you had been there did Ludlam come in?

A. I cannot exactly say how long.

Q. Five minutes, or an hour or two?

A. I think it was about one o'clock when he came in.

Q. Who came with him?

A. Turner.

Q. Brandreth you found there?

A. Yes.

Q. Did Mac Kesswick come in by himself?

A. No.

Q. Who came in with him?

A. There was another man came in with him; I cannot say what his name was; I should know him if I saw him again.

Q. You are sure Turner and Ludlam came in together?

A. Yes.

Re-examined by Mr. Serjeaut Vaughan.

Q. I think you have told us your going there was quite accidental, that you did not know Pentridge before, and did not know there was any meeting there?

A. I did not know of any meeting there.

Q. How came you to go into the parlour; who desired you to go into the parlour?

A. Mrs. Weightman went into the parlour, and told them there were some Butterley chaps there.

Q. Mrs. Weightman went while you were in the kitchen, and told them in the parlour there were some Butterley chaps there?

A. Yes.

Q. And upon that you went in?

A. Yes.

Q. At whose desire?

A. She asked whether they would have any objection that we should come in.

Q. Then you said, that you communicated to them in the parlour, that you were constables, when you heard the sort of conversation that you mentioned?

A. Yes.

Q. Upon which they threatened you in the way you have described?

A. Yes.

Q. You heard the names of Mr. Jessop, Mr. Goodwin, and Mr. Wragg, as persons who were to be murdered?

A. Yes.

Q. You have been asked why you did not mention that to them afterwards; had you any reason to know whether Mr. Goodwin and Mr. Jessop, and the persons at the works, were at that time prepared to resist any attempt that might be made upon them?

A. I cannot say whether they were or were not.

Q. How many special constables had been sworn in to protect the works?

A. I cannot say.

Q. Ten, twenty, thirty, or how many?

A. There might be thirty.

Q. Who had been sworn in on the night before?

A. Yes.

Q. Do you know how they came to be sworn in; you were one of them?

A. I was one of them.

Q. You have told us it was to defend the Butterley works?

A. Yes, it was.

Q. So that that precaution had been taken?

A. Yes.

Q. You say that they threatened to shoot you?

A. Yes.

Q. You said before this, sixpence was subscribed; you do not recollect that any thing was said about overturning the government?

A. No.

Q. Do you recollect when any verses were read?

A. Yes.

Q. How soon after that; how long after you had been in the room were those said?

A. A long time; a good bit I had been in.

Q. Was that after the subscription?

A. Yes, it was after the subscription.

Mr. Serjeant Vaughan. I did not ask him as to the song originally. Do you recollect them?

A. Yes.

Q. Repeat them?

A. " Every man his skill must try,
He must turn out and not deny;
No bloody soldiers must he dread,
He must turn out and fight for bread;
The time is come you plainly see,
The government opposed must be."

Q. What was done with that?

A. It was distributed about the room.

Q. Were they written copies or what?

A. I wrote mine myself.

Q. Do you recollect who produced that?

A. Brandreth.

Q. Did other people write as well as you?

A. Yes.

Q. Copies were taken and written, and distributed in the room?

A. Yes.

Mr. Cross. Will your Lordship permit me to put one question upon this, as to the verses. You say you took a copy of these verses; did you take them from the mouth of Brandreth, or copy them from another paper?

A. I copied them from another paper.

Q. For what purpose did you take a copy?

A. Because the rest were taking them; I did not know what I was taking it for, but because the rest were taking it.

Q. All the company took copies did they?

A. I cannot say whether all the company did, but many of them did.

Q. Did Cope?

A. Yes, I believe Cope had one.

Q. Martin?

A. No, I do not think Martin had; I do not know.

Q. Have you got your copy now?

A. No.

Q. Did you take it to Mr. Goodwin, or any of your masters at the works?

A. No; I got it off by heart; I burnt mine.

Q. When did you burn it?

A. Either the next day or the day afterwards, I cannot tell which.

Q. You got it by heart that day?

A. Yes.

Q. And burnt it on the following day, the Tuesday?

A. I cannot say which day it was.

William Smith sworn.

Examined by Mr. Clarke.

Q. Where did you live in June last?

A. Wingfield Park.

Q. What business are you?

A. A frame-work knitter.

Q. Do you know the prisoner at the bar?

A. Yes.

Q. Do you know his son Isaac?

A. Yes.

Q. Tell me whether you recollect, on Monday the 9th of June, seeing his son Isaac and any persons with him, with any thing upon their shoulders?

A. Yes, I saw them go from home.

Q. Which way were they going?

A. Down the lane just below their house, towards Boden-lane.

Q. Who were the persons whom you saw go?

A. Old Isaac, and young Isaac, and William.

Q. I speak of the afternoon; did you see young Isaac Ludlam?

A. Yes.

Q. And Joseph Taylor and Benjamin Taylor?

A. Yes.

Q. Where did you see them going that afternoon?

A. Coming down Boden-lane, into Park-lane, towards James Taylor's.

Q. Were they carrying any thing at that time?

A. Bits of poles.

Q. How many do you think they had?

A. Three or four a-piece.

Q. What sort of poles?

A. The poles the same as the pikes were made of.

Q. Like pike shafts?

A. Yes.

Q. They had three or four of those a-piece?

A. Yes.

[*Several pikes were produced.*]

Q. Were they such sort of poles as those?

A. Yes.

Q. Had they any pikes on them at that time?

A. No.

Q. Was the bark off them at that time?

A. Yes, I think it was.

Q. They were carrying them you say towards James Taylor's house?

A. Yes.

Mr. Justice Abbott. He has not told us what time of the day this was.

Mr. Clarke. In the afternoon.

Mr. Justice Abbott. I have not heard him say so.

Mr. Clarke. About what time of day was it?

A. About five o'clock in the afternoon.

Q. Did you see any thing of either of them that night again?

A. Yes.

Q. Did you see the prisoner with either of them?

A. Yes.

Q. What o'clock was that?

A. When I saw him was between eleven and twelve o'clock perhaps.

Q. Between eleven and twelve at night?

A. Yes.

Q. You saw the prisoner?

A. Yes.

Q. Did you see whether his son Isaac was with him then?

A. Yes, he was there.

Q. Did you see Samuel Briddon?

A. Yes.

Q. And William Ludlam?
A. Yes.
Q. Were they all together?
A. Samuel Briddon and old Isaac were mostly behind?
Q. Which way were they going when you saw them?
A. To Pentridge-lane-end.
Q. Where were they going from at that time?
A. I do not know where they came from; I never saw them till there, not after they started from home.
Q. How far was it from Ludlam's the prisoner's house?
A. About a mile I should think.
Q. Had they any thing with them at that time?
A. Yes, they had poles with spikes to them?
Q. Were they such things as those?
A. Yes.
Q. Had they each of them one?
A. Yes.
Q. Did you afterwards go to the house of John Wilkinson with anybody?
A. I set out to go up Boden-lane.
Q. With whom?
A. Henry Taylor and Samuel Taylor.
Q. They went with you?
A. Yes.
Q. To go from where?
A. To go from home.

Mr. Justice Abbott. To go from home to what place?
Mr. Clarke. To the house of John Wilkinson; you set out with those persons to go to John Wilkinson's.
A. Yes.
Q. In your way there did you meet with anybody?
A. Yes, I met with a party of men before we had gone far up the lane.
Q. What lane?
A. Boden-lane.
Q. Who were those men?
A. James Taylor and George Weightman, Benjamin Taylor and Joseph and Miles Bacon.
Q. Anybody else?
A. James Hopkinson and Abraham James.

Vol. II.   K

Q. You met those persons?

A. Yes, and Samuel Marriott.

Q. Was any thing said to you by any of them at that time?

A. Yes; when they met us they demanded us to go with them.

Q. What did you say to that?

A. I refused going.

Mr. Justice Abbott. Did you all refuse, or only you. I did not hear whether you said we or I?

A. We all three refused.

Mr. Clarke. Who were you all?

A. Henry Taylor, Samuel Taylor, and myself.

Q. Upon your refusal, what was done?

A. They gave us a spike a piece, and we went down the lane with them.

Q. Where did you go to with them?

A. Down to Boden-lane-end.

Q. Did you go to any person's house?

A. Yes; the party agreed that I should go to let Henry Taylor's family and my own know that we were going.

Q. Did you go?

A. Yes.

Q. Did you return?

A. James Taylor followed me up to the house, and brought a pike with him.

Q. Did that occasion you to return?

A. Yes.

Q. Where did you go to then?

A. We went down to the party.

Q. Where was that?

A. Down to Boden-lane-end.

Q. What party do you mean?

A. The party I had before met in the lane.

Q. I think you said Samuel Marriott was with you?

A. Yes.

Q. Was he carrying any thing?

A. A bag of bullets.

Q. Did Marriott keep that bag of bullets, or deliver it over to anybody else?

A. He delivered it to George Weightman.

Q. Where did you proceed to then?

A. Down the Park-lane to John Marriott's.

Q. Is that the wire-mill?

A. Yes.

Q. Did you meet with any persons there?

A. Yes.

Q. Did you find any persons when you got there?

A. After we had been there awhile, a party came down the yard.

Q. What number do you think?

A. I do not know how many there were.

Q. Was there anything done at Marriott's?

A. Yes, they demanded a gun.

Q. What did Marriott do on the gun being demanded of him?

A. He got up; he refused to give it them.

Q. What did they do or say on his refusing to give it them?

A. They said they would break the door open if he did not give them the gun.

Q. What did he do then?

A. He came down the stairs and gave them the gun.

Q. Had any thing been said about Marriott's gun at that time?

A. I do not know that there had; I did not hear it.

Q. Was there anything said afterwards about his gun?

A. I cannot recollect that there was.

Q. Had Marriott a gun?

A. Yes.

Q. Was he called for?

A. I cannot say that they called for him.

Q. Did he go with you?

A. No.

Q. Was there anything said about his going with you?

A. I cannot particularly say that they did say anything, they might.

Q. You say they took the gun?
A. Yes.
Q. Having got this gun, what became of them, where did they go?
A. They went up to William Lister's.
Q. Before they went to Lister's, did you attempt to get away from them?
A. In the wire-mill yard.
Q. What prevented your getting away from them?
A. James Taylor.
Q. How did he prevent you?
A. He stood behind me.
Q. Had he anything in his hand?
A. A gun.
Q. You say you proceeded with them to Lister's?
A. Yes.
Q. What did they do there?
A. They demanded his gun.
Q. Was he in bed?
A. Yes.
Q. Did he deliver them his gun?
A. Yes.
Q. Immediately?
A. No, not immediately.
Q. What did he say when they first demanded his gun?
A. I do not know what he said particularly, but he would not give it them.
Q. What did they do upon his refusing to give his gun?
A. They went round to the kitchen windows and broke the windows; I did not go *no* further than into the yard, but I heard the windows smash.
Q. Was the prisoner Ludlam with you all this time?
A. No.
Q. What had become of him?
A. I do not know what had become of him, he had not been with us.
Q. Do you happen to know whether they got Lister's gun?
A. Yes, they got his gun.

Q. Whom did you go to next?
A. Mr. Sellars's.
Q. Does he live near Pentridge-mill?
A. Yes.
Q. From this place you went to near Pentridge-mill?
A. Yes.
Q. How far is that from the wire-mill?
A. Near the mill.
Q. What did they do when they got to Sellars's?
A. They knocked him up to go with them; he got up.
Q. Did he go?
A. Yes.
Q. Where next did you go to?
A. Mr. Fletcher's.
Q. Where did he live?
A. At Pentridge-lane-end.
Q. What did they do there?
A. Demanded his gun.
Q. Did he get up too?
A. I do not know whether it was he who got up, some of them got up.
Q. Some of the people in the house?
A. Yes.
Q. Did they get any gun there?
A. Yes.
Q. Any thing besides the gun?
A. His man.
Q. Where next did you go to?
A. Forwards, into Pentridge-lane.
Q. Do you know James Turner.
A. Yes.
Q. Did you go into his house?
A. I saw a man come out of his house, and him come out too.
Q. They went in, and he came out with them?
A. Yes.

Mr. Justice Abbott. Was that so?
Mr. Clarke. He said so.
Mr. Justice Abbott. No: you did not ask him, whether

that was so—you said so; but the witness did not; he said yes, to what you said. I wish you would ask him.

Mr. Clarke. Had any persons come out of the house?

A. Yes.

Q. What became of Turner?

A. He came out and joined the party.

Q. Where did you go to next?

A. We went up into the lane.

Q. Into Pentridge-lane?

A. Yes, we were formed into rank there.

Q. How many of you do you think were got together then?

A. I do not know.

Q. Who formed you into rank there?

A. The captain.

Q. Who was he?

A. I do not know his name, they called him the captain.

Q. Did you know any of the persons who were there, at the time you were formed into rank?

A. There was William Turner.

Q. Had he any thing with him then?

A. He had a gun.

Q. Did any body assist the captain in forming you into rank?

A. William Turner.

Q. When you were formed into rank what became of you?

A. We went towards Pentridge.

Q. Did you go to any persons then in Pentridge?

A. I do not know that I did, I never went out of the road.

Q. Did you hear?

A. I heard a rattling at a door.

Q. In Pentridge?

A. Yes.

Q. Were any other persons brought up to you to join you in Pentridge?

A. I do not know that there was, there might be.

Q. Did you see the prisoner Isaac Ludlam there?

A. I do not know as I did.

Q. In any part of the march, as you were going on?

A. I saw him at Butterley.

Q. Did you see him before you got to Butterley?

A. No, I do not know that I did.

Q. In what part of the ranks were you?

A. Nearly the last.

Q. Do you happen to know who went behind you?

A. Isaac Ludlam and Samuel Briddon were the last always.

Q. They went behind you?

A. Yes.

Q. They came in the rear?

A. Yes.

Q. Do you happen to know what they were doing there behind?

A. No, I do not, they never said *nothing* to me.

Q. Did you make any offer to leave them as you were going along?

A. Not there.

Q. Where did you?

A. At Codnor.

Q. Do you know a place called the Coburn quarry?

A. Yes.

Q. It is a stone quarry?

A. Yes.

Q. Do you know who occupies that quarry; who had that quarry at the time you are speaking of?

A. Mr. Thomas.

Q. Did he work it?

A. No, it was not worked much then?

Q. Had it been working?

A. Yes, some time before.

Q. Who had worked it?

A. Isaac Ludlam.

Q. What distance is it from Isaac Ludlam's house?

A. I do not know how far it is; do you mean the quarry?—400 yards.

Q. You got away, I think you said, at Codnor.

A. No, I did not get away; I meant to make my escape there at the glass house.

Q. What prevented your making your escape there?
A. Isaac Ludlam was out of doors.
Q. What was he doing out at the door?
A. We supposed he was guarding the prisoners.
Q. What did he appear to be doing?
A. He was sheltering under the eaves.
Q. Was it raining?
A. Yes, very hard.
Q. Did you see him?
A. Yes.
Q. Had he any thing in his hand?
A. Yes, a spike.
Q. Did that prevent your escaping?
A. Yes.

Mr. Cross. Do you mean the pike, or the rain, or the man, by the word that?

Mr. Clarke. The man; he said so himself.

Mr. Denman. He should say so himself, and not you for him.

Mr. Justice Abbott. Ask him again, that will save trouble.

Mr. Clarke. What prevented your escaping?
A. Isaac Ludlam, standing under the eaves with a pike in his hand.
Q. Then Isaac Ludlam standing there prevented your escaping?
A. Yes.

Cross-examined by Mr. Cross.

Q. What did he do to prevent your escaping?
A. We supposed the man was keeping guard there.
Q. But neither by word nor deed did he prevent your escaping?
A. No, he said nothing to us?
Q. You were forced into the ranks against your will?
A. Yes.
Q. He was not present, and took no part in that?
A. No.
Q. As you marched along through the different places

you have mentioned, till you got to Butterley you saw nothing of him?

A. Yes, at Pentridge-lane-end?

Mr. Justice Abbott. Where was it you saw him at Pentridge-lane-end?

A. I saw him just before James Turner's.

Q. What do you mean by just before James Turner's?

A. Just before his house.

Q. Was that at the time you said that the people went out, and James Turner came out?

A. Yes.

Thomas Turner sworn.

Examined by Mr. Gurney.

Q. Do you live in Southwingfield?

A. No, not at present.

Q. Did you live there in June last?

A. A little out of Southwingfield.

Q. Have you been taken into custody on this business?

A. Yes.

Q. And have remained in custody?

A. Yes.

Q. On the evening of Monday the 9th of June last, were you at your father's house?

A. Yes.

Q. Did you go from thence in company with any other persons?

A. Yes.

Q. At about what time?

A. About nine o'clock, or a little before.

Q. In company with whom?

A. Samuel Ludlam and John Walker.

Q. To what place did you go?

A. To the meeting-house in Southwingfield.

Q. Is that near the gates of Colonel Halton?

A. Yes.

Q. Whom did you see there?

A. William Turner and George Weightman, whom we knew, and a strange man with them.

Q. Whom did you afterwards find that strange man to be?

A. The Nottingham captain.

Q. What was his name?

A. I did not hear his name mentioned?

Q. Do you now know that it was Brandreth?

A. Yes.

Q. Had Brandreth and George Weightman and William Turner any arms?

A. Yes.

Q. What, guns?

A. Each a gun.

Q. Was William Turner doing any thing with that gun?

A. Yes.

Q. What was he doing?

A. Loading it with a bullet.

Q. Did George Weightman say any thing?

A. Yes.

Q. What did he say?

A. He said, " Come, lads, I expect an engagement very soon."

Q. Did he say where and with whom?

A. Yes, with Mr. Jessop's men at Butterley furnace?

Q. Was any thing said to you by William Turner?

A. Yes.

Q. What was said?

A. William Turner said that was the captain, the strange man.

Q. To whom did he say that?

A. To me, I asked him.

Q. Did he tell you from whence the captain had come?

A. No.

Q. Where did Turner and Brandreth and George Weightman go to?

A. To Hunt's Barn?

Q. Did you and those with you follow to or near to the barn?

A. Yes, near to it.

Q. Were there any persons assembled at the barn?

A. Yes.

Q. How many in number, do you think?

A. I do not justly know; perhaps a score, or something better.

Q. Were they armed or unarmed?

A. Armed.

Q. How?

A. With different sorts of weapons?

Q. What sort of weapons?

A. Pikes and guns.

Q. By pikes do you mean such pikes as those?

A. Yes.

Q. Besides the pikes which the men had in their hands, did you see any other pikes piled up against the barn?

A. Not by the barn; I did not go to the barn, but there were a few up against the hedge side.

Q. Besides the persons you have named to me who were there, did you see William Barker?

A. Yes.

Q. John Hill?

A. Yes.

Mr. Justice Abbott. Where were they?

Mr. Gurney. I am speaking of the place near Hunt's Barn.

A. Yes.

Q. Was Robert Turner there?

A. Yes.

Q. Manchester Turner?

A. Yes.

Q. Charles Swaine?

A. Yes.

Q. Were all those armed?

A. Robert Turner, I cannot say whether he was armed or not; all the rest were, I know.

Q. Did Brandreth the captain say any thing to you where you were going to?

A. Yes, he said we must go to Nottingham forest, where there would be a great quantity of people meet us.

Q. Did Brandreth and Turner then do any thing with respect to the body of men that were there?

A. They put us in rank.

Q. Do you mean like soldiers?

A. Yes, two and two.

Q. Did you receive any thing to carry?

A. Yes.

Q. What?

A. A bag of bullets.

Q. From whom?

A. George Bramley.

Q. He was one of the party?

A. Yes.

Q. How many do you think you then amounted to?

A. There might be something better than a score.

Q. Were you then ordered to march?

A. Yes.

Q. By whom?

A. By Brandreth.

Q. For what place?

A. For Mr. Topham's ground, what is called Topham's close.

Q. Before you got to that place did you stop at any house?

A. Yes, James Hardwicke's.

Q. Before however you marched, you have told me, there were some pikes lying there; were there more pikes than one?

A. Yes, I believe there were.

Q. Did any persons carry more pikes than one, so as to have surplus arms?

A. They might, but I do not remember.

Q. Was any thing taken from Hardwicke's?

A. I do not know.

Q. Where did you go to next?

A. Most of the party went to Henry Tomlinson's: I and a few others did not go.

Q. Did you then go to Topham's close?

A. Yes.

Q. Had either of the party said whom you were to meet at Topham's close?

A. Yes, George Weightman.

Q. What did he say?

A. He said that we must march to Topham's close, and that the Pentridge people would meet us there he expected.

Q. Did you halt at Topham's close?

A. Yes.

Q. Who joined you there?

A. Isaac Ludlam.

Q. The prisoner?

A. Yes.

Q. Who with him?

A. His two sons, young Isaac and William.

Q. What had they with them?

A. Spikes.

Q. Such as those?

A. Yes.

Q. Did any other persons come with them?

A. There might, but I did not see any others.

Q. Did the Pentridge people join you there?

A. No.

Q. When you found they did not join you there, was any thing agreed to be done?

A. Yes.

Q. What?

A. George Weightman said he would take the bullets and go by Coburn quarry and the wire-mill.

Q. What was he to do?

A. And if he met the Pentridge people coming there he was to turn them back to Pentridge-lane-end.

Q. Did he and others quit your party for this purpose?

A. Yes, I suppose so.

Q. They quitted your party professedly for that purpose?

A. Yes.

Q. Did George Weightman take the bag of bullets along with him?

A. Yes.

Q. Where was the party that you staid with marched to?

A. To Mr. Elijah Hall's.

Q. Who then commanded you?
A. Brandreth.
Q. Did he command you throughout the night in short?
A. Yes, most of the commands were given by him.
Q. When you got to Mr. Hall's what was done?
A. There was a gun taken and his son forced away.
Q. Did he give up the gun willingly?
A. No.
Q. What was done to make him give it up?
A. Brandreth said if he did not give the gun they should break the house open for it.
Q. Did any persons go into the house?
A. Yes.
Q. How many.
A. There were a good many in the house, I did not take particular notice how many.
Q. Was Brandreth one?
A. Yes, and a good many others.
Q. A gun was taken, and young Elijah Hall was forced to go with them?
A. Yes.
Q. To whose house did you go next?
A. Mr. Walker's.
Q. Was any thing taken away from his house?
A. Yes, a pistol.
Q. What kind of a pistol?
A. It appeared to be a brass pistol.
Q. Who had that pistol for the rest of the night?
A. Brandreth.
Q. To whose house did you next go?
A. Mr. Bestwick's.
Q. Whose next?
A. Samuel Hunt's.
Q. When you got to Samuel Hunt's did you break in, or were you admitted without?
A. I cannot say; there was admittance in when I got there.
Q. What had you given you there?
A. Bread and cheese and beer,

Q. I should have asked you a question, while you were at Mr. Hall's do you remember Barker saying any thing?

A. Yes.

Q. What did he say?

A. He said he had wished for that day to come for long, but it had come at last.

Q. Was the prisoner with you at that time at Elijah Hall's?

A. Yes.

Q. When you marched on to Hunt's was he still with you?

A. I did not see him till we got there.

Q. Did you see him while you were at Hunt's?

A. Yes.

Q. With the pike in his hand still;

A. Yes.

Q. After you had had your bread and cheese and beer at Hunt's, did you march away?

A. Yes.

Q. Did Hunt and his servant Daniel Hunt go with you?

A. Yes.

Q. To whose house did you next go?

A. Mrs. Hepworth's.

Q. Did the prisoner go with you there?

A. Yes.

Q. What was done at Mrs. Hepworth's?

A. There was a gun brought from there.

Q. What was done when you arrived in the first place?

A. In the first place Brandreth went up to the back door and began thundering.

Q. Did the people of the house open it upon that?

A. No, there was no answer made to that.

Q. What was then done, did they open the door?

A. Brandreth called for some one to come and break the door open.

Q. Upon his saying that, what was done?

A. Samuel Hunt went up with a stone, and threw it against the door.

Q. What sort of a stone did it appear?

A. It appeared to be like the coping of a wall.

Q. Did that force it open?

A. No.

Q. Upon that was any attempt made at the window?

A. Brandreth left that door, and went to a window.

Q. Was the window forced?

A. The window was broken when I got there; I did not see it broken.

Q. The kitchen window?

A. Yes.

Q. Did you hear Brandreth say any thing to the persons within?

A. I heard Brandreth tell the persons within, to give him the arms out, and open the door and let them in.

Q. Did the persons within comply with his demand?

A. No.

Q. What did he do then?

A. He then fired in at the window.

Q. What mischief did that do?

A. It killed Robert Walters.

Q. Mrs. Hepworth's servant?

A. Yes.

Q. Did you remonstrate with him upon this?

A. Yes.

Q. Did you do so in the hearing of the party?

A. Yes; there were people round about.

Q. What did you say to him?

A. I went up to the window and saw Robert Walters lying upon the floor, and I said he should not have shot that poor innocent lad.

Q. What answer did he give you?

A. He said it was his duty to do it, and he would do it, and if I said any thing more, he would blow my brains out.

Q. Did he give you that answer publicly, and in the hearing of the party?

A. Others might hear it as well as I.

Q. Have you any doubt they did hear it?

A. They must have heard it.

Q. After this was done, did you get any arms from Mrs. Hepworth's?

A. Yes, a gun.

Q. Was Ludlam with your party all the while this was transacting at Mrs. Hepworth's?

A. I cannot say whether he was there all the time.

Q. Did you see him there?

A. Yes; I saw him go into the yard.

Q. With the party?

A. Yes.

Q. To what place did you then march?

A. To Pentridge-lane-end.

Q. Did you there meet any other party?

A. Yes.

Q. Were they armed?

A. Yes, some of them.

Q. In the same way as your party were?

A. Yes.

Q. Was Joseph Weightman, the younger, one of that party?

A. Yes.

Q. Was Thomas Weightman one?

A. Yes.

Q. Was Benjamin Taylor one?

A. Yes.

Q. Was Joseph Taylor one?

A. Yes.

Q. And Samuel Taylor?

A. James Taylor.

Q. Was Samuel Taylor?

A. Joseph and Benjamin.

Q. What place were you next marched to?

A. We went forward to the lane-end.

Q. To whose house?

A. I did not go to any body's house.

Q. Did the party go to any house?

A. There was a party went to Wheatcroft's.

Q. Was that at Buckland hollow?

A. Yes.

Q. Did you hear any noise of what they were doing?

A. Yes; I heard a disturbance.

Q. What did they appear to be doing?

A. They appeared to be thundering at doors.

Q. Did you hear them do that also at the houses of Pentridge-lane-end?

A. Yes; I heard them rattling at folks houses, and calling them up.

Q. What were they getting from them?

A. I understood they were getting their arms and their men, what they could.

Q. After you had done all that, to what place did you next go?

A. To Pentridge from thence.

Q. As you were going to Pentridge, do you remember your captain saying any thing about what men he wanted?

A. He was falling us in altogether, and he asked whether there were any men who had been soldiers, or in the militia, or knew discipline, that if there were, they must turn out and keep the men in order.

Q. Did any man turn out upon that?

A. Yes.

Q. Who?

A. Charles Swaine.

Q. Were the men then put in order?

A. Yes; they were put in rank, two and two.

Q. By whom?

A. By Brandreth and William Turner, and this Charles Swaine.

Q. Among the houses that your party went to, was Mr. William Booth's one?

A. Yes.

Q. Was any poney taken from thence?

A. I believe there was.

Q. Whom did you see taking that poney out, or leading it out?

A. I saw George Weightman with it, at the yard gate.

Q. Did Weightman desire you to help any man upon it?

A. Yes; he asked me to give a man of the name of Storer, a leg upon it; he pretended to be ill.

Q. Was he one of the persons who had been taken out of his house?

A. I did not see him taken out, but I understood he was.

Q. You understood then in the party that he was taken out of his house?

A. Yes.

Q. Did he remain on?

A. Not far.

Q. What became of him?

A. He tumbled off and lay in the street.

Q. To what place were you then marched?

A. To Butterley furnace.

Q. When you arrived there, did Mr. Goodwin, one of the managers of the works, come out to you?

A. Yes.

Q. Did you hear any thing that passed between Mr. Goodwin and Brandreth, or any other of your party?

Q. I heard him say something, but did not hear what it was.

Q. After that, to what part were you next marched?

A. To Ripley town-end.

Q. What was done there?

A. Brandreth ordered us to halt, and to give three huzzas.

Q. Did you do so?

A. Yes.

Q. For what purpose was that?

A. I did not understand for what purpose it was.

Q. Ripley town-end is upon the high road to Nottingham?

A. Yes.

Q. To what place were you then marched?

A. To Codnor.

Q. That is in the high road?

A. Yes, I believe it is.

Q. Did you stop at any house there?

A. Yes.

Q. At what house?

A. A public-house they call the Glass House.

Q. What was done?

A. Brandreth went to the door and knocked and called them up, and ordered them to fill some drink for us.

Q. Was drink supplied?
A. Yes.
Q. To what amount?
A. Eight and twenty shillings.
Q. Did you all go into the house there, or only part of you?
A. I cannot say; I went into the parlour.
Q. Did a great many go in?
A. Yes, the house and parlour were almost full.
Q. Did any person remain outside that you saw?
A. Not that I saw.
Q. From thence where did you march?
A. To Langley mill.
Q. Before you got there, were any men fetched out of a barn?
A. Yes.
Q. How many?
A. Three.
Q. Were they forced to go with you?
A. I understood so; I did not see them forced.
Q. Were they taken with you?
A. Yes, they were.
Q. When you got to Langley mill did you meet any person returning as from Nottingham?
A. Yes.
Q. Whom?
A. George Weightman upon a poney.
Q. Was that Mr. Booth's poney?
A. Yes, I understood so.
Q. The poney you had lifted Storer upon?
A. Yes.
Q. Had you known of George Weightman leaving the party before that?
A. I knew he had left it, but not where he had gone to.
Q. What report did George Weightman make to your party, when he met them?
A. The party surrounded him, and asked him what was going on at Nottingham, and he told them that every thing was going on very well; that the town was taken,

and the soldiers would not come out of the barracks, and we must march forwards as fast as we could.

Q. Upon that did you march forwards?
A. Yes.
Q. How far did you march with them?
A. Two or three miles beyond Eastwood.
Q. Then you left them?
A. Yes, I did.
Q. When you left them, were they still marching on towards Nottingham?
A. Some few; very few.
Q. Who were leading them?
A. Brandreth and William Turner were together when I saw them.
Q. How far did Isaac Ludlam go with your party?
A. I cannot say.
Q. You saw him at Codnor?
A. No, I do not know that I saw him at Codnor.
Q. What was the last place you recollect having seen him?
A. I do not remember having seen him after we were at Mrs. Hepworth's yard; I might see him, but I cannot recollect.
Q. At what time in the morning was it that you left?
A. It might be between nine and ten in the morning.
Q. Then you had been with them from nine or ten at night, till between nine and ten in the morning?
A. Yes.
Q. As you were marching along, and stopping, and so on, in the course of the night, was it said among you all where you were going to?
A. No, I cannot recollect any body but Brandreth saying where they were going to.
Q. Do you remember his saying where you were going more than once or twice?
A. No, I cannot.
Q. Had you any weapon with you as you went along?
A. Yes.
Q. What was it?
A. A pike.

Q. Who gave it you?

A. Samuel Ludlam gave it me when I gave him the bullets.

Q. You parted with the bullets to Samuel Ludlam, and then he parted with them to George Weightman?

A. Yes.

Cross-examined by Mr. Denman.

Q. What was it that Brandreth said about where you were going?

A. He said we were going to Nottingham forest.

Q. Did you hear that said by him more than once?

A. No, I cannot say that I did.

Q. Whereabouts was it you heard him say that?

A. Before we started from Hunt's Barn.

Q. The prisoner joined you sometime after that?

A. Yes, after that.

Q. You saw him go into the yard at Hepworth's?

A. I saw him in the yard.

Q. You are sure of that, are you?

A. Yes.

Q. Do you recollect his dropping behind anywhere?

A. No.

Q. Where was Brandreth stopping at the time that unfortunate thing occurred, of the shooting of the boy?

A. At the window.

Q. By the outer door?

A. At the back side of the house.

Q. Do you know the age of the prisoner's two sons; how old they are?

A. I cannot say.

Q. They are both grown men, are not they?

A. They are both young men.

Henry Tomlinson, sworn.
Examined by Mr. Gurney.

Q. I believe you are a farmer, residing at Southwingfield park?

A. Yes.

Q. On the night of Monday the 9th of June, did any body of men come to your house?
A. Yes.
Q. At about what time?
A. Half-past nine or a quarter before ten.
Q. How many in number do you think?
A. There appeared to be between thirty and forty.
Q. Were they armed?
A. Yes.
Q. In what manner?
A. Some with guns, some with spikes.
Q. By spikes, do you mean such weapons as those?
A. Yes.
Q. What did they do at your house?
A. They went up to the door; I called "halloo"! and asked what they wanted; they said they wanted me and my gun.
Q. What answer did you give them?
A. I told them they must have neither; they said they would; I told them my gun was gone to Ashover to be mended.
Q. What reply was made to that?
A. They said if I did not open the door, they would break it, and find my gun, or else they would search my house.
Q. Upon this threat did you open the door?
A. Yes, I opened the door.
Q. Whom did you see?
A. There were two men entered the house, one called the captain, the other I did not know the name of; but before them I saw William Turner.
Q. Did the person who entered, whom you describe to be the captain, turn out to be Brandreth?
A. Yes, and William Barker.
Q. You knew Turner and Barker before?
A. Yes.
Q. Did you speak to them?
A. Yes, I spoke to them, and said, "well William are you one," and they answered "yes."
Q. Did any of the party say any thing to you?
A. I went into the house with them.

Q. Did the party use any threats of any kind?

A. That was when I came out of the house; the captain said I must go with them.

Q. Did you give them your gun?

A. Yes I did; and then the captain said I must go with them.

Q. What answer did you give him?

A. I told him I would not.

Q. What was said upon that?

A. He said I must go with them; I had better go that night than stop while morning.

Q. Did he say why?

A. For he said there was a great gang coming from Sheffield, and a great cloud coming out of the North, that would sweep all before them.

Q. What did you say to this?

A. I told him I would not go, and he presented his gun, and swore he would shoot me.

Q. Did he tell you where he was going to?

A. Yes, he said they were going to Nottingham.

Q. Did he say by what time they were to be at Nottingham?

A. By half-past eight or nine, as I understood.

Q. What else did he say?

A. He said they should need to go no farther than Nottingham, for London would be taken before they got thither.

Q. Did they at last force you to go?

A. Yes.

Q. Did you propose what you should carry?

A. Yes; I wanted to carry my own gun, but the captain would not let me.

Q. What did he say?

A. That I must carry a spike.

Q. Was a spike put into your hand?

A. Yes.

Q. Were you marched away?

A. Yes.

Q. Did you manage to get away from them soon?

A. Yes, George Weightman bade me give him my spike, and he let me go back again.

Q. Were you and he acquainted?

A. Yes; and I said it was a very lonesome place to leave my wife by herself; and he said I should go a little way and then turn back again.

Q. Did he go on with the party when you returned?

A. Yes; about three hundred yards off he took the spike, and let me go back.

Q. Which way did they then march?

A. They marched right forwards, making towards Nottingham as they talked.

Mr. Elijah Hall senior, sworn.

Examined by Mr. Serjeant Copley.

Q. I believe you are a farmer and miller, and live in Southwingfield-park?

A. I am, I live there.

Q. Do you remember on Monday night the 9th of June, at what time you got to your house?

A. About eleven o'clock.

Q. From your mill?

A. Yes.

Q. Did you fasten up the house?

A. The house door was fastened as I got in.

Q. After you had fastened the house door, did you hear any persons on the outside?

A. I heard the footsteps of two men.

Q. Did they say any thing to you?

A. One of them asked whether any men had been there that night.

Q. You were then on the inside of the house?

A. On the inside.

Q. What answer did you make?

A. I told them there had.

Q. What did they reply?

A. They asked me if they had taken any guns away, and I told them they had.

Q. After that conversation did they go away?

A. They did.

Q. Did you afterwards open the house door?

A. I did.

Q. How soon?

A. A very few minutes.

Q. Did you see any persons?

A. I did not immediately on opening the door.

Q. How soon?

A. In a very few minutes, in a very short time indeed.

Q. Where were they?

A. Coming into the yard.

Q. Were they few or many?

A. There appeared I thought about thirty, perhaps more or less.

Q. Were you at the time on the outside of the house?

A. I was.

Q. How far from the door?

A. Not ten yards.

Q. Were the men armed or unarmed?

A. They had pikes, guns, and one of them had a sword.

Q. You say you were about ten yards from the door, did the men see you?

A. They did.

Q. What did they say?

A. I asked them what they wanted there at that time of night.

Q. What answer did they make?

A. They said they wanted fire-arms.

Q. What answer did you make?

A. Some of them said they wanted a bigger loaf and the times altering; I told them it was not in power to do either; I also told them I had no fire-arms for them.

Q. While this conversation passed, did any person inside the house do any thing to the door?

A. Some person inside the house fastened the door.

Q. What did the people outside the house do when you said you had no fire-arms?

A. They said they knew I had, and demanded them, and told me I had better deliver them up quietly to prevent further mischief, and my house from being fired.

Q. Any thing else?

A. About that time there was a gun fired about half a mile off.

Q. In which direction?

A. The west.

Q. Was that Frichley?

A. Yes.

Q. Frichley is in a direction towards Pentridge?

A. No, in the opposite direction.

Q. After the gun was fired, what did they do?

A. They demanded guns.

Q. They repeated the demand for fire arms?

A. Yes, and began to force the door.

Q. Before they began to force the door, or while they were forcing the door, did they say any thing further about what was going on?

A. Not that I recollect.

Q. Did they get into the house?

A. There was a gun given to them through the window.

Q. Was that the window of the room in which your son slept?

A. It was.

Q. After the gun was given to them what passed?

A. I told them I hoped they would go away quietly, as they had promised me at first.

Q. Upon your saying that what answer was made?

A. They said I must go with them.

Q. What did you say?

A. I told them I would not.

Q. Upon your saying you would not, was any answer made or any thing said?

A. Some of them said he has sons, we will have them; on which the captain said if he has sons, we will not take the old man; they then desired me to open the door, and fetch my sons out: I told them I could not, being outside as well as themselves.

Q. What was done then upon that?

A. They then ordered me to command it to be opened, and on refusal they began to force it.

Q. On your refusal?

A. Yes.

Q. Upon their endeavour to force the door what was done?

A. Some of them said, "captain how must it be?" after they had made several fruitless attempts with their pikes at the door, the captain said, "blow it in pieces."

Q. What was then done?

A. The door was then opened by some person inside.

Q. Did any body go in upon the door being opened?

A. There did.

Q. How many?

A. To the number of a dozen or more; twelve or more.

Q. Did the captain go in?

A. He did.

Q. Did you go in also?

A. I did.

Q. What took place inside when you and they went in?

A. The captain ordered me to fetch my sons out of bed. I told him I would not.

Q. Was the bed room up stairs?

A. Yes, it was; upon which he said, "if you will not, I will blow your brains out."

Q. Had he a gun in his hand.

A. Yes, he had.

Q. What did he do?

A. He gave me two thrusts in the side with the muzzle of his gun, and presented it at me; Thomas Turner cried out, "do not shoot." The captain then took a candle from some person in the house, and lighted it at the fire, and he and several others went up stairs.

Q. Into the bed room?

A. Yes, into the bed room where my son slept.

Q. Could you hear in the kitchen what passed up stairs?

A. I could hear a great noise; I could hear one person threaten to hash them up, if they would not get up.

Q. Did you hear any thing more upstairs, except the noise and the expressions you have mentioned?

A. No.

Q. What did they do?

A. They brought one of my sons down into the house place.

Q. Down stairs?

A. Yes.

Q. Which of your sons?

A. Elijah.

Q. Was he quite dressed when he came down, or only partly dressed?

A. Only partly.

Q. Did he bring down the rest of his clothes with him?

A. I think not.

Q. Did he finish his dressing in the house?

A. He did.

Q. Whilst he was completing his dressing in the house place, can you tell us any conversation that passed?

A. I asked the captain where he was going, that is, where he was taking my son.

Q. What answer did he give?

A. He said he was going to Nottingham; that he believed Nottingham was given up at that time; that there was a general rising throughout the country, from whence their object was London, to wipe off the national debt, and begin again afresh.

Q. Among the party outside the house, did you see the prisoner at the bar Isaac Ludlam?

A. I did.

Q. Inside the house, did you see Isaac Ludlam the younger, his son?

A. I did.

Q. Did you see William Ludlam inside the house?

A. I did.

Q. Did you see Manchester Turner?

A. I did.

Q. Robert Turner?

A. I did.

Q. John Walker?

A. I did.

Q. William Walker?

A. I did.

Q. Thomas Turner?

A. I did.

Mr. Justice Abbott. Did you see all of them within the house?

A. Yes, all within the house, except the prisoner.

Mr. Serjeant Copley. Was anything said in the course of the conversation about the consequence of what they had done?

A. I asked them if they knew the consequences of what they were going about.

Mr. Justice Abbott. Of whom did you ask that; of any particular person, or of the party?

A. Of the party.

Q. Outside or inside the house?

A. Inside the house.

Mr Serjeant Copley. What answer did they make?

A. They said they knew the consequence; it was hanging what they had done already; they were determined to go on.

Mr. Justice Abbott. Do you know who said that?

A. No, I do not.

Cross-examined by Mr. Cross.

Q. It was the party inside the house that spoke in that way, that they were determined to go on?

A. Yes.

Q. The prisoner was outside?

A. Yes.

Q. Was there a light inside?

A. Yes.

Q. And that was strong enough to enable you to see them?

A. No, it was not.

Q. How was it you saw him then?

A. There was light enough outside the house to enable me to distinguish him.

Elijah Hall the younger sworn.

Examined by Mr. Serjeant Copley.

Q. You are the son of the last witness, and lived with your father in Southwingfield park, on the 9th of June?

A. Yes.

Q. Do you remember any party coming to your house that night?

A. Yes.

Q. Did you hear them outside the house?

A. I did.

Q. Did you afterwards hear them inside the house?

A. Yes.

Q. While they were outside the house was any gun given out of the window?

A. Yes.

Q. Of your room?

A. Yes.

Q. After they had got into the house did any of them come up into your bed room?

A. They did.

Q. Can you tell us about how many?

A. I cannot say positively, there were several came up.

Q. When they came up there, what did they say or do?

A. They demanded me to get out of my bed and go along with them.

Q. Was Jeremiah Brandreth one of those that came into the room?

A. He was.

Q. When they demanded you to to get out of your bed and go along with them, what else did they say?

A. They told me they could not wait of me, that I must make haste.

Q. Did you get up?

A. I did.

Q. Did you dress yourself in the room or how?

A. I partly dressed myself in the room.

Q. And then you went down?

A. Yes.

Q. When they told you to get up and go along with them, did they say any thing as to what they would do if you would not get up?
A. They threatened to murder me if I did not.

Q. Was it in consequence of that conversation and that threat that you got up and went?
A. It was.

Q. After you had finished your dressing below stairs did they compel you to go?
A. They did.

Q. Did you ask them yourself any thing about where they were going?
A. I did.

Q. Whom did you ask, which of the party?
A. I cannot recollect which it was.

Q. What answer did they give you?
A. They told me that they were going to Nottingham.

Q. Did they tell you what they were going to Nottingham for?
A. That they were going to meet a great party of other men on the race course at Nottingham.

Q. Did they tell you what for—what they were going to do?
A. They told me they were going to break the laws and to pull down the parliament house.

Q. Did they tell you what you were to get when you got to Nottingham?
A. They told me I was to have a deal of money when I got to Nottingham.

Q. Did they tell you how much?
A. They told me there would be 100 *l.* for every man that got there.

Q. Did you consent to go, or did you refuse?
A. I refused.

Mr. Justice Abbott. He has said that he was compelled to go.

Mr. Serjeant Copley. After you left the house where did you go to next?
A. First to Isaac Walker's.

Q. Did you make any attack upon Isaac Walker's house?
A. They did.

Q. What did you get there?
A. A gun and a pistol.
Q. After you had got the gun and the pistol at Isaac Walker's house, what place did you go to next?
A. To Henry Bestwick's.
Q. Did they make any attack upon Bestwick's house?
A. They did.
Q. Did they get any thing there?
A. They got a gun.
Q. Where did they go to from Bestwick's house?
A. To Samuel Hunt's at the lodge; to Southwingfield park.
Q. A house they call the lodge?
A. Yes.
Q. Which Samuel Hunt occupies?
A. Yes.
Q. Did they stop there?
A. I was not there at the first.
Q. When you got there did you find them in the house?
A. They were.
Q. What were they doing in the house when you got there?
A. They were bringing out the bread and cheese.
Q. Who was bringing out the bread and cheese?
A. The servant girl or Samuel Hunt himself, I do not know which it was.
Q. Did you see Samuel Hunt there?
A. I did.
Q. Had they any thing else besides the bread and cheese?
A. Some table beer to drink.
Q. How long did they stay there?
A. They did not stop long.
Q. When they went away from there, did Samuel Hunt go with them?
A. He did.
Q. Has Samuel Hunt a man called Daniel Hunt?
A. He had at that time.
Q. Did he go with them?
A. He did.
Q. Had Samuel Hunt any arms?
A. His man took a gun with him.

Q. You have told us this party went first from your father's house to Isaac Walker's, from Isaac Walker's to another house, and from that to Hunt's, I want to know whether Isaac Ludlam was of the party?

A. Yes, he was.

Mr Justice Abbott. At each of those places?

A. Yes.

Mr. Serjeant Copley. Where did the party next go to?

A. They went from there to Mrs. Hepworth's.

Q. What did they do when they first got to Mrs. Hepworth's?

A. They made a great disturbance at the kitchen door.

Q. What passed?

A. The family got up and asked them what they wanted, they told them they wanted men and arms.

Q. What answer was returned from the inside of the house?

A. They told them they should neither have men nor arms there.

Q. What was then done?

A. Some of the party went to the kitchen window and broke it open.

Q. After the kitchen window was broken open what was done?

A. There was a gun fired.

Q. By whom?

A. By the Nottingham captain.

Q. Into the kitchen?

A. Yes.

Q. Was any body shot by it?

A. Robert Walters was shot by it.

Q. Was Isaac Ludlam of the party at that time?

A. I did not see him present when the gun was let off, but I saw him before we left the house in the back yard; I did not see him at the present time when the gun was let off.

Q. How long might you be about the house in the whole?

A. A very few minutes.

Q. After the shot was fired, what then happened?
A. They demanded Mrs. Hepworth's gun.
Q. Was it given to them?
A. It was given to them.
Q. Upon the gun being given, what did they do?
A. They went away.
Q. Where did they then go to?
A. They went from there to Pentridge-lane-end.
Q. Did they attack any houses at Pentridge-lane-end?
A. They did.
Q. Did they go from thence to Buckland Hollow.
A. Yes, some part of them did.
Q. Did they make any attack there?
A. I did not see any.
Q. Did you hear any?
A. I heard some thunders at the door.
Q. At Wheatcroft's?
A. Yes.
Q. Did that party that went down to Wheatcroft's again return?
A. They returned to Pentridge-lane-end.
Q. Did you then go up to Pentridge?
A. We then went up to Pentridge, and they attacked several houses in Pentridge.
Q. While they were attacking those houses, some of those houses in Pentridge, what did you do?
A. I made my escape.

Mr. Isaac Walker sworn.
Examined by Mr. Reader.

Q. Where do you live?
A. At Wingfield park.
Q. What are you?
A. A farmer.
Q. At any time on Monday night, the 9th of June, after you were in bed, were you disturbed?
A. Yes.
Q. At what time of night was that?
A. About half past eleven o'clock.

Q. Were all your family a bed?
A. They were.
Q. What disturbed you?
A. A dog barking.
Q. Did you get up?
A. Yes.
Q. Did you go to the window?
A. Yes.
Q. What did you observe?
A. A parcel of men coming up the yard.
Q. About what number?
A. I supposed about forty.
Q. Were they armed or not?
A. Armed.
Q. What with.
A. Those kind of things (pikes) and guns.
Q. Did they come up to your house?
A. Yes, they came to the front door.
Q. What did they do?
A. They demanded entrance; I asked them what for, they said they wanted my fire-arms.
Q. What answer did you give them?
A. I asked them what they wanted them for; they said that was no business of mine, they were determined to have them; they demanded a gun and a brace of pistols.
Q. What answer did you give them?
A. I told them I had a gun, but I had no pistols; they presented a piece at me, and said they would fire at me.
Q. Did more than one person present a piece?
A. Only one.
Mr. Justice Abbott. You were standing at the window at this time?
A. Yes, at my bed-room window.
Mr. Reader. The window was open?
A. I pushed up the sash; they said they would fire at me if I did not immediately open the door; upon that I went down and opened the door.
Q. Did any person say any thing to you?
A. Some of the party told him not to fire, but to give me time to put my clothes on.

Q. Then you went down and opened the door?

A. Yes, and I gave them the gun; I took the gun down with me, and gave it them, and they went away then.

Q. What became of you?

A. I was going up stairs again, I heard them rap at the door again, I went back, and they said they knew I had one pistol.

Q. You went back and opened the door again?

A. Yes, I did; they said they knew I had one pistol, if I had not two, and that they were determined to have that and all; they demanded a servant man also.

Q. What did you say to that?

A. I told them I had none; they said they knew I had, and they would have him.

Q. Had you a servant man?

A. No.

Q. Did you tell them so?

Q. Yes, and they went away then.

Mr. Justice Abbott. You gave them the pistol did you.

A. Yes, I did.

Mr. Reader. On their demanding the pistol a second time you gave it them?

A. Yes; they said they would make me glad to give it them.

Q. What sort of a pistol was it?

A. A brass barrelled pistol.

Q. Look at the prisoner, Isaac Ludlam, did you see him there?

A. Yes, I believe he was there.

Q. Have you any doubt about it?

A. No.

Q. Had you known him before?

A. Yes.

Q. Where was he at the time this passed?

A. Under my window, but rather to the right of it.

Mr. Justice Abbott. You saw him there?

A. Yes, I saw him, I knew his voice.

Mrs. Mary Hepworth sworn.
Examined by Mr. Reader.

Q. Where do you live?
A. At Southwingfield park.
Q. Have you a farm there?
A. Yes.
Q. Were your family disturbed on the night of the 9th of June last?
A. Yes, between eleven and twelve o'clock.
Q. Were you and your family in bed?
A. We were in bed at the time.
Q. Of what did your family consist?
A. Two servant men, Fox and Walters; my son William Hepworth, and two daughters.
Q. What disturbed you?
A. A noise at the door.
Q. What kind of a noise?
A. A loud knocking at the door, as loud as thunder; I suppose with the pikes.
Q. Did you get up?
A. I got up immediately.
Q. What did you do when you had got up?
A. They demanded men.
Q. Did you go to the window?
A. I went down stairs and stood in the kitchen; they kept up the noise at the door and the window of the kitchen.
Q. The door and the window were both in the kitchen?
A. Yes; and then they came to the front of the house and demanded men and guns.
Q. Then they went to the front of the house?
A. They did not go from thence, there were others came in front of the house.
Q. What were they doing in front?
A. Knocking at the door, and demanding men and guns.
Q. Did you make any answer to that demand?
A. I told them they should not have any. I went up stairs again, and I told them that from the window.
Q. Did you open the window?
A. Somebody had done that. I told them they should have none; that they were doing very wrong.

Q. Did you go down stairs again?

A. I did. The window was broken open.

Q. The kitchen window?

A. Yes, the back kitchen window; and a man was immediately shot.

Q. In what way was the window broken open?

A. The shutters were forced into the room, and the glass fell both ways.

Q. Immediately as you came you heard what?

A. A man was immediately shot.

Q. What man was that?

A. Robert Walters.

Q. Where was he at the time he was shot?

A. He was set down stooping, as if he was putting on his boots.

Q. How long did he live?

A. Perhaps ten minutes; I cannot exactly say.

Q. After Walters was shot, what more passed?

A. They called out for men and guns. I told them I could not let them have them. The gun had been hid in the cellar, and I ordered my son to go and give it them, or I imagined we should all be murdered.

Q. Did he give it them?

A. He gave it them out of the window: they desired to have the but end forward.

Q. When they had got the gun, did they desire to have any thing else?

A. They still said they must have the men.

Q. You were then in the kitchen?

A. Yes, I was.

Q. What did you do?

A. I went up stairs and told them they had shot one, was not that sufficient for them.

Q. Did they then go away?

A. They went away when they had got the gun.

Henry Hole sworn.

Examined by Mr. Reynolds.

Q. On the 9th of June last, were you a labourer at Pentridge-lane-end?
A. Yes.
Q. Were you disturbed on the night of the 9th of June?
A. Yes.
Q. About what hour?
A. About twenty minutes before twelve o'clock.
Q. Had you been in bed, and did you get up?
A. Yes.
Q. Did you go to your window and see any body?
A. I went to my window and put my head out, and said, "halloo, who is there, what do you want."
Q. What was the answer?
A. The answer was, "we want you to volunteer yourself to go with us, or else we will break the door down and murder you."
Q. Did you go and open the door?
A. I went down and opened the door, and I saw four men.
Q. Do you know the names of any of those four?
A. I know Joseph Weightman and Joseph Topham.
Q. Was any thing said to you by any one of them?
A. I asked them where they were going, they said they were going to Nottingham.
Q. For what purpose did they say?
A. I said if they were going to Nottingham I could not pretend to go with them, for I had no money to carry me there, nor I had no money to take care of my family while I was gone.
Q. Was any answer made to that?
A. They said I needed no money; that they should keep me on roast beef and ale, and there was people fixed to take care of every body's families that would come in two days or under.
Q. Were you then obliged to go?
A. They said I had better go that night than stop till morning.

Q. Did they give any reason why you had better do so?

A. That they would come out of Yorkshire like a cloud, and take all before them; and those that refused to go would all be shot, they said.

Q. What did you do?

A. I dressed myself and went out.

Q. Was any thing given to you?

A. A pike.

Q. Any thing like this?

A. Yes, like that which lies this way; I carried it a little way, and said if they were going to Nottingham I was not able to carry it, it was so heavy; and if they did not take it I should hurl it down.

Q. Where did you go?

A. I went on the turnpike road towards John Sellars's.

Mr. Justice Abbott. Did you throw it down?

A. Yes, I did.

Mr. Reynolds. Was any thing done at John Sellars's?

A. When I got against John Sellars's, I saw John Sellars and his apprentice coming from against his own door.

Q. From whose door?

A. John Sellars.

Q. Did any other number of persons join you?

A. I heard some others coming over the meadow from Mrs. Hepworth's.

Q. Did they join you?

A. They joined us at Mr. Fletcher's.

Q. When you were at Mr. Fletcher's who was there, was Brandreth there?

A. Yes, I saw him.

Q. Who else?

A. William Turner and Manchester Turner, Isaac Ludlam and William Ludlam.

Q. By Isaac Ludlam, do you mean that man?

A. Yes.

Q. The prisoner?

A. Yes.

Q. Any body else?

A. Joseph Weightman and Joseph Topham; and I saw Samuel Hunt as we were going out of the yard.

Q. What was done at Mr. Fletcher's, was any thing taken from him?

A. Yes, there was a man and a gun taken.

Q. Was that man's name William Shipman?

A. Yes.

Q. From Mr. Fletcher's where did you go?

A. We went a little on the turnpike road; there we were divided. Brandreth and the biggest party of men went to the row of houses.

Q. To what row of houses?

A. What they call George Turner's; they are George Turner's and his sons.

Q. Whereabout was that?

A. At Pentridge-lane-end.

Q. What became of the other party; where did they go?

A. Me and Samuel Hunt, and eight or ten others, went towards Samuel Booth's.

Q. Was any thing taken from Samuel Booth's?

A. They took Samuel Booth's son, Hugh Booth.

Q. Did Brandreth's party join you again there?

A. Yes, he joined us before we went away from there; Brandreth, not his party.

Q. Was Isaac Ludlam the prisoner of your party who went to Booth's, or not?

A. No, I believe he was not; I did not see him.

Q. Did you go to Mr. Wheatcroft's, in Buckland Hollow?

A. Yes.

Q. What was done there?

A. The door was broken open, and three men and a gun were brought away.

Q. Did you return back to Pentridge-lane-end?

A. Yes.

Q. Did you there meet the other party?

A. Yes.

Q. Was any thing done there?

A. Yes, we were formed into ranks there, three deep?

Q. Where were the persons put who had guns, and those that had spikes?

A. The biggest part of the musquets in the front, the spikemen in the middle, and a few musquets behind.

Q. When you were thus formed, was any thing said?

A. The word of command was given to march.

Q. Who was in command?

A. Brandreth.

Q. Where did you then go?

A. We went along the road towards Pentridge.

Q. Did you see any thing of George Weightman?

A. I saw George Weightman as we were going out of Pentridge, on William Booth's poney.

Q. Did you hear it stated where he was going with the poney?

A. I heard it stated among them that he was going to Nottingham, to let their friends know that they were coming?

Q. Did you go onwards to the Butterley works?

A. Yes.

Q. Did you see Mr. Goodwin there?

A. Yes.

Q. What passed?

A. I saw him come out of the office.

Q. Did he say any thing?

A. First Brandreth and William Turner knocked at the door, and then he came out of the office.

Q. What did he say?

A. He called about for his men, and he said there were a great many too many already, without they were for a better purpose upon a better subject.

Q. Was the prisoner Isaac Ludlam there then?

A. I cannot recollect seeing him.

Q. Upon Mr. Goodwin saying that, what further passed?

A. There was a man in the rear said, " You have no business there," which I took to be John Bacon.

Q. Said to whom?

A. To the men; to the captain; " you had better turn off;" they turned off and marched towards the Coke Hearth.

Q. The captain turned off?
A. He first, and they all followed.
Q. Did you then proceed to Ripley?
A. Yes, there we were halted.
Q. Did you go afterwards on to Codnor?
A. Yes.
Q. Did you go to the Glass House public house?
A. Yes.
Q. What sort of a night was it at this time?
A. A very wet night.
Q. Did the party go into the public house?
A. Yes.
Q. Was any body at the door?
A. I saw Isaac Ludlam while they were at the door, stand at the door with a musquet in his hand.
Q. Where were you when you saw him?
A. I came to the door to look out.
Q. Had you been in?
A. I had been in the back kitchen.
Q. How did he appear to be standing, in what way?
A. He appeared to be standing against the wall, with a musquet in his hand.
Q. How long did you stay at the Glass House at Codnor?
A. About half an hour.
Q. Do you know whether Isaac Ludlam continued at the post at the door?
A. No, I cannot say for any thing any further.
Q. You saw him there?
A. Yes, I did.
Q. Did you go afterwards to Mr. Raynor's?
A. Yes.
Q. Was any person taken from Mr. Raynor's?
A. Yes, they took his man and his gun, and a pitching fork, and perhaps more.
Q. While you were at Codnor, did you see any person of the name of John Bacon there?
A. Yes.
Q. At the Glass House?
A. Yes.

Q. Did he say any thing?

A. I heard him say, the government had robbed them and plundered them of all that ever they had; that that was the last shift they ever could make.

Q. Was any thing more said by Bacon at that time?

A. I do not recollect any thing.

Q. You had something to eat there, had not you?

A. I had nothing; some of them appeared to be eating, but I believe it was what they brought with them.

Q. Was any thing said about a bill?

A. Yes, I saw a bill given to the captain and John Bacon.

Q. Had they had something to drink there?

A. Yes.

Q. Some ale?

A. Yes.

Q. Was any thing said about the payment of that bill?

A. I heard them say it would be paid in a fortnight when the job was over.

Q. Who said that?

A. Either the captain or John Bacon, I cannot say which.

Q. Had any of the other party gone to any other public house?

A. Yes, there was a party went to a public house called the French Horn.

Q. Is that at Codnor?

A. Yes.

Mr. Justice Abbott. How does he know that?

Mr. Reynolds. Did you meet any other party as you left the Glass House?

A. There was a party came from Hartsay to the Glass House, and after we left the Glass House a party came from Swanwick.

Q. What was done after the parties met; were you formed again?

A. No, there was no regular form that I can recollect?

Q. Did you go on afterwards to Raynor's?

A. We afterwards went in along the Nottingham road to Raynor's; there we were halted.

Q. At Raynor's a man and a gun and a pitching fork were taken?

A. Yes.

Q. Did you go from Raynor's towards Langley mill?

A. Yes.

Q. When you were near Langley mill did you see George Weightman?

A. I saw George Weightman on William Booth's poney.

Q. In what direction was he coming?

A. He was coming from towards Nottingham.

Q. On the turnpike road?

A. Yes.

Q. Did he go and speak to any body?

A. As he went past us I heard him say, " March on my lads, all is right; they have bombarded Nottingham at two o'clock this morning, and it is given up to them."

Q. Did you march on?

A. Yes.

Q. Did you go in the course from Langley to Eastwood?

A. Yes.

Q. In going that way, had you any conversation with a person of the name of Barnes?

A. Yes, we were halted at Eastwood.

Q. What was it Barnes said to you?

A. I asked him what they were going to do when they got to Nottingham; he said, they had fixed up a fresh government at Nottingham, and they was going there to defend it until the other counties came into their terms.

Q. What further did he say?

A. He said he had never been set down.

Q. Did he say any thing about London?

A. He said it would be soon all over, for by a letter he had seen yesterday, the keys of the Tower would be given up to the Hampden Club party, if they were not already.

Q. What else did he say?

A. That he had never been set down since four o'clock yesterday morning; I asked him what he had been doing.

Q. What did he tell you?

A. He said he had been providing guns, pikes, and ammunition.

Q. Did you see the prisoner at the bar during the time of your march from place to place?

A. Yes, most of the time; I cannot say that I always saw him.

Q. Whereabout was he?

A. He appeared to be in the rear chiefly.

Q. What was he doing in the rear?

A. He seemed to walk in the rear to keep the men up together apparently, he and James Taylor.

Q. Did you observe what he was doing?

A. That is all the observation I made from what I saw him do.

Q. That appeared to be his chief employment during the time you saw him?

Mr. Denman. He does not say that was his employment.

Mr. Reynolds. Did you make that observation upon him which you have stated?

A. Yes.

Q. How did he seem employed?

A. He seemed to walk in the rear, to keep the men up.

Q. What numbers were there about Langley mill?

A. I should think about two hundred in the party I was with.

Q. Did you at any time when you were at Eastwood make any attempt to get away?

A. Yes.

Q. Were you prevented by any body?

A. Brandreth came up to me with a gun, and said, if I did not go into the rank again he would shoot me; I perceived that he had got a gun, and I stepped up to him with a stack paring knife, and said if he offered to present his gun, I would hack his head off.

Q. What then?

A. He stood a short time and turned off, and I then marched off.

Q. Did you return?

A. When I had walked fifty or sixty yards, I heard a cry of "do not shoot."

Q. What became of you, did you look back?

A. Yes, I looked back, and I saw Brandreth with the gun at his shoulder pointed at me; Thomas Turner took hold of him, and drew the gun off.

Q. On your return did you meet any other number of persons?

A. I met a party of about fifty; a few with guns and spikes, but the chief part were colliers unarmed.

Q. Which way were they going?

A. They were proceeding after the others along the Nottingham road.

Q. How long had you left the others when you met them?

A. Not long.

Q. Did you meet any other party?

A. I saw another party, but I did not meet them; I went by the bank to miss them.

Q. What number might they consist of?

A. There might be sixty or there might be more.

Q. Were they proceeding the same way?

A. No, they stood still when I first saw them; then they proceeded along the same road.

Q. In the way for Nottingham?

A. Yes.

Q. Had they any thing with them?

A. They appeared to be some of them armed, but I was not very nigh, and I could not judge exactly.

Cross-examined by Mr. Cross.

Q. The first house you went to was Booth's?

A. No.

Q. Which was the first house?

A. John Sellars's.

Q. You stood by with the rest?

A. At John Sellars's I did.

Q. Were you in sight of Sellars?

A. I saw him come from his door.

Q. And he could see you?

A. I cannot say that.

Q. Were you near enough to be seen by him?

A. Yes.

Q. As you stood with a pike?

A. No, I had not.

Q. With the weapon you have mentioned?

A. I had no weapon at that time.

Q. You afterwards went with them to Booth's, did not you?

A. Yes.

Q. Were you in any other house with them besides those two?

A. Yes, I was at Mr. Wheatcroft's.

Q. Were you in any other?

A. I just looked into a house up at Pentridge, where I saw some people smoking, and the Glass House.

Q. At all those different outrages, you appeared as one of the party?

A. I was amongst the party.

Q. And you never announced to any of the persons who were so visited, that you were amongst them against your will?

A. It was against my will.

Q. We do not doubt that my friend at all; but you did not say so at any of the houses that were attacked?

A. No, I cannot say that I did.

Q. You told us of a violent speech made by Bacon in the back kitchen at the Glass House; Isaac Ludlam the prisoner was not present at that time?

A. I never saw him in the kitchen; I cannot say that I ever saw him there; but when I went to the front door there I saw him stand.

Q. What part of this body of people were you in; near the front or the rear?

A. Along the march I was not always in one place when we were not in rank; sometimes in the middle and sometimes along the rear.

Q. So that Isaac Ludlam, the prisoner, was very often out of your sight?

A. Sometimes he was out of my sight, and sometimes in.

Q. He changed his place perhaps as much as you?

A. I cannot say much as to that; he was in the rear when I saw him.

Q. He was generally the last?

A. He was the last, or very near it; there were he and James Taylor.

Q. Seeing him there you suppose it was to keep the people up?

A. It was said by the company many times that he was.

Q. He was not present when that was said, was he?

A. I cannot say.

Q. What you know of his keeping up the rear, was chiefly what you heard said?

A. Yes, and seeing him there.

Q. You did not see him?

A. No, except standing at the Glass House.

Q. But you are not positive you did not see him in other parts?

A. No; but when I recollect seeing him he was there.

Q. But if I understand you right, you did not see him often in that situation?

A. He was there when I saw him; I cannot say more than I have.

Q. This is of importance to him, and affects his life, therefore you will excuse my pressing you upon it whether you saw him often?

A. No, I cannot say that I did see him often there.

Q. Had you known him before?

A. Yes I had; I wish I had never known none of them.

John Dexter sworn.

Mr. *Denman.*—Do not you live in the parish of Pentridge?

A. Yes; I beg your pardon, Buckland Hollow is in Heage.

Mr. Richardson.—Is Heage a parish, or in any other parish?

A. It is within the parish of Duffield.

Mr. Denman.—Duffield is a very large parish?

A. Yes.

Q. Containing different townships?

A. Yes.

Q. Do you know how many townships there are in it?

A. No.

Mr. Richardson.—Is the town of Heage at some distance from Buckland Hollow?

A. Yes.

Mr. Denman.—What is Buckland Hollow, a single house?

A. Yes.

Q. There is a township of Heage?

A. Yes.

Mr. Richardson.—This is a sufficient description of the place of abode, I submit.

Examined by Mr. Richardson.

Q. Were you in the month of June last servant to Mr. Wheatcroft?

A. Yes.

Q. On the night of the 9th of June were you disturbed?

A. Yes.

Q. At what time?

A. About twelve or between twelve and one.

Q. What were you disturbed by?

A. By a desperate noise I heard in the yard, and the first word that I heard was——

Mr. Cross.—My Lord, we are referring to the statute of Queen Anne, we have not quite abandoned the objection with respect to the description of this witness; it is provided, that a list shall be delivered to the prisoner, specifying the names, professions, and places of abode of the witnesses; the question is, whether the place of abode of this witness is sufficiently mentioned in the panel; the place of abode is described in these words, " of Buckland

Hollow, in the parish of Duffield, in the county of Derby." Now the evidence is this, that Buckland Hollow is the name given to a single house where the witness lives, and that the parish of Duffield contains a great many townships; now that being the case, I conceive this is not a sufficient description of the place of abode within the meaning of the statute which directs the place of abode to be described. I apprehend the correct mode of describing the place of abode of any person is by describing the township in which he lives, and that there is no other correct mode of describing a person's place of abode in a country situation; if it were sufficient to describe the witness's place of abode as it is here described, it might be sufficient also to say of the parish of Duffield, or it might be sufficient to say of the county of Derby, and it might be contended, that describing the place of abode of the party to be in counties would be sufficient to satisfy the directions of this Act. In a parish containing a number of townships and a numerous population, it can hardly be expected that the prisoner can be enabled to obtain proper information respecting the residence of the party so as to enquire about him, unless the township is mentioned; for these reasons I submit, my Lord, that this witness has not been so described in the copy of the panel given to the prisoner, as will authorize the prosecutor to call him as a witness.

Mr. Denman.—My Lord, I apprehend this objection is well founded; this person is not described as living in the township of Heage to which Buckland Hollow belongs, but in general terms as living in a very large parish, and that parish it appears comprehends many townships, of which one is the township of Duffield, being the name of the parish. I do not know whether I can put this better than by illustrating it in a supposed case from the place where my learned friend Mr. Cross resides, from the town of Manchester, which is not, I believe, a parish of itself, but a township belonging to the parish of Salford. Now, suppose that any person was to be described as dwelling in James-street, or any street in the parish of Salford, I would submit to your Lordship whether that could be considered as a proper description within this act of parliament. My Lord, I apprehend it is of the highest importance that this provision of the statute be strictly and punctually enforced in every instance; and if your Lordships should see that by the rule laid down in any particular instance there be a possibility of introducing a relaxation of this particular provision, I am sure that your Lordships would feel bound to reject such a rule as might lead to such general consequences. Now my Lords, the question is, whether the party here has a fair opportunity of knowing where the person so described resides; he knows John Dexter of the township of Heage, but he knows no John Dexter of the township of Duffield, and I do not know why those persons were to be considered as cognizant that the township of Heage is part of the parish of Duffield, it appears to me the description of the lone house should be first adopted, and that if any municipal division should be inserted that should be the smallest and least general and the most special the circumstances of the case will admit. If a man resided in the town of Derby, I should doubt whether it would be sufficient to say so; I should think that the parish also ought to be inserted, for that a prisoner ought to have the opportunity of knowing who are the parties to come against him, and of knowing by what witnesses, he might be able to contradict him as to facts he might be likely to prove, or the character of the man who was to come as a witness; it appears to me, with great deference to your Lordships, that this principle as to description cannot be disputed, and that if it is likely to lead to such consequences as I contend, your Lordships will not admit any rule which can be so followed up.

Lord Chief Baron Richards. Mr. Attorney General, you need not give yourself any trouble; the Court do not feel the least doubt upon the subject. The witness is described as of Buckland Hollow, in the parish of Duffield; and he swears that he is of Buckland Hollow, in the parish of Duffield; how can he be described more particularly?

Mr Justice Abbott. Certainly every witness must be described, so as to be found; and the question is, whether this is not a sufficient decription. Buckland Hollow, I apprehend, according to the testimony of the witness, to be a place very well known; I do not know that its being inserted to be in the parish of Duffield, and in the township of Heage too, would have enabled persons to find it the better.

Mr. Justice Holroyd. It is evident that Buckland Hollow was a good decription, and sufficient to be known by the person for whose information the statute directs the notice to be given; the only object of requiring the description of the party to be given, is that the prisoner, or those acting for him, may know where to find him.

Mr. Justice Dallas. It appears to me, not having the least doubt upon the subject, casting my eye upon the notices, that they are all in this way; if this be bad, all are bad; I do not find township in any one.

Mr. Denman. I beg your lordship's pardon; if your lordship looks at the next; " Samuel Daykin, of Wood Linkin, in the township of Codnor," *non constat* that there is a township in other cases.

Mr. Justice Dallas. You may find a single instance; but I have not the least doubt upon the point; I pointed out that perhaps unnecessarily.

Mr. Richardson (to Dexter.) You stated that you were disturbed about twelve at night, by a great noise in the yard?

A. Yes.

Q. Were you in bed?

A. Yes; the first word I heard was, " come Dexter get up, we must take you along with us." I got up and went to the window.

Q. What did you hear or see then?

A. The first word I heard was, " come down and open the door, we must have you along with us;" they said that again.

Q. From the window could you see any persons in the yard?

A. Yes, they stood just before the door, as it might be here, as I was looking out of the window.

Q. Did you go down?

A. I told them that I should not open the door; some one made answer, telling me, that if I would not come down and open the door, they had shot Hepworth's man, and they would also shoot me. I told them that they might shoot on, for I should not come down and open the door; they answered again, telling me, that I had better come down and open the door, or else, if I would not come down, they would break the door open.

Q. Did you still refuse to open it?

A. I did; and immediately two men began to break open the door.

Q. What did you do?

A. The instant I saw two men go to break open the door, I went to call the young man out of the garret.

Q. Did they succeed in breaking open the door?

A. Whilst I was upon the garret stairs, the door smashed open.

Q. Was the door forced on the outside?

A. Yes; I heard a louder knock than I had heard before, and the door broke open with it.

Q. Did any persons come in upon the door being forced open?

A There was I suppose, as many as half a score entered the house.

Q. Were they armed?

A. They then called to me, to ask me whether I would come down stairs; I told them I hoped they would give me time to dress me; I came down part dressed, and found that part of those that came into the house were armed.

Q. With what were they armed?

A. Spikes and spears, and guns and pistols.

Q. Were you forced to join them?

A. I asked them to let me remain; they told me that positively I must go, and therefore I had better get myself dressed; I went up to dress myself, and when I came down again, they were charging the gun which was taken off the top of the house.

Q. Which was taken from your master's house?
A. Yes, our gun.
Q. Were you compelled to join them?
A. Yes.
Q. Were any other persons taken with you from the house?
A. Yes, two men.
Q. What were their names?
A. William Wheatcroft and Samuel Levers; I had only resided in the house that night.
Q. Fellow servants of your's?
A. The one a blacksmith, the other a fellow servant.
Q. They were compelled to join?
A. Yes, they were.
Q. What was said to you before you left the house?
A. We asked them what their intention was, and why were they acting in that manner; they said that they were going to ease the nation of that burthen it had so long groaned under.

Mr. Justice Abbott. Do you know who said that?
A. Both Manchester Turner and the captain.
Mr. Richardson. Do you mean Brandeth by the captain?
A. Yes.
Q. From Mr. Wheatcroft's house, you proceeded to Pentridge-lane with the party?
A. Yes.
Q. Were you joined there by another party?
A. Yes, that remained at the lane end.
Q. Were they drawn up in any way?
A. They put us in ranks when we joined.
Q. Who put you in ranks?
A. The captain and Manchester Turner were the two active men.
Q. Do you know Isaac Ludlam, the prisoner?
A. Yes.
Q. Was he there?
A. Yes.
Q. Where was it you first saw him?
A. At Pentridge-lane-end, when they had formed us.

Q. When the two parties joined?

A. Yes.

Q. You were then formed by the captain and Manchester Turner in ranks?

A. Yes, three deep.

Q. Did the prisoner say anything to you there?

A. Yes, he did; that it would be better for us to go.

Q. Has he any sons?

A. Yes, he told us there were two of his sons of the party.

Q. Did he say where they were going to?

Mr. Justice Abbott. What did he say?

Mr. Richardson. What did he say?

A. He told me that they were going to Nottingham, and that there was a parliament chose ready when they got there; and that the party in Nottingham would break into the houses and take away the soldiers arms, and that Nottingham would be all taken by such time as we got there.

Q. Did he say anything more?

A. Yes, he said respecting us all going, that we had better all go, for that those that remained behind, there would be a party come out of the North that would take or sweep all before them.

Q. Any thing more?

A. As we were going along, it was talked of in the party that if Mr. Jessop did not surrender or give up his men, they would take away his life; who it was that said that I do not know.

Q. Was the prisoner near at the time that was said?

A. Yes.

Q. Was he near enough to hear that?

A. Yes.

Q. Was any thing further said about the nature of the insurrection?

A. I do not recollect any thing in particular.

Q. Did not you during the time of your proceeding forwards——

A. I did not go much further.

Q. Where about was the prisoner Isaac Ludlam when the party marched on?

A. He was in the rear.

Q. How was he armed?

A. With a spike or a spear, which it was I cannot say.

Q. Was it a thing like one of these?

A. Yes, it was.

Q. He marched in the rear.

A. Yes; and the right hand man of three the greater part of the time; the rear guard.

Q. Forming the rear guard?

A. They went abreast three in the rear guard.

Q. There was a rear guard of three, of which he formed the right hand man?

A. Yes.

Q. Was he close to the ranks or a little way behind them?

A. A little distance when they halted a little; he marched up to them; he was a little way behind them.

Q. Did you endeavour to get away?

A. Yes.

Q. Where was it?

A. In Pentridge-lane; I turned behind once when they were going forwards and stopped behind, and he said "come we must have you forward, you must come along with us."

Q. Who was he?

A. The prisoner, Isaac Ludlam.

Q. He was the man who said so, was he?

A. Yes.

Q. Did you make any further attempt to get away?

A. I tried two or three different times, and found it impossible to make my escape in the rear; and when we had got into Pentridge, I went forward and said, "come come, it will not do to stay here all night, what are they about so long;" and I went down a yard as if I was going to call a person, and made my escape down the yard.

Q. I think you stated that you attempted two or three

times to get away in the rear, but found it impossible; what was it rendered that impossible?

A. It was Isaac Ludlam and the two men that were with him that prevented me.

Q. When you say Isaac Ludlam, do you mean the elder or the younger?

A. The elder.

Q. The prisoner at the bar?

A. Yes, the prisoner at the bar.

Cross examined by Mr. Denman.

Q. Who were those two men?

A. I cannot say.

Q. You have been in the volunteers I should think?

A. In the local.

Q. How far were you from the rear?

A. I walked in the rear.

Q. What was it he said, " come—you must come along with us?"

A. Yes.

Q. Manchester Turner and the captain were the two who talked in the way you have mentioned?

A. The principal men in putting them in rank.

Q. They appeared you say to be the most active men?

A. Yes.

Q. You say, I think, that some one said it was talked that if Jessop did not give up his men so and so?

A. Yes.

Q. That was the expression?

A. Yes.

Mr. Serjeant Vaughan. He did not say " some said it was talked."

Mr. Denman. He says so now.

Mr. Justice Abbott. I have it, that it was talked by some one in the party.

A. There was some one in the party said, that if Jessop did not give up his men he would be murdered.

Mr. Denman. Who was that?

A. I cannot say.

Q. Where was he?
A. The one close by my side.
Q. When you were marching?
A. No; when we were halted.
Q. You were all about as you pleased there?
A. We were talking one with another, and with Isaac Ludlam, and with the serjeant.
Q. Who was the serjeant?
A. Manchester Turner was called the serjeant there.

Re-examined by Mr. Richardson.

Q. At the time of this observation, was the prisoner near?
A. Yes.
Q. Was it made in his presence and hearing?
A. Yes.

William Booth sworn.

Examined by Mr. J. Balguy.

Q. Did you live at Pentridge-lane-end on the 9th of June last?
A. Yes.
Q. Do you remember being disturbed at any time on that night?
A. Yes.
Q. At what time?
A. Between twelve and one o'clock.
Q. What were you disturbed by?
A. By a parcel of men.
Q. What did they do to disturb you?
A. They were knocking very loud at the door.
Q. In consequence of that did you get out of bed and go the window?
A. They called "halloo," and I got up and went to the window.
Q. Did you open the window?
A. Yes, I opened the window and asked them what they wanted.

Q. What answer did they make to you?

A. They said I want you and your gun.

Q. What answer did you make?

A. I said I have no gun: they said " then I must have you; come down stairs and open the door, or else I will shoot you."

Q. Was this all said by one man, or were there many voices?

A. I believe it was all said by one man.

Q. Did you go down stairs?

A. I said, " I cannot go, I am ballotted for the militia, and I must attend at Derby to day."

Q. This was before you came down stairs?

A. Yes.

Q. What answer was made to that?

A. They said, " come down stairs and open the door, we will protect you from the militia; or else I will shoot you."

Q. Did you then go down stairs?

A. Yes, I went down stairs and unbolted the door.

Q. What happened upon your unbolting the door?

A. Part of the door fell into the passage.

Q. What was the occasion of that?

A. The occasion of that was the violence the men had used at the door.

Q. The violence which had been used before you came down stairs?

A. Yes.

Q. Upon the door being opened, whom did you see?

A. I saw a number of men rush in at the door.

Q. How many?

A. Six or eight.

Q. Armed or unarmed?

A. Some were armed with guns.

Q. Were the others armed with any thing?

A. Some that stood at the door were armed with spikes.

Q. Were all that came into the house armed?

A. I will not say whether all were or not.

Q. The spikes were weapons like those on the table?

A. Yes, they were.

Q. What passed when those persons came into the house?

A. The captain of the company asked me where my clothes were I took up stairs.

Q. Who was the captain?

A. A man that they called Jerry.

Q. You were not dressed at that time?

A. No, I was not.

Q. What did he say?

A. " Go and put them on immediately;" I went up stairs immediately to put my clothes on; they lit a candle, and followed me up.

Q. How many of them followed you up?

A. Four or five.

Q. Do you know who they were?

A. Yes, one was the captain, and William Turner; they were all that I knew; those two were all that followed me, as I knew.

Q. What passed when you got up stairs?

A. They asked me what I had been doing, as I was not dressed; I told them I had made what haste I could; " Make haste," he said, " or else I will shoot you."

Q. You got dressed?

A. Whilst I was dressing me, I did not get on fast enough for them; and they said, " Make haste; you seem to wish us to shoot you;" and I said, " I had rather you would not." Then I only stopped to put either my waistcoat and my breeches on; they drove me down before them into the house; I went and set me down on the squab, and offered to put my boots on, and to lace them; and the captain said, " If you offer to stop to lace your boots, I will shoot you."

Q. Did they at last force you out?

A. Yes, I was forced out of the house before them?

Q. Did they put any thing into your hand?

A. No; when I was going out of the house, there was some man called me by my sirname, and said, " Have not you a gun;" and I said, " No, I have not, nor never had since I was here."

Q. Upon your saying that you had no gun, what did they say?

A. They said I must take a fork; I said I could not find any fork: and they drove me out of the yard, and took me to a man along the ranks who had a gun, and told him to take care of that man as a prisoner.

Q. Did you march on with them from that place?

A. Yes.

Q. Where did you go to?

A. We went Pentridge way, and went to Mr. Storer's?

Q. I will not ask you what passed there; do you remember a gun being fired any where?

A. Yes, for a signal to alarm them at Butterley.

Q. Where was it fired?

A. Against the meeting-house, near to a close belonging to Andrew Moore.

Q. Do you know Mr. William Booth?

A. Yes.

Q. Where does he live?

A. Near the top of Pentridge?

Q. Do you remember his poney being brought out?

A. Yes.

Q. What was done with the poney?

A. George Weightman brought the poney out of the yard, and went back to Mr. Booth's barn; the captain told him to take that poney and ride to Nottingham forest, and see how they were coming on, and to come back to Langley mill and bring them tidings.

Q. Having got Mr. Booth's poney, do you remember marching forwards to Butterley?

A. Yes.

Q. To the works at Butterley?

A. Yes.

Q. In what order did you march to Butterley?

A. We marched two deep to Butterley.

Q. Do you know the prisoner Isaac Ludlam?

A. Yes, I dare say I should know him?

Q. Look at him?
A. Yes, I saw that man there.
Q. Where did you first see him?
A. I saw him before we got to Butterley?
Q. What had he?
A. He had a spike.
Q. In what situation was he?
A. He was fixed in the rear to keep the men up, so that they could not get away.
Q. With the prisoner in the rear keeping the men up, you marched to Butterley?
A. Yes.
Q. What passed when you were at the works at Butterley?
A. The captain in front of the men marched up to the Butterley gates, and rapped at the door?
Q. I will not ask you particularly what passed there; from thence where did you go?
A. We went up into the turnpike road, and then along the turnpike road to Ripley, over the coke hearth.
Q. From Ripley did you go to Codnor?
A. Yes.
Q. Did the prisoner march with you from Butterley to Codnor?
A. Yes, I saw him several times?
Q. Was he always in the same position when you saw him?
A. Yes.
Q. What was that?
A. Keeping guard in the rear.
Q. Where did you go to at Codnor?
A. We called at a house they called the Glass House.
Q. A public house?
A. Yes.
Q. Did you all go into the public house?
A. No; the prisoner said to the captain, "There must somebody stop on the outside, to take care that the men did not get away; for that a great many of them would go away, if there was not some person to take care of them on the outside."

Q. Who remained on the outside?
A. Isaac Ludlam.
Q. The prisoner?
A. Yes.
Q. You mean the outside of the Glass House public house?
A. Yes.
Q. Had he a spike at that time?
A. He had a gun delivered to him during the time he stopped there; I saw him have a gun at the time I came out of the Glass House.
Q. What had he when you went in?
A. He had a spike when I went in.
Q. When you came out he had a gun?
A. Yes.
Q. Was he the only person who remained outside?
A. No, I think I saw his son likewise.
Q. Was the son armed as well as the father?
A. I cannot say whether he had any arms with him when he was by the side of the party or not. I saw him through the window during part of the time.
Q. Was it raining while you were in the public house?
A. Yes, it rained very hard.
Q. From the public house at Codnor where did you go to?
A. We marched on the road for Langley mill.
Q. Is that in the way to Nottingham?
A. Yes.
Q. Did the prisoner march along with you?
A. Yes, I saw him several times in his old situation.
Q. Between the Glass House and Langley mill?
A. Yes.
Q. What do you mean by his old situation?
A. Still continuing in the rear.
Q. Did you go further than Langley mill?
A. Yes.
Q. How far did you go?
A. I went beyond Eastwood, a little way.

Q. What became of you then?

A. I got away about half a mile beyond Eastwood, and turned back.

Q. Did you see the prisoner all the way to Eastwood?

A. I saw the prisoner beyond Eastwood; when I was turning, the prisoner was going forwards.

Q. Do you mean with the party?

A. No; he was behind the party then.

Q. How far behind the party?

A. The party was got out of sight, over the hill, the greatest part of them.

Hugh Booth sworn,

Examined by Mr. Solicitor General.

Q. I believe you live at Pentridge-lane-end?
A. Yes.

Q. You are the son of Samuel Booth?
A. Yes I am.

Q. Do you remember, on Monday night, the 9th of June last, being disturbed in the night?
A. Yes.

Q. About what hour?
A. Between twelve and one.

Q. What was it that disturbed you?
A. A party of men came to the door.

Q. What did they do at the door?
A. They came and knocked at the door two or three times.

Q. What did they say?
A. They called out for me.

Q. What did they call out?
A. They called out 'I want you; I want Hugh Booth.'

Q. Was any answer given to that?
A. Yes; my father got up and wished them to go without me.

Q. What did they say upon his wishing them to go without you?

A. They said they would **not** go without me, that if my

father would not get up and open the door, they would break down the door and shoot him.

Q. Did they say any thing else?

A. I got up and went down to the door, as they wished me to go with them.

Mr. Justice Abbott. In what way did they express their wish, that you should go with them?

A. There was a man offered me a spike, to go with them in the ranks.

Mr. Solicitor General. What did they say when you came to the door?

A. They said they were going to Nottingham.

Mr. Justice Abbott. Do you know who it was that said they were going to Nottingham?

A. Isaac Ludlam.

Mr. Solicitor General. The prisoner?

A. Yes.

Q. He was at the door?

A. No, he was a little way off the door.

Mr. Justice Abbott. By Isaac Ludlam, do you mean Isaac Ludlam the elder, or the younger?

A. The elder; that man who is there.

Mr. Solicitor General. Was it mentioned where they had been at?

A. They came from Mr. Fletcher's to our house.

Q. You say they threatened to shoot you, was any thing else said?

A. I did not hear any thing else.

Q. You say they gave you a spike?

A. They wanted me to have one, but I would not take it.

Q. Who wanted you to have a spike?

A. Miles Bacon.

Q. What did they do to you?

A. They wished me to go into the ranks.

Q. Who ordered you to go into the ranks?

A. Isaac Ludlam.

Q. The prisoner?

A. Yes.

Q. Were you forced to go into the ranks?

A. Yes, at Pentridge-lane-end.

Q. Where did you go to from Pentridge-lane-end?

A. I went as far as Butterley; I went up Pentridge from there.

Q. Upon your coming to Pentridge, did you stop?

A. Yes.

Q. The whole body halted?

A. Yes.

Q. Do you remember, at that time, the prisoner saying any thing to you?

A. Yes.

Q. What was it he said?

A. I asked him where we were going, and he said 'it is brought to a head at last, we are going to Nottingham.'

Q. After this, did you go on to Pentridge?

A. Yes.

Q. Do you know a person of the name of John Bright?

A. Yes.

Q. Did you go to his house?

A. Yes.

Q. That is in Pentridge?

A. Yes.

Q. You say you stopped at John Bright's?

A. Yes.

Q. Whilst you were stopping at John Bright's, had you any conversation with Ludlam?

A. Yes.

Q. By Ludlam, do you mean the prisoner?

A. Yes.

Q. What passed between you and him, when you were at John Bright's?

A. I asked him again where we were going.

Q. What did he then say?

A. He said we were going to Nottingham; he said there was a parliament formed at Nottingham, and we were going to guard them.

Q. Any thing more?

A. He said 'the business will all be done before we get there.'

Q. Had you any conversation there with any others of the party?

A. There was a young man with a blue coat and blue trowsers.

Q. Had he any arms?

A. Yes, a sword.

Q. Do you know his name?

A. I have heard since that his name is Manchester Turner.

Q. Did you observe any thing else about his person?

A. No; I did not see any thing particular.

Q. He was of the party, however?

A. Yes he was.

Q. What part was he taking?

A. They called him serjeant.

Q. What induces you now to say, you believe him to be Manchester Turner?

A. By his blue dress.

Q. Have you seen him since?

A. No.

Q. There was a person of this description whom they called serjeant, with a sword?

A. Yes.

Q. Had you any conversation with him?

A. I did not ask him any question.

Q. Did you hear him say any thing?

A. Yes.

Q. What did you hear him say?

A. He said they were going to Nottingham, to unload the burthen that England had so long borne.

Q. Where did you hear him say that?

A. Against John Bright's.

Q. Whilst you were at John Bright's, besides this conversation, was any thing done there?

A. I saw John Bright bring a fork out.

Q. Was any thing else done whilst you halted there?

A. I did not see any thing else.

Q. Was any gun fired?

A. There was a gun fired before we got to John Bright's house, just before.

Q. Did you know why the gun was fired?
A. No.
Q. From Pentridge, where did you march to?
A. Towards Butterley.
Q. Had the prisoner any arms?
A. Yes.
Q. What had he?
A. A large staff, with a spike at the end of it.
Q. Such an one as this?
A. Yes.
Q. Where about did old Ludlam walk?
A. He was walking in the rear.
Q. In your way to Butterley did you observe him doing any thing?
A. He was very forward in pushing the men along.
Q. You went on in this way to Butterley?
A. Yes.
Q. When you came to Butterley, were you of the party that went round by the works?
A. Yes, I went round to Butterley?
Q. Were you halted at Butterley?
A. Yes.
Q. Do you remember seeing Mr. Goodwin?
A. Yes.
Q, Do you remember any thing being said by Mr. Goodwin?
A. Yes.
Q. Who was the leader of the party?
A. William Turner and a man called the Nottingham captain.
Q. Did you hear either William Turner or the Nottingham captain say any thing to Mr. Goodwin?
A. Yes.
Q. Which of them?
A. The Nottingham captain.

Mr. Justice Abbott. Is it necessary to repeat this?

Mr. Solicitor General. Only as introductory to another fact, my Lord; I will take it short; What did he say?

A. Mr. Goodwin asked him what he wanted, and he said we want your men.
Q. Mr. Goodwin made some answer to that?
A. Yes, he told him they would not have any.

Q. What became of you?
A. I went into Mr. Goodwin's office.
Q. How did you get into Mr. Goodwin's office?
A. I saw the door open while the party halted, and I walked in.
Q. You made your escape from them?
A. Yes.
Q. And did not join them again?
A. No.

Cross-examined by Mr. Denman.

Q. Did you carry any arms?
A. No.
Q. None the whole way?
A. No.
Q. The captain and Turner were the active people?
A. Yes.
Q. At the works it was that the captain came and made that demand of Mr. Goodwin?
A. Yes.
Q. Was that the first you heard of the captain?
A. No.
Q. You heard of him long before that?
A. Yes.
Q. How did he walk, in front of the whole, or how?
A. Sometimes in front, and sometimes in other places.
Q. As you had no arms, were you in the ranks?
A. Yes.
Q. Were you near the front?
A. I was near the rear.
Q. Who was your right hand or left hand man?
A. James Turner.
Mr. Justice Abbott. Right hand or left hand?
A. Sometimes right, sometimes left.
Q. He was against you?
A. Yes, my Lord.

Mr. George Goodwin sworn.

Examined by Mr. Serjeant Vaughan.

Q. I believe you were managing clerk of Messrs. Jessop's iron works at Butterley?

A. Yes.

Q. On the 8th or 9th of June special constables were sworn in at the works; those works?

A. They were.

Mr. Justice Abbott. On the 7th was not it?

A. On the 7th.

Mr. Serjeant Vaughan. On the evening of the 9th did you make any observations or see any thing?

A. Yes; during the course of the 9th, at the time we were on duty with the constables, we heard guns fired.

Q. At what time of the night might it be?

A. I think the first I heard was about twelve o'clock, or a little before.

Q. How long did that continue?

A. The guns, till day-light I think; I heard three or four guns and horns blowing.

Q. At what time did you dismiss your constables, supposing things to be more quiet?

A. The greater part a little before three o'clock in the morning of the Tuesday.

Q. After you had dismissed your men, did you observe any body in particular coming by your premises?

A. Yes; Mr. Jessop and myself came down with a party of men, those that were armed with pikes, to the office; it was then a little after three o'clock, perhaps a quarter; we observed first a man riding past on horseback, George Weightman, riding very quick past.

Q. Did you know George Weightman?

A. Yes.

Q. Did you speak to him?

A. I did; I called to him to stop.

Q. Did he stop?

A. No, he did not; he merely looked and went on.

Q. How soon after that did you observe any other person?

A. Almost immediately; in a very few minutes.

Q. What number of persons?

A. About one hundred.

Q. In what state; how were they moving?

A. They were marching on the road from Pentridge in regular military order.

Q. Do you mean in rank?

A. Yes, two abreast.

Q. Had they any arms or weapons with them?

A. They were armed, the greater part with guns, that is, some with guns, many with spears and pikes, and a few that had no arms.

Q Did they stop at your works as they approached them?

A, They did; they marched up to the door of the iron works, and there stopped and halted.

Q. Upon their halting did you speak to any of them?

A. I did; I spoke to the captain at the head of them, and asked him what he wanted, what was his object there.

Q. Whom do you mean by the captain?

A. Brandreth.

Q. What answer did you receive from him?

A. " We want your men." I told him they should not have any of them; that they were too many already, excepting they were going for a better purpose.

Q. Did you recognize amongst them any persons whom you knew?

A. I did.

Q. Mention the name or names of any you recognized?

A. Isaac Ludlam the elder.

Q. The prisoner at the bar.

A. Yes.

Q. What was he doing, how was he placed with reference to the men?

A. He was in the front rank as it was then, what would have been the rear when they were marching.

Q. In what part of it?

A. Near the right flank near the office.

Q. Upon seeing him him, did you say any thing to him?

A. I did; I said, "good God, Isaac, what are you doing here, upon such an errand as this?" I urged him to leave them.

Q. What did you say?

A. I told him he had got a halter about his neck, and he would be hanged if he did not leave them; "go home," I said.

Q. Upon your saying that, did he make any reply, or did you do any thing to him?

A. I took him by the shoulders and turned him with his face towards the office, and pushed him.

Q. For what purpose?

A. That he might make his escape into the office.

Q. Would he have had an opportunity of getting into the office, if he had had a desire of so doing?

A. Certainly, for I was beside him in the ranks; he had the same opportunity as I had.

Q. Did he make any observation to you upon your saying that?

A. Yes, he said "I cannot go back, I am as bad as I can be; I must go on."

Q. Was that all that passed between you two?

A. Yes, most of it.

Q. Had you any conversation with any other person there?

A. Yes; with James Taylor; I spoke nearly to the same effect to him.

Q. Did anybody go into the office?

A. Three.

Q. Three of them escaped from the ranks?

A. Three of them, during the time Ludlam and I were talking, escaped into the office.

Q. Do you remember a man of the name of Booth?

A. Yes; he was one of them, and there were two others.

Q. After they had escaped into the office, what became of the captain and the rest of the men?

A. After looking at each other for a short time, he gave the men the word "march," and took them away.

Q. Brandreth did?
A. Yes.

Q. Which way did they march upon moving?
A. They marched on the road to Ripley from Butterley which is in fact the road towards Nottingham.

Q. Is that the road to Codnor?
A. It is.

Q. After this party had left you, did you, soon afterwards, see anybody else?
A. Another party came shortly afterwards.

Q. Did Ludlam go with them, or did he remain?
A. Ludlam went off with the first party; when Brandreth gave the word, he marched off with the rest.

Mr. Justice Abbott. By Ludlam, do you mean the prisoner?
A. Yes.

Mr. Serjeant Vaughan. How soon after they had marched did you observe anybody else?
A. In about a quarter of an hour, I observed another party coming into Pentridge.

Q. Did you observe anybody on horseback?
A. That was a little distance of time after the second body; in about half an hour after, or less, I observed William Weightman coming past on horseback.

Q. In what direction was William Weightman going?
A. In the direction of Nottingham.

Q. The same direction the others had taken?
A. Not exactly the same direction, but a nearer road.

Q. Had you any conversation with him?
A. I had.

Q. Without going into the conversation, had he any thing with him, and did you take any thing from him?
A. I took this bag of bullets from him *(producing it.)*

Q. How was he carrying them?
A. He had them upon his horse; he had on a blue smock frock, and the smock frock in part covered the bag.

Q. Do you know what quantity there are?

A. About eighty-four pounds.

Mr. Justice Abbott. How many charges?

A. I fancy there may be from 1500 to 2000.

Mr. Serjeant Vaughan. Are they all the same bore, or suited to different bores?

A. There are a great variety of sizes suited to different bores.

Q. Is there anything else besides bullets in the bag?

A. There are some moulds for cartridges.

Q. Do you mean something of that sort?

A. Yes, those were in the bag.

Q. Was there any cartridge paper?

A. There was paper in the bag.

Q. Was that paper fit for those purposes?

A. Yes, fit for the purpose, though not the best.

Q. Were those bullets given up to you, or were they taken by you by force.

A. They were taken; he resisted till he found it was of no use. I think the man with the bullets passed about four o'clock.

Cross-examined by Mr. Cross.

Q. You were very much surprised at seeing the prisoner at the bar amongst them?

A. I certainly was surprised at seeing him.

Q. A man, perhaps, whom you had known and respected?

A. A man whom I had known for several years.

Q. And a man whom you wished well to no doubt.

A. Certainly.

Q. He appeared in great agitation, I think, from your description?

A. Yes, he was a good deal agitated when I spoke to him.

Q. I dare say you thought he did not know well what he was about?

A. No in fact I did not think about it.

Q. You had no clear idea yourself what they were about, had you?

A. Yes, certainly.

Q. You met with no resistance from the account you give?

A. No not from him, or any of them.

Q. Nor any attempt of violence to you.

A. When I spoke to Taylor he made an attempt to cock his piece.

Q. But as to these hundred warriors, you set them at defiance?

A. Yes.

Q. Unarmed as you were?

A. I was armed; I had a brace of pistols in my pocket.

Q. But they could not see them?

A. No, they could not of course.

Q. Did you tell the prisoner that if he quitted the ranks, you were able to protect him from any violence of his captain or the others?

A. I did not tell him that; but I conceived his life would have been in as little danger as my own: having offered him protection, I should have afforded it at the hazard of my own.

Q. How could he know his life was safe, when his captain had shot another man?

A. I cannot answer that.

Q. Though confident of your own safety, you cannot undertake to say that he considered himself safe?

A. I did not consider myself confident of safety. I considered myself in danger; but I considered it his duty to face the danger the same as myself; being in the situation I was, I felt it my duty.

Q. That is your argument upon the subject; it may or may not be correct. Without attempting any violence, they all marched away?

A. Certainly; they did not attempt any violence there: I have described pretty accurately every circumstance which did pass.

Re-examined by Mr. Serjeant Vaughan.

Q. You have been asked, whether you had any idea of what they were about; how many special constables had you sworn in on the Saturday before?

A. About one hundred and fifteen or one hundred and sixteen.

Q. In expectation of what?

A. In expectation of an insurrection certainly.

Q. Had you made any preparations at the office?

A. Yes, on the Monday afternoon we got thirteen pikes made to arm the men.

Q. You thought it necessary to make some arrangements to defend the works?

A. Yes.

Mr. Justice Abbott. You have the fact; I think you need not go into the reasons.

Mr. Cross. You had thought proper to manufacture some pikes for the defence of yourselves and your property?

A. Yes.

Q. And had a stock of pikes upon your premises?

A. We had thirteen pikes made on the afternoon before the insurrection, with which the constables were armed.

Mr. Serjeant Vanghan. Were they made for the constables?

A. Yes.

Mr. John Storer sworn.

Examined by Mr. Clarke.

Q. You are a farmer at Pentridge, I believe?

A. Yes.

Q. On Monday the 9th of June last, were you disturbed after you had gone to bed?

A. Yes.

Q. At what hour was it?

A. About one o'clock, I think.

Q. What was it that disturbed you?

A. A body of armed men.

Q. How did they disturb you, in what way?

A. They presented guns at the windows, and threatened to shoot me.

Q. Did you go to the windows?

A. Yes, on the first of my hearing them, on the first alarm.

Q. And you saw the guns presented at you?

A. Yes.

Q. Was any thing said to you, or did you say any thing to them first?

A. "Damn your eyes come and go with us, or we will shoot you."

Q. That was addressed to you from those armed men?

A. Yes.

Q. Did you observe at that time what number there might be?

A. Twelve or fifteen.

Q. Did you say any thing to that, when they said, "damn your eyes, come and go with us, or we will shoot you?"

A. Yes; I asked them if there was no excuse, they said, not.

A. Could you distinguish who any of the men were at that time?

A. I could distinguish one; one was William Turner.

Q. Was he armed?

A. Yes, he had a gun.

Q. Did they enquire for any thing else besides you?

A. They said there was me and two or three more in the house, and me and a gun they were determined should go with them, and they would shoot me and all in the house if I would not go; that the captain had just shot Hepworth's man: thinking I must be shot if I did not go, I told them if they would give me a little time I would go.

Q. What did you do then?

A. I began to dress myself.

Q. Whilst you were dressing yourself, did they say any thing to you?

A. They told me that if I did not make haste they would make me as I could not go.

Q. Did you see who it was that said that?

A. No; they were outside the house, and I cannot say.

Q. Did you finish dressing yourself?

A. Yes.

Q. What did you do?

A. I took an old gun and went to them

Q. Did you go out of your house?

A. Yes.

Q. What was said to you when you went out with your gun?

A. They asked me if it was loaded, I told them not.

Q. Did they ask you any thing else?

A. They asked me whether I had got any shot and powder, I told them a little shot; they said it did not mean, they should have powder and ball sufficient.

Q. What was said or done after this conversation?

A. We went through the yard to a gate leading into the lane.

Q. What was said then?

A. I told them I was not fit to go, I had been very unwell the day before.

Q. What was said to that?

A. I told them I could not carry the gun any further: they said it must go by the baggage. I asked them where the baggage was; they said they had not any, but they should have; they then waited in the lane——

Q. Did they say nothing after that, how they were to have baggage?

A. No, they did not.

Q. Did they give any reason why they should have baggage?

A. They did not say.

Q. You went into the lane?

A. Yes.

Q. Did you make any enquiries of them where they were going to?

A. They said they were going to Nottingham; that it was a general rising; that twenty-five or thirty thousand were coming from Sheffield; that there would be several hundred thousands assemble that day; that liberty would be gained, and an end of slavery.

Q. Can you tell who it was that said this?

A. I do not know; it was a person in the midst of them.

Q. Was any thing said as to what would be done to those who did not go to Nottingham?

A. They said that they must all go or be shot.

Q. You say you got into the lane; when you got to the lane did you observe any more persons?

A. No.

Q. What did you observe?

A. They stopped in the lane, waiting for the captain.

Q. Do you know the prisoner Isaac Ludlam?

A. I did not see him at that time.

Q. They told you when you got into the lane they were waiting for the captain?

A. Yes; and a body of men down the lane-end.

Q. Whilst you were in the lane, did the captain and a body of men come up?

A. Yes, they came up in about twenty minutes.

Q. How many do you think there were?

A. I thought them about a hundred.

Q. Had they any arms with them?

A. Yes.

Q. What sort of arms?

A. Guns and pistols.

Q. Of the same sort as those upon the table?

A. Yes.

Q. Were they such instruments as these?

A. Similar to them.

Q. When that body came up, did you see any thing of the prisoner?

A. Yes, I then saw him.

Q. Had he any arms?

A. He carried a very long pike.

Q. When the captain and the body of men came up, what was done?

A. The captain ordered the men to fall in three deep.

Q. Was any direction given how they were to fall in?

A. Those with guns were ordered to fall in in the front.

Q. How were the others?

A. The pikes behind.

Q. Was there any thing said about any other persons besides those with the pikes and the guns?

A. Yes; the captain and the principal men held a consultation.

Vol. II.   P

Q. Who were those principal men, do you recollect?

A. William Turner, and a young man that appeared to have but one eye.

Q. Was that the man they called Manchester Turner?

A. Yes; they called him lieutenant.

Q. They consulted together?

A. Yes.

Q. What was said when they had consulted together?

A. The captain then asked whether there were any men that could do their exercise, if they could they must fall out and be made non-commissioned officers of.

Q. What was done then, did any of them fall out?

A. Yes, some did fall out.

Q. Were any serjeants or any non-commissioned officers appointed?

A. Yes, I believe some were appointed, but I was rather too far off to know.

Q. Having done this, what was done next?

A. There was an advance guard appointed and a rear guard.

Q. Do you happen to know who was appointed to command the advanced guard?

A. I do not know.

Q. Do you happen to know who was to command the rar guard?

A. Yes, Isaac Ludlam.

Q. The prisoner at the bar?

A. Yes.

Q. Was any thing done after this arrangement was made?

A. The captain ordered them to march.

Q. Where did they proceed to?

A. They marched towards Pentridge.

Q. What did they do when they marched through Pentridge?

Mr. Justice Abbott. Towards Pentridge I understood him.

Mr. Clarke. What was the next thing as you marched towards Pentridge?

A. They stopped to break open houses, and bring men and guns out.

Q. Did you get on to Pentridge?

A. Yes, we got to Pentridge.

Q. What happened to you there?

A. I then feigned myself ill, I wished to get from them?

Q. In consequence of that, what was done with you?

A. They said they would all do in that way.

Mr. Justice Abbott. Who said that?

A. A man in the midst of them; I did not know his name, and somebody said " shoot him."

Mr. Clarke. Did you know who that was?

A. No, I did not; the captain appointed two men to take hold of me, one by each arm.

Q. What did they do with you?

A. They led me in the midst of the men up Pentridge?

Q. How long did you continue to go in that manner led by the two men; how far did you go?

A. Till we got to Mr. Booth's house.

Mr. Justice Abbott. What is Mr. Booth's christian name?

A. William Booth.

Mr. Clarke. What was done when you got there?

A. They got Mr. Booth's poney out, and saddled and bridled it.

Q. What did they do with you?

A. They set me on the poney.

Q. What happened when you were put upon the poney?

A. I was not willing to go with them, and I fell off.

Q. After you had fallen off, what became of you?

A. The captain ordered them to face to the right, and march, and they left me.

Q. You saw no more of them?

A. No, I did not.

Cross-examined by Mr. Denman.

Q. Did you see the prisoner about the time that you yourself got away?

A. I saw him frequently.

Q. Just before you got away?

Q. I cannot particularly speak to that.

Q. Some of them ill used you at the top of the town I understand.

A. No, they did not particularly ill use me; they threatened to shoot me.

Q. Did you see the prisoner about that time?

A. I cannot recollect that I did.

Q. Did you see him about the time they were ill using you?

A. I have no doubt he was very near; I saw him in Pentridge.

Q. Do you recollect his interfering and begging the captain to let you go?

A. By no means.

Q. The captain was using the violent language you describe?

A. Yes.

Q. From first to last?

A. He did not use it all; there were others used it besides him.

Q. I ask whether he was not during the whole time using that kind of language towards you?

A. Yes, he frequently did.

Q. Did any of them interpose to have you set at liberty?

A. I do not know that they did.

Q. Do not you recollect any of them mentioning to the captain that you were a sick man, and not fit to go, and that it would be cruel to compel you?

A. No; I said to the captain he had better shoot me, and have done with me, and he says, " Damn him—leave him—we can do without one."

Q. Was Shipman there at that time?

A. I did not see.

Q. Was Hole there at that time?

A. I did not see him.

Q. Was Thomas Turner near at that time?

A. I do not know Thomas Turner.

Q. You have no recollection of any of those persons interfering at all in your favour?

A. Not in the least.

Q. Did they go away after the captain said that?

A. Immediately.

Q. The captain said when you said you were ill and wished to go off, that if you went all would do in the same way?

A. Yes; that was at the bottom of Pentridge before we got into the town.

Q. Then he talked of putting a pike through you?

A. Some of the men did; I do not know which it was.

Q. How far might you go with them altogether?

A. Not a mile; I should think about three quarters.

Q. Who was it put you upon the poney?

A. George Weightman was one, and the other I did not know.

Q. They lifted you up by the captain's command, I think you say?

A. I do not know that it was by the captain's command.

Q. Did not you say that he desired it?

A. No, I do not know that he commanded it.

Mr. Justice Abbott. Did you say in answer to some question put to you that you did not know Thomas Turner?

A. No, I did not.

William Roper sworn.

Examined by Mr Gurney.

Q. Where do you live?

A. At the stand on the race-course Nottingham Forest.

Q. How near to the town of Nottingham?

A. I think about three quarters of a mile.

Q. On the evening of Monday, the 9th of June, were you at Nottingham?

A. Yes.

Q. At about what time did you return home?

A. About half past eleven I think.

Q. Was any person with you?
A. Yes.
Q. Who?
A. William Percival.
Q. When you got upon the Forest, did you observe any body of men?
A. Yes.
Q. How many in number do you think?
A. I met first of all two, and after that two more, then a single one, and after that several more.
Q. Had those persons any arms?
A. None at all that I saw.
Q. Then did you come in sight of any body of men?
A. Yes.
Q. Amounting to about how many?
A. As nearly as I can guess about a hundred.
Q. Did any persons from amongst them approach you or follow you?
A. Yes.
Q. How many?
A. About ten or twelve.
Q. Did they meet you or follow you?
A. They followed me and Percival.
Q. What had they in their hands?
A. They had poles.
Q. Do you mean such poles as those would be?
A. Yes.
Q. What did they do with those poles?
A. They brought them down to a charge.
Q. To a level against you and Percival?
A. Yes.
Q. Did they make any demand of you?
A. They asked us where we were going?
Q. Did they afterwards permit you to pass and go on?
A. Yes.
Q. After you had got into your own house, did any number of men come to your house?
A. Yes.
Q. Could you say about what number?
A. They seemed to me to be the same men.

Q. Did they demand any thing from you?

A. Yes.

Q. What did they demand?

A. They asked me first of all whether I had got any firearms in the house? I told them yes; they told me I must deliver them up to them; I told them that I would not; they said if I did not deliver them up, they should be under the necessity of breaking the door open, and taking them by force.

Q. What reply did you make to that?

A. I told them that if they did that, I should blow the first man's brains out that came in, let him be who he would.

Q. I presume after that they did not break in?

A. No.

Q. How long did they remain about the house?

A. This was about one o'clock when they demanded the arms, and about two they left.

Captain Frederick Charles Philips sworn.

Examined by Mr. Serjeant Copley.

Q. I believe you are an officer in the 15th dragoons?

A. I am.

Q. Were you quartered at Nottingham barracks on the 9th of June.

A. Yes, I was.

Q. Were the troops ordered into the town of Nottingham on the evening of that day?

A. About ten o'clock that evening they were?

Mr. Justice Abbott. That is a very general question; what number were ordered in?

A. About two companies of infantry, a part of my troop, with a field officer.

Mr. Serjeant Copley. Was that in consequence of directions you received from the magistrates?

A. It was.

Q. Had you been in the town in the course of that day yourself?

A. I do not believe I had; I do not exactly recollect.

Q. How long did you remain in the town with the troop?

A. About half an hour; hardly half an hour.

Mr. Justice Abbott. I did not understand the witness to say he went in?

A. Yes, I went in; I commanded a part of my own troop; but there was a field officer who had the command of the whole.

Q. At the expiration of that time did you return to the barracks?

A. Yes, we did.

Q. In the course of the following morning were you alarmed at any hour?

A. About half past six on the following morning I was ordered out with a party of men to go with Mr. Rolleston and Mr. Mundy in pursuit of the rioters.

Q. Mr. Mundy and Mr. Rolleston are magistrates?

A. Yes, they are.

Mr. Justice Abbott. Both those gentlemen accompanied you?

A. Yes, they did.

Mr. Serjeant Copley. Did either of those magistrates sleep in the barracks that night?

A. There was a magistrate in the barracks all night.

Q. What road did you take?

A. The Pentridge road.

Q. Did you see any armed men on the road or near the road.

A. About half a mile before I got to Eastwood, I saw some armed men on the road to the right, making their escape across some fields.

Q. How were they armed?

A. They appeared to be armed with some pikes.

Q. I understand you those had left the road?

A. Yes.

Q. Did you send any person in pursuit of them?

A. I went across one field myself, and found I could not overtake them, and then I returned to the road and went on to Eastwood.

Q. After you had passed through Eastwood, did you observe any body of men upon the road?

A. Yes, between Eastwood and Langley mill I observed a party of about sixty on the road.

Q. Were they armed or unarmed?

A. They were armed most of them; the greater part of them were armed.

Q. What were they doing?

A. At the time that I saw them, they were standing upon the road; and one man attempted to form them up in opposition to us, but they paid no attention to him, and immediately fled across the fields, some to the right and some to the left.

Q. Did you pursue them?

A. Yes, we did; I ordered the dragoons to pursue, and to take as many prisoners as they could.

Q. How many prisoners were brought in?

A. I think about six-and-thirty.

Q. Were any pikes or other arms found or taken?

A. Yes, there were.

Q. Found upon the men, or taken on the side of the road?

A. There were five or six men taken armed, some with musquets and some with pikes; the rest of the arms had been thrown away by the rioters; they were collected together and put into a cart, and taken to the Nottingham gaol.

Q. The rest of the arms you stated to have been picked up, did they consist of pikes?

A. Of pikes and guns, chiefly of pikes.

Q. Did you examine for the purpose of ascertaining whether the guns that were picked up were any of them loaded?

A. Yes, they were.

Cross-examined by Mr. Denman.

Q. They fled in all directions?

A. Some to the right and some to the left.

Q. In the utmost confusion?

A. Yes.

Q. Eighteen men took thirty-six prisoners?

A. Assisted by the constables; there were some constables that assisted in taking them.

Re-examined by Mr. Serjeant Copley.

Q. Did you meet the High Sheriff of Derbyshire and the Chesterfield yeomanry?

A. Yes, after we had taken these men, we met them on the road.

Mr. Attorney General. My Lord, that is my Case on the part of the prosecution?

Lord Chief Baron Richards. We shall not go any further to-night.

Adjourned till to-morrow morning, eight o'clock.

SPECIAL ASSIZE, DERBY.

Thursday, 23d October, 1817.

Isaac Ludlam was set to the Bar.

MR. CROSS.

May it please your Lordship,
Gentlemen of the Jury,

THE Prisoner at the Bar stands charged before you with the crime of High Treason, in levying war against the King; and in support of this charge it was stated to you in the outset by the Attorney General, that levying war was a question of law. I shall not dispute that proposition now, and I trust the Attorney General will not dispute the corollary, as I may say, which results from that proposition; namely, that the question whether the prisoner at the bar has levied war against the King, is in the particular case a question of fact. Neither shall I waste any time in disputing whether in the absence of an actual levying of war against the troops of the King, a person may not be guilty of levying war against the King by levying insurrection for a general purpose: But there is a distinction arises out of the two cases, which I trust in the consideration of the case of the prisoner at the bar you will never forget; if a man be taken in the fact of actual warfare against the King's troops, there is no room for enquiry into his motives; but the principle of law which my learned friend the Attorney General has stated to you, brings us to this question, whether or not there was a general purpose, a general definite purpose in the mind of the man who is brought before you for trial; and what I alone have objected to with regard to the law upon these subjects, is the danger of our adopting the definitions of men learned in the law for rules as inflexible as the statute law itself. If a learned writer upon the law has said that levying an insurrection for a general purpose is levying war, that is a very good guide for the judgment of courts of justice, but it is guide and direction only, and it is not to be taken to the letter as if it were statute law; for if it were so, and there were a special clause in the statute of Edward III, which we have been obliged to discuss so much, saying that he who levies insurrection for a general purpose shall be deemed to levy war, then, Gentlemen, the words general purpose would still require interpretation with reference to the particular case, otherwise suppose there were a general insurrection to repel a foreign invasion, that would be an insurrection for a general purpose, and would be within the definition of the writers upon the law ef England, but it would not be within the statute of levying war against the King.

Gentlemen, I feel no anxiety on account of the prisoner at the bar in respect of any precise distinctions between fact and law, because I feel not the least jealousy of the Court before which you are impanelled to try the prisoner; on the contrary, I beg leave to say, that if my life, my property, and all the interests that are dear to me were at stake upon the decision, there is no tribunal existing upon the face of the earth, or ever did, before which I would sooner trust and repose every thing that is dear to me, than before the learned Judges who sit in this place; but, Gentlemen, the reason of my anxiety is this, lest when the law is so generally stated to you it should appear as if you had nothing to try but whether the prisoner at the bar was personally concerned in these transactions; that is the reason, and that is the only reason of my anxiety for keeping awake your attention to the distinction between the questions of law and of fact.

Gentlemen, I conceive the question with regard to the prisoner at the bar upon this occasion for trial is substantially this, did the prisoner intend to levy war against the King for a general purpose, aye or no, but for a definite purpose; for it will not be contended I think that it would be sufficient to charge a man in an indictment that he did levy insurrection for a general purpose, and then produce evidences to state that there was a levying of war. It is incumbent upon the prosecutor in a charge of high treason like this not merely to use the words general purpose, the most indefinite of all objects, but it is incumbent upon the prosecutor to state the special general object which was proposed to be accomplished by the prisoner at the bar, in order that the Court and Jury may form some judgment whether it is such a general purpose as the law of England has in contemplation when it has deemed that a levying of war; levying insurrection must be with a general purpose in order to be deemed a levying of war.

Gentlemen, having taken leave to say thus much upon the matter of law, in this case, I will beg leave now to call your particular attention to the evidence, which tends to fix an intention so highly culpable, as that which is imputed to the prisoner at the bar. Now let us see, first of all, how these unfortunate transactions began: it appears that to the village of Southwingfield, an obscure place, where, from any thing that we have heard, none but villagers, in the condition of common labourers reside, and a few farmers, from about the distance of sixteen miles there came a man of a most extraordinary character and disposition, an utter stranger, for any thing that appears in evidence, to the prisoner at the bar; he seated himself at noonday, on the sabbath, in a public house, inviting the presence and attention of all the villagers of the place, to come and hear what he had to state, and to promulgate. He sat in a public room in the house; there lay a map before him; he was called a captain, according to the evidence of the witnesses; and I shall have something to observe upon the testimony of those witnesses, but if I omit to do so, I know the prisoner will suffer nothing from my omission, for I have witnessed already the wisdom and manly eloquence with which I have the good fortune to be supported in these struggles, therefore if I should omit any observation upon the testimony of those witnesses, or any other part of the case, advantageous to the prisoner at the bar, I am sure that omission will be more than supplied by my learned friend who supports me; but, gentlemen, I say supposing the fact to be as represented by the witnesses, that this extraordinary man presented himself at that public house, in the situation that I have described to you, it seems, and we can only collect his representations by scraps and parcels from what was picked up from the expressions of the prisoner at the bar, and has been given in evidence against him, and what could be picked up from the expressions of others; as far as we can discover, he represented that there was coming from the North, an overwhelming torrent of population and insurrection, and that the effect of it would be, to sweep every man in their train, and that he who did not go, would be shot; that he who waited till the torrent arrived and came over him, would be carried away in the society of strangers, and those with whom he could neither associate nor converse. These were the representations, false indeed as they turned out, false in fact; but these were the representations that were held out to these unhappy people; no secret, gentlemen, there was no plot in the dark, with which these poor villagers had any thing to do; no conspiracy which you are to find out by their overt acts; it was a publication of the purpose; there was a proclamation by this man, inviting the villagers to come forward. Why, gentlemen, none of you would have been deluded by this imposture, I dare say; but that is not the question; was it a delusion that might impose on ignorant and illiterate labourers, such was the prisoner at the bar, that is the question. We all know that some years since, a man appeared in London, and he gave out that the world was to be at an end in the course of a few days time; the well informed part of mankind paid no credit to the prediction, but I believe a large proportion of the lower orders believed him, and made preparations for the event; nothing is so easy, as to induce a great proportion of the lower orders, to believe the most absurd reports, if asserted with the most audacious boldness.

Gentlemen, while this man was seated in the public house, it appears that various persons entered it from time to time; any person that accidentally passed the door; the two first witnesses would have you believe, and let us suppose that was the case, that they were at liberty to enter and hear all this, and were invited to hear it. Gentlemen, if that evidence be true, then it is quite clear that many innocent men were drawn into that room, and drawn into conversation with that extraordinary man, who made his appearance amongst them, when he had been there a considerable length of time; the evidence represents to you, that this poor creature was taken to the house, or went to the house in company with the other person, who is convicted by the second verdict at this place; they went into the room; how the prisoner came to go with William Turner into that room, no evidence can explain; but let it not be presumed that there is no defence upon this trial, because there is no evidence. Gentlemen, in a case of crime of such complexity as this, it is of more importance to observe, to weigh well, and to consider all the circumstances of the case, than to hear the testimony of witnesses. How can he prove under what circumstances he fell into the company of these persons; under what circumstances William Turner persuaded him to go there; he has two sons, you have heard they are implicated with him in this charge, and their names are found in this indictment, their lips are sealed by that proceeding, and they cannot with any effect, be adduced as witnesses on his behalf; his wife, the law will not suffer to give evidence for him. I am not meaning, God forbid I should presume, to impugn the wisdom of the law; no man is wiser than the law, and the law has so settled it, and therefore the prisoner's wife cannot be called as a witness. Why then gentlemen, the lips of every one nearest to him, being sealed upon this occasion, what are we to do on his behalf, but to observe upon the evidence; I say then we cannot account for his going into that room, but I do with all deference submit, that we are not, in the absence of all evidence to that fact, to presume that he went there for a criminal purpose.

Then, Gentlemen, being there, these two suspicious witnesses who have led up this prosecution, tell you that a paper was produced by William Turner, containing what? that is but very indistinctly explained. I wish we had that paper here, that we might know exactly what it did contain, and exactly what it was that the prisoner read; but it has been stated that it was something like this, a list of all the persons in the village who possessed a gun, or any other offensive weapon; that was the paper. It would therefore, I presume, contain the names of every housekeeper whose peace was invaded by these dreadful proceedings, on the night of the 9th of June. It would represent, one would suppose, that those persons had arms, but whether it represented to the prisoner at the bar, who read that paper, that those persons were already prepared to proceed upon the expedition to which I shall by and by advert, the evidence does not say; and therefore, for anything that appears, the prisoner was drawn to that spot a perfect stranger to the transactions, and was induced to read a paper he had never seen, the contents of which he had never heard before, and the information of which tended rather to carry on and extend the delusion that was to be practised upon himself, and upon the other unfortunate villagers of the place. It did then, we may take it, represent that all these persons were ready to supply their arms to the intended purpose, whatever that purpose might be. Well, Gentlemen, beyond that—beyond the reading of that paper, it is not pretended that at that meeting any act was done by the prisoner, or any one thing said by him in furtherance of any common purpose.

So much then, Gentlemen, for the transactions of the day that preceded the outrages, so far as they concern the prisoner. The next we hear of the prisoner, is, that he was seen with his two sons the following day going to a particular spot, where there were many others, about nine o'clock at night. Now let us consider what might be the condition of the mind of the prisoner at the bar, and his two miserable sons who were at that time in his company. It had been given out, you find, that this overwhelming insurrection was coming down from the North; that every man must go or be shot; that the effect of it would be plenty and abundance; there was death on one hand, and food on the other. That was the representation that was made to them; and that to such a height had the insurrection risen, that it was utterly irresistible; that a parliament was actually sitting at Nottingham; and that the special object for which they were to assemble, was not to make war against the King, not to fight his troops, but to guard that phantom of a parliament which this deluder from Nottingham had made them believe actually existed and sat there. Gentlemen, under these impressions I conceive it was that this miserable man and his two sons were deluded to enter upon this march to Nottingham.

Now it appears that among all the persons who set out, there were two classes; there were three, I may say.—There were, besides those drawn in by delusion, the men who have been convicted, and whom, in deference to the verdicts which have been pronounced, we must take to have been guilty of the criminal intention imputed to the full extent; there was another class of persons. you find, who were dragged out of their beds, or out of their houses, or met upon the highways, and were compelled by force and threat of instant death, to join their ranks. That was a degree of compulsion utterly irresistible, to be sure; and the law excuses any man, who under such circumstances, did march among the ranks of those persons; but it is a hard case, Gentlemen, upon a man, if, for instance, one of the witnesses, I forget his name, who was walking on the highway, and who therefore had no witness of the manner or circumstances under which he was drawn into the body, if he had been brought before you at this bar, he must have been infallibly convicted of high treason, if this evidence be sufficient; although he was forced into the ranks, and a pike put into his hand against his will, yet the fact of finding him there in those ranks, would be damning evidence against him; he had no witness to call, and he had no defence to make against the charge, but those observations which the law of England permits his counsel to make before the jury who try him. Let it not then be said, that the defence lies all in observation, and that there is no evidence. I submit that the observations require from you the most attentive and careful consideration.

Then, Gentlemen, again, I say the evidence is silent as to the pressure of circumstances that brought this man and his two sons into the ranks, except those speeches of intimidation, to which I have taken leave already to allude. Then proceeding onwards, you never find any act of outrage or of hostility committed by the prisoner in person. That poor fellow Hole, who had the good fortune to escape from the ranks, into which he was pressed against his will, under the terror and menace of immediate death, tells you of the difficulty he had to make his escape; that he might have been shot dead upon the spot, and an attempt was made by their outrageous and desperate leader to carry that threat into execution, and he was prevented doing so only by the act of one who had more humanity. Gentlemen, the prisoner at the bar had seen that desperate man carry his threats into execution; he had heard, if he had not seen, that he had laid an innocent creature dead at his feet. The prisoner knew all this, and he followed with his two sons in silence, taking no active part or lead whatever; but in the course of time, and upon that march, you find that their desperate captain ordered him into the rear with two others, to close up their ranks. It was at his peril that he obeyed; it was at the peril of immediate death that he did perform that duty, and under these impressions it was that he did discharge something like a duty in the rear of the ranks of these unhappy beings, that were driven like a flock of sheep to slaughter at the town of Nottingham.

Well, Gentlemen, under these circumstances they proceeded onwards, and they got to the works at Butterley, and there they were seen by a person of the name of Goodwin, who tells you, that he conjured the prisoner to leave their ranks, that he admonished him of the dreadful consequences that would attend his going to Nottingham with these people; well, what does he say of the prisoner; he was in a dreadful agitation of mind; he was embarrassed, and knew not what to do; and, gentlemen, Mr. Goodwin did not know of the fatal shot which had taken place; Mr. Goodwin did not know of the threats of being shot for disobedience, and this unfortunate creature was in the dilemma, either to accept the invitation of

Mr. Goodwin, which he wished to have done, or to proceed; it was in the presence of the captain, for Mr. Goodwin had just spoken to the captain himself; then the prisoner must either have quitted the ranks at the hazard of being shot dead upon the spot, as he thought, or at all events if he had escaped, he would have been separated from the dearest objects of his heart, his sons, and he must have left them hostages in the hands of that dangerous and desperate leader. Gentlemen, we sitting in cold blood here, under the protection of the law, may form a very rational judgment what a man under these circumstances ought to do; but that was not the case; then Gentlemen, do not consider that the prisoner had the same opportunities of judging and deciding as you have; the law was not present to protect or to encourage him; there was no magistrate present in the country, as far as appears, even on the Sunday or on the Monday, while that man was alarming the minds of the people, persuading them that they would be overwhelmed by a cloud of insurrection from the North, and utterly ruined if they did not run to Nottingham for protection; where were the ministers of the gospel, who might have removed that delusion from the minds of the people? where were the constables; where were the justices of the peace! all was dead, sleeping, and inert; there was no law; there was no minister of law and justice. I am not imputing blame, but there was no one present to protect these unhappy villagers from that fatal and foolish delusion which that impostor from Nottingham had practised upon them. Well then, Gentlemen, he did not quit the ranks; he did not forsake his children when he was accosted by Mr. Goodwin, but he went on; how far did he go on, Gentlemen? a few miles; and what became of him then and of his sons; they took the advice of Mr. Goodwin; they availed themselves of the first opportunity they had, and they fell away from the ranks, and they did not go to Nottingham. Now that is the history of the conduct of this unfortunate man in these unfortunate transactions.

Then, Gentlemen, this view of the facts brings us back

to the question, which I have submitted to your consideration. Is it upon this evidence proved to your satisfaction, that the prisoner at the bar had a settled purpose in his mind of deposing the King from his royal state and majesty, levying war against him, and overturning by his assistance the laws, constitution, and government of this country? if any thing short of that was done by the prisoner at the bar, then he is not guilty of this charge. What was the intention of the prisoner, it will be said, if that was not it? I will tell you what I conceive was his intention; he did believe what was stated to him of this overwhelming insurrection; he was persuaded it was irresistible; he was persuaded that death would be the consequence of a refusal, and he at last lent a reluctant consent, but not to fight the King's troops; not to make war against our beloved King, but he was consenting to go as far as Nottingham, and then he knew well that he would ascertain whether there was any truth in the story, which had been stated throughout the country, and if he found there was no parliament for him to guard, no overwhelming torrent from the North, he had nothing then to do but to walk home again; that was his motive, and he would not willingly lose the society of his two dear children, who were in these ranks.

Gentlemen, such things have occurred in this world, and they have occurred not very long ago; it is now but two years since, what may be called an insurrection, did happen in a neighbouring country; not pouring from the North, but from the South. You may recollect, that at that period, an extraordinary and desperate man had set his foot upon the south coast of France, and there arose an insurrection so overwhelming, that the General who commanded the King's troops said, " I cannot turn the ocean with the palm of my hand, and I must swim with the tide;" he said he could not help himself: the judgment of Europe however has been formed upon his case, and all mankind seem to have agreed, that there was no doubt where the point of honour lay with that officer. But, Gentlemen, supposing during the influx of that overwhelming torrent, one of the officers of that most enterprising leader, who had excited and raised that insurrection, had gone into a country village, and said, " Here is an overwhelming torrent coming from the South, it will be here in two days; you had better all go to Lyons for safety, there is a parliament sitting there; here, take a pike in your hands, and depend upon it if you get there in time you will have money and subsistence; if you do not go you will be shot dead upon the spot." Gentlemen, what should we in England have said, if the French government had extended the hand of justice to such miserable and deluded villagers, for such no doubt there were. The French government did not do so. The French government overlooked those helpless creatures, who were thus forced, or seduced, or intimidated into the ranks of that great rebel; but no one of them was brought to trial or to public justice for what he had done. Oh, but here! here they must! there are no other victims of treason. I do not mean to say, nor in all that I address to this court, and to you, do I ever mean to insinuate the smallest degree of blame to the public prosecutors, for bringing this matter under the consideration of a court and jury. Gentlemen, the hurry and impetuosity of argument, of the compassion we must all fell, when the life of man is at stake, will occasionally draw us into an observation, without seeing all the bearings and tendencies of what one accidentally throws out; but, Gentlemen, it so is. I do not mean to say, that therefore the prosecutor has selected objects, but one feels almost a necessity, when the prime mover is out of sight, to look for him elsewhere, than among these obscure villagers; some public enquiry must have taken place, we are here upon enquiry, the Attorney General has had all the exparte information before him, and he has felt it his duty, and so would every one, every lawyer, in that high station which he so eminently fills, to submit these matters to the consideration of a jury. There was evidence enough, no doubt, for the Grand Jury to present a bill of indictment against all the parties concerned in that transaction; but then, last and most important of all, comes your duty to select which was the traitor, and which was the deluded instrument of the treason; two have been already convicted; they were proved, the one to have been the leader, and the other the second in command, in this insurrection. The prisoner at the bar, is now the first of those unhappy villagers, upon whom these incredible delusions were practised on the Sunday, executed on the Monday, as it has been stated, and practised without the interposition, advice, persuasion, or caution, either of the law, or any of its ministers.

Gentlemen, with these observations, I leave the life of this unhappy man in your hands; with him, it is an issue of life and death; but I say, as was said to you before on the part of the prosecution, do your duty with firmness; I have no doubt you will. Do not, however, permit yourselves to be intimidated into an apparent acquiescence in former verdicts; do not suffer yourselves to be intimidated, lest your neighbours will reproach you for not punishing treason; let no such thought sway your judgments. Consider coolly, patiently, and impartially, that this poor creature who stands before you, must be considered, till you have pronounced your verdict, as an innocent man. That he is not guilty of this crime, unless in your consciences you are fully satisfied, that to the utmost extent of intention imputed to him, he did really go for the purpose of making war against the King. If you think, that instead of going for that purpose, he was hurried away by misrepresentation, falsehood, terror, and an overwhelming influence, then his mind was not guilty; his heart was with his children, and his heart was still with his Sovereign.

EVIDENCE FOR THE PRISONER.

Mr. William Eaton, sworn.

Examined by Mr. Denman.

Q. This man, Isaac Ludlam, has been now in gaol for several months?

A. Yes.

Q. With several other persons, his neighbours and others?

A. Yes.

Q. Have you had an opportunity of knowing what his general character has been, as a peaceable, harmless, and inoffensive man?

A. During his confinement he has so conducted himself.

Q. Do you know what his general character has been upon those subjects?

Mr. Justice Abbott. Did you know him before?

A. No, I never knew him before.

Mr. Denman. I believe his two sons have also been in your custody?

A. Yes.

Q. I beg to ask you, whether towards those sons he has conducted himself as an affectionate father?

A. He certainly has, as far as my observation has gone.

MR. DENMAN.

May it please your Lordship,

Gentlemen of the Jury,

As my learned friends who conduct these prosecutions on the part of the Crown, have thought that the public justice of the country has not yet been satisfied, and that it is necessary to bring this third prisoner as a culprit before you, it is now my duty, for the third time, to address a jury on the charge preferred, and upon the case which has been made out in evidence; and I am well assured, Gentlemen, that what has passed upon this occasion will not fail to have impressed upon your minds, if indeed they were not fully convinced before, how extremely necessary it is to distinguish, with the utmost particularity, the nature of the proof in the several cases, and the circumstances of each individual; to bear in mind that you are trying a fellow subject upon the evidence that affects himself alone; to discard all prejudice, all prepossession, from whatever source it may proceed; and to look to the case of this unfortunate man, as if no other person had been brought to answer a similar charge. If any illustration could add force to a truth so evident, it might be found in the correction given by my learned friend, the Attorney General, to an hypothesis, which I before suggested; for it demonstrated that in this very transaction there were actual instances of those, who though apparently involved in all the guilt that attached on any of the parties, yet bore a heart as innocent of every crime as any of the Gentlemen whom I have the honour to see before me. It may be recollected that when I imagined facts that might have occurred in the rebellion of 1745, he mentioned Elijah Hall the younger, as a person who appeared indeed with a pike in his hand, who was found in that assembled body which held the violent language stated, and was made privy to all the illegal purposes avowed, and yet incurred no guilt; because the circumstances and intentions under which he was there, excused him from the imputation. In addition to what was advanced by my learned friend Mr. Cross upon that subject, I would beg to call your particular attention to the precise facts affecting the witness Henry Tomlinson. It has been proved on every trial that he was taken from the lone house where he resided with his wife, was dragged a considerable distance with the riotous multitude, and compelled, according to his expression, to be one of them for a time, increasing their numbers and their forces, and actually bearing the weapon of mischief in his hand, when their intentions were unequivocally proclaimed. Now, Gentlemen, suppose that any constable, any magistrate, any officer had come up with that party, before Tomlinson had found the opportunity of retreating from it, in what situation would be have been discovered? and to what suspicions would he not have been exposed? He was in the ranks—he was with arms in his hand—he was obeying the orders of the captain and commander. If then he had been apprehended and accused, if, like this unfortunate man, he had stood before you upon the charge of high treason, how could he have established his defence? His wife, as you have been truly told, could not have appeared as a witness in his favour; no other living creature, except the persons indicted with him, could possibly possess the knowledge requisite to manifest his innocence, and though entirely blameless, he would have been overwhelmed by unanswerable proofs of the most enormous crime. Gentlemen, is it possible to suggest a stronger or a more convincing case? and having put it, let me ask with confidence whether I have not stated also the case of my unfortunate client?

Two selections, Gentlemen, have been already made. The captain has already been pronounced a traitor, and he who appeared as his lieutenant has been condemned for conspiring with him, and for acting in the prosecution of his treason. But with respect to this third man, and with respect to every other man, who shall hereafter appear at this tribunal, allow me to impress upon you the extreme importance of cautiously guarding against that, which is so likely to follow from the course adopted. I fear that your minds may be familiarized to the subject by degrees, and acquiesce in the gradual extension of your notions of guilt, to a point they ought never to attain. I deprecate the argument, that though the second may not be quite so bad as the first, yet the difference is not very great, and having condemned the one, therefore we shall do no great harm in refusing to acquit the other; for it may then be deemed a legitimate consequence, that the third shall follow the fate of the second, though somewhat less strongly implicated; the fourth man may approach within one shade of the third, and so on, to the end of the chapter; while perhaps if the last man had been first called to answer, and the evidence had been confined to the real nature of the crime alleged, you would have treated with the ridicule it deserved, the charge against him. Let not the line of proceedings that has been pursued mislead your honest judgment; it is not by degrees of comparison between the offences of different prisoners that you are to be led to a conclusion of guilt against any; but you are to look at each case as it stands by itself, supported by that evidence alone which undertakes to bring home the accusation to the particular individual before you.

What then is the case, Gentlemen, against this particular individual, and what are the facts which have been proved upon his trial? With regard to their general nature, we have given very little trouble upon the subject; and with regard to the particular intention which is supposed to have actuated the mind of Isaac Ludlam, that is of necessity rather a subject of observation upon the evidence that has been delivered, than it can be of proof, on our side the question. Gentlemen, it is stated by two witnesses, upon whom I shall presently observe, that this prisoner was found in a room with Brandreth the Nottingham captain, when schemes of riot and confusion at least were talked over, and when mischief was debated. It has been constantly opened to you, and if that evidence be true, it is most certainly undeniable, that that was not the first meeting which had been held amongst the conspirators; I say if that evidence be true; but I shall satisfy you that you would betray your trust as jurymen, if you paid the smallest attention to it :—but for a moment and for argument's sake, admitting its truth, there had been former conspiracies in which some of the parties had been concerned, though I know not whether this prisoner is meant to be treated as a party to them. Of these former conspiracies, all mention is suppressed; all particulars are concealed from you by the Crown. Why is this course pursued? Why are we in the dark upon a subject so interesting and important? and you will remember, that this challenge is not now for the first time thrown out. I have made the observation twice before, and yet this case rests precisely on the same foundation as before, namely, the evidence of Martin and Asbury, on which I shall not fail to offer my observations when I come to consider the particulars related by the several witnesses.

Gentlemen, we all know how much the country was agitated and disturbed; we all know that the distresses of the poor had driven them to a state of desperation, that they were all hungry and miserable, and to a certain degree, discontented. Such dispositions, in the lower orders, are the materials with which artful and abandoned men can best effect their purposes of treachery and mischief. It is evident, that the leader, of whom so much has been said, was acting, by these means, upon the minds of the ignorant villagers; it is clear that this leader was himself deceived, and that he was also in other hands; why are those hands still kept invisible? why is a veil still spread before the mysterious machinery which set the lower agents in motion? Whether this was the act of base spies and wicked informers, whose trade it is to report nothing but danger and alarm, who find their interest in creating the mischiefs which they were only appointed to detect and prevent; or whether for general purposes of mischief, some traitors of deeper views, had engaged these wretched men in their plans; in either case, government had full information of the origin of all that passed; it is essential, to a fair understanding of the facts, that the root of them should be laid bare; and yet that information is studiously withheld from the minds of the jury impanelled to decide this cause, according to the truth, and the whole truth.

Gentlemen, when I name that unfortunate convict, Jeremiah Brandreth, the captain of this host of paupers, it is impossible not to reflect upon the peculiar character which appears to belong to him. I may spare the Court the trouble of hearing a second time, my own observations upon him, because I have since found him so wonderfully depicted by a noble poet of our own time, and one of the greatest geniusses of any age, that I shall take the liberty of now reading that prophetic description. It will perfectly bring before you his character, and even his appearance, the commanding qualities of his powerful but uncultivated mind, and the nature of his influence over those that he seduced to outrage. Gentlemen, it is from the poem of "The Corsair," which I dare say many of you have read, that I shall beg to extract a portrait of that Brandreth, as minute, as accurate, as powerful, as if the first of painters had seen him in his hour of exertion, and had then hit off his likeness; at first, indeed, it describes a kind of military reputation, which did not exist here;

"Who is that chief? his name on every shore
Is famed and feared; they ask, and know no more."

But mark what follows:

"With these he mingles not but to command,
Few are his words, but keen his eye and hand;
His name appals the fiercest of his crew,
And tints each swarthy cheek with sallower hue;
Still sways their souls with that commanding art,
That dazzles, leads, yet chills the vulgar heart.
What is that spell that thus his lawless train
Confess and envy, yet oppose in vain;
What should it be, that thus their faith can bind?
The power, the nerve, the magic of the mind—
Link'd with success, assumed and kept with skill,
That moulds another's weakness to its will;
Wields with their hands, but still to these unknown,
Makes ev'n their mightiest deeds appear his own."

Then he speaks of his person:

"Unlike the heroes of his ancient race,
Demons in act, but gods at least in face;
In Conrad's form seems little to admire,
Though his dark eye-brow shades a glance of fire.
Robust, but not Herculean, to the sight,
No giant frame sets forth his common height;
Yet in the whole, who paused to look again,
Saw more than marks the crowd of vulgar men.
They gaze and marvel how, and still confess
That thus it is; but why, they cannot guess.
Sunburnt his cheek, his forehead high and pale,
The sable curls in wild profusion veil;

" There breathe but few, whose aspect could defy
The full encounter of his searching eye.
There was a laughing devil in his sneer,
That roused emotions both of rage and fear;
And where his frown of hatred darkly fell,
Hope withering fled, and mercy sighed farewell."

Gentlemen, I am sure you will forgive the length of this beautiful extract, on account of its singular aptitude to this extraordinary person; it really seems as if the poet who drew such a picture must have known the original. Now, Gentlemen, in the history of the transaction, Brandreth is first introduced to your notice at the public house, surrounded by several individuals; amongst the rest, this Isaac Ludlam is stated by the two witnesses first called to have made his appearance; whether he did or not, I cannot pretend to say, and I rather think I shall convince you that these witnesses are entitled to no credit. But supposing he was there, and remained a part of Sunday, and that several things which are stated actually passed, does that prove him concurring in any conspiracy which this captain might have formed for any wild, indefinite, or absurd purpose? on the contrary, one of these witnesses expressly declares, that during the six hours he staid there, he does not know that any thing was said about the government in the prisoner's presence; he says, that when the prisoner entered, the map was in Brandreth's pocket; he says, that nothing was said in his hearing about killing the vermin; and that the miserable doggrel verses, as to every one trying his skill, were repeated before he came, and were not afterwards mentioned. That is the account of the first witness of Ludlam's share in the interview at the public house. If you look to Shirley Asbury's report, you will find it so confused, so full of prevaricaton and contradiction, that I hardly know how to recite it to you, such a tissue of manifest falsehoods was never attempted to be imposed by the most impudent witness on the most credulous jury. Both of them tell you they had been recently sworn in as special constables, for the protection of their masters, and that they went accidentally to the public house; can you believe that? and that in this house and in a public room they heard revolutionary plans discussed in a room open to the most general inspection, and to which all mankind had access. My learned friend, however, has an ingenious paradox, which struck me at first as a little singular, but which was necessary, as a theory, to account for the facts which these witnesses undertook to prove; he makes the general remark, that there is nothing improbable in their being extremely public and unreserved in their disclosures, for they were on the eve of breaking out into insurrection, and they wished to have it generally understood how bold and decisive their measures were to be. Now that is not to me a very satisfactory explanation; conspiracy in general is more reluctant to expose itself, " it shames even to shew its dangerous face by night;" but that such disclosures should be made with a loud voice, in the full light of day, is a statement so contrary to experience as to call for a new theory to make it even credible. I remember it was observed on the trials in 1794, that the persons then accused of treason, were fond of magnifying their numbers, and boasting of what great things they had the means of effecting; but not when the sun was in the Heaven, not when such announcements would have called down immediate interference on the part of the magistracy and the government; but privately, cautiously, and in a clandestine manner, so as to give encouragement to each other, without attracting the notice of the superior powers. Such was the observation in 1794, and it was rational and consistent; would not the same conduct have been pursued here, if similar intentions had been entertained? I maintain that it would, upon the evidence of these two men themselves; for though they tell you that the intention to commit riot and outrage was loudly and fearlessly proclaimed, yet they swear in the same breath that they themselves were threatened with destruction if they whispered a syllable of the secret to any one. These things have both been stated by these witnesses upon their oaths: and I ask you upon yours, whether it is possible that both can be true? How can human ingenuity reconcile two such answers? Oh, they spoke of revolution freely and openly; they had no desire to conceal their plan, on the contrary, they wished a general terror to be spread by its being universally foreseen. Then why did you conceal it? you, the witnesses who seem to have been admitted for no other purpose than to disseminate the expectation? mark the answer—because they threatened to put us up the chimney if we said a word about it, and because we were enjoined to secrecy by the terror of instant death.

Another thing appeared, Gentlemen, in the evidence of the special constables, which, for the sake of the prisoner, I remarked with pleasure, for in my mind it utterly destroys their credit: "you tell us that being a special constable you heard some talk about your masters being murdered, those masters whose bread you were eating, and for whose protection you had just been sworn into your office; now when you heard, from that conversation, that the danger was imminent and near, why did you not give them immediate warning, and afford them the means of providing for their safety?" You will allow the question to be a fair and natural one; it has received a great variety of answers, which are not unworthy of examination. The first answer is, "they threatened to cram me up the chimney, when I told them to remember that I was a constable, and that it was wrong to go on with this sort of conversation." That perhaps might be a very good reason for not enforcing their remonstrances there, or proceeding to apprehend so numerous a party; but it seems rather an insufficient one for not telling the story when they got home. Why was not that done? Oh, they did not tell the story when they got home, because these persons " threatened them so very hard;" they said they would take the lives of anybody that told. Now, that, I have proved, cannot be true, for the same man cannot at the same moment desire that the same affair shall be both public and private, they could not intend at once to avoid detection by its secrecy, and scatter consternation by its publicity.

These reasons then being found extremely weak and insufficient, another is to be found. " Come witness, you see that these pretexts will impose on nobody, tell us at length your real reason." Why, then, if I must speak the truth, we did not know that we had any right to communicate to our masters the design to attack and murder them." Asbury declared that to be as true as any thing he had sworn besides; which is the only answer I give him credit for. That all the rest was as true as that account, I firmly believe; but, is that an account that you, Gentlemen, can possibly believe? that these special constables, who were appointed but the day before, for the express purpose of protecting their masters' lives and property, could have the smallest doubt whether it was their indispensible duty to go and make an immediate disclosure of what they say they heard? The men have sworn it, but juries are to look at probabilities as well as assertions; they are to take the whole case and every part of it, and if by the utmost stretch of credulity they cannot bring themselves to trust to what is nominally sworn, but never can be satisfactorily proved, they will not only obliterate that fact from their minds, but every other which proceeds from the same polluted source. Between hearing a thing stated, and judging it to be proved, the difference is wide indeed; and Gentlemen, in this case you will be anxious to scan with jealousy every particle of evidence, assigning to it its just weight in the scale, and its due effect on all the surrounding proofs.

It was evidently necessary to provide another reason, and it was hit upon yesterday for the first time. Having kept it to themselves on the former enquiries, both these men happened to discover it on the same day. " Why did you not apprize Mr. Goodwin of his danger? Because, they say, they thought it unnecessary, since he had already taken the alarm, he had appointed special constables, and had his forces on the alert to repel any attack." Now, Gentlemen, when danger is expected, and where persons are sworn in as constables for the special purpose of repelling it, at some indefinite period, do you think it possible that these persons should hear that, what might be distant and doubtful, was approaching and certain, that their throats are to be cut to-morrow night, and that they, the selected guardians of their master's safety, should bury in their own bosoms such important intelligence? "The people from Sheffield and Chesterfield were to come at ten o'clock;" fixing even the precise hour of their intended arrival to destroy the gentlemen at the Butterley works, and yet the special constables disclosed nothing on the subject, because those gentlemen knew they were to be attacked. But does it require to be a special or any constable at all, for a servant to disclose to his master that his life is to be sacrificed to-morrow, does it require to be any thing but a man to warn a fellow-creature of his impending danger? Forgive me, gentlemen, for intreating you for one moment to make the case of these wretched witnesses your own,— would you, could you have known such a fact, and concealed it? and the question is equally material, whether the witnesses are perjured in stating that the project was to be kept secret, or made public. My learned friends, with an extravagant tenderness towards these men,—I mean the witnesses, not the prisoners, though this prisoner is much more entitled to tenderness, and I should have liked to see a little of that candour exercised towards him, which is so largely lavished on these two witnesses; my learned friends find a charitable excuse for them, which they have not pretended to advance for themselves. " Oh, they say, they had not quite the firmness to make the disclosure;" and for want of it, the matter proceeds to extremities, and terminates in a war, which is extinguished by eighteen hussars and a single magistrate. The events of that night must take their character from the preceding designs; and these rest on the honesty of these two miserable witnesses alone. They alone describe what passed at that extraordinary meeting—extraordinary in all its parts—improbable in its general bearings—strange in all the language that occurs—unparalleled, from the circumstance of being attended by constables, one four hours and another six, without making the slightest objection then, or any disclosure afterwards; but more marvellous than all, in the nature of the proof which has been applied to it. Consider a moment how it might have been proved, if true. Cope was present with these men, who is a witness in the list delivered, who has been examined out of Court on the part of the crown, and who is not called to support this tottering testimony. Elsden was present, what he could have proved is well known to the crown; but neither is he called here to confirm the two accomplices. For upon their own shewing, gentlemen, I put it broadly and distinctly to you, that accomplices they are, nor can that proposition be disputed. There is no doubt that if there was treason committed, they were accessaries before the fact: it is ridiculous, on any other principle, to suppose that they could hear of overturning the government, if they did so, and that they should subscribe their money to dispatch messengers to Nottingham. If they heard any thing of what they swear to, they heard all; you must take the whole or no part of their narrative. Their own account therefore makes them accomplices in the strictest sense of the word, and requires the fullest confirmation. They might have been confirmed by Cope and Elsden, if their story has any truth in it; but neither Cope nor Elsden are brought as witnesses before you.

But this palpable deficiency of proof is supplied by an ingenious argument: you will be told that we for the prisoner, by calling some of the persons who were present, ought to have convicted the two witnesses of falsehood. To that I answer, that it is the duty of my learned friends to make out their case, and not for me to disprove it before it is made out; they are to establish and confirm, and something must be set up that demands contradiction, before I can be called upon to contradict it. The burthen of proof is entirely upon them, and if any part of that proof fails, the prisoner is entitled to a verdict of acquittal at your hands.

But even if I were bound to contradict them, and had had the amplest means of doing so in the first instance, what situation am I placed in now? Is there an individual who was present at that meeting, that is not put upon his trial as a traitor? Neither the sons of the prisoner, nor any one to whom it is imputed that he listened to all this improper conversation, can possibly be called as a witness for the prisoner, for the plain and conclusive reason, that that they are all made prisoners themselves; and that being charged as conspirators upon the same indictment, they are of course incompetent to appear in favour of any party indicted.

Equally ingenious is another argument in reserve. We shall be asked, why we do not call Mrs. Weightman, who kept the White Horse, to contradict that, which no man of common sense can believe? Why, Gentlemen, if we had called her, what could she have proved? could she have proved that the witnesses or others were not there? By no means; I do not dispute the fact; and probably they were there; it is not the fact of their going to a public house, and taking a pint of ale, and staying four or five hours, by which I am affected. I should indeed be affected, and the prisoner's life might be sacrificed, if you were to believe, which I am sure you will not, these witnesses' account of what passed while they were in the parlour. That portion of the evidence is alone material, and as to that, however gross the fabrication, Mrs. Weightman could not have detected it; for she is not stated by any one to have been once in the parlour during the whole time this talk was going forward. Then how can I be told, with a grave face on the part of the crown, that I might have called the others, and that I might have called Mrs. Weightman? She knew nothing of what passed in the room, for she was never there; and all the persons who were in the room are disqualified and reduced to silence by the conduct of the crown, which has made them defendants, upon these proceedings.

The necessity of confirmation is still felt, and other circumstances are resorted to. I cannot serve my client so well as by adopting a few observations of my learned friend, Mr. Serjeant Copley, in a late trial, upon this subject of confirming accomplices. To me they seem conclusive; and I have sometimes noticed these cases of confirmation adduced at the bar, in a manner more like mockery of the human understanding, than a serious proceeding in a court of justice. It is said, an accomplice is to be believed in all he testifies, when confirmed in some things and not in others; that if he states correctly where he breakfasted, and where he dined, and where he played at cards in the evening; as to all which indifferent matters he will be sure to receive enough confirmation, he must therefore be believed, though unconfirmed in all the material points he may choose to depose. I know my learned friend will say, that no prosecutor would ever call an accomplice, if he could be confirmed in all particulars, because those who could so confirm his testimony, could themselves have given unsuspected evidence of all he said. But here are persons present at this meeting, Cope and Elsden, who could have told us every word that passed; it was important to throw all possible light upon this obscurity; but the accomplices remain unsupported by two persons who were present, who are in the list of witnesses for the prosecution, but are not presented to the scrutiny of a court of justice. I remember once, because a woman had had greens for dinner, I think about a year before the time she was speaking as a witness, that was considered as a confirmation of the accomplice, who had said that he had greens for dinner at that time; but, Gentlemen, it is obvious, that the breakfast, and the dinner, and the supper, may be all rightly recorded, while every material fact is wholly destitute of foundation. But you shall hear how Serjeant Copley dealt with the observation: speaking of Castle, the witness for the crown on Watson's trial, he remarks, " It is said he is confirmed, and because he is confirmed in some facts, you are therefore to believe him in the rest. This is a position, which lawyers are in the habit of stating in a very unqualified manner; but it is not a position which can be maintained to this extent, according to any principle of common sense." You cannot fail to agree with these observations. He proceeds with the same good sense: "There is no man who tells a long and complicated story, like that which you have heard, who may and must not of necessity be confirmed in many parts of it; the witness was upwards of eight hours in giving his evidence, and of course stated many facts which no man denies, which have been in all the newspapers for weeks and for months past, and because he is confirmed in certain particulars, you are therefore required to believe the whole of his story to be true." Fortunately for the purposes of justice, the jury addressed by Serjeant Copley did not believe the whole or any part of that man's story; and now let us see whether you can believe this. Here the accomplices are supposed to be confirmed by the subsequent transactions; that is, by the rising in the evening of Monday. Now, Gentlemen, if this Asbury had gone to Mr. Goodwin, as he ought, on the Monday morning, and Mr. Goodwin had said, I cannot believe you, the thing is improbable, and you are not a man to be believed; the rising on the Monday evening would indeed have become a striking confirmation of a suspicious report; but when the story of the design is never told till days and weeks and months after the execution; when the deliberation about levying war is never heard of, till long after the war has been levied and put down, and hundreds of people had been examined by the magistrate; any story, however false, of the origin of the mischief on the Sunday, must have met with full confirmation from the events of the Monday. This is the explanation I give of, it in my own mind. On the Monday night something we will not now dispute, whether a war, a rebellion, an insurrection or riot, notoriously takes place; it is publicly known to be prompted and commanded by a man called the Nottingham captain, and it may perhaps be proved that these two witnesses were with that man on the Sunday, when he was supposed to have prepared the proceedings that ensued. Their conduct is naturally called in question: what, you special constables, you who had been just sworn in to protect the Butterley works, and the lives of your masters, how came you to be in company with this leader, at a crisis so pregnant with danger! Oh, I will tell you all. Gentlemen, do you not believe that they told much more than all, to purchase their own security, and shared their own guilt with others, who were not really implicated? Is not that a probable explanation, and can an accomplice under such circumstances, find credit with the jury? Supposing that you had resided near the place, and that these men, to injure you, or to save themselves, had chosen to swear that you were at the Sunday's meeting, how could you have contradicted them? They might have defied you to get rid of any story they thought proper to invent against you; unless you happened to have left your house with that caution in defence of your innocence, which belongs to guilt alone, unless you had provided a distinct alibi, before you took your Sunday's walk, the thing would have been as distinctly and undeniably proved against you, as it is against Isaac Ludlam by these two witnesses.

If, then, Gentlemen, the confirmation resulting from the fact of the rising, is a little disposed of by these remarks, several other points of confirmation might have been established, of which nothing is to be found. Verses are said to have been recited, and copies taken away; we have seen no copy produced—it might have been. If Asbury burnt his copy, having committed the verses to memory, there were many others. My learned friend, the Attorney-General, says, these verses are dangerous things; they are not very fine poetry to be sure, but they might be set to fine tunes, and then they might produce as great a sensation in a rebel army, as during the French revolution. The imputation is, that these people were copying them out with delight, and making charms and amulets of them; and that they did produce a grand effect upon their minds: but is there one single man who says that he heard one single expression out of them employed during the rising? Could it have happened if these Tyrtæan strains excited so much enthusiasm, that no witness should have heard a single scrap of them, either sung or said? How do I know but that Asbury made these verses himself? I think he is as likely to be their author as any other man; nothing is rendered more probable by his swearing it; and his familiar acquaintance with the nonsense he recited savours of a father's partiality.

Gentlemen, there was another document, a map. It has not been exhibited at least; if there, it might or might not have been found, and I do not put that as a very strong argument, though that is a confirmation which the case admitted. Another remark is of more consequence; money was collected, and they sent Weightman on horseback to Nottingham, and he set out upon his journey, in the day time, on a Sunday, when people are most abroad, on that public King's highway between Pentridge and Nottingham: did any one see him on his horse going or returning? Such a confirmation might reasonably have been expected; and the absence of any collateral proof in this case is ten thousand times stronger than in any other, on account of the diligence and acuteness which have been for so many months employed, with the fullest command of information in detecting every particle of this alleged conspiracy. From several quarters the clearest confirmation might have been obtained, if the story was true, there is none from any; and these accomplices, according to the rules of courts of justice, are therefore to be discarded with disgrace from your recollection, and the case must be left to the other parts of the evidence.

On the Monday night, it is not denied, that this poor man joined the party: and you will do my learned friend and me the justice to observe, that we have not wasted time by troubling you with idle contention on clear matters. We called no evidence; from the nature of the case it was impossible: we have not, as we might, if we supposed you had taste for such entertainment, fatigued your attention by long cross-examinations, for the sake of raising a laugh, or of betraying ignorant witnesses into confusion, and trifling mistakes, but we meet the evidence on the fair ground of reason and probability; and upon that ground we refer it to your honour and your oath.

Gentlemen, this prisoner is the third who has been selected for trial. With regard to the propriety beginning with the first, there can be no difference of opinion. If treason was committed, Brandreth was the most deeply implicated in it: if war was levied, it was levied by him; and whether he originated that treason, or was the tool of others, as I most firmly and conscientiously believe, he would stand equally without excuse in the eye of the law. Other circumstances appeared against him; and above all, that unfortunate one on which any jury would dwell with regret, I may say with prejudice, the shooting of that poor innocent boy. That act of violence perhaps was brought forward with rather too much zeal; but it could not fail of pointing out the determined leader in a scheme of mischief, by his unrelenting sternness, and his daring and impetuous temper. The second was the man whom they called lieutenant; and these two were certainly walking by the side of the others; the lieutenant took an active part, and did that, which I was sorry to hear proved against him, when he threatened the life of Mr. Raynor. There was mischief and danger in what he said; but I think it was pressed a little too strongly against him; for whether it was treason or not, all these circumstances might have equally occurred. And it is singular, that in every case, my learned friends, not satisfied with the proof of treason alone, though that is the only charge, have connected it with some independent circumstance, which can have no other effect than to make the jury look less favourably on the general character of the prisoner under accusation. The murder was thus made the prominent part of the first case; the menace of the second; and on the present occasion this prisoner is selected on account of a fact, which if proved, has nothing to do with treason, I mean the suspicion cast upon him, of having deceived and deluded his own sons, and tempted them to walk in those dangerous footsteps, which have led him to the jeopardy in which he stands. Gentlemen, I sincerely wish my learned friend had not made that statement; and am disposed to think, that when the bustle of these proceedings, and the passions they naturally excite, are at an end, he himself will repent of having done so. It has no bearing on the question, nor at all increases the probability of the charge being true; but besides, I am sure that you will consider it is as unfounded in fact, as cruel and inhuman in its application. What, Gentlemen, a father to mislead his sons to the commission of crimes, by which their lives are forfeited? Examine the evidence, and even if this poor man is to go to the scaffold, and suffer that death which would be the result of your verdict of guilty, if you could bring yourselves to pronounce it; if he is to perish with his two sons, and to see them suffer the same ignominious and cruel death; even then, Gentlemen, he might have been spared the additional torment of being reproached with betraying them into that fatal snare : his memory should not have been unnecessarily stigmatised with a crime, the most revolting to human nature; and which your own feelings tell you, ought not to be imputed without proof the most direct and irresistible. Is there such proof, Gentlemen, in this case? I say no; I assert that this man is no more proved to have led his sons, who are grown up men, into this unfortunate affray, than to have been led there by them. I have just as much right to assume that they dragged this poor helpless grey-headed man to the assembly they all joined; and the probabilities are all in my favour, as my learned friend has to assume that he induced them: your knowledge of human nature and of your own hearts will convince you, that this is the most probable history. We have no direct proof what it was that acted on their minds, whether the boys first went, or followed; but we do know, that the young are more prone to such enterprizes than the old; and every father will reject the imputation that the parent should have wantonly seduced his children into guilt and danger.

What has been truly and wisely observed by my learned friend Mr. Cross, is particularly applicable to this branch of our enquiry. Let it not be supposed that we have no defence, because we have no evidence; who has deprived us of our evidence? The crown. It is the crown who has charged the two sons as fellow conspirators with their father; their lips are sealed, for they may themselves be brought to trial to-morrow. With respect to this prisoner, you will not expect from him the declaration, when his sons may so soon be placed in his present unfortunate situation, that their crime was aggravated by the enlistment of their aged father: if he should offer any address to you, (whether he will, I know not) but I am sure his silence upon this subject, the reluctance of a father to accuse his offspring, ought not to operate against himself; from that silence, which his paternal affection may suggest, you will not uncharitably presume that he led his sons to be cruelly butchered, when it is far more likely that he went to watch them, to bring them home at the earliest moment of their repentance, and that he also yielded to the overpowering force of their extraordinary leader. He witnessed his violence, and heard his menaces; and if these two miserable witnesses can be justified on account of fears, which must have subsided when they quitted his presence, how much more is the same protection to be extended to a feeble and unhappy father, who because his sons have unfortunately joined a tumultuous body of rioters, follows them to that scene of danger, and is overpowered by the frantic cruelty of their desperate captain. I repeat then, Gentlemen, that that imputation is not made out by any evidence, it is mere imputation; the one mode of considering the case is just as probable as the other; it is made impossible for us to refute it, for we are deprived of our evidence; but it derives no support from any thing that has been proved. I recollect but one occasion when he mentions his sons at all, and then his expression is, that they are along with them. Can any inference be drawn from that expression? Supposing him to have yielded to the violence and fury of the man that led them, and his sons to have done the same, is that inconsistent with such an expression? He might state the fact, as his own motive for having joined the multitude.

I really trembled at the opening, and expected to hear it proved, that in pursuit of some long matured treason, he had been beating up for recruits in his own family, and came with the dignity of an ancient baron, bringing his sons to serve in the wars; but the proof relieved me, for there is nothing to shew any anterior notion on the subject, but his reading the paper produced by Turner. If true, that admits an easy explanation, by supposing him the only scholar who could read; but it is proved only by the two wretched accomplices; upon whom I have already wearied you with my observations.

Now, Gentlemen, is there any thing to contradict the statement I make to you? No doubt this man held a pike, he was with the party in the rear-guard, according to that language of military science employed by the witnesses, which the volunteers and local militia have made so current amongst us. He said to one man, " you must go with us, we cannot spare you;" these are his acts; but that there is not a single word respecting his motives, I appeal to the evidence, which will be detailed to you by the learned judge. Some of the witnesses, I know, who speak under the influence both of resentment and alarm, and cannot help exaggerating the circumstances by which their safety has been compromised, say that he was pushing a man forward more than once; but they mention no names; those that were so prevented from escaping, must have been unwilling to proceed, and do not stand in the situation of accomplices; yet not one of them is called to prove the fact, except, I think, one William Smith; and now I wish you to be particularly attentive to the way in which that person was examined, and gave his answers. He deposed, " that the captain formed the men into ranks; this was a little beyond the wire-mill; that William Turner, the lieutenant, assisted; he had a gun. We went towards Pentridge, and at Pentridge we rattled at several doors. Did you see the prisoner in any part of the march? the answer is, I do not know that I did, till we got to Butterley." So that this active person, this third in command, was never seen by William Smith, who knew him well, for the whole distance from the wire-mill where he joined, to Butterley. At Codnor the witness offered to leave this body of men; and here the imputation to be raised by William Smith's evidence is, that he was prevented from retiring by Isaac Ludlam. I hope you understand me, I state it quite fairly. And I beg you to observe how Mr. Clarke, who managed the examination with the greatest address, contrived to introduce this inference. After bringing the witness to the Glass House at Codnor, he suddenly enquires of him, " Do you know Coburn quarry?" "Yes."—" Well, who worked Coburn quarry?" " It was not in work at that time at all."—" Well, but did the prisoner Isaac Ludlam ever work in it?" " Yes; it was worked sometime before by Isaac Ludlam."—" And how far is it from his house?" " About three or four hundred yards." Now having by this machinery introduced the name of Isaac Ludlam, by means of the Coburn quarry, which he did not work at the time, then my learned friend takes a short turn to the Glass House at Codnor, and makes him answer that the prisoner was standing at the door there with a pike in the rain under the eaves. Then follows the question, " Did that prevent your escaping?" I think that was not quite a fair way of putting the question, for the answer might have been true, and the impression produced by it entirely false. He ought to have been asked what did prevent him; and then if the prisoner did any act with that intention, the evidence would have been regular and material. But this, which would have been the proper course, is not adopted, and the evidence is left by my learned friend to receive that interpretation which suspicion may attach to it. But my friend Mr. Cross did not leave it in that degree of doubt, he boldly pressed the point home, and asked in his examination what Isaac Ludlam did to prevent the witness from escaping. Gentlemen, you heard the witness declare upon his oath, that Isaac Ludlam neither said nor did any thing, but only that he had some supposition of his own about it. Gentlemen, is that the way that the lives of men are to be sacrificed? is it thus that charges of high treason should be proved? on loose and insufficient evidence so pieced together, by the dexterity of an advocate, as to give a mere imagination the semblance of a fact? Are innocent men in this manner to be sworn out of the world? Gentlemen, I hope you have remarked this; I think you could not fail to remark the course of that examination; and I am confident you feel with me, that the result amounts to nothing.

Now, Gentlemen, whether he was a little more or a little less active in his obedience to the captain, I confess, appears to me, under such circumstances, very immaterial, for the captain and Turner were clearly assuming the lead, marching out of the rank; Brandreth acting in the highest place, and Turner in the second, and this poor man's name was hardly mentioned on their trials; he was in the rear of all; is he to be made the third in command, in activity and forwardness, merely because William Smith saw him at the door with a pike, and because to some other person he said, "no, I cannot let you go?" Indeed it was not so strong an expression as that, but only " you must go forward with us." Two other men were in this rear rank, who are represented to be fully as active as he; those no doubt were younger men, and one of the witnesses says James Taylor, and the prisoner, and another, were the rear guard. Now I ask you, whether, in all reason and probability, it was not James Taylor and the other, who were keeping the men together? The mistake is easy, and there is no proof of the prisoner's any otherwise consenting to the acts of the mob, than as he accompanied them to watch over the safety of his sons, and to bring them home as soon as possible!

The few words that passed between Mr. Goodwin and the prisoner, are also pressed with considerable vehemence against him. I confess that short conversation strikes me in a different light, and whatever suspicion it may excite in you, or the Attorney General, still I am sure you will see that it is nothing more, and it is not by suspicion, but by convincing proof, that this man is to be condemned of the basest and heaviest of crimes. Gentlemen, Mr. Goodwin, with a feeling that does honour to his humanity, seeing a peaceable old man, whom he knew so well, walking among these persons prepared for outrage, exclaimed with surprise, " Good God, Isaac, are you there? go home, the law will be too strong for you; you have a halter about your neck; I will give you protection, come into my office." It was a friendly and a generous offer; but if he had accepted it, he must have left his sons behind; they were not within hearing at the moment; and if the prisoner had made any effort, for the purpose, of addressing them, what think you would have been the conduct of the captain? Do you believe he would have tamely permitted them to withdraw? or would he have hesitated to repeat the outrageous act he had committed at Mrs. Hepworth's? do you doubt, that if he had seen this man, who is represented as his rear guard and the third officer, attempt to desert, he would have laid him low at his feet? his two sons might have shared his fate; at all events, they would have been left as hostages in the hands of an exasperated leader, exposed to his dangerous revenge, and hurried into his violent courses. I think there is something distressing in this man's answer to Mr. Goodwin's solicitation; " I have gone too far, I cannot retract; I must go on;" it marks the agitation of a man alarmed for himself, and for those most dear to him, and deterred by the immediate fear of death alone, from accepting the proffered shelter so suitable to his grey hairs. Mr. Goodwin says, we would have hazarded our own lives in his defence, after offering to protect him; and I give entire credit to the sentiment; but though this man had not the courage and promptitude of mind to accept that refuge, at the moment, from fear for himself, or from affection to his sons, or from both motives acting at once upon a timorous mind, for God's sake, let not that be taken as proof of high treason; when nothing is disclosed inconsistent with the views taken by my learned friend and myself, of the leading features of this case, and of the object with which the prisoner first joined this party.

Gentlemen I do not trouble you by going particularly through the evidence, though I hope you will attend to every part of it, when it is summed up by the learned judge; keeping the two opposite suppositions in your minds, and comparing them with the evidence, as it goes along. You will then see whether our explanation of motives is not at least as probable as that which my learned friend has so unnecessarily brought forward, calculated as it is to excite a prejudice against the prisoner, in the minds of the jury; but not at all more calculated to prove him guilty of this particular crime, than if it was to receive any other legal description; and therefore I think most unfit to be pressed against him, upon the present occasion.

Another general observation seems fairly to arise out of the evidence. One or two witnesses have stated that the prisoner said something about a parliament being held at Nottingham, and that the party were going to guard that parliament. Now suppose anything of that sort to have been said by him, what was it more than adopting the expressions he heard from those around him, telling his neighbours, who like himself were compelled to accompany them, what he had heard these people say they were about? Is not that the fair account to be given? supposing an unfortunate necessity to have constrained any of you to join a violent and outrageous party, and that you were kept along with them, by fear or affection; if any of your friends had been compelled to join you, and had enquired what is all this hubbub, where are you going, and what are you about? you would naturally have repeated the information you had heard; would have said, that they had talked of a parliament at Nottingham; and that you, that is the party, which you, like the prisoner had been forced to join, were going to guard that supposed parliament, to get a bigger loaf, or to attain any other object, which had been discussed in his presence. Does it follow from his repeating these pretences, that he concurred in them, and meant to be active in demolishing the constitution of his country? This imaginary parliament at Nottingham, is a new speculation; we heard of it on no former trial; it is one of the many delusions which this unfortunate captain was made to practise on his followers, by the persons who employed him; it was no object of this prisoner's; there is no expression of such a kind traced to him, during any part of his life; and as to the reading of that paper, if you can believe it upon the evidence of these witnesses, it is fairly explained by supposing he read it without adverting to its meaning or consequences, because no other of the party was learned enough to do so. The time of his leaving that party is not in evidence; he might have left it before Asbury and Martin, or have stayed after them; they were all drinking there, it was a public party, and if so rash and absurd a conversation took place, the hearers might naturally suppose there could be no formed intention upon the subject, and that nobody could be mad enough to talk of such a design in a public house, if they had really contemplated its execution.

Gentlemen, in enforcing the probable supposition that the prisoner went among the rioters, for the purpose of being near his sons in the hour of peril, I have, perhaps, gone farther than I need; for when you find parties alarmed and controuled by a man, who has the power to wield them to his purposes, it is too much to say that every one of them is bound to give an account of himself and his own intentions. It is for the Attorney General, it is for him who prosecutes, for him who charges that criminal intention which constitutes the treason, to satisfy you that it exists in the particular case; and I perhaps have gone out of the way in arguing that his motives might be innocent, since there has been no unexceptionable evidence from any quarter, to persuade you to believe them guilty.

On the law that is applicable to this case, I will not dissemble, Gentlemen, that I find myself under some difficulty; I should have paussd before I renewed that discussion, if my learned friend, the Attorney General, had not felt it necessary, in a most ingenious, a most elaborate and subtile argument, to revert to that subject, and answer the reasonings before adduced, thus treating it as a question still open to farther investigation. For my own part, Gentlemen, I cannot help bowing under the weight of authority, though my reason may remain unconvinced; but when I am told, by a learned counsel, that such and such arguments refute an opinion, I most honestly and conscientiously entertain, I cannot shrink from the contest. I will set my reasons in array against his, and shew you why his opinion ought not to prevail. I know my inability to contend with my learned friend, but I will, on such a challenge, descend into the lists once again, and renew the combat in so good a cause.— On a late occasion, my learned friend began with stating, that what amounts to a levying of war, must be a question of law; that was his first maxim. I can only state again, from my Lord Hale, that he entertains exactly the opposite opinion, expressly declaring that what is a levying of war, is in truth, and must be a question of fact alone. I will state also what is said in Mr. East's book of pleas of the Crown, from the manuscript summary already spoken of, 'It must in general be difficult in the inception of intestine troubles, to fix the period when opposition to the established government shall be said to wear the formidable appearance of insurrection, and to constitute what in the terms of the Act, is called a levying of war against the King; it is strictly, therefore, a question of fact to be tried by the jury under all the circumstances.' Such is the text drawn from the purest authorities, that is the law of the land; does it or does it not contradict the assertion of my learned friend the Attorney General, and which of us is right? When I am accused of contending against grave authorities, my learned friend must take his share of that censure, for his argument is at variance with the greatest. Sir Matthew Hale says, " what shall be said to be a levying of war, is in truth a question of fact, and requires many circumstances to give it that denomination, which it may be difficult to enumerate or to define;" but because it is difficult to enumerate and define what the circumstances are beforehand, therefore I contend, in opposition to that doctrine, that it must be a question in each case for the jury; and if that were otherwise, if the judges are at liberty, in violation of the plain letter of the statute of Edward the III, to take upon them to create treasons by construction, and ingraft a new offence upon it, I say the statute had better not have passed; instead of securing the subject, it would only lead to what Sir Matthew Hale calls a new set of constructive and interpretative treasons; which we ought to be very wary in multiplying, for no man can say where it will end.

My learned friend speaks in the language of panegyric of the judges who have pronounced opinions upon that subject; and I am not disposed to speak of the late judges, Mr. Justice Foster in particular, and Lord Chief Justice Holt, in any terms but those of the highest respect. But Mr. Justice Foster does not affect to lay down his opinion as a matter of authority, because he states it, for he founds it on decisions, to which he refers as the premises on which his conclusion rests. To us, who are in the habit of boasting that the law is the perfection of reason, it can never be improper to inquire, whether authorities are consonant with reason, or whether they support the inference, and above all, whether they can be reconciled with the words of the Act of parliament, from which alone the judges derive their power. Then see what the act provides: "As the justices of our Lord the King assigned in divers counties have adjudged persons guilty of treasons, for divers causes unknown to the law, may it please our Lord the King, and the great and wise men of the land, to declare the pains of treason in this present parliament." The statute then lays down, that compassing the death of the King is treason, and so is levying war against the King in his realm. It then enumerates and defines other acts, which shall also be deemed treason, and proceeds to that most remarkable provision, that if any new case shall arise, the judges shall not presume to decide it, but shall refer it to the King and his Parliament to pronounce whether it be treason or not. Upon this clause Lord Coke speaks in language the most forcible and pointed; "If that be not within the words of this Act, then by force of a clause hereafter, it cannot be adjudged treason, until it be declared treason by parliament, which is the remedy in that case which the makers of the law provided." But, gentlemen, you well know that the judges are not the makers of the law, but the expounders; they are not to legislate, but to interpret what is really doubtful, which this Act is not; for the same Lord Coke lays it down, that " nothing is left to the construction of the judge, if it be not specified and particularized before by this Act. A happy sanctuary or place of refuge for judges to fly unto, that no man's blood and ruin of his family do lie upon their consciences against law!" And all this for a clear reason, which he had before announced in language which, though rather quaint, is neither inelegant nor unfeeling, and which I will take the liberty of reading to you. " All this was done in several ages, that the fair lilies and roses of the crown might flourish, and not be stained by severe and sanguinary statutes." This then was the object of King Edward III, and his parliament and I ask you whether this object was not violated, when, in opposition to such express provisions, instead of going to the Parliament for a declaration of new treason, the judges in the reign of Henry VIII, declared that the rising of workmen to enhance wages, was a levying of war against the King in his realm. That is the foundation of the whole system of constructive treason, and the authority to which the cases all refer; for the judges of late times, whom we all agree to honour, did not deduce their opinion from the statute itself, but thought themselves bound to hold that opinion, because Henry the eighth's judges formerly professed a similar one.

Now, gentlemen, let me suppose that this Act had passed only the last summer, instead of five hundred years ago, with this enactment, that nothing should be treason but what is there rehearsed; if the parliament had said to judges, we make this Act for the purpose of defining and restricting your powers, and preventing you from extending the letter of the law, by any construction whatever; if you, Gentlemen, had been impanelled as a jury to try whether a particular offence described in the Act had been committed, what would have been your surprize at hearing from any judge, that you had no right to attend to what parliament had done;—that though parliament had referred the question to your conscience and judgment, you must act on the conscience and judgment of the court? Upon such an occasion, the question arising for the first time on a recent Act, I presume no jury would be disposed to pay much deference to that doctrine: but after a lapse of ages, the abuse becomes inveterate; and though commencing in bad times and continuing in the worst, at last it assumes the character of that very law which it repeals, and judges and juries forgetting their sacred functions, and thinking only how to please and flatter the crown, conspire to render it incurable. The first authority is under Henry the VIIIth, the second under Charles II, and from that time the subject is continued to the case of Damaree and Purchase, which my learned friend on this occasion has abstained from mentioning; that case, I still confidently submit, cannot be law. Sir Matthew Hale says, it is a question of fact, a special verdict is found stating all the facts; for whom? the judges. What have judges to do with the facts? they are for the jury to decide. Even supposing it proper for a judge to define to the jury what a levying of war is, that it is a rising for a general purpose; having stated that, they had no right to go farther; they should have said, tell us whether these men joined in a rising to effect a general purpose? But it could not be correct for the judges to pronounce why the prisoners abused the Presbyterians the friends of the then government, and cried " down with the meeting-houses, and up with " Doctor Sacheverel!" If, indeed, Queen Anne being in possession of the crown to the disparagement of her brother, the Pretender's right, their hostility to meeting-houses was a mere pretence for cloaking designs against her government, that covert intention would have properly given a treasonable character to their outrages. But that, like all other questions of intention, should have been left to the consideration of the jury, and could, on no just principle, be decided by the judges. You have heard before of the drunken porter Purchase, who joined these rioters, in perfect ignorance of their object, saying only he would go as far as any of them in the cause; and I will read what Mr. Justice Foster says of his offence. Damaree was pardoned, and three of the judges thought Purchase was not guilty, nine of them I suppose holding that he was guilty; this man likewise was pardoned; both were pardoned; which gives fair reason to suppose that the construction of law which condemned them was doubted at the time. "The case of Purchase (says Mr. Justice Foster) came far short of Damaree's, both in a legal and a moral view;" what was Damaree's offence, in a legal view? high treason. There cannot be degrees of high treason. Treason is a higher felony than murder, and murder a higher felony than larceny, but there are no degrees of high treason;" this man's offence therefore comes far short of treason, in Mr. Justice Foster's opinion; he agrees with the three judges who dissented. I am very well content to take the opinion of Mr. Justice Foster in diminishing the mass of treason, in lessening the great evil arising from constructive treasons, and the more so, because he thought the authorities in favour of such constructive treasons, too strong to be resisted in general. This is the opinion which Lord Hale avowed, lamenting that constructive treasons should ever have been adopted; and though he defers to the authority of his brother judges, withdrawing his own sanction from the propriety of extending the law to any case not expressly named in the statute.

My learned friend's quotation from Lord Chief Justice Holt, I own surprised me. If that was the only Case to be found since the revolution, and in honest times, it does but little towards removing us from our position. He says, "there may be a levying of war against the King, without immediate danger to his person," that I never disputed; for if, in old times, the Prince of Wales, or any of the leading nobles of the realm, had engaged in a conspiracy, and proceeded to take a castle, though the King was not within it, or attack the royal forces, though not under the immediate orders of the King, war might be levied and treason committed. But does that admission conform to the construction, that pulling down brothels is levying war against the King; is it possible to connect these two cases, by any reasonable analogy? yet that was war according to the servile judges of the reign of Charles II. L..d Chief Justice Hale dissented; and where judges dissent from the authority of their brethren, so closely intervoven with their own, there cannot be a stronger argument in favour of the justness of that principle, which induces their separation. In another case the judges were equally divided, and left the law uncertain; but with that, I will not trouble you; my object is to expose the weakness of the argument drawn from Lord Chief Justice Holt's expression, on the trial of Sir John Friend, " There may be a war levied, without any design upon the King's person, or endangering of it, which, if actually levied, is high treason; as for example, if persons do assemble themselves, and act with force, in opposition to some law, which they think inconvenient, and hope thereby to get it repealed." Now that is not the point decided; it is no more than an example by way of illustration; why it would not be high treason to conspire to levy war, unless that war was actually levied. Sir John Friend had thus shaped his defence; "you charge me with compassing the King's death; and you prove merely, that I conspired to levy war against him; now, conspiring to levy war is not high treason, unless it is actually levied." This was true, but not applicable; for the Chief Justice encounters it by a very satisfactory answer, "You are not indicted for levying war, but for a treason of a different class: you are charged with compassing the death of the King, and a conspiracy to levy direct war, though none were levied, is an overt act, and evidence of an intention to compass his death." And then he states the whole distinction between direct and constructive war. I am so far from feeling, that this little incidental example affects the general reasoning we have advanced, that I think the citation of it, a striking argument of the little confidence reposed by my learned friend, in the correctness of his own propositions.

On the present occasion, no notice has been taken of Damaree and Purchase's case; and having said already, what I thought right about it, I have only to request that you will bear the arguments in mind. But, in defining, by what criterion a levying of war shall be distinguished from a riot; it is contended, that if the object be not private and peculiar, and referrable to the interests of the individuals acting, but of a more general nature, it shall cease to be riot, and pass by the name of war. I admit that to be a distinction, but I deny that it is the only one, or at all times conclusive. In truth, it only draws the line between treason and one particular description of offence which bears some resemblance to it. To make treason, a peculiar purpose will not do; the purpose must be general; but an intelligible purpose is supposed in either case. That distinction is introduced by the statute of Edward III, which declares, that if people shall ride armed over the country merely to make war against one another, though that justly might be considered levying war, yet it shall not be levying war against the King. Though it is the King's duty to preserve the laws from being invaded, and the country from being endangered by civil commotions; yet it is expressly declared, that such private quarrels, however furious and extensive, shall not be treason. To constitute treason, the quarrel must be against the state, and when it is conducted with competent force, it becomes a levying of war against the King. This definition however is questioned on the other side; the success of the enterprize is pronounced immaterial; and most undoubtedly so it is; but it is moreover asserted, that the means need not be competent to effect the object proposed: another attack on high authority, for I can refer to the present Lord Chief Justice of England, for the language I employed. " It is not necessary, (said his lordship) that there should be an armed force, for it is laid down with great propriety and good sense, that if any force be raised competent to the purpose, that shall be considered by law, as a levying of war." In this proposition, my learned friend finds something absurd :—competent to the purpose, he exclaims, " that can never be an ingredient in the definition of treason; for if the purpose be revolution, and the force competent, the offenders could not be brought to punishment, since the competent force would subvert the old government, and the new one would feel nothing but gratitude to the insurgents who established it." I must honestly confess, without meaning anything uncivil to my learned friend, that does strike me as much more like a quibble than an argument: for to be competent to a purpose, is not the same thing as being sure to effect it; and we know that means are frequently set in motion competent to an end which they do not attain, because injudiciously employed, or accidentally defeated, or overpowered by superior force. As to the treason of compassing the death of the King, the most trifling act, presenting a pinch of snuff, if there be poison in it, might accomplish that purpose: any act revealing the treasonable mind is sufficient: but in levying war to subvert the State, something like a competency to the purpose; something like a rational proportion, between the instruments and the object, is rendered necessary by that statute, which is the polar star to guide all our decisions upon this subject.

I find in my notes another observation which I think I have already answered. It was urged, where levying war is mentioned in the statute, a direct war against the person of the King cannot be alone contemplated, for that would have been already comprised in the provision against compassing his death. But I have already admitted, that cases may exist; as, where his castle or his troops were assailed in his absence by a rebellious force,—which would amount to a clear levying of war against the King, without the contemplation of violence against the royal person; there is therefore no inconsistency in providing against both cases.

In his general discussion of the law, my learned friend has now resorted to a new and very refined piece of logic, raised on a particular phrase in the Act, and I was unfortunate enough to interrupt my learned friend when he first produced it, not really knowing there was such a word in the act. The prisoner is tried for levying war against the King in his realm; that is the charge against him in the language of the legislature; but in a clause at the conclusion, a different language is introduced, and applied to all the treasons enumerated; "and it is to be understood that in the cases above rehearsed, that ought to be adjudged treason which extends to our Lord the King and his Royal Majesty." These last words, by a curious legal manœuvre, are attempted to be imported into the earlier part of the statute, which would then be read thus: "it shall be treason to levy war not only against the King, but also, as a distinct offence, against His Royal Majesty;" and then the construction is to be raised. But this would equally apply to all the other treasons; " imagining the death of our Lord the King, or our Lady the Queen, of their eldest son and heir, violating the King's companion," and so on; bringing false money into this realm, counterfeit to the money of England, and all the others. I do most strenuously contend against this inference and strain of wit, for it would lead to consequences far more extravagant, than any the most constructive judges have ever thought of. It would extend to every opposition to a sheriff, who executes civil process in the King's name, and so conducts one of the most important functions of the royal authority; it would be treason to commit the slightest violence against the peace of our Lord the King, his crown and dignity; and though no intention to endanger the royal person or to interfere with his government were harboured, his Royal Majesty would be infringed, on this supposition, and a war be levied against him in his realm by every riot, trespass, and assault committed within his dominions.

So much, Gentlemen, for what my learned friend advanced; but observe also how much he passed over. I heard nothing urged by him against the argument arising out of the several riot Acts, which I trust you have not forgotten. I repeat that yet unanswered question; If to assemble for the purpose of breaking down all inclosures, and so on, was levying war against the King, why was the Act of Edward VI passed? By that Act, when twelve persons or more assemble for the purpose of changing the religion established, and of breaking the law, they shall be guilty of high treason, not in all cases, but only in case they continue together for a certain period of time, and do not disperse after proclamation made. That law enacted in the reign of Edward VI, re-enacted with alterations in the reign of Queen Mary, and again put in force by an Act against rebellious riots in the reign of George I, never could have been made if the offences described were high treason before. I wait for a reply, for I have heard none yet; and I shall beg your attention to that reply, when it falls to my learned friend's turn to address you.

These statutes suggest another illustration of my leading principle; they prescribe certain penalties against persons assembled to the number of twelve or more. Suppose it had been handed down to us, that in an arbitrary reign, soon after the first of those laws was enacted, some judge had thus addressed a jury: " Gentlemen, you see it declared by this Act, that twelve persons meeting, shall incur the penalties of the Act; now the danger is the same in an assembly of eleven, though not within the words it is within the mischief of the law, and the judges therefore have agreed to make that treason by construction."—Perhaps the Act might have said, that judges should have no such power, that all construction should be excluded; but no matter, Lord Chief Justice Jefferies, when he went the western circuit, and destroyed by wholesale the unfortunate men who had been with the Duke of Monmouth, always recognised the principle, that within the legal meaning of that Act, eleven were equal to twelve. Gentlemen, could this be endured? would any jury submit to it? It is not to be supposed that in such times as these, such a thing could be attempted; but it is against adopting, in humane and enlightened times, the sanguinary practice of reigns half barbarous, that I appeal to reason, common sense, and law. With the opinions, gentlemen, which I entertain, I might, if the course of proceeding were different, carry this important point to the consideration of a Court of higher resort, and obtain a decision from judges of higher authority, but that cannot be done here;

the argument must be stated in the course of my appeal to you, or not at all. You have heard the contention on both sides; and I ask you confidently, have I argued the point on fair principles, and have they received a satisfactory answer? My learned friends rely on argument, inference, and construction; I stand upon the plain letter of a most intelligible statute, which ordains, that no construction of law shall ever be applied to it, and that any case which is not mentioned therein, shall be disposed of, not by the judges who had formerly abused their power, but by our Lord the King and his Parliament.

This is my answer to the elaborate arguments, which the learned Attorney General found it necessary to adduce; in reply to our clear and simple legal propositions, to my own mind, the answer we have offered, carries complete conviction; but the decision rests with you.

Having thus argued the law, observed on the facts, and gone through the evidence as well as I can, not pretending to specify every little circumstance, and admitting (which it would be folly to deny) that there has been great and outrageous mischief committed and threatened in Pentridge and the neighbouring parishes, in the first place, are you satisfied that you can truly call the tumult a levying war against the King in his realm; in the second place, as to this poor unfortunate man, walking with a pike in his hand, with all the motives that so evidently actuated him, is he sufficiently proved to have partaken of any general purpose, to be considered guilty of the enormous offence of high treason? These are the questions to be tried, and you will try them calmly and dispassionately. I am sure, that if you feel it a case of doubt, if you feel that the prisoner has not been fairly and conclusively affected by the evidence, of that doubt you will gladly give him the advantage. Such would be the direction of learned judges in any case; but in this, the most important of all, it is your peculiar duty to watch with jealousy, the extension of the letter of so clear a law, and to be perfectly convinced in the words of my Lord Coke, that the evidence is brought home to the prisoner, not probably, but proveably; not by arguments and inferences, and strains of wit, but by plain, direct and manifest proof, before you return a verdict of condemnation. If the smallest tittle of that proof should be wanting, you are bound by the oath you have taken, to acquit the prisoner. But, Gentlemen, in this case, wherever we turn our eyes, we are encountered by fresh doubts, doubts at least upon the law, doubts on the character of the transactions, doubts on the effect of the evidence, doubts on the credit due to the accomplices from whom it proceeded, doubts as to the motives, doubts as to the expressions. The prisoner was but a few hours with the party: when he left, we do not precisely know, but it was certainly before the dragoons came up; and in the absence of all direct and positive evidence, I submit that so many doubts on the one side, amount to absolute certainty on the other. On retiring from the box, and minutely examining the evidence, if your minds cannot be clearly and fully satisfied that this unfortunate man was guilty of the high offence imputed to him, you will rejoice in the verdict you must then pronounce. By whom these few poor unhappy and miserable wretches were corrupted and seduced from the path of duty, we are still entirely uninformed; was not that a doubt worth removing? No such attempt has been made, and it casts upon the whole proceeding, a cloud of the blackest suspicion. You will ask yourselves why it has been kept back, and not convict a man upon evidence thus managed and selected, and upon a few circumstances picked out of a long series of transactions, without knowing the origin and source of all, and who it was that tempted the miserable captain to betray these ignorant villagers into guilt and ruin.

It will then, gentlemen, be your happy privilege to give a turn to these prosecutions; this victim must be saved by your verdict; for the proof is manifestly defective, and the case abounds with doubt. I revert not to the past; but how enviable is your distinction, how blessed the lot that Providence has cast upon you! The waters of wrath are beginning to subside; it is for you to hold out the olive branch, the auspicious symbol of pardon, hope, and joy. Yours will be the blessing of the peace-makers, yours will be the blessing of the merciful, who shall obtain that mercy which they extend to others. You will feel, with exalted pleasure, that your feelings can be reconciled with your duty; you will return to your homes with undoubting consciences, and embrace your families with arms unstained by blood; you will leave to your children, as their best inheritance, the memory of that just and humane verdict, the record of your honesty, your firmness, and your independence, which will be the pride and glory of your latest posterity, as long as that constitution endures, which is indebted for its life, its health, and its excellence, to the trial by Jury.

Mr. Justice Abbott. Isaac Ludlam, if you wish to say anything in addition to the observations of your Counsel, you are at liberty to do so; and this is the proper time for you to do it.

Isaac Ludlam. I will leave it to my Counsel, my lord.

REPLY.

Mr. SOLICITOR GENERAL.

May it please your Lordship,

Gentlemen of the Jury,

IT now becomes my painful duty to reply to the observations which have been made on the part of the prisoner by his Counsel; and to call back your attention from the powerful appeal which has been made to your feelings, by my learned friend who last addressed you, to that which you alone have to consider upon the present occasion, the facts and the law as applicable to this Case. Gentlemen, your decision is not to be influenced by those feelings, which every man must entertain upon an occasion like the present towards the unfortunate prisoner at the bar; nor is your verdict to be affected by any thing which has taken place upon former trials, or by what may succeed the present; your decision is to be formed upon the facts of this particular Case, and to those alone your attention will be by me directed.

Gentlemen, the situation which I fill upon the present occasion precludes me, even if my inclination were not in unison with my duty, from addressing any topics to you, which can either excite your prejudices or your feelings. To my learned friends who addressed you for the prisoners, that is reserved, and properly so; but to me, the single duty remains of calmly, temperately, dispassionately, without attempting, as I have already said, to rouse your prejudices or to influence your feelings, addressing what I have to say upon this subject to your understandings, and to your understandings alone.

Gentlemen, I had expected, from the discussions which have already at so much length taken place in the course of these trials, that I should not have had the task of addressing you again upon the subject of the law of the Case; and for a great length of time in the course of this trial, during the whole indeed of the speech of the learned counsel who first spoke to you, and the greater part of my learned friend Mr. Denman's address, I was confirmed in the notion, that the point was at rest, and that it would have been perfectly unnecessary for me to say one syllable upon the law, as it applies to the charge now preferred against the prisoner at the bar, and that I might confine myself to what I humbly apprehend to be your province and your duty upon the present occasion.

Gentlemen; what is the constitution of the trial by jury, of which every Englishman is so proud, and the pre-eminence of which he boasts, over all the legal institutions of other countries? It is, that the prisoner accused of a crime shall be tried by twelve of his fellow-subjects, who are to determine upon the facts; and that the judges of the land, persons of education, of experience, of learning, who have made the law of the country their peculiar study, are to explain that law, and state it to the jury who are assembled, as you are, to decide upon the guilt or innocence of the person accused; but that with the judges, and with them only, shall be confided the exposition of the law upon which those jurymen are to act; and I must confess, that with all that respect which I and every man must entertain for the talents and abilities of my learned friend who last addressed you, and which have been so conspicuously displayed upon the present trials, I was surprised to hear him urge, upon the first trial, and to hear it repeated upon the present, that there is a distinction with respect to the crime of high treason; for such there is, if he be correct; that there is, I say, a distinction in the trial of the offence of high treason, from every other which can be brought before you for your decision; and that, upon that most heinous of all crimes in our penal code, you are to judge, not only of the facts but of the law of the case; I say, I was surprised, because I verily believe it was the first time that such a proposition ever was laid down in a Court of justice; it is unconfirmed by any former decision, and unsupported, I will venture to say, by a single authority or writer on the subject. I therefore beg leave to state to you with great humility, but at the same time with the utmost confidence, that I shall be confirmed in what I say by the judges who preside upon this occasion, that that is not the law of the land, but that the crime of high treason is to be tried like every other crime; you are to hear, from the learned judges, what, in point of law, constitutes the offence, and then you are to be the judges whether the facts proved bring the prisoner's case within that law or not.

Gentlemen, my learned friend, in his argument on the law, which he has resumed to day, has stated to you, that the language of the Act of parliament is plain, with respect to levying war against the King, and that you are the proper persons to judge of the construction of that Act of parliament. What authority does my learned friend produce for this ? Who, by the constitution of the country, is to expound the meaning of an Act of parliament upon any subject ? Is it you, who from your situation in life, and from your pursuits and studies, cannot be supposed to understand correctly the laws of the country, or the expositions of Acts of parliament ; or is it the learned judges of the land ? Gentlemen, I beg leave to state, that with respect to the construction of this or any Act of parliament (if the construction were doubtful in this case, which I will shew you that it is not ;) if this Act of parliament, instead of having been passed so many centuries ago, and having received so many decisions upon it, had passed the last session, still you are bound to receive the exposition of it, from the learned judges; that you are not yourselves to put the construction upon it, but to receive it from those by whom by the law it is directed to be explained ; therefore taking my learned friend's instance, if this was the first case tried upon this Act of parliament, you would be bound to receive the construction to be put upon that Act, from the judges who preside upon this occasion. But that however is not the fact here; and though my learned friend considers it as a misfortune upon the prisoner at the bar and those to be tried, that this Act passed so long ago, and that decisions have taken place, which have left no doubt upon the law of the Case; yet you, on the contrary, and every one who hears me will, I am sure, congratulate yourselves that this is not the first Case, and that the learned judges are not for the first time considering this Act of Parliament and its construction, but that they have before them decisions upon it, unvaried from their commencement down to the present period, acted upon, century after century, till at last the current of decisions is so clear and uniform, that no writer upon the subject entertains the slightest doubt upon it.

Without tiring you or fatiguing the Court with citing authorities upon that which has been already so ably laid down in this place, upon the former trials, I will state, in the language of a former Chief Justice of the King's Bench, that the uniform decision, the decision from the very time this Statute has passed down to the present, has been, that an insurrection of the sort (I call it an insurrection) which has taken place in this Case, is most certainly and unquestionably high treason within the law as it stands. Gentlemen, I will just read to you a passage from the argument of the Chief Justice in the Case of Purchase and Damaree, who joined with others in pulling down meeting houses: " when a multitude is assembled, and force used, not for any private end or revenge, but upon a pretence which is public and general, it has, *in all ages*, been adjudged a levying war against the King, and high treason." I am citing this from the Chief Justice's argument and judgment in that Case, in the reign of Queen Anne; and he states, as you hear, that to have been adjudged in all ages a levying war against the Crown, and high treason; and the other learned judges upon that occasion had no doubt upon the law. My learned friend has most ingeniously endeavoured to satisfy you that three of the judges differed in that Case from the others; but in what did they differ? not upon the law of the Case, but upon the facts found; they doubted whether Purchase had been sufficiently shewn to have been privy to the design the other parties had in view, and therefore they doubted, upon the whole, whether he was guilty of the high treason, imputed to him; but they had not the least particle of doubt upon the general law; the whole of them concurred that if he was a party to the transaction, and privy to the views of the others, he was as much guilty of high treason as the rest, for that the law of high treason, as applicable to that Case, was unequivocal and clear.

Then my learned friend has stated that, which as a lawyer I confess I was again surprised at; he stated upon the former occasion, which I then omitted to notice, that it was most clearly a question for the jury; for if it were not why did they find a special verdict in the Case of Damaree and Purchase? why, that very circumstance shews, that my learned friend's principle is wrong; he said he did not understand why they found a special verdict, and referred it to the judges for their decision. I will tell him why; it was because they did not consider themselves, and were not the judges of the law; they said, we will find the facts upon this occasion, because we doubt how far the law may apply to those facts, and had rather that the judges should decide upon the law; and this is not peculiar to high treason; every charge brought before a jury for trial, involves a question of law and fact; the law must define what the offence is, and then the jury must decide whether the facts bring the particular case within that principle of law, and if they doubt upon that question, then it has been the practice to refer that question to the learned judges, who are to decide upon that law; for illustration:— Take a common instance; I dare say many of you have been in the habit of serving upon juries at the assizes; a man is there indicted for burglary; who is to determine what a burglary is? we must refer for that purpose to what the law says shall constitute the offence of burglary, and the judge, acting upon that law, will tell the jury it must be a breaking of the house in the night time, with an intent to commit felony; the judge therefore would say to the jury, such is the offence of burglary, and then he would observe upon the facts proved, and would say, that if the jury were satisfied upon those facts, that the man broke into the house, that he broke into it by night, and with the intent to commit felony, that it would be their duty to convict the man; but the jury, in such a case, are not to act upon their own conception of the law; thus, suppose a question to arise, whether the man broke the house, and it be proved that he thrust his hand through the window (which has been adjudged a breaking;) whether that be a breaking in law is a point for the judges to decide, and upon whose opinion therefore the jury are bound to act, without considering the consequences which may follow upon their verdict; but upon the fact of the man's putting his hand through the window, the jury are the only judges. I hope I have made the distinction intelligible, and whilst upon this part of the subject, I should observe, that the Attorney General did not, according to my recollection, use the expressions which are imputed to him; he did not tell you that, whether there had been, in point of fact, a levying of war or not, is for the judges; but that, what is a levying of war within the meaning of the Act of parliament, is for them to consider, but that then it was for the jury to determine whether the facts brought the case within that law; such was the proposition of the Attorney General; and that proposition, I beg leave to maintain, as that which is the law of the land, and by which you are to be guided upon the present occasion.

Then, without tiring you with any laborious examination of all the authorities upon the subject, (because I cannot help thinking, to use an expression which I have heard in the course of these trials, from the highest authority, as much simplicity as possible is desirable, with respect to the statement of the law to you,) I venture to state to you, without having recourse to the technical language used upon this indictment, that if there be a rising of a considerable number of persons armed, in order to carry into effect some general public purpose against the government of the country, and against the laws as established in the country, that is high treason. My friend, Mr. Denman, said, why, if a general public purpose is to be the criterion, then, if this country were invaded; (I think that was the case he put) and a number of persons were assembled for the public purpose of repelling that invasion, that is high treason. Why really, my learned friend's good sense must have instantly seen the misapplication of his instance; it is to be a public purpose *against* the law and government of the country; whereas, the instance he puts is that, in which they are acting *with* the law, and *in support* of the government. How then does it apply?— If you should be satisfied, after I have commented upon the evidence, that this was a rising *to support* the laws and the government, undoubtedly you are bound to acquit the prisoner; but if the purpose be that, which I am sure I shall be able to satisfy you, it was (though, when I say I am sure, do not rely upon that assurance, because you are to decide upon the evidence,) but if I satisfy you, that the purpose was to arm themselves *against* the constituted authorities of the kingdom, and to effect a change in the laws; I say, that constitutes the offence of high treason, and is nothing short of high treason; and therefore, the only questions as I apprehend upon the present occasion, will be, whether there was this rising; whether the insurgents had that intent; and whether the unfortunate man at the bar concurred in the common object? those are the three points which you should keep steadily in view. Has there been a rising of armed persons? what has been the object; has it been against the laws and government of the country? If you can satisfy yourselves upon these two points, upon which I am sure you will entertain no doubt, then I agree with my friend Mr. Cross, who first addressed you; you have that most solemn and important duty imposed upon you, to consider whether the prisoner, Isaac Ludlam, was a party concuring in these objects, and acting with a view to their completion.

Gentlemen, in considering this question, I am as anxious as my learned friends can be, that you should consider it with reference to this case, and to this case only. I regret myself, that any allusion has been made by my friend Mr. Denman, in the way in which he has made it, to the former cases which have been tried. I doubt whether the Attorney General, in the fair and candid opening which he made of this case, made the slightest allusion to the convictions which have taken place; they are not unquestionably to operate upon your minds, and I trust they will not; but if they are not to operate to the prejudice of the prisoner at the bar, unquestionably they are not to be used in his favour. The argument is not to be used, that, because the persons have been already convicted, if a third case presents itself, in which it is clearly proved that the party against whom the charge is made is guilty, you are therefore to acquit the third prisoner; the consequences to follow upon your verdict, if a verdict of guilty are in the breasts of other persons, and you have nothing to do with them. It has been said by my learned friend, in the outset of his address to you, that it seems public justice is not yet satisfied, and that a third person is now presented to you for trial. Gentlemen, the course adopted by my learned friends on the other side, of challenging separately, made it necessary for us to proceed step by step, and to take single individuals for trial; it was impossible for us to try them together, and therefore it became necessary that your attention and that of the county should be wearied by taking them singly; when justice will be satisfied, it is for other persons to consider. I am sure, that speaking for myself, and for my friend the Attorney General, it is not our wish, (indeed, wish we can have none upon the subject,) that any greater number of examples, or any greater number of convictions should take place, than clearly will satisfy the justice of the case; but we are presenting, as we apprehend, before you, those persons who took the most active part in the transaction, who in many respects were the leaders, if I may use the expression, of this insurrection which took place, and who by their presence, and by their conduct, animated and excited those who were joined with them to the attainment of their object, and endeavoured, as well by their example as by their conduct, to assist in the completion of it. Therefore, do not let your minds be affected by the consideration of any circumstances extraneous to this case: keep your attention steadily and uniformly to the case before you.

Complaint, I recollect, was made by my learned friend, (who chooses to allude to these things, and therefore forces from me the observation), complaint was made, when the first man was tried, that we had selected the man who was the leader in the transaction, and we were accused of a sort of management of the proceedings upon this occasion in having taken him first. But now, when we come to try another man, that unquestionably is no longer imputed to us, but they say it was the natural course to have taken; and that, inasmuch as the ringleaders, as they are styled by my learned friends, have been already convicted, then you are to guard your minds against proceeding step by step, from the stronger to the weaker case, lest you should at last thereby be led to the conviction of a person who had little to do with the transaction. Gentlemen, your province is to try, whether Isaac Ludlam, the prisoner at the bar, is guilty, or not, of high treason. Dismiss from your minds the recollection that any former trial has taken place; dismiss from your minds the recollection of Brandreth and William Turner, and recollect that you are trying this person only; and that, whether other persons have been tried, or not, is not to weigh a feather in the scale: and that you are to determine this case upon its own merits alone, and upon the evidence produced in support of this case, or in answer to it on the part of the prisoner.

Having divested your minds of all prejudice, of all feelings of compassion, except as they are produced by the evidence in the particular case, let us come now to consider, as I trust I shall do, calmly and dispassionately, the evidence produced in this case; and if I am betrayed into any apparent warmth upon the occasion, believe me, that I have no object whatever, but that public justice should be done. It is not my wish that one fact should be strained, one inference drawn against the prisoner at the bar, except as it is fairly and legitimately warranted by the evidence which has been produced in the case. Then what are the questions which you have to try? First, was there a rising? the fact is not disputed, it is admitted; indeed it has been proved by such overwhelming evidence, that no man alive can doubt about it; that on the night of the 9th of June there were considerable bodies of armed men acting in concert, forcing arms from the houses of the persons they attacked, compelling men into their ranks, and all proceeding with one common object towards Nottingham; that is a fact which cannot be disputed; nor is it attempted to be so. What was their object? Have you any doubt about that? Have you any doubt that at the meeting on Sunday the 8th of June, at the White Horse, this rising was in contemplation, that preparations were made for it, and that the object was to overturn the present government? the evidence on this point of intention, is not confined to the meeting which took place on Sunday the 8th of June, for you have declarations made from time to time in the course of their progress, that such was their object, and that they expected success in taking possession of the town of Nottingham.

Gentlemen, if such be the rising and such the object, then we come to the part Isaac Ludlam took in this transaction; and here bear in mind the defence attempted to be made for him; there is not a single witness to contradict any fact we have proved; it is therefore clear he was in that body, and acting with that body, as I shall by and by shew to you; then what is the defence attempted to be made? bear that in mind, and then follow me in the facts proved upon this occasion. My friend, Mr. Cross, puts his defence upon the ground of compulsion; Mr. Denman says it was either compulsion or fatherly affection which induced him to follow this party, in order to draw from it, as soon as he possibly could, those two unfortunate young men his sons, who it appears also took a part in the transaction; therefore the defence set up, is either compulsion or paternal affection. Gentlemen, would to God they could have proved either upon this occasion, because I am sure it would have been a most satisfactory conclusion for you to have arrived at, if you could with honest minds, and in a faithful discharge of your duty, have acquitted the prisoner at the bar of the present charge. Now let us see how the facts stand, and whether it is possible to contend that either the one motive or the other actuated the mind of the prisoner at the bar, in the part which he took in these transactions.

On Sunday the 8th of June, there is a meeting at the White Horse at Pentridge, at which Brandreth, William Turner, and many other of the persons whose names you have heard in the course of this trial, met. You have heard many observations upon the testimony given by the two witnesses who have proved that transaction; it will be for you certainly to consider the weight which is due to them. I must confess it appears to me, that little or no inroad whatever has been made upon their credit, by the observations which have been made; and I could not help observing (but it will happen to us all when we are arguing untenable points) the difficulties by which my learned friend Mr. Denman was pressed in arguing that question; he says, if they spoke truly we might have confirmed them, and that they on the prisoner's part could not contradict them, in any part, because, he says, all the persons who were present at that transaction are named in this indictment, and therefore they are precluded from calling them; and yet in the very same breath he told you that we had an opportunity of calling Cope, Booth, and Elsden. He has also the opportunity of calling them if he pleases, and yet he does not choose to do it. My friend says, he has not a possibility of calling any witnesses to contradict the facts, and yet those persons are competent witnesses. Mrs. Weightman, who keeps the house, is a competent witness; I know not what family she has; there is a little girl mentioned; those persons might have been called to contradict Martin and Asbury, if they could have been contradicted; and they are not called.

My friend says, why did you not call some of those persons to confirm them? I will tell you why; because if two witnesses prove a fact satisfactorily, it would be (I was going to use my friend's own expression) ridiculous; it would be vain to prove it farther. We might have called all the persons whose houses were attacked, and every person who knew any thing of the transaction, and your time might have been occupied much longer in hearing these facts proved over and over again; but we did not consider that consistent with our duty. I assume then as a fact, proved by Martin and Asbury, that Isaac Ludlam was at that meeting, because they do not venture to call any body, not even Mrs. Weightman, to contradict it. I say therefore, that fact is perfectly clear; and when a fact is proved by positive testimony, it receives still further confirmation, if it could be contradicted and is not attempted to be so; a fact proved by two witnesses which could be contradicted if it does not exist, receives confirmation from no attempt made to offer such contradiction.

Isaac Ludlam, it appears, went to this meeting in company with William Turner; and you will please to recollect they are both Southwingfield men. William Turner is a Southwingfield man, and so is the prisoner at the bar, Isaac Ludlam. What object had he in going there? was it accidental his going there? did he appear to be unacquainted with the object? did he appear surprised at finding Brandreth, who was a stranger to that part of the country, there. Was he a stranger to him upon that occasion? and when we are told some other persons might have sent Brandreth, I say that the evidence shews that these persons, in the prosecution of their designs had recourse to this man Brandreth, to head them upon this occasion, knowing him to be of the character which has been described.

Not only is Isaac Ludlam there, but what does he do when he is there. You have enquiries made from Turner as to the state of arms in the neighbouring parishes, and he boasts of the forward manner in which the Southwingfield men are conducting themselves, Ludlam himself being a Southwingfield man, making no comment or observation upon that, and therefore admitting in fact that the Southwingfield men, of whom he was one, were thus ready and forward, procuring pike shafts in the open day, which has been proved in evidence; and proved to have been done by persons nearly connected with the prisoner, namely his sons. The prisoner is a man whose faculties are matured, does he remonstrate against what is going forward? does he say, this is a most improper meeting, I will have nothing to do with it; I will not enter into the scheme or the plan, nor shall my sons? remember however that neither of his sons was there, those sons who were supposed to have entered without the consent of their father, and for whose protection he is supposed to have followed; it is the father, and the father alone who is there, and who reads the paper produced by Turner; and what is the deliberation upon that occasion? it is that they are to rise the next night. It is also stated that pikes are prepared, which are in a stone quarry near Ludlam's house. What were pikes prepared for? if this was an enterprise which had just come into the heads of these persons who were there, how came this preparation? It was, that they might arm the persons who were to accompany them on the following night, and terrify other innocent persons into their ranks, that they might create terror as well by their arms as by the number that might accompany them.

Gentlemen, can you doubt about the object of that meeting? My friend has made some observations upon the verses recited; which indeed are most important, for they shew to demonstration what was the object they had in view; it was to animate the persons assembled to an opposition to the government, which fortunately still exists; for the concluding lines are,

"The time is come you plainly see,
When government opposed must be."

And what are the first lines,

" Every man his skill must try,
He must turn out and not deny;"—

He shall not refuse his assistance, and we will compel him to turn out; and upon that they afterwards act.

" No bloody soldiers must he dread;—"

And therefore they were to prepare themselves for an opposition to the King's troops, and for that warfare in which they must necessarily be engaged the moment they were opposed by the troops.

"He must turn out and fight for bread:"—

Such was the language to be used to induce persons to enter the ranks: But, was that the inducement to this prisoner at the bar? had he to fight for bread? have you not in evidence that he was carrying on the occupation of a stone-getter? and have you any proof that he was in want of bread, or that he had suffered those privations under which so many of the lower classes unfortunately laboured during the last winter? No; but this was the argument, the incentive to be held out to those persons who had been suffering those privations, to induce them to join, and to carry into effect those plans which persons having no such pressure upon them were actually contemplating.

"The time is come you plainly see,
When government opposed must be:"—

Those were the lines which were recited by Brandreth, and which were handed about the room in the way which has been described; have you then the least particle of doubt that they were conspiring at that time to rise the next night to carry into effect the purpose they plainly declared upon this occasion? But not only does that purpose appear by the verses, but by the various declarations made, "that no good was to be expected from the government;" "that good could be alone expected from a revolution and a change of affairs:" and the like; such was the language used both before and after Isaac Ludlam was there.

The scheme was, that they should direct their march to Nottingham Forest: they were told by Brandreth, that persons were to be there to meet them; and that persons would come from Chesterfield and places in the North, to unite with them; and a fact took place which shews Nottingham was their object, for Joseph Weightman was dispatched from this meeting, and money was collected to bear his expences to go to Nottingham, and to see whether the people were prepared to receive them on the following night. Are these facts attempted to be contradicted? If Ludlam was not there, and did not concur in these transactions, I say, the evidence of the people in the house might have contradicted it; and if Ludlam was not there, he might have shewn by other testimony where he was. If he had been (I know not any thing of his character) but if he had been in a place of public worship; if he had been attending that duty, instead of coming to this meeting in the afternoon, that might have been proved; if he had been at home, that also might have been proved by some one or other of his family, and therefore it must, I think, be taken as proved beyond the possibility of a doubt, that he was in that room, and that he took part in the discussions. Mr. Denman said, indeed, that they could not call Mrs. Weightman, since the fact was probably that Ludlam was at her house, and that he might have gone there for the purpose of taking his beer; but she might have proved that Brandreth and the other persons were not assembled in the parlour; and that it was a fabrication that there was such an assembly of persons at her house during that day; and therefore her absence confirms the testimony of Martin and Asbury upon this occasion; and nothing which has been said, in my mind, weakens the strength of their evidence.

It is said, however, they were special constables; and why did not they impart this to their masters? Why, Gentlemen, you have it proved, that public as this meeting was for the reception of their friends, the persons introduced into this parlour, and invited to join, were either persons who were their friends, or on whom they thought their threats could have an effect; and these two persons who had been sworn in on the night of Saturday preceding the riot, were sworn in, in expectation of a riot at the Butterley works on Monday; which shows that it was believed such a rising would take place on the Monday, or at some other time. Then, with respect to these persons, Martin and Asbury, they certainly did not, as my learned friend stated to you in his opening, conduct themselves as you or I should have done under similar circumstances; but when you recollect the circumstances in which they were, and the threats that were used; when you recollect that they knew that their masters were prepared for the attack, I say it is not at all unnatural that they should not communicate this. You heard them examined; you saw their demeanor; and it is for you to judge whether there is any thing in their evidence or in their manner at all impeaching the evidence they have given, as to the transactions at the White Horse.

Then, Gentlemen, was Isaac Ludlam compelled to go to the White Horse on the Sunday? was compulsion exerted upon him, when he read that paper produced by William Turner? was it paternal affection to prevent his sons taking a part in this business? they were not there; it was he, and he alone; and yet he is supposed by Mr. Denman to have acted throughout from compulsion, or from paternal affection, to prevent his sons engaging in this matter, as they afterwards did.

But, if this acted upon him on the Sunday, what was it operated upon him on the Monday night, compulsion? Is it in proof that this party ever was near his house to compel him; did they go to Isaac Ludlam's house, as they did to Elijah Hall's, knock him up, insist upon his arms, and insist upon it that if he did not go, his sons should accompany them; nay, more, what arms had he upon that occasion? had Isaac Ludlam a pistol or a gun, which they had forced him to take from his house in order to accompany them? No; the very first time himself and his sons are seen, they are seen apart from any body of the conspirators; they are coming by themselves to Topham's close, and there join the party; and with what arms? with pikes; those pikes which it had been boasted the day before, at the meeting at the White Horse, had been in preparation by the Southwingfield people; and for which they had the hardihood to procure shafts in open day: those deadly instruments which you saw. But the strong observation I am making, is this; if there had been compulsion and force to compel him to join this party, how is it that he joined them at a distance from his own house, at a time when no attack had been made upon it; at a period when, for aught that has been proved (and it could have been proved if the fact were otherwise) the party had never been near his house that evening; and he is seen coming with his two sons; those sons whom the argument is, he anxiously wished to quit the party, and whom he followed in order to prevent their committing any thing which might subject them to future punishment. Yet, to guard and protect these sons, Isaac Ludlam comes armed with one of those instruments they had provided; common sense cannot endure the observation; it was evidently neither compulsion nor paternal affection that induced him to join the party.

But as we proceed in the progress of that march, which those persons made that night, the supposition becomes still more preposterous; for when I come to point your attention, as it will be my duty to do, to the different facts as they took place that night, and the conduct of Isaac Ludlam, there is an end to all notion of compulsion, and an end to every other motive except the participation in the common design, which they all had, of marching to Nottingham for the purpose of opposing the present government, and of overturning it, if they could by possibility effect it. In the march, when they compelled persons to join them, they took care to have some of their partizans in the rear, to prevent any from making their escape, and Isaac Ludlam was appointed as one of the persons of the rear guard; for such was the expression used by one of the witnesses; he was the right hand man of the rear guard, for the purpose of preventing the escape of any persons whom they forced into their ranks.

After he had joined them in Topham's close, with his two sons, they proceeded to Elijah Hall's; there you will recollect what took place; and my learned friend said he would take that, as an instance and test by which Isaac Ludlam was to be tried upon this occasion. He says, and I unquestionably concur with him, you must be satisfied that the mind of the prisoner went along with his conduct. He says, Elijah Hall walked with them with a pike in his hand, and if he had been taken prisoner while marching with them, the case would have been proved apparently against him. Undoubtedly, the single act of his marching with them, and having a pike in his hand, prima facie and unexplained, would have fixed him with the crime of high treason; but what is the fact as it appears with respect to Hall? why, that he was forced into the ranks; that nothing but the danger to which he was exposed compelled him to go with them; if that is the case with Isaac Ludlam, he is not guilty of this offence; but I put the case to you, and you must see that the whole evidence points that way; that he went voluntarily; that no compulsion was used; and that when he had gone, he was the most active of the party, with the exception of William Turner and the captain who led them; that he was in the most important situation, namely, in the rear of those who marched; and that it was his part in the transaction to keep the insurgents together in their places in their march.

They next went to Isaac Walker's, and Bestwick's, and so on; and then there is that which my learned friend did not wish to introduce upon this occasion, but which we must introduce, I mean the unfortunate death of that young man Robert Walters. The prisoner Isaac Ludlam was there. If paternal affection or compulsion had led him there, what induced him to proceed, when he found that where threats would not have the effect of compelling persons to bring their arms, the captain had recourse to actual murder? why did he not then recede from the party? but so far from retiring from them, you will find that he afterwards takes an active part in compelling a person of the name of Dexter, and a person of the name of Hugh Booth, to join them, and that too by the recital of the horrible act which had been just before committed.

Gentlemen, they marched on from Mary Hepworth's, and came to Pentridge-lane; and there one party halted, while another went down to Buckland Hollow, to compel Dexter to join their ranks. Who was of that party that went down to Buckland Hollow? the prisoner Isaac Ludlam. Dexter was compelled by them, in the manner you have heard described, to join their ranks, and he happens to have been very near to Isaac Ludlam in the course of their march; recollect what it was that Isaac Ludlam said upon that occasion. Mr. Denman says, that the Attorney General in his opening laid too much stress upon the circumstance of this man's two sons being of the party, as shewing his concurrence and his activity in the prosecution of the design. Why, you have evidence of it, you have the evidence of what he said to Dexter upon that occasion, which shews, that so far from those two sons of his having gone against his consent, and acted against his parental authority in joining that party, almost the first expression he uses to Dexter is, that he has two sons of the party; in order to induce Dexter to join them, by shewing what strength they had, and with what zeal and activity he was proceeding; "that they were going to Nottingham; that there was a parliament chosen against they got there; and that he expected it would be taken by the time they got there;" he then proceeds in the rear, and there is no obstacle whatever to prevent his escape, for he might have departed at any time, without being seen by the captain or William Turner, or any other person in the front of the body; but instead of doing so, he himself presents, with those persons who composed with him the rear guard, the principal obstacle to the escape of those who desired to get away; he was the only person, with his companions the rear guard, who actually prevented the design of those wishing to escape from being carried into effect. Dexter told you that he attempted to escape in his way up Pentridge, and what prevented him? who was the person that hindered his escaping from this party, by whom murder and devastation had been already committed, and who were in full march towards Nottingham, to execute the purpose which, it appears, not only from the conversation at the White Horse, but from the expressions of this prisoner himself to Dexter, that they had in view? Dexter says, "I stopped behind going along Pentridge-lane, and the prisoner said, 'Come, we must have you forward; you must go on with us; you must not stop; we must have you with us;'" his act and his expression therefore, upon that occasion; shew he was fulfilling the duty to which he was appointed, to the utmost of his exertions, and he actually prevented Dexter from escaping, and compelled him to march on. Dexter had afterwards an opportunity of escape, and instantly embraced it; but there was nothing in the whole progress of this march, which prevented Isaac Ludlam's retiring at any time, but he went on acting throughout. His position you must never forget: he is, from the very time he joins them, from first to last, in the rear of this body.

They then proceed towards Pentridge; and in Pentridge or in Pentridge-lane, Hugh Booth is compelled to join them. You recollect the opposition he made at the time the house was attacked; he came down to them; he expostulated with them, and was actually forced into the ranks by the prisoner, Isaac Ludlam. What! Isaac Ludlam, who was acting from compulsion! Isaac Ludlam, who was merely accompanying these parties for the purpose of protecting his sons, and of withdrawing them from the expedition in which they had embarked! This Isaac Ludlam is one of the most active of the whole party, and actually forces Hugh Booth into the ranks; and upon that occasion used an expression, which if there were any thing wanting in the case, demonstrates that this expedition had been long in his contemplation; for he expresses his satisfaction that it is brought to a head *at last*. " We are going to Nottingham; it is brought to a head at last?" What is brought to a head at last? what is it he exults in? it is, that the insurrection had actually broken out, and that he was himself accompanying it; that this favourite object, which he had long in view, was actually brought to a head. " It is at last brought to a head, and we are going to Nottingham!" Such is the expression of Isaac Ludlam to Hugh Booth, at the time he is forcing him into the ranks; and after this, may I not ask whether this man was not willingly and voluntarily engaged in this transaction? if there were nothing else in the case, this very circumstance proves the active and willing part he took in the transaction; it is decisive evidence of the active mind and the willing consent of this man to the plan; and that it was a thing, not that he had embarked in for the first time that night, but which he had long meditated, and to him it was matter of satisfaction that it was at last brought to a head, and that he was accompanying them in a scheme, which had been so long in contemplation.

Hugh Booth goes on with them to another and most important scene, as it affects the prisoner at the bar; I mean to the Butterley works, where they are accosted by Mr. Goodwin. You will recollect the account given by Mr. Goodwin of that transaction; Isaac Ludlam was still in the rear; he is the last man in the ranks, and therefore with him, as I have so often observed, there was no difficulty of escape, nothing to encounter in order to enable him to evade the party, with whom he was at that time marching. Would to God he had followed Mr. Goodwin's advice; it is true, he had then completed his offence, and had been guilty of high treason; but still, if he had then taken the advice of Mr. Goodwin, he would have shewn that, which never comes too late, he would have evinced some repentance and contrition for the offence of which he had been guilty, and in which he was a participator. Mr. Goodwin points out to him the consequences, so that this is not a man ignorant of what might follow; he knows that if their expedition shall fail, and government shall not be overturned, he has committed the heaviest offence a subject can commit against the state; he has all this set before him; he has it presented to his view by Mr. Goodwin; but his answer is, "No, no, I cannot go back; I am as bad as I can be, I must go on." No, Gentlemen, he was not as bad as he could be; he might have been worse, and was worse in the subsequent part of the transaction; for that subsequent part will shew, that so far from this expostulation having any effect upon him, it soon evaporated from his mind. Mr. Goodwin said to him, "Good God, Isaac, what do you do here upon such an errand as this; go home, you have got a halter about your neck, you will be hanged if you do not leave them and go home." With all this before him, mark his conduct in the subsequent part of the transaction; and indeed, what was his conduct there? what prevented his going into Mr. Goodwin's office, where he would have been protected. Mr. Goodwin actually gave him a shove to go forwards; he knew that the Butterley works were armed, for George Weightman said that they expected an engagement there; the knowledge of that fact shews why they did not attack them; he knew that there was a protection there, but his answer is, " No, no, I cannot go back; I am as bad as I can be, I must go on;" and go on he does. Why then, Gentlemen, not only has this man voluntarily gone with this party from the outset; not only has he accompanied them with his free will, but when he has an opportunity afforded him, when he might have receded and escaped, he declines the offer; he pursues the object with the rest of the party, and he takes a prominent part, a sort of military duty, as connected with this unfortunate transaction; and you will find presently what he does when they come to an inn at Codnor, some hours after this interview with Mr. Goodwin had taken place.

He proceeds with the party as far as Codnor; where you will recollect it being a rainy night, and they having marched several miles, many of them went into a public house called the Glass House, to take refreshment; upon this rainy night, where is Isaac Ludlam after this march, did he go in to take refreshment? No, he had another duty assigned him, and he himself proposed that duty; for it is proved by William Booth, (not the Booth who made his escape at Codnor, but William Booth, who had also been compelled to follow them,) that Isaac Ludlam himself addressed the captain, saying, " we must take care the men do not get away, and we must keep guard at the door, or they will go." Such was the conduct of Isaac Ludlam; true and faithful was he to that duty which he conceived he owed to this party, but faithless to the higher duty which he owed to his country; he takes upon himself this duty; he stands at the door to prevent the escape of any of those persons whom they had compelled to embark in this transaction, and what is very material, though he had been previously armed with a pike, yet while guarding this door, he is provided with a more deadly instrument and a more effectual one for the purpose with which he was entrusted; he has a gun, keeping guard as a centinel at the door, in order to prevent the escape of any of those who had unwillingly accompanied them, and who were desirous, if they could, to have made their escape, and not to have proceeded any further.

Then, Gentlemen, after these facts are proved, after they are proved by testimony, not attempted to be contradicted, what becomes of the reasons assigned by my learned friends; the one, that he acted from compulsion, and the other, that he followed, from the duty he owed to his sons, to endeavour to prevail upon them to depart from this party which they had accompanied. Does he ever remonstrate with his sons? does he ever say to them, "Oh! you are embarking in a transaction which, if successful, is against the laws of your country; but which, if unsuccessful, will bring you to an ignominious end; I exhort you, as you regard your safety and my feelings, depart from this assembly of people." Not a word of the kind, but on the contrary, he appears to glory in the thing; do not think I am using too strong an expression, it is for you to say what effect you give to his words, at the time he said to Dexter " his sons were with him."

Then as to compulsion; you will recollect that he was first seen at a distance from his house, at which this party never could have been at all; recollect the manner in which he was armed when first seen, that he has a pike, which had been prepared for the very purpose of the insurrection; recollect the manner in which he marched, from the beginning to the end of their progress, that he was always in the rear, and never attempted to escape; recollect, the exhortation he received from Mr. Goodwin, when he might have withdrawn from the party with ease, and his declining that opportunity; but recollect above all, that after that when at Codnor, when in expectation that some of these persons may escape from the party, he was the very person to propose the guarding the door, and that he actually took upon himself the performance of that office, and that he thereby prevented persons escaping, who would have been otherwise inclined to do so.

Then, Gentlemen, addressing you as men of sense and men of integrity, can you doubt that the three points I stated for your consideration, are distinctly and clearly proved; have you any doubt that there was a rising and insurrection; have you any doubt that their object in that rising and insurrection, was to proceed to Nottingham, for the purpose of overturning the government? And here attend to what was taking place at that time at Nottingham; the object of the party from Pentridge, was to go to Nottingham, to join a large body of men in the Forest, and to take Nottingham; it is in proof to you, that on that very night, a considerable body of men assembled at the Forest at Nottingham, some of them armed with pikes like these men, and threatened to attack the house of Roper, to get his fire arms; but at the hour of three, finding these men did not come up, having been delayed in procuring arms, they dispersed; but at that very important period of time, at Nottingham, was carrying on that very design which at Pentridge, at Ripley, and at other places, was also at that time in prosecution.

Gentlemen, I will not fatigue you with further observations upon the general object of their march; upon the preparation of bullets, which were taken possession of by Mr. Goodwin; or by stating George Weightman's being dispatched on the way to Nottingham for tidings; of his return, and the false account he gave; all this goes to the general plan and general purpose, which has hardly been attempted to be denied, even in argument, certainly not attempted to be disputed by proof. Then as to the prisoner at the bar, I have enumerated the particular facts which affect him, and I think that these facts, so proved, can leave no doubt upon your minds that he was a party in the transaction, and that he was concurring in the common object and design; if so the whole charge as exhibited upon this Indictment, is made out against him. And here allow me to repeat, what I stated in the outset; let not any considerations weigh with you, except that duty which is now cast upon you, namely, the investigation of the case of the prisoner Isaac Ludlam, as it respects the offence imputed to him; do not be led away by any false feeling that a verdict of acquittal, contrary to the evidence, can be consistent with your duty, or can prevent you hereafter feeling a reproach. Gentlemen, all of us concerned in the trial of this important case, have most anxious and painful duties to discharge; but the best consolation, after the trial is over, to all of us, will be, that in the respective parts assigned to us, we have kept steadily in view that duty, which we were called upon to execute; and your best consolation will be, that regarding the solemn obligation under which you now act, you have executed the duty imposed upon you faithfully and with integrity; and if you have done so, whether it be a verdict of guilty, or a verdict of acquittal, your consciences can never reproach you.

SUMMING UP.

MR. JUSTICE ABBOTT.

Gentlemen of the Jury,

Isaac Ludlam the elder, the prisoner now at the bar, is charged before you with the offence of High Treason. The charge is of the most serious nature, most important to the prisoner at the bar, and most important to the public justice and the safety of the country; some additional importance has been given to it by the great learning, talents, and zeal that have been displayed, particularly on the part of the very learned gentlemen, to whom the life of this person and his defence here have been entrusted. I must however take leave to say, the case does not appear to me to involve in it any questionable proposition of law, and I am sorry to say, neither does it appear to me to involve any very doubtful or difficult considerations of fact.

The indictment, Gentlemen, charges that this prisoner, together with many others named in it, and others not named, did wilfully, maliciously, and traitorously assemble themselves together, and levy and make war against our Lord the King within his realm, and that being so assembled together, arrayed, and armed against our Lord the King, they did with great force and violence parade and march, in a hostile manner, in and through divers villages, places, and public highways, and did maliciously and traitorously attempt and endeavour by force and arms, to subvert and destroy the constitution and government of this realm as by law established. This, Gentlemen, is the charge in the first count of this indictment; there is a second count, which charges a compassing and intention to depose the

King from the style, honour, and kingly name of the Imperial Crown of this realm; another, which charges a compassing and intending to levy war against the King in his realm, in order by force and constraint to compel him to change his measures and councils: And as acts, manifestations, and proofs of each of these intentions, it is alleged that this prisoner and others met and consulted together, and devised means for the accomplishment of their purpose, to raise an insurrection against the King in his realm; provided arms and ammunition, marched and attacked the houses of divers persons, seized their arms, and compelled them to unite with them in levying war against the King.

These, Gentlemen, are the charges in this indictment. The first, as I have already stated to you, is the charge of levying war against the King; the others are charges of intention; but the acts alleged to have been done in the furtherance of that intention, are those acts which constitute the levying of war in this case, if there has indeed been any war levied; you may therefore, as it seems to me, with great safety, consider your attention in this case as confined to that first count, which is the most plain and simple, namely, to the charge of levying war against the King.

This offence, Gentlemen, of levying war against the King within his realm, was declared to be high treason by that ancient statute passed in the reign of King Edward the third, to which so much allusion has been made in the course of what you have heard from the counsel for the prisoner. The statute begins by reciting, that " whereas divers opinions have been before this time in what case treason shall be laid, and in what not; the King, at the request of the Lords and of the Commons hath made a declaration in the manner as hereafter followeth, that is to say, when a man doth compass or imagine the death of our Lord the King, or of our Lady his Queen, or of their eldest son and heir; or if a man do violate the King's companion, or the King's eldest daughter unmarried, or the wife of the King's eldest son and heir ; or if a man do levy war against our Lord the King in his realm, or be adherent to the King's enemies in his realm, giving to them aid and comfort in the realm or elsewhere, and thereof be proveably attainted, of open deed, by the people of their condition." It further declares, that " if a man do counterfeit the King's great or privy seal, or his money ; and if a man slay the chancellor, treasurer, or the King's justices of the one bench, or the other justices in Eyre, or justices of assize, and all other justices assigned to hear and determine, being in their places, doing their offices ; and it is to be understood, that, in the cases above rehearsed, that ought to be judged treason which extends to our Lord the King and His Royal Majesty." Then it provides " that because many other like cases of treason may happen in time to come, which a man cannot think nor declare at this present time, it is accorded, that if any other case supposed treason which is not above specified, doth happen before any justices, the justices shall tarry without any going to judgment of the treason, till the cause be shewed and declared before the King and his parliament, whether it ought to be judged treason or other felony." Then it proceeds " and in case any man of this realm ride armed, covertly or secretly, with men of arms against any other to slay him, or rob him, or take him or retain him, till he hath made fine or ransom for to have his deliverance, it is not the mind of the King nor his Council that in such case it shall be judged treason, but it shall be judged felony or trespass, according to the laws of the land of old time used, and according as the case requireth."

You see therefore, Gentlemen, that by the tenor of this ancient statute, those offences only are to be considered as treason, which relate in some way to the King and to his Royal Majesty; private quarrels and private objects are declared not to be treason; it has, ever since the passing of this statute, uniformly been held, that where the object is public and national ; where the attack is against the constituted government and authority of the realm, of which the King is the head and chief, that is high treason against the King, within the meaning of this Act.

Gentlemen, much of very learned argument was addressed to you on the part of one of the learned counsel for the prisoner, against what he called constructive and interpretative treason; and you have been cautioned with the zeal and freedom that belong to, and are commendable in an English advocate standing for the life of a prisoner at the bar, not to lend your aid to any strained construction or interpretation of the law. Gentlemen, it seems to me, that in this particular case, adverting to the charge, and to the evidence which has been adduced, the argument and the caution were alike needless, for the charge, as it is preferred by the indictment, as it is stated to you by those who conduct the prosecution; and as it is attempted to be proved by the evidence, (but of which you are to judge) is a charge, that an assembly of persons met together and armed themselves, for the purpose of assailing and endeavouring to overturn the established government of the country, and actually moved forwards for the accomplishment of that object; this is the charge, and that such an assembly, acting in such a manner, and for the accomplishment of such an object, is a levying of war against the King, who is the head and chief of the government, is a proposition, which no court or judge, nor any writer on the law of England has ever questioned; in every court, and on every occasion where the point has arisen, this proposition has been laid down and acted upon, as a clear and unquestionable proposition of law. It is not creating a new treason out of offences provided for by other statutes; for those statutes will all be found, upon close examination, to embrace offences far short of this. It is not made an ingredient in the offence described in any one of them, as far at least as I have been able to learn, that the persons who are the objects of them, should assemble with arms in their hands; an armed assembly may, perhaps, be within the purview of some of those statutes; but an unarmed assembly may also under certain circumstances; whereas the levying war against the King, can be accomplished only by an armed assembly; the distinction is therefore, Gentlemen, as it appears to me, plain and clear, and I cannot see that this case does involve in it any proposition of law, on which any lawyer can doubt.

Such, Gentlemen, being the law, as it may be applicable to the case, several questions will arise for your consideration, for your judgment, and for your decision; with your judgment, and your decision upon them, it is far from being the intention of the Court to interfere. You have been very properly told, that you are to consider in this case; first, whether there has been, in point of fact, an insurrection of armed men, committing acts of violence and outrage; has such an insurrection actually taken place? If it has, then, secondly, what was its object; was the object of the insurgents to assail, and endeavour to overthrow the established government of the state? if there was such an insurrection, with such an object, the crime of high treason, in levying war against the King, has been committed. But then another question arises also for your consideration; was the prisoner at the bar, for his case, and his alone, is now the object of your enquiry; was the prisoner at the bar a party concerned in that insurrection, and having in common with others that unlawful intent? And in considering those questions, Gentlemen, you will exercise your own judgment, uninfluenced by any thing that has passed upon the trials of any other persons; uninfluenced by any thing that you may suppose is to come out hereafter upon the trials of others; the enquiries that have already taken place, have been decided upon by persons in the condition of life of yourselves, acting, as no doubt you will do, honestly. The further enquiries, if any shall be made, will be made by other persons, who will act for themselves, and exercise their own judgment on the evidence to be laid before them, with reference to the particular person who may be the subject of charge; you will exercise your judgment on the particular case, which is made the subject of your consideration. If, Gentlemen, considering these questions, and the evidence that has been laid before you, you shall not be satisfied in your own minds, that there was such an insurrection, with such an object, or being satisfied there was such an insurrection with such an object, you shall not be satisfied that the individual at the bar was a party to it, you will pronounce with pleasure your verdict of acquittal; but if, upon consideration of the evidence, you shall be satisfied, not only that there was such an insurrection, and with such an object, but also that the prisoner at the bar was a party concerned in it, then, however painful it may be, you will, I have no doubt, discharge your duty like men, and pronounce him guilty.

Gentlemen, in considering this case, you will apply your minds to the evidence that has been laid before you, uninfluenced by any thing which may have taken place on any other occasion, or by any surmise of matter not in proof or laid before you. If the prisoner has unfortunately joined himself, in your opinion, to such an insurrection, and made himself a party to it; it is not material to this case, whether he was first induced so to do by the person who is named to you, or by other persons; or who may have been the original mover of that conspiracy; all that is irrelevant and immaterial; for if any man takes part actively in a conspiracy of this kind, although he comes into it at a late period of its existence, he is nevertheless answerable for his own acts, and for his own conduct; and if his acts and his conduct should involve him in the guilt of high treason, he must be so pronounced, although there may be others equally guilty with him.

Gentlemen, having made these general remarks, for the purpose of guiding your attention, and assisting you (for that is my object) in the enquiry which you are to make, I will now read over to you the whole of the evidence which has been given; and upon which, and which alone, your judgment is to be formed; making, perhaps, as I shall go along, some few remarks upon particular parts of that evidence, and making two or three general remarks at the end.

Gentlemen, the first witness who is called, is a person of the name of Anthony Martin, who appears to have been in the employ of gentlemen of the names of Outram and Jessop, who are very considerable iron-founders in this county, and carry on their business at some works, which are called the Butterley works: he says, " I was in their employ in the month of June last; upon the 8th of June, between nine and ten in the morning, I went with a man of the name of John Cope, who is another workman in the same employ, to a croft below the White Horse, a public-house at Pentridge, when a little girl came out of the White Horse to John Cope, and I went in with him. This house, the White Horse, was kept by a person of the name of Nanny Weightman. I went into the house place first; then she asked John Cope to go into the parlour, and I went in with him: on going into the parlour, we found Jeremiah Brandreth, George Weightman, Joseph Weightman, another Joseph Weightman, John Bacon, Thomas Weightman, Ormond Booth, and some other persons; others kept coming in; there might occasionally be as many as twenty in the room at once;" not always, but at times, that being probably about the number that the room would contain: he says, " Brandreth was sitting in the centre of the room by a table, the prisoner was there," not when the witness went in; he going in at an early hour, but " the prisoner came in between one and two o'clock, attended by another person, of the name of William Turner. The prisoner and Turner live in the parish of Southwing-field, about a mile from thence." He says, " the subject of the conversation was about overturning the present government; I cannot tell that that was stated after the prisoner came into the room, but it was said by the captain before." You find, however, by the testimony of the next witness, that something of that kind was probably said after the prisoner came in: he says, " after the prisoner came in, William Turner pulled a list out of his pocket, and the prisoner read it. William Turner said, they had a list of all the pikes and guns and swords in their parish;

and he wanted to know, where the guns and pikes were that belonged to the Pentridge and to the Ripley people." Then he says, " the prisoner at the bar read this list," which William Turner, it seems, took out of his pocket: " it was an account of arms, and from what people's houses they were to fetch them." Not the arms which they had, but the names of persons, and the situation of the houses where arms might be found, which they proposed to take away. He says, " after the paper was read, there was a conversation about pikes; and the prisoner said, there were pikes in a stone quarry; that they had forty pikes in a stone quarry." It does seem they must have contemplated something, you will be to say what, before this day. " The prisoner," he says, " was a stone-getter; I did not hear any thing that the prisoner said, but whilst he was there they were talking about a revolution, and how they were to proceed: then they talked of starting for Nottingham; Brandreth, the captain, had a map before him; there were some dots and pricks of places where they were to meet, and to which they were to proceed. The map was in Brandreth's pocket, when the prisoner and Turner came in; and I cannot tell whether it was produced afterwards." You see, therefore, that what passed about the map, passed without the knowledge of the prisoner: " they talked after that," he says, " that they were to take the town of Nottingham, and then return back, and make barracks of Butterley works; and they said they would make all the men go that they met with, and those that would not go they would shoot." Then he says, " Brandreth repeated some verses before the prisoner came in; I think they were not repeated afterwards;" and he repeats those verses. Whatever is said in the absence of the prisoner, is no otherwise important against him, than as you may judge from what he afterwards says and does, whether he entertains the same object and intention as that which was entertained by the persons using those expressions; then what they say is material, as against him; if you think that he had not the same object as they had, then what they said is not material as evidence against him. The verses they repeated are these:

> " Every man his skill must try,
> " He must turn out and not deny;
> " No bloody soldier must he dread,
> " He must turn out and fight for bread.
> " The time is come you plainly see—
> " That government opposed must be."

These verses therefore you see, Gentlemen, are a plain indication and declaration, that every man must turn out to try his own skill, entertaining no fear of the soldiers, but to oppose the government, in order to relieve the people, and to fight for bread; that is one of the expressions used.

Some allusions have been made in the course of what has been said, calculated to excite pity in your minds, and in the minds of others, as if all this that took place was the effect of oppression, of irresistible oppression; of poverty and of distress: we have not however, Gentlemen, heard, in the course of the evidence before you, that any one of the individuals who have been named, was at that time labouring under any particular urgency of poverty: that there was much distress in many parts of the country, we know; probably some in that part of the country; but it does not appear that any of those particular individuals did at that moment suffer the pressure of poverty. Then he says, " Brandreth appeared as the leader of the party. William Turner was talking about a plan, about drawing the badger. John Cope said, he heard that they had a plan, he wanted to know what it was; then Turner told him, that it was to lay a bundle of straw before the door, and then set it on fire, and that the badger would come out, and they would shoot him." Now, Gentlemen, such a plan as that, was private and personal; and if the object of the meeting, the insurrection which is afterwards spoken of, was only to destroy such a particular individual as is here alluded to, or several of them, that would be private and personal, and not high treason; but when they do assemble together, we hear nothing of this attempt spoken of, in those very improper terms, to take away the life of an individual; but they leave his place of residence, and set out upon a very different object. He says, " William Turner was speaking about how they were to assemble together; and what time of the night they were to start; and where the pikes were: during the time I was there, several persons came in and out from time to time; I went away between three and four, and left the prisoner there, and Turner and Brandreth;" so that the prisoner appears to have come to this place somewhere between twelve and one, perhaps as late as one; to have staid there for at least the period of two hours; to have been left by the witness who is called before you; consequently, whether he staid any longer or not we have no evidence. He says, " a man of the name of Mac Kesswick came in while I was there, and asked the captain how he was; he said he did not know him; he asked him whether he did not recollect his coming a little way with him on the road. Brandreth on being reminded of that," it seems, " did recollect him: Brandreth then asked him how he was, and Mac Kesswick turned himself round and said, he thought there were too many in the room for that business." His opinion seems to have been, that the business on which they were met to consult was not fit for the presence of so many persons; " the conversation," he says, " was public in the room during all the time I was there; there was no secret made of it; I had been sworn in a special constable on the Saturday night before, to protect my masters' property, in case of any riot or disturbance; that," he says, " is what I understood to be the object for which I was sworn in.

Then, upon being cross-examined, he says, " I was sworn in for the purpose of keeping the peace at Butterley works, in case of there being any disturbance; they were talking at the public house about making barracks of the Butterley works; if any thing was said as to any mischief designed against my masters, I do not recollect that." The other witness says he does recollect it, and it very often happens, that two persons being present in different parts of a room, at a conversation, one may hear one part and the other another, or one man may recollect what he has heard and the other may not. Then he says, "After I left that place, I went home; I went to work next day." Then he is asked, whether he told Mr. Goodwin what he had heard at the alehouse; he says, "It had been narrated about the place before, about Butterley works; I thought therefore there was no need; I cannot say how many were sworn into office; I do not know what is become of Cope," that is, John Cope; "he has been taken into custody, but liberated again, I suppose. The prisoner came to the house with Turner; there were three of them came in one with another, within a small trifle of each other; they all came in at the door together; I was sitting in the parlour at the time; I was not in the parlour all the time they were there. I was in the house part some part of the time; I went there only for amusement; I had nothing to do with this matter; I spoke to them about it, but they threatened to cram me up the chimney; I was not hindered at all from going; I did ask Cope to go, but he did not choose to go, and I stopped till he went, and he and I, and Asbury and Elsden went away together. I told them I was a constable; I was afraid if I said any more, after they threatened me that they would put me up the chimney; I thought what they were doing was not right, but I said nothing to Cope about it; Cope said something about this matter, but I said nothing to him and he said nothing to me about the business; he asked me to go to Pentridge; that he had a little business to do when there; he was talking amongst them, but I do not recollect what it was." Then he says, "The prisoner was not taking any very active part that I heard, further than reading the paper. I waited for Cope and Shirley Asbury and Elsden. I do not know whether Cope had any business to transact at this meeting; he said he had a little business to do at Pentridge, but he did not tell me what it was; he was talking amongst the rest, but I cannot recollect what he said, nor what a many others said. I was six hours in the room, but I did not know what Cope's business was there; I did not see him take any active part in what was going on in the room. The prisoner and Turner were stating that there were pikes in a stone quarry;" that, therefore, is mentioned by the prisoner; then he says, "There was a collection to send Weightman to Nottingham." He is asked whether he contributed any thing, and he says, "I did not, and nobody asked me. The prisoner was not in the room when the money was gathered; I cannot recollect whether he was there when they talked about taking Nottingham." Inquiry was made whether those verses were part of the contents of the paper, or whether there was any thing else that might tend to explain them; he says, "They were the whole of the verses, and there was nothing else connected with them."

On his re-examination, he says, "Weightman was to go to Nottingham, to see whether the people there were ready to join them, and to bring back a particular account that night, and money was collected to enable him to go." He says further, "that there were threats held out, that if any man should tell any thing about them, they would call on him another day;" that was the nature of the threat.

The next witness is Shirley Asbury; he says, "I am an engine fitter at Butterley, in the service of Messrs. Jessop and Company, and was so in June; on the 8th of June I went to the White Horse at Pentridge, about twelve o'clock, in company with John Elsden; we found there Cope, Anthony Martin, Brandreth, Mac Kesswick, John Moore, Edward Moore, William Smith, and several others in the room; I did not know all of them, but there were about twenty in all. I saw the prisoner there; he came in with Turner; the prisoner and Turner are both Wingfield men. Turner produced a paper consisting of what guns they had; what guns such and such people had." He says, "Their names were mentioned, but I do not recollect them; Turner delivered the paper to the prisoner, and he read it over to the company; then William Turner seemed to say that the Wingfield people were more forward than the Butterley, for they went out to get pike-shafts in the day;" and he said, "that they had about forty pikes in a stone quarry, for men that would volunteer; he did not say where that stone quarry was; the prisoner was present when this conversation passed. Turner said they were to go first to Wingfield; they were going to draw the badger in the first place; they were to take a bundle of straw, and set it on fire, and as soon as it was set on fire, he would come out, and then they were to shoot him. Colonel Halton was mentioned as this person, whom they thus stated they intended to shoot. William Turner said that they had vermin to kill, and every one must kill their own vermin. I cannot recollect that I heard the prisoner say any thing more than reading the paper over. Nottingham was mentioned by Brandreth; he said they were to go to take Nottingham, and every one was to have plenty of rum, and a hundred guineas when he got there. William Turner also mentioned it." Now if William Turner mentioned it, it must have been mentioned after the prisoner Ludlam came in, as they came in together. " I cannot recollect that any body but Brandreth and Turner used those expressions; William Turner said there would be no good done till such time as the Government was overthrown. I do not remember any body else mentioning this. They were to go to Nottingham in the first place; they were to take Nottingham; and they were to go down the Trent by the Trent boats to Newark from thence, and to take Newark, and then to make the best of their way to London to overturn the Government; that there would be no good done till they had overturned the Government; this was talked of from the time I went till the time I came away. They said, they had no doubt they should succeed in what they were going to undertake. I came away about four o'clock; they spoke it up to all in the room loud enough for all to hear; they were to set out at ten o'clock the next night," and at ten o'clock some persons accordingly did set out; " it was proposed that George Weightman should be sent to Nottingham, and a subscription was made for him to pay his expenses; he was to set out that night, and after he had been at Nottingham, he was to come home again; money was collected for the purpose while I was there; Brandreth produced a map, and he pointed out and pricked out the places where they they were to go to; Brandreth wanted a barrel of gunpowder produced, so that he might learn them how to make cartridges; it was mentioned that they had a barrel; only one barrel of gunpowder was spoken of; they had no other ammunition but gunpowder, but Brandreth said that there were plenty of churches on the road that they might get lead from; there was to be a party to meet them from Sheffield and Chesterfield, and to join them; and they were to go to Butterley."

On his cross-examination he says, " It was not mentioned that when they started they were to meet a quantity of men at Nottingham before the money was gathered for Weightman to go to Nottingham; I do not recollect that any thing was mentioned before, but it was mentioned after; I cannot recollect that there was any thing said about overturning the Government before the money was collected, but there was something said afterwards; I do not know whether the prisoner was there at the time the money was collected; I gave sixpence, but I did not know what it was for; I put it upon the table; I saw the rest give sixpence, and so I gave; I cannot say whether all gave or not; Cope gave sixpence I believe." Then he is asked whether Martin gave any thing, and he says, " I do not recollect that he did; he might; I cannot state who gave and who did not; I cannot recollect whether the prisoner was in the room when the money was gathered or not; I do not know whether any thing was said about a revolution or overturning the Government before the money was gathered; I do not know whether the verses were recited before or after that; the map was not produced till afterwards; I do not recollect any thing about a cloud from the North." I do not think he had spoken to such an expression, though I think it is mentioned by one of the witnesses afterwards. " I can remember Sheffield and Chesterfield being mentioned, but I cannot recollect whether it was before the money was collected or afterwards; I never heard the name of Oliver mentioned there at all; I have heard it mentioned since, but it was a long time after that meeting; the names of Jessop, Goodwin, and Wragg, were mentioned: it was said that Sheffield and Chesterfield were to meet the Wingfield men at Butterley, and they were to take the place and to kill Mr. Goodwin, Mr. Wragg, and Mr. Jessop: I do not know whether Cope heard this; Martin was in the room; I did not tell Mr. Jessop, nor Mr. Goodwin, nor Mr. Wragg, they were to be shot." He says, upon being asked what he meant by saying this had been mentioned before; " this revolution had been talked of;" according to his account there had been a conversation before in this neighbourhood; then he says, " I did not know there was any thing of the kind before I went to the White Horse; I did not tell Mr. Jessop, Mr. Goodwin, and Mr. Wragg, they were in danger; I did not know that I had any right to tell, for they talked of putting us up the chimney; we told them that we were constables, and there was a talk of murdering us too; they said if we mentioned any thing we should be rammed up the chimney, and likewise that we should be murdered, and my fear prevented my telling; I saw Mr. Goodwin the next day, and also Mr. Jessop, and Mr. Wragg; I might have told them, but I did not trouble my head about it, because I was sworn in the night before to protect our master's property; the Sheffield and Chesterfield people were to come the next night." Upon being asked how he came to go to this public house, he says, " I was taking a walk towards Butterley with John Elsden; and we went to Swanwick and had two pints of ale; and he asked me whether I would take another walk; I said I had no objection to go to Pentridge, for I had never seen it." According to his own account therefore he was a stranger to that place; " I asked him if he would have a pint of ale there, and he said yes, and in consequence of that I went to the White Horse; that was in my way home." This is the way in which he accounts for being there; he says, " they did not make it any secret at all that every one would be obliged to go; they began to talk in this way very soon after I went in, but I did not go into the parlour till some time after I first went in; I might be in the house about half an hour before I went in; I went there about twelve o'clock; I did not like the company; I might have come away if I had tried; I told them I was a constable; I cannot tell the constable's oath; I think Ludlam came in about one o'clock; Turner came with him; I found Brandreth there; Mac Kesswick and another man, whose name I do not know, came in together."

On his re-examination, he says, " I did not know Pentridge before this time, and did not know there was any meeting there; we went into the kitchen first, and Mrs. Weightman went into the parlour and told them there were some Butterley chaps there, and asked whether they would have any objection to our coming in :" this accounts for his going into the parlour. Elsden might be known to her, though the witness was not, or she might learn that they came from Butterley from their conversation. " I told them we were constables, and told them to beware, and then they threatened us in the way I have described; I heard the names of Mr. Jessop, Mr. Goodwin, and Mr. Wragg, as persons who were to be murdered; a great many had been sworn in as special constables, twenty or thirty, or it might be more;" then the verses he recites in the same words as the other witnesses had done; he says, " they were distributed about the room; I wrote my copy myself; other people wrote theirs; Brandreth produced them;'" then he says, " I copied the verses from another paper, because the rest were taking them; I did not know what I was taking it for; many took copies; all, however, did not take copies; I think Cope did, but that Martin did not; I did not take my copy to the works, but burnt it either the next day or the day afterwards; I got it by heart that day."

These two witnesses, you see, Gentlemen, have detailed a great deal of conversation held partly before the prisoner at the bar came in, and partly afterwards, relating to the procuring of arms, to a rising of the people, to a journey to Nottingham to bringing about a revolution, to the overturning of the Government; much comment has been made upon the testimony of these two persons, and they have been represented to you by the counsel for the prisoner, as persons not worthy of belief, and whose testimony ought to be altogether discarded. Gentlemen, it is your province to consider what credit is due to the testimony of particular witnesses; but in considering that question, if in the result of the whole of this evidence, you should think it material to do so, you will bear in mind that there is no imputation whatever cast or attempted to be cast, on the former lives, conversation or habits of either of these two persons; it was known many days before the first trial upon this subject took place, that they were to be examined; this is now the seventh day since they were first examined in this place, and gave evidence to the effect of what I have stated; if any thing could have been found out relating to these persons, relating to their former lives, to their former habits or their former conduct, which could have been brought forward to impeach them, it is reasonable to suppose that that would have been done; but there is none; but it is urged, that the story they tell is so improbable, and that they have been each of them guilty of so great a violation of moral and legal duties, as that, on that account only, they shall be held unworthy of credit. Now see and consider a little, upon their own account, how that stands; they were constables it is true, sworn in however only the night before, and that not for the general purpose of keeping the King's peace, but for the particular purpose of protecting the property of their masters; they say they did not very well understand what was their duty as constables; you will consider whether they ought to have understood it; with respect to making a communication to their own masters, they say this matter had been much talked of before, and they surmised that if they had communicated it, they should have communicated not a great deal more than was known, for they knew that their masters did expect an attack upon their works, and did expect a riot, from the fact of their having caused them and others to be sworn in as special constables; and they tell you too, that in this room, threats were held out, that if any person should divulge what was passing there, he should be visited another day. It is said, those threats are inconsistent with the notions of a public talking in this room; but you will recollect, the persons coming into the room, were persons in a particular condition in life, many it appears, conversant with what was going on; it will be for you to say, whether all those motives, operating in combination on the minds of those persons, may not so far excuse them in your judgment, for not having disclosed what they had heard, as to induce you to give credit to them; or whether, from the circumstances I have mentioned to you, and the observations made by the learned counsel, the circumstance of their not communicating what it would have been better they should have communicated, you are prepared to say, that those two persons come into this place to relate to you, upon their oaths, falsehoods, and fictions, and inventions, in fact to commit wilful and corrupt perjury, and that for the purpose of taking away the life of an innocent fellow creature.

The next witness, Gentlemen, who has been called, is a person of the name of William Smith. You perceive the evidence now proceeds to detail to you what actually did take place; the former evidence was only as to conversations about what was to take place; he says, " I live in Wingfield-park; I am a framework knitter; I know the prisoner and his son Isaac. On the 9th of June, I saw old Isaac and young Isaac, and William and Joseph Taylor, and Benjamin Taylor, coming down Boden-lane towards James Taylor's; they were then carrying poles, three or four a piece, they were like pike-shafts; they had at that time no iron upon them, but I think the bark was upon them." He says, " this was about five in the afternoon; between eleven and twelve o'clock at night, I saw the prisoner and his son Isaac, Samuel Briddon and William Ludlam; the prisoner and Samuel Briddon were mostly behind; they were going to Pentridge-lane-end; I do not know where they came from; they were about a mile from the prisoner's house." The prisoner is here, you be under no force or constraint, but going, as far as we can judge from the circumstances, voluntarily to join this party. "They had poles with spikes to them, each of them had one; I set out to go up Boden-lane, with Henry Taylor and Samuel Taylor, to go to John Wilkinson; we met a party on our way before we got far up the lane; there were in that party, one James Taylor, George Weightman, Benjamin Taylor and Joseph, Miles Bacon, James Hopkinson, Abraham James, and Samuel Marriott; they demanded us to go with them; I refused going; we all refused; then they give us a spike a piece, and we went down the lane with them to Boden-lane-end; all the party agreed that I should go to let Henry Taylor's family and my own know, that we were going; James Taylor followed me up to the house, and brought a pike with him; that occasioned me to return; we went down to the same party that we met in the lane; Samuel Marriott was then carrying a bag of bullets; he delivered the bag to George Weightman; we then proceeded down the Park-lane to John Marriott's house, the wire-mill, and after we had been there awhile, a party came down the yard; I do not know how many; they demanded a gun there; Marriott refused giving it; they said they would break the door open if he did not give them the gun; and he came down the stairs and gave them the gun; they then went towards William Lister's; in the mill-yard I attempted to get away from them; but James Taylor prevented me; he stood behind me with a gun in his hand; I went with them to Lister's; they demanded his gun, which he at first refused to give them; they then went round and broke the kitchen windows; I only went into the yard, but I heard the windows smash." He represents himself therefore as being an unwilling partaker in these scenes. "They got his gun which he afterwards produced; the prisoner was not with us at this time; we next went to Mr. Sellars's, near Pentridge mill, which is near a mile from the wire-mill, and knocked him up to go with them; he got up and went; we went next to Mr. Fletcher's, at Pentridge-lane-end; they demanded his gun, and they took his gun and his man; I saw James Turner came out of his own house; they went in, and he came out with them, and joined the party; we then went up into Pentridge-lane, and we were formed into rank there; the captain formed us into rank; William Turner assisted the captain in forming us into ranks; we then went towards Pentridge; I did not go out of the road; but I heard a rattling at the doors; I do not know that I saw the prisoner there, but I saw him at Butterley; I was nearly the last in the ranks; Isaac Ludlam and Samuel Briddon were the last in the ranks always; I do not know what they were doing; they said nothing to me; at Codnor I offered to leave them." Then he says something about a place called Coburn quarry, which does not appear material for your consideration, as it does not point distinctly to the prisoner. Then he says, " at Codnor I tried to make my escape, but I was prevented by Isaac Ludlam; he was out of doors, and we supposed he was guarding the prisoners; he was sheltering under the eaves; it was raining very hard; he had a spike in his hand near the door, and that prevented my escape."

Then upon being cross-examined as to this about the prisoner preventing his going, he says, " We supposed he was keeping garrison there, but he said nothing to us." You will judge afterwards from the testimony of another witness called, whether this supposition was well founded, and whether the prisoner was, or was not keeping garrison at his own suggestion. Then he says, " I saw the prisoner just before the house of James Turner at the time the people went in, and James Turner came out." He speaks to him therefore first as to seeing him with a pike in his hand at eleven or twelve at night, then at the house of James Turner, then at the house at Codnor, where he conceived him to be keeping garrison to prevent his going out.

The next witness is Thomas Turner; he says, " I was taken into custody upon this business, and have remained in custody. On the evening of the 9th of June last I was at my father's house, and went from thence at a little before nine, in company with Samuel Ludlam and John

Walker, to the Meeting House in Southwingfield, which is near Colonel Halton's gates; there we saw William Turner and George Weightman, whom we knew, and a strange man, whom we afterwards found to be the Nottingham captain; I did not hear his name mentioned then, but I now know that it was Brandreth." He is the man spoken of by all the witnesses as the person who took the lead upon this occasion. " They had each of them a gun; William Turner was loading his with a bullet; George Weightman said, ' Come, lads, I expect an engagement very soon with Mr. Jessop's men at Butterley Furnace.' I asked William Turner who the strange man was, and he said, that was the captain; he did not tell me where he came from; they three went to Hunt's Barn, and we followed; a number of persons were assembled at the barn, perhaps a score, or something better; they were armed with pikes and guns; a few pikes were lying against the hedge side; among the persons there, I saw William Barker, John Hill, Robert Turner, Manchester Turner, and Charles Swaine; I am not sure whether Robert Turner was armed, but all the rest were I know; the captain said, ' We must go to Nottingham Forest, a great quantity of people would meet us there.' They put us in rank two and two; I received a bag of bullets to carry from George Bramley, one of the party; at that time we amounted to about a score; the captain ordered us to march for Mr. Topham's ground, what is called Topham's Close; before we got there we stopped at James Hardwick's; I do not know whether any man carried more pikes than one; after having stopped at James Hardwick's, most of the party went to Henry Tomlinson's, but I and a few others did not go there; I went to Topham's Close; George Weightman had said he expected the Pentridge people to meet us there; we halted there, and the prisoner and his two sons, Isaac and William, joined us there." He also introduces the prisoner at the bar as coming forwards with his two sons, and another person, to join them at Topham's Close, not as having been brought there under force; he says, " I did not see any one come with them, but there might be; the Pentridge people did not join us there; George Weightman said he would take the bullets, and go by Coburn quarry and the wire-mill, and if he met the Pentridge people coming there, he was to take them back to Pentridge-lane-end; he and others quitted our party for that purpose; George Weightman took the bullets with him; then we marched to Elijah Hall's;" Elijah Hall, you recollect, is called. "His gun was taken, and his son forced away; he gave his gun very unwillingly; Brandreth had said if he did not give the gun they should break the house open for it; and he and a great many others went into the house; we went next to Mr. Walker's; there a brass pistol was taken away, and Brandreth had that pistol for the rest of the night; we next went to Mr. Bestwick's, and then to Mr. Samuel Hunt's, and there we had some bread and cheese and beer; whilst we were at Hall's, Barker said he had wished for that day to come for long, but it had come at last; the prisoner was with us at Elijah Hall's; and I saw him at Hunt's with a pike; we marched from Hunt's; he and his servant went with us; we then went to Mrs. Hepworth's; the prisoner was with us; there a gun was taken; in the first place, Brandreth went up to the back door, and began thundering; there was no answer made, that I heard; Brandreth called for some one to come and break open the door, and Samuel Hunt went up with a stone and threw it against the door, but did not force it open; Brandreth left that door, and went to the kitchen window; when I got there, the window was broken, but I did not see it done; I heard Brandreth ask the persons within to give him the arms out, and open the door and let them in; the persons within did not comply with this demand, and he fired in at the window, and killed Robert Walters; I spoke to him about it, and said, he should not have shot that poor innocent young fellow; he said, it was his duty to do it, and he would do it; and if I spoke any thing more about it, he would blow my brains out; others must have heard that as well as I; after this we got a gun; I cannot say whether the prisoner was there all the time this was transacting, but I saw him go into the yard with the party." The prisoner is therefore one of the party who made the assault upon the house of Mrs. Hepworth; but perhaps not one of those who was close to it at the time that the gun was fired, which occasioned that unfortunate death.

He says, " Then we went to Pentridge-lane-end, and there we met another party, some of them were armed in the same way as we were. Joseph Weightman the younger, Thomas Weightman, Benjamin Taylor, Joseph Taylor, and James Taylor, were of that party; we went forward to the lane end. I did not go to any body's house, but a party went to Wheatcroft's, at Buckland Hollow; I heard a disturbance; they appeared to be thundering at doors." There is afterwards a witness called from Buckland Hollow, who states what actually passed there. " At Pentridge-lane-end I heard them rattling at folks's houses, and calling them up; we went to Pentridge from thence; as we were going along, the captain asked whether there were any men who had been soldiers, or in the militia, or knew discipline; that if there were any, they must turn out and keep the men in order; Charles Swaine turned out, and the men were put in rank by Brandreth, William Turner, and Charles Swaine; William Booth's was one of the houses that they went to; a poney was taken from thence; I saw George Weightman with it at the yard gate; he asked me to give Storer a leg on ; Storer pretended to be ill ; I understood in the party he was one of the persons that had been taken out of his house; he did not remain on long; he tumbled off, and lay in the street; we were then marched to Butterley Furnace. Mr. Goodwin came out to us; I heard him say something to Brandreth, but could not hear what it was; we were then marched to Ripley town end; there Brandreth ordered us to halt and give three huzzas; we did so, but I do not know for what purpose; we were then marched to Codnor, and there we stopped at a public house called the Glass House; Brandreth went to the door and knocked, and called the people up, and ordered them to fill some drink for us; drink was supplied to the amount of eight-and-twenty shillings; I went into the parlour, but I cannot say who else went in; from thence we marched on to Langley mill; before we got there, three men were fetched out of a barn; I did not see them forced out; they were taken with us; when we got to Langley mill, we met George Weightman upon the poney I had helped Storer upon; the party surrounded him, and asked how they were going on at Nottingham; he said they were going on very well, the town was taken, and the soldiers would not come out of their barracks, and we must march forwards as fast as we could; we marched on; I went with them two or three miles beyond Eastwood, and there I left them; when I left them, very few were marching on towards Nottingham; I do not recollect seeing the prisoner after we were at Mrs. Hepworth's yard;" but it seems other witnesses speak to seeing him later than that. " I left them between nine and ten in the morning; I do not recollect any body but Brandreth saying where we were going to; I had a pike, as I went along with them; it was given me by Samuel Ludlam, when I gave him the bullets; he afterwards parted with the bullets to George Weightman."

On his cross-examination, he says, " Brandreth said before we started, that we were going to Nottingham Forest; I do not know that he said that more than once; the prisoner joined us after that; I do not know the age of his two sons; they are both grown men." This witness, you see, Gentlemen, details to you a great number of acts of violence and outrage committed by these parties; great crimes committed by many of them; crimes, however, which, unless their object was that which has been stated to you so often, would not amount to the crime of high treason.

The next witness, Gentleman, is Henry Tomlinson, who is a farmer at Southwingfield Park. He says, " On the night of the 9th of June, about half past nine, or a quarter before ten, a party of between thirty and forty men came to my house armed with guns and spikes; I went up to the door, and asked what they wanted; they said they wanted me and my gun; I told them they must have neither; they said they would; I told them the gun was gone to Ashover to be mended; they said if I did not open the door they would break it, and find my gun, or else they would search my house; I opened the door; I saw William Turner and Brandreth; they entered the house, and also William Barker; I said to Turner, 'Well, William, are you here,' and he answered, 'yes;' 'are you one of them,'—'yes.' I used the same expressions to Barker also, and had the same answer; I went into the house with them, and when I came out, the captain said I must go with them; I told him I would not; he said I must, I had better go to-night than stop till the morning, for there was a great gang coming from Sheffield, and a great cloud coming out of the North that would sweep all before them; I told them I would not go; he presented his gun, and swore he would shoot me; he said they were going to Nottingham; they were to be there by half past eight or nine, as I understood; he said we should not need to go further than Nottingham, for London would be taken before they got there; at last they forced me to go; I wanted to carry my own gun, but the captain would not let me; he said that I must carry a spike, and a spike was put into my hand; I got away from them soon; George Weightman bade me give him my spike, and he let me go back again; I said to him it was a very lonesome place to leave my wife by herself; and he said I should go a little way, and then turn back again; I went with them about three hundred yards; George Weightman took the spike from me, and suffered me to go back, and they marched right forwards towards Nottingham."

The next witness is Elijah Hall, senior, a farmer and miller at Southwingfield Park. He says, " on Monday night the 9th of June, I got home about eleven o'clock from the mill; the door was fastened," that is after he got in the door was fastened; " then I heard the footsteps of two men on the outside; one of them asked whether any men had been there that night; I said yes; they asked whether they had taken any guns, and I said yes." He said this evidently to get rid of them, to make them believe he had received a visit from others before. "After that they went away; a few minutes after they were gone, I opened the door; I did not see any body immediately on opening the door, but soon after I saw people come into the yard; about thirty of them; I was then not ten yards from my door; they were armed with pikes and guns, and one of them had a sword; I asked what they wanted at that time of night; they said they wanted fire-arms; some said they wanted a bigger loaf and the times altered; I told them it was not in my power to do either; I also told them I had no fire-arms for them. Whilst we were talking, some person within fastened the door; when I said I had no fire-arms, they said they knew I had, and demanded them; they said I had better deliver them up quietly, to prevent further mischief, and my house from being fired. About the same time a gun was fired about half a mile off, in the direction of Frichley; after the gun was fired, they again demanded arms, and began to force the door; then a gun was given to them through the window, and I told them I hoped they would go away, as they had promised at first they would do; they said I must go with them: I said I would not; and some of them then said, he has sons, we will take them; upon this the captain," that is Brandreth, "said, if he has sons we will not take the old man; then they desired me to open the door and fetch my sons out; I told them I was outside as well as they, and therefore I could not do it; then they ordered me to command it to be opened," he being the master had a right to command it, "and on my refusal, they began to force it; some of them said, captain how must it be, after they had made several fruitless attempts, he said, blow it in pieces; upon that," he says, " the door was opened by some one within, and about a dozen or more went in; and the captain and myself also went in. The captain ordered me to fetch my sons out of bed; I told him I would not; he said if you do not, I will blow your brains out; he had a gun, and he gave me two thrusts in the side with the muzzle of it, and presented it at me; Thomas Turner cried out, do not shoot."

Thomas Turner had gone with them perhaps willingly but he appears upon this and on one other occasion, I think, to have acted in such a way as to entitle him to a merciful consideration, which is probably the reason you see him here as a witness and not as a prisoner. Then he says, " the captain then took a candle from some person in the house, and lighted it at the fire, and he and several other persons went up stairs into the bed room where my sons slept; I heard a great noise: I heard some person threaten to hash them up if they would not get up; they brought my son Elijah into the house-place, partly dressed, he finished dressing when he came down; I asked the captain,"—who is their leader, and may be supposed to speak their sentiments, if you find them in any measure concurring with him,—" where he was going to take my son;—he said he was going to Nottingham, that he believed Nottingham was given up at that time, that there was a general rising throughout the country; from whence their object was to go to London to wipe off the national debt, and begin again afresh;" that is, to overturn the whole government of the country. " I saw the prisoner at the bar among the party outside the house;"—the prisoner, therefore was outside and not inside;—" I saw inside the house Isaac Ludlam the younger, his son William Ludlam, Manchester Turner, Robert Turner, John Walker, William Walker, and Thomas Turner. I asked the party, did they know the consequences of what they were doing? they said, they knew the consequences, it was hanging what they had done already; they were determined to go on; I do not know which of them it was that said this."

Then, on his cross-examination, he says, " It was the party inside the house who said they were determined to go on; the prisoner was outside; there was light enough outside the house to enable me to distinguish him;" so that he was not present when the language was uttered.

Elijah Hall, junior, says, " I heard the people outside the house, and afterwards in the inside; while they were outside, a gun was given them out of the window of my room; after they had got into the house, several of them came up into my bed room, and demanded me to get out of my bed and go along with them. Brandreth was one of them. They told me they could not wait of me, I must make haste; I got up and partly dressed myself in the room; I then went down. They had threatened to murder me if I did not get up. I finished my dressing below stairs, and went with them; they compelled me; I asked one of them where they were going to, I do not know who it was; he told me they were going to Nottingham, to meet a great party of other men on the race course; they were going to break the laws and pull down the parliament house; they told me I was to have a deal of money when I got to Nottingham, that there would be one hundred pounds for every man that got there; after we left the house we went first to Isaac Walker's; a gun and a pistol were got there; then we went to Bestwick's; there they got a gun; from thence we went to Samuel Hunt's, at the lodge in Southwingfield Park; I was not there at the first; when I got there they were in the house, and the servant girl or Samuel Hunt was bringing out the bread and cheese, and they had some table beer to drink with it; we did not stop long; Samuel Hunt went with us from thence, and his man Daniel Hunt; Daniel Hunt took a gun with him; Isaac Ludlam the prisoner was of the party at each of those places;"—so that he was with the party and acted with them on many of the occurrences which took place;—" we went next to Mrs. Hepworth's; they made a great disturbance at the kitchen door; the family got up and asked what they wanted; they said they wanted men and guns; they were told they should have neither there; some went to the kitchen window, and broke it open, and a gun was fired off by the Nottingham captain into the kitchen, and Robert Walters was shot by it. I did not see the prisoner at the present time when the gun was fired, but I saw him before we left the house in the back yard; I was about the house only a few minutes; after the shot was fired, they demanded Mrs. Hepworth's gun, and it was given to them; then they went away to Pentridge-lane-end, and attacked some houses there; some went from thence to Buckland Hollow;

I heard them thunder at the door there, at Wheatcroft's; then they returned again, and then we went up to Pentridge, where they attacked several houses; while they were attacking those houses I made my escape from them and returned home."

Isaac Walker, who is a person who had been before mentioned, says, that he lives at Wingfield, and is a farmer there; he says, " About half past eleven o'clock on Monday night the 9th of June, I was disturbed by a dog barking; I got up and went to the window; I saw a parcel of men coming up the yard, about forty in number, armed with pikes and guns; they came to the front door and demanded entrance; I asked them what for; they said they wanted my fire arms; I asked them what they wanted them for, and they said that was no business of mine, they were determined to have them; they demanded a gun and a brace of pistols; I said I had a gun but I had no pistols; some person presented a piece at my bed room window, and said he would fire at me if I did not immediately open the door; upon that I went and opened the door; some person told him not to fire, but to give me time to put my clothes on, and I took the gun down and gave it them, and they went away; I was going up stairs when I heard them rattle at the door again; I opened the door, and they said they knew I had one pistol if not two;"—they seem to have got pretty good intelligence what arms the Wingfield people had; here is a Wingfield man, and it appears from the testimony of the two first witnesses, that William Turner produced and the prisoner read a paper containing an account of the arms which the Wingfield people had, and where they were to be found; —" they said they knew I had one, and they were determined to have that and all; they demanded a servant man also; I told them I had none; they said they knew I had, and they would have him; I again said I had none, and they went away; I gave them the pistol; it was a brass barrelled pistol; the prisoner was there, I knew him before; I saw him under the window a little to my right hand;"—he speaks therefore to the prisoner being one of those concerned in this violence and outrage committed at the house.

Mary Hepworth is next called: she says, " I have a farm at Southwingfield Park; I was disturbed between eleven and twelve o'clock on the night of the 9th of June; I and my family were in bed at the time, two servant men, Fox and Walters, my son William, and two daughters, composed my family; we were disturbed by a thundering at the door; I got up immediately; they demanded men; I went down stairs and stood in the kitchen; they kept up a noise at the door and the window, and demanded men and guns; I went up stairs again; somebody had opened the window; I told them from the window that they should not have any; I said that they were doing very wrong; I then went down stairs again; the kitchen window was broken open, and Robert Walters was immediately shot; he was sitting down, stooping as if putting on his boots; he lived for about ten minutes; they then called out again for men and guns; I told them I could not let them have them; the gun had been hid in the cellar, and I told my son William to give it or we should all be murdered; he gave it to them; they still said they must have a man; I went up stairs and said to them, one man has been shot already, is not that sufficient for you; upon this remonstrance they proceeded no further, but went away."

Henry Hole says, " On the 9th of June last I was a labourer at Pentridge-lane-end; I was disturbed about twenty minutes before twelve; I got up and went to the window, and asked who is there, what do you want; we want you to volunteer yourself to go with us, or else we will break the door open and murder you; I went down and opened the door; I saw four men, Joseph Weightman and Joseph Topham were two of them; I asked them where they were going, they said to Nottingham; I said if they were going to Nottingham I could not pretend to go with them, for I had no money to carry me there, nor I had no money to take care of my family while I was gone; they said, I needed no money, they should keep me on roast beef and ale; and there were people fixed to take care of every body's families that would come in two days or under." It should seem, according to the testimony of the first witnesses, that they were convinced of the certainty of success of this enterprize, and they said to this man that there would come persons in two days at the farthest:—" they said, I had better go that night; that they would come out of Yorkshire like a cloud, and would carry all before them; and those that refused to go would all be shot; I dressed myself and went out; a pike was forced upon me; I carried it a little way, and then said if they were going to Nottingham I was not able to carry it, it was so heavy, and if they did not take it I should throw it down, and I did throw it down; then I went on to John Sellars's, and I saw him and his apprentice coming from his door; I heard some others coming over the meadow from towards Mrs. Hepworth's; they joined us at Mr. Fletcher's; I saw Brandreth there, and William Turner, Manchester Turner, the prisoner, William Ludlam, Joseph Weightman, Joseph Topham, and Samuel Hunt, as we were going out of the yard; a man and a gun were taken from Mr. Fletcher's; William Shipman was the man's name; from Mr. Fletcher's we went a little way on the turnpike road, and there we were divided; Brandreth and the biggest part of the people went to the row of houses which is called George Turner's at Pentridge-lane-end; I and Samuel Hunt and eight or ten more, went towards Samuel Booth's; Hugh Booth, a son of Samuel, was taken; Brandreth joined us before we went away from there, but not his party; then we went to Buckland Hollow, Mr. Wheatcroft's; the door was broken open, and three men and a gun were brought away; we then returned back to Pentridge-lane-end; we there met the other people; we were formed into ranks three deep; the biggest part of the musquets were put in front, the spike men in the middle, and a few musquets behind; the word of command was given by Brandreth to march; then," he says, " we went along the road towards Pentridge; I saw George Weightman as we were going out of Pentridge on William Booth's poney; I had heard it said among the company, that he was going to Nottingham to let their friends know that they were coming; we went onwards to the Butterley works; I saw Goodwin there; Brandreth and William Turner knocked at the door, and then he came out out of the office; he called about for his men, and he said there were a great many, too many already, without they were upon a better subject; I do not recollect seeing the prisoner there; a man in the rear, whom I took to be John Bacon, said, you have no business here, you had better turn off; we turned off and marched towards the Coke Hearth; we then proceeded to Ripley, and there we were halted; we then went on to the Glass House public house at Codnor, it was a very wet night; a party went into the house; I saw the prisoner stand at the door with a musket in his hand; I had been in the back parlour, and I came to look out; we staid there upwards of half an hour, then we went to Mr. Raynor's; they took his man and his gun and a pitch-fork, and perhaps more; at the Glass House I heard John Bacon say, the Government had robbed them and plundered them of all that ever they had; that that was the last shift they ever could make; some of them had some ale there. I saw the bill given to the captain and John Bacon, and I heard one of those two, either the captain or John Bacon, say it would be paid in a fortnight, when the job was over. A party from Hartsay came to the Glass House, and after we left the Glass House, a party came from Swanwick;"—it appears that different parties met in the course of their march;—" we afterwards went along the Nottingham road to Raynor's, there we were halted, and from thence we went towards Langley mill, there I saw George Weightman on William Booth's poney, coming from towards Nottingham; as he went past us, I heard him say, march on my lads, all is right, they have bombarded Nottingham at two o'clock this morning, and it is given up to them;"—all this was untrue, no doubt, but it was said probably with a view to encourage them to go on;—" we marched on towards Eastwood, and there we were halted; I asked Barnes what they were going to do when they got to Nottingham; he said they had fixed up a fresh government at Nottingham, and they were going there to defend it, until the other counties came into their terms; it would be all soon over, for by a letter he had seen yesterday, the keys of the Tower would be given up to the Hampden Club party, if they were not already; and that he had never sat down since four o'clock yesterday morning; I asked what he had been doing; he said he had been preparing guns, spikes, and ammunition. I saw the prisoner most of the time I was there; I cannot say I always saw him; he appeared to walk in the rear chiefly, as if to keep the men up together." This witness tells you, " I conceived from what I saw him do, this was his chief employ; there were about two hundred about Langley mill; I attempted to get away while we were at Eastwood; Brandreth came up to me with a gun, and said if I did not go into the rank again, he would shoot me; I stepped up to him with a stack-paring knife, and said if he offered to present the gun, I would hack his head off; he stood a short time, and turned off, and I then marched off; when I had walked fifty or sixty yards, I heard a cry of, do not shoot; I looked back and saw him with a gun at his shoulder presented at me, Thomas Turner;"—that is the young man whom I mentioned before, as having appeared to conduct himself with great humanity, on more than one occasion;—" took hold of him and drew the gun off; on my return, I met a party of about fifty, a few with guns and spikes, but the rest appeared to be colliers unarmed, they were proceeding after the others along the Nottingham road; I saw another party, but I went by a bank to miss them;"—those therefore appeared to be in addition to the Hartsay and Swanwick party, and those who had come from Pentridge and Wingfield;—" I saw them proceed along the same road, in the way for Nottingham; some of them appeared to be armed, but I was not very nigh, and I could not judge exactly."

Then, upon being cross-examined, he says, " John Sellars's house was the first we went to; I saw him come from his door; I afterwards went with them to Booth's, and I was with them at Wheatcroft's and the Glass House;

at all those places I was amongst the party; I did not say at any of the houses I was there against my will; I did not see the prisoner in the kitchen at the Glass House; I was not always in the same place when we marched, I was sometimes in the middle, and sometimes I was in the rear; sometimes the prisoner was out of my sight, and sometimes in; he was in the rear when I saw him;"—that is, whenever he did see him, it was there;—" it was said many times by the company, that he was keeping up the rear; I do not remember seeing him but in the rear, except sitting at the Glass House; I had known him before:" therefore there can be no doubt about his person.

Then the next is John Dexter, who lives at this house called Buckland Hollow; he says, " I was disturbed about twelve at night, by a desperate noise in the yard; the first word I heard was, Dexter, come get up, we must have you along with us; I got up and went to the window; I saw people in the yard just before the door; I said I should not open the door; some one made answer, that if I would not come down and open the door, they had shot Hepworth's man, and they would shoot me." Now here, as in the case of the younger Hall, you have the testimony of a man who is forced to go, and gets away as soon as he can. " I was told, that if I would not come down and open the door, they would shoot me; I told them that they might shoot on, for I would not come down; they again said, I had better come down and open the door, or they would break it open; I still refused, and immediately two men began to break it open; the instant I saw that, I went to call the young men from the garret; whilst I was upon the garret stairs, the door smashed open; half a score persons entered the house; they then called to me, to ask me whether I would come down stairs; I told them I hoped they would give me time to dress; when I went down, I found part of the men armed and part not; they had spikes, spears, guns, and pistols; I desired to be allowed to remain; they told me that positively I must go, and therefore I had better get myself dressed; I went up to dress myself, and when I came down again they were charging my master's gun, which they had taken from the house; I and William Wheatcroft and Samuel Lewis were compelled to go; we asked before we left the house, what their intention was, and why they were acting in that manner; they said that they were going to ease the Nation of that burthen it had so long groaned under;"—declaring their intention to be to execute a purpose of the most public nature, before conceived;—" from Mr. Wheatcroft's house I proceeded to Pentridge-lane with the party; we were joined there by another party; they were in ranks, and the captain and Manchester Turner put us in ranks; the prisoner was there; I first saw him at Pentridge-lane-end;"— now you have his declaration;—" he told me he had two sons of his in the party; that we were going to Nottingham, and that there was a parliament chosen ready when they got there; that the party in Nottingham would break into the houses, and take away the soldiers arms; and that Nottingham would be all taken by such time as we got there; he said we had better all go, that a party was coming out of the North, that would sweep all before them;"—here therefore you have a declaration of the prisoner himself, that their object was to go to Nottingham; that something which he calls a parliament was assembled there; that their object was of the same kind as that which has been spoken to by the other witnesses, as being declared by Brandreth, by Manchester Turner, and by others:—" As we were going along there was a talk by some one of the party, but I do not know who, that if Mr. Jessop did not give up his men they would take away his life; the prisoner was near enough to hear that; when the party marched on, the prisoner was in the rear; he was armed with a weapon like those on the table;"—those were some pikes, Gentlemen, that were lying on the table;— " he was the right hand man of the three the greater part of the time; they were a rear guard; at Pentridge-lane I stopped behind once." You will see whether the prisoner is acting as a rear guard or not; you will observe that when a man is placed in the rear, he has little to do to quit the party but to stand still, and they will march on without him. " At Pentridge-lane, when they were going forward; I stopped behind once; the prisoner said, we must have you forward, you must come along with us;"—actually preventing his going away.—" I tried two or three different times, and found it impossible to make my escape in the rear, and in Pentridge-lane I got away in front; I went down a yard, as if I was going to call a person, and made my escape; I tried in the rear two or three times, but the prisoner and the two men that were with him prevented me;"—according to the account of this witness therefore, the prisoner is acting in the way mentioned by some others; marching in the rear for the purpose of compelling those who might have been brought against their will into the party to remain with it, and actually prevents this witness from leaving the party when he was desirous of doing so.

Upon being cross-examined, he says, " I do not know the names of the other two who walked in the rear; they appeared the most active men; some one said, that if Jessop did not give up his men he would be murdered; Manchester Turner was called the serjeant."

Then, on his re-examination, he says, " At the time of this observation the prisoner was near, and it was made in his presence and hearing."

The next witness is William Booth. He says, " I lived at Pentridge-lane end on the 9th of June last; I was disturbed between twelve and one o'clock by a parcel of men knocking very loud at the door; they called me up; I went to the window and asked what they wanted, they said, you and your gun; I said, I have no gun; they said, then we must have you, come down stairs and open the door, or else I will shoot you. I believe one man said all this; I said I cannot go, I am ballotted for the militia, and I must go to Derby to-day; they said, come down stairs and open the door, we will protect you from the militia, or else I will shoot you; I went down stairs and unbolted the door, and part of it fell into the passage; this was occasioned by the violence that had been used at the door; upon the door being opened, I saw a number of men rush in at the door, to the amount of six or eight;—

some were armed with guns, and some that stood at the door were armed with spikes, like those on the table; when they came in, the captain of the company asked me where my clothes were, I said, up stairs; he said, go and put them on immediately; I went up stairs immediately to put my clothes on; they lit a candle and followed me up, four or five of them; the captain and William Turner were all that I knew; when I got up stairs, they asked me what I had been doing, that I was not dressed; make haste, he said, or else I will shoot you, you seem to wish us to shoot you; I said, I had rather you would not;—as soon as I had put my clothes on, I went and sat me down on the squab, and offered to put my boots on, and to lace them, and the captain said, if you offer to stop to lace your boots I will shoot you; they then forced me out of the house before them; some one called me by my sirname, and asked me whether I had a gun, I said no, I had not, nor never had since I had been at that house; then they bade me take a fork; I said I could not find my fork, and they drove me out of the yard, and took me to a man in the ranks who had a gun, and told him to take care of that man as a prisoner; we went first to Mr. Storer's; a gun was fired against the meeting house, as a signal to alarm them at Butterley. I know Mr. William Booth, I remember his poney being brought out by George Weightman; the captain told him to take it and ride to Nottingham forest, and see how they were going on, and to come back and bring tidings;"—he sends this man, therefore, to that place, which had been before mentioned, Nottingham forest, and to come and bring them tidings;—" to meet them at Langley Mill; we then marched forward, two deep, to Butterley. I know the prisoner at the bar, I saw him there before we got to Butterley; he had a spike in his hand; he was in the rear to keep the men up, so that we could not get away; with the prisoner in the rear, and the captain in front, we marched up to Butterley gates, and rapped at the door; from Butterley we went to Ripley, and from thence to Codnor; in our march, I saw the prisoner several times, keeping guard in the rear; he was always in the same position when I saw him keeping guard in the rear; at Codnor we called at a house called the Glass House;"—you recollect other witnesses have said they supposed the prisoner to be stationed at the door of the Glass House for the purpose of keeping guard to prevent others going away; that they saw him there, and supposed that to be his object; now you will see what this man says,—" we called at a house called the Glass House, the prisoner said to the captain, there must somebody stop on the outside to take care that the men do not get away, or a great many will go away, if there is not some person to take care of them; and the prisoner did stay at the outside."—If you give credit to what this witness says, the prisoner did take his station at the outside as the others had supposed him to do, for the purpose of preventing those who might wish not to proceed further, escaping; and he did so at the suggestion of himself to Brandreth;—" he had had a gun delivered to him during the time he stopped there; when I went in he had a spike;" he says, " I think I saw his son likewise, I cannot say whether he had any arms or not; it rained very hard while we were at the public house at Codnor: we then marched on the road for Langley Mill. I saw the Prisoner several times in his old situation between the Glass House and Langley Mill, he still continued in the rear; I went beyond Eastwood a little way; I got away about half a mile beyond Eastwood and turned back; I saw the prisoner beyond Eastwood, when I was turning he was going forwards; he was behind the party; the greater part of them had got out of sight over the hill."

The next witness called, Gentlemen, is Hugh Booth, a son of Samuel Booth, of Pentridge-lane-end; you recollect it was proved, that Hugh a son of Samuel Booth, was taken from his father's house, and compelled to join this party; he says, " On the 9th of June last, I was disturbed between twelve and one by a party of men who came and knocked at the door two or three times; they called out, I want Hugh, I want Hugh Booth; my father got up and wished them to go without me; they said they would not go without me; that if my father would not get up and open the door, they would break the door down, and shoot him: I got up, and went to the door, and a man offered me a spike to go with them in the ranks; the prisoner said they were going to Nottingham; he was a little way from the door; they said they came from Mr. Fletcher's to our house; the prisoner ordered me to go into the ranks, and I was forced to do so; we went up to Pentridge, and stopped there; the whole body halted at that time; I again asked the Prisoner where we were going, he said, it is brought to a head at last, we are going to Nottingham; we then went to John Bright's house, there I had some conversation with the prisoner; I again asked him where we were going, and he said there was a parliament formed at Nottingham, and we were going to guard them; he said, the business will all be done before we get there;"—declaring again, if you believe the testimony of this witness, an object corresponding with that detailed to you, in the evidence of the others, namely, the object of guarding some meeting like a parliament, which it was supposed was to assemble, which could only be by taking the power from that Parliament in whom by the law of the land it is vested, and vesting it in others;—he says, "there was a young man in a blue coat and trowsers, who had a sword, and whose name, I have since heard, is Manchester Turner; he was of the party, and he said they were going to Nottingham to unload the burthen that England had so long borne; this was said at John Bright's; there was a gun fired just before we got there from Pentridge; we then marched towards Butterley, the prisoner had a large staff with a spike at the end of it; he was walking in the rear, and was very forward in pushing the men along; we went round to Butterley, and halted there; there we saw Mr. Goodwin; William Turner and the Nottingham captain were the leaders of the party; I heard the Nottingham captain speak to Mr. Goodwin; Mr. Goodwin asked him what he wanted, and he said we want your men; Mr. Goodwin told him they should not have them; I went into Mr. Goodwin's office; I saw the door open while the party was halted, and I walked in and escaped from them, and did not join them again."—This young man was a person who had been called out of his bed and compelled unwillingly to join their party, and at these Butterley works, seeing the door of the office open, he took the first convenient opportunity which presented itself, went in and remained no more engaged, or appearing to be so, in these transactions.

On his cross examination, he says, " I carried no arms the whole way ; the Captain and William Turner were the active men."

Then the next witness called is George Goodwin, who is the managing clerk of Mr. Jessop's works, who certainly does give very material and important evidence as it affects the prisoner at the bar; he says, " On Saturday the 7th of June, Special Constables were sworn in to protect the works."—It does appear from this, as well as from some circumstances he mentioned afterwards upon his cross-examination, that he had anticipated there might be some attempt to force open the works belonging to his masters, and the first two witnesses who are examined assign that as a reason for not making the disclosure which seemed to have been expected ;—he says, " on the 9th of June, at night, while on duty with the constables, we heard guns fired; the first I heard was a little before twelve o'clock, and between that time and day-light I heard three or four guns and the blowing of horns; a great part of the constables were dismissed a little before three in the morning of Tuesday;"—they seemed to have supposed that when day-light arrived there would be nothing attempted.—" Mr. Jessop and myself came down with a party that were armed with pikes to the office; a little before three o'clock I observed George Weightman riding past very quick; I called to him to stop, but he did not; he looked over and went on ;"—you may recollect what the other witnesses told you, that George Weightman was sent to Nottingham on Mr. Booth's pony to bring intelligence ;—a few minutes after, I observed about a hundred persons marching on the road from Pentridge in regular military order, two abreast, armed with guns, spears, and pikes, a few had no arms; they marched up to the door of the iron works, and there stopped and halted; I spoke to the Captain, who was at the head of them, and asked what was his object in halting there; he said, we want your men; I told him they should have none; that they were too many already, except they were going for a better purpose; I recognized among them the prisoner at the bar; he was in the front rank, as it was then, what in the march would have been the rear; I said to him, good God, Isaac, what are you doing here on such an errand as this; I urged him to leave them; I told him he had a halter about his neck, and he would be hanged if he did not immediately go home;"—he not only urges him by words to do this, but he endeavours to force him;—" I took him by his shoulders, and turned him with his face towards the office, and pushed him, that he might make his escape into the office; he had an opportunity of escaping if he chose;" he might have done so in the same way which Hugh Booth the young man did.—" The prisoner was much agitated, and said, I cannot go back; I am as bad as I can be; I must go on;"—this is the language which the prisoner at the bar uses when remonstrated with by that friend, who is anxious to give him an opportunity of redeeming himself, if possible, by taking no further part in these transactions;—but he says, " I cannot go back; I am as bad as I can be; it is too late to go back; I must go on." You will consider whether those expressions do not plainly import a mind conscious of all that he was doing, and conscious that he was one of those engaged in that plan of which he spoke, and of which they all spoke.—He says, " I spoke to nearly the same effect to James Taylor; three of them, during the time Ludlam and I were talking, escaped into the office; Booth was one of them. The captain and the party looked at each other for a short time, the captain then gave the word of command, and they marched along the road to Ripley, which is the road to Codnor; the prisoner went off with the first party, and in about a quarter of an hour after I observed another coming from

Pentridge; in about half an hour after the second party, I saw William Weightman on horseback, riding in the direction of Nottingham; from him I got a bag of bullets, of about 84 pounds weight;"—this is a preparation of ammunition;—"there might be from 1,500 to 2,000 bullets; there were a great variety of sizes, so as to fit the bore of different muskets and pistols; there were some moulds for cartridges, and paper in the bag, fit for the purpose, though not the best."—It appears that William Weightman was not willing to deliver up this bag to him; he made some resistance, but Mr. Goodwin overpowered him, and took it.

On his cross examination, he says, " I was surprized to see the prisoner at the bar amongst them; he was a man I had known for several years, and I wished him well;"— that he did wish him well, is plain from the expressions he used, but which had not the effect in prevailing upon the prisoner;—" he was much agitated when I spoke to him; I met with no resistance from him or any of them; I was armed; I had a brace of pistols in my pocket; I considered the prisoner in as little danger as myself;"—he is asked, whether he felt confident of his own safety, and he says, " I considered myself in danger, but I considered if the prisoner had gone, that he would not have been in greater danger than myself; he would have had all the means of safety I had."

Then he says, on re-examination, " I had sworn in an hundred and fifteen or sixteen special constables on the Saturday before, in expectation of an insurrection; they were armed with pikes;"—it was very fit and very proper, that when Mr. Jessop and Mr. Goodwin expected an assault from a number of persons, they should put arms into the hands of their own servants to protect their property from the assault that was expected.

The next witness, Gentlemen, is John Storer, a farmer at Pentridge; he says, " On the 9th of June I was disturbed after I was gone to bed, about one o'clock, by a body of armed men; they presented a gun at the windows, and threatened to shoot me. I had gone to the window

and threatened to shoot me; I had gone to the window on the first alarm; one of them said, 'Damn your eyes, come and go with us, or we will shoot you.' There were about twelve or fifteen of them; I asked them if there was no excuse; they said, none. William Turner was one of them; he had a gun; he said there was me, a gun, and two or three more in the house, and me and the gun they were determined should go with them; and they would shoot me and all in the house if I would not go; that the captain had just shot Hepworth's man. I told them, I would go with them, if they would give me a little time to dress myself; they told me, that if I did not make haste they would make me so that I could not go; I cannot say who said that. I finished dressing myself, and I took an old gun, and went to them out of the house; they asked me if it was loaded; I told them, not; they asked me if I had any shot and powder; I told them, a little shot."
"They said it did not mean; (a word, I believe, importing, did not signify;) they should have powder and ball sufficient. We then went on by the yard to a gate leading into the lane; I told them, I was not fit to go, I had been very unwell the day before, and I was not willing to go; I told them I could not carry the gun any further; they said it must go with the baggage; I asked them where the baggage was; they said, they did not know then what they should have; then we went into the lane; they said, they were going to Nottingham; it was a general rising; that twenty-five or thirty thousand were coming from Sheffield; that there would be several hundred thousands assemble that day; that liberty would be gained, and an end of slavery; this was said by a person in the midst of them, I do not know by whom. They said all must go, or be shot."—Gentlemen, I cannot forbear making a remark upon this expression, "liberty would be gained, and an end of slavery; all must go, or be shot." The very first step taken by these people, the first purpose that they are arming themselves for, in the recovery of the lost liberty of the country, is, to take away the life of all those who will not join them, and become parties in

their scheme; for they declare in words, that those that will not join them shall all be shot.—" We stopped in the lane waiting for the captain. They told us, when we got into the lane, they were waiting for the captain and a party down the lane end. They came up in about twenty minutes; I thought them about a hundred, armed with guns and pikes similar to those on the table; when the body came up, I saw the captain; he carried a very long pike; he ordered the men to fall in three deep; those with guns in the front, and those with pikes behind. The captain and the principal men held a consultation; among them were William Turner, and a young man that appeared to have but one eye, whom they called Manchester Turner, whom they called lieutenant. After they had consulted together, the captain asked whether there were any men that could do their exercise; if they could, they should fall out, and be made non-commissioned officers; some did fall out; I believe some were appointed, but I was in the rear too far off to know. There was an advanced guard and a guard in the rear; the prisoner was to command the rear;"—which is exactly what all the other witnesses have spoken to his doing.—" Then the Captain ordered them to march; they proceeded towards Pentridge; they stopped to break open houses, and bring men and guns out at Pentridge. I feigned myself ill; I wished to get from them; they said they would all go in that way; and somebody said, 'shoot him.' The captain appointed two men to take hold of me, each by one arm; they led me in this way up Pentridge, to William Booth's; there they got out his pony, and saddled and bridled it, and then they set me on the poney; I was not willing to go with them, and I fell off; the captain ordered them to face to the right, and march; then they left me, and I saw no more of them."

Upon being cross-examined, he says, " I saw the prisoner frequently; I cannot say particularly whether I saw him just before I got away; they did not ill use me, they threatened to shoot me; I did not see the prisoner at that time, but I have no doubt he was very near, for I saw him frequently at Pentridge. The captain frequently used very violent language towards me. I told him he had better shoot me, then he would have done with me; and he said, ' damn him, leave him, we can do without one;' they went away immediately. I had proceeded with them about three quarters of a mile. George Weightman was one that put me upon the poney, the other I do not know."—In answer to a question put by me, he says, " I did not know Thomas Turner;" it seems by the testimony of Thomas Turner, that he was the other man who gave him a leg up.

The next witness is William Roper. You will observe, Gentlemen, that in the evidence which has already been given you, an expectation at least appears to have been entertained by many of the persons engaged in these transactions, that they were to be joined by a considerable party at Nottingham Forest, and at Nottingham; now whether they acted under that expectation, or whether that expectation was well or ill founded, would not make any difference; men who engage in treason are not the less traitorous because they expect others to unite in that treason; nor are they the less traitors because they are deceived in their expectation; but the object on the part of the Crown, in calling forwards this William Roper, is to prove that this expectation of an assembly on Nottingham Forest, was not altogether without foundation; he says, " I live on the race course, Nottingham Forest, about three quarters of a mile from the town of Nottingham. On the 9th of June I was returning home from Nottingham about half-past eleven o'clock, a person of the name of Percival was with me; when I got on the Forest, I met, first of all, two men, and afterwards several more, they had no arms that I saw; and then I came in sight of a body, as nearly as I can guess, about a hundred; about ten or twelve of them followed me and Percival, with poles in their hands, brought down to a charge against us, and asked us where we were going; after a conversation they permitted us to go on. After I had got to my house, a number of men came to it, they seemed to be of the same party, and they acted pretty much in the same way; they asked if I had got any fire-arms in the house, I told them yes; they told me I must deliver them up to them; I said, I would not; they said if I did not deliver them up, they should be under the necessity of breaking the door open and taking them by force; I said if they did I should blow out the brains of the first man that came in, let him be who he would; they did not break in; this was about one o'clock when they demanded the arms, and about two they departed."—This therefore does, you see, go, if you give credit to it, to prove that there was, in fact, this very same night, a large assembly of persons at Nottingham Forest, much smaller than those persons whose particular acts have been detailed, expected, but still that there was a considerable assembly.

Captain Philips, an officer in the 15th dragoons, says, "I was quartered at Nottingham barracks on the 9th of June; about ten o'clock that evening two companies of infantry, a part of my troop, with a field officer, were ordered into Nottingham, in consequence of being sent for by some of the magistrates;"—what was going forward there at that time is not in proof; you are only to take it that they were sent for; "we remained in the town about half an hour; I went in the command of part of my own troop, and there was a field officer who had the command of the whole; at the expiration of that time we returned;" he says, "about half past six the following morning I was ordered out with a party of men to go with Mr. Rolleston and Mr. Mundy, two magistrates, in pursuit of the rioters; both those gentlemen accompanied me; a magistrate had slept in the barracks all night; we took the Pentridge road. About half a mile before I got to Eastwood, I saw some armed men on the left hand of the road making their escape across some fields; they appeared to be armed with pikes; we pursued them a little way but could not overtake them; we then went on through Eastwood, and between Eastwood and Langley mill I observed a party of about sixty on the road; the greatest part of them were armed; they were standing in the road, and one man attempted to form them up in opposition to us; but they paid no attention to him, and fled across the fields immediately, some to the right and some to the left. I ordered the dragoons to pursue and to take as many prisoners as they could; I think about thirty-six prisoners were brought in; there were five or six taken armed with muskets, and some with pikes; the rest of the arms, consisting of pikes and guns, chiefly pikes, had been thrown away by the rioters, and were collected and put into a cart, and taken to Nottingham gaol; we examined the guns that were picked up, and found them loaded."

On his cross examination, he says, " they fled in all directions in the utmost confusion."

Then on being re-examined he says, " some time after that, we met the high sheriff of Derbyshire and the Chesterfield yeomanry."

This, Gentlemen, is the whole of the evidence that has been laid before you, on the part of the Crown, to support the very serious charge which is preferred against this prisoner; no evidence is aduced in answer to it; no witness is called to contradict any fact spoken to by any of the persons examined on the part of the Crown, or to impeach the character or credibility of any one of them; but it is contended on the part of the prisoner, and rightly contended, that he is not to be called upon to answer, but that the question is, whether the evidence which you have thus heard, is in itself sufficient to satisfy you, not that he was guilty of riot, of outrage, of breaking open houses, or of any practices of that kind, but that he was guilty of this crime of High Treason, in levying war against the King, and if this evidence has not satisfied you that he was guilty of that charge, then without any answer either by evidence or otherwise, you will find him not guilty. He has called one witness, who is the gaoler of this county, who says, that during the time the prisoner has been in confinement he has conducted himself peaceably and orderly, and with the greatest affection towards those two sons who appear, according to the evidence, to have been of this party; their conduct, however, is not now the subject of enquiry.

Upon this evidence, you have, as I before mentioned, to

consider three questions. Has there been an insurrection; a rising of armed men, marching and committing acts of violence? I can hardly state that to you as a question, because the whole of the evidence conspires to prove it; and indeed the fact is not controverted by the prisoners counsel.—Next, was the object of these persons to assail and endeavour to overturn the established Government of the Country? Now what their object was you are to collect, as well from their acts as from their expressions and declarations; what the object of an individual was, is to be collected from his own declarations and expressions, and from his own acts; what was said by others in his absence, and out of his hearing, ought not to affect him, unless what he has himself said and himself has done, shew to your satisfaction, that he too was a party embarked in the same designs as are expressed by others; many expressions of his own, proceeding from his own lips, have been given in evidence against the prisoner, and they are most important for your consideration.—Then the third question is, Was the prisoner at the bar a party concerned in that rising, and having the same object? You have heard what he himself said to two of the witnesses, and what they said to one another, that Nottingham was their object; there was to be a new parliament; they would have little to do when they got there; thousands would join them, and so on; always expressing a confident hope that the present Government would be overturned, and some new system of government established.

It has been urged, that the means which these persons possessed were wholly inadequate to the end they proposed, and that it is absurd to suppose that the government of the country could be overturned by such an assembly of persons as this, even with the aid they expressed themselves to expect; but, Gentlemen, the question is not, whether their design was likely to succeed, but whether they entertained it. The improbability of success may be used as a sort of argument to shew that a person does not entertain a design imputed to him, because in general, it is not likely that a man will entertain a design which there is no probability of his executing; but if you find, from the evidence, that he is actually embarking in that design, and declaring that he entertains it, there is then no room for the argument, which might otherwise be adduced as to the improbability of its success; if you find he was embarked in it, the improbability of success makes no difference in the crime; they expected, as it appears, a much greater force to assemble than did assemble; they were acting probably on some delusion, whether at the instigation of their own immediate friends, or of others, is not material; the question is not, whether they had ground for hoping for success, but the question is, did they or did they not, and particularly did the prisoner at the bar, engage in the acts imputed to him, with the design charged by this Indictment; namely, the design of endeavouring to overturn the Government: if you think he did, then you cannot otherwise discharge your painful duty than by pronouncing him guilty. You will consider calmly, temperately, and dispassionately, the evidence which has been laid before you; you will weigh the remarks which have been made; you will discharge your duty according to your own judgment, and your oaths; and be assured, nothing can confer upon you greater comfort in life, or better hopes hereafter; nothing can confer any greater blessing upon yourselves, your family, your posterity or your country, than a faithful, upright, and conscientious discharge of that painful duty which it has fallen to your lot to execute.

> The Jury withdrew at ten minutes after two, and returned in ten minutes with their Verdict, pronouncing the prisoner GUILTY; and that he had not to their knowledge any lands, &c. at the time of the offence committed.

THE TRIAL OF GEORGE WEIGHTMAN.

SPECIAL ASSIZE, DERBY.
Thursday, 23d October 1817.

The Prisoner was set to the Bar.
The Jury returned by the Sheriff were called over.

JOHN BUXTON, farmer, challenged by the prisoner.
Thomas Buxton, farmer, challenged by the crown.
Robert Millington, farmer, challenged by the prisoner.
George Toplis, farmer, challenged by the prisoner.
William Allsopp, farmer, challenged by the prisoner.
Peter Buxton, farmer, challenged by the prisoner.
John Oldfield, farmer, challenged by the prisoner.
William Ashmore, farmer, fined £.10; but fine afterwards remitted.
Joseph Gould, farmer, excused on account of illness.
George Bankes, miller, challenged by the prisoner.
William Swan, farmer, sworn.
Thomas Lomas, farmer, challenged by the prisoner.
John Rogers, farmer, sworn.
Anthony Broadhurst, farmer, not a freeholder, &c.
Roger Sheldon, farmer, sworn.
Joseph Needham, farmer, sworn.
George Bagshaw, farmer, sworn.
Richard Shaw, farmer, challenged by the prisoner.
John Millwood, farmer; not properly described in the panel.

Richard Thompson, horse dealer, challenged by the crown.

Thomas Travis, farmer, challenged by the prisoner.

John Matkin, butcher, challenged by the prisoner.

German Dean, farmer, challenged by the crown.

John Thomson, farmer, challenged by the prisoner.

Thomas Slater, farmer, challenged by the crown.

Francis Hayne, farmer, challenged by the prisoner.

Wigley Hodgkinson, farmer, sworn.

George Hodgkinson, farmer, sworn.

Nathaniel Wheatcroft, coal merchant, challenged by the prisoner.

John Ward, farmer, sworn.

William Stone, joiner, challenged by the prisoner.

Nathaniel Hall, farmer, challenged by the prisoner.

William Brownson, shopkeeper, challenged by the crown.

John Endsor, farmer, sworn.

Thomas Gould, farmer, challenged by the prisoner.

Thomas Deakin, farmer, sworn.

John Bagshaw, farmer, challenged by the prisoner.

Robert Bagshaw, farmer, not a freeholder, &c.

Isaac Bennett, farmer, challenged by the prisoner.

George Holmes, farmer, challenged by the prisoner.

Robert Johnson, mercer, challenged by the prisoner.

Robert Simpson, miller, challenged by the prisoner.

Robert Tarrand, grocer, challenged by the crown.

Joseph Hodgkinson, miller, sworn.

Thomas Drinkwater, gentleman, challenged by the crown.

Randle Taylor, gentleman, challenged by the prisoner.

John Barnes, the younger, cotton spinner, sworn.

THE JURY:

William Swan.	George Hodgkinson.
John Rogers.	John Ward.
Roger Sheldon.	John Endsor.
Joseph Needham.	Thomas Deakin.
George Bagshaw.	Joseph Hodgkinson.
Wigley Hodgkinson.	John Barnes the younger.

The Jury were charged with the prisoner in the usual form.

The Indictment was opened by Mr J. Balguy.

Mr. SOLICITOR GENERAL.

May it please your Lordship,

Gentlemen of the Jury,

FROM the Indictment which has just been opened to you by my learned friend Mr. Balguy, you are informed of the nature of the charge which is now preferred against the prisoner at the bar; namely, that he is accused of the crime of high treason; and the anxious duty is imposed upon you, of determining, after you shall have heard the evidence, whether that charge be well founded or not.

It will be my duty in the few observations which I shall have the honour of making to you upon this occasion, to state to you, very shortly, my apprehension of the nature of the charge against the prisoner at the bar in point of law; and then to state to you, with as much brevity and perspicuity as I can, the facts, which I believe will be proved to you in evidence upon the present occasion; but before I make this statement, let me request you to discharge from your minds any thing that you may have heard in the course of the trials which have preceded the present, and to dismiss from your recollection the result of those trials, and to come to the present investigation with free and unbiassed minds, resolved to do that which you know it is your duty to do; to decide upon the guilt or innocence of the prisoner at the bar, upon the evidence and the evidence alone, which shall be adduced upon the present charge.

Gentlemen, with respect to the nature of that charge, I shall content myself with stating to you, very shortly, what I apprehend it consists of, with all due deference to the high authority under which you are acting, and by which you will be ultimately guided; and unless you find my notions upon the subject confirmed by that authority, you will most properly, when you come to the consideration of this case, dismiss them from your minds, relying, as you are bound to do, upon that authority only.

But after the discussions which have already taken place, I consider it the safest and best course, without troubling you with an historical account of the law of Treason, or fatiguing your minds with the recapitulation of cases and decisions upon the subject, to state to you shortly what the nature of the principal charge against the prisoner at the bar is, to which charge you are to apply the evidence.

Gentlemen, the species of high treason which it is alledged this prisoner has committed, is that of levying war against the King; to make out that charge, it will be sufficient to satisfy your minds that there was a general rising or assembly of an armed multitude, that they intended by force to effect some general public object, inconsistent with the Government of the country, as established by law; and if that be proved to your satisfaction, it will be, in point of law, a levying of war against the King in his realm. There must be a rising or an assembly of a considerable number of persons. It is not essential, although on the present occasion it will be proved, that such persons were armed, for, if they were not armed, yet if they were in such numbers as to cause such terror and alarm as was likely to effect their object, that their object was treasonable, would be a levying war, but that circumstance will not be material for your consideration, because the case is, that there was a multitude of armed persons on this occasion. I say, if it shall be proved there was this assembly of armed persons, and they intended by force to effect that which we attribute to them, namely, an alteration in the constitution as established by law, it constitutes the offence of levying war against the King; and it is the high treason charged against the prisoner upon this Indictment.

Gentlemen, having stated to you thus much with respect to the nature of the charge, you will have no difficulty whatever in applying the evidence which will be given to it, and be able in the result, to come to a conclusion, whether those things which I state to you are essential to constitute the crime of high treason, appear in the present case; and whether the prisoner at the bar be shewn to be one of those persons so acting against the law, and so bringing himself within the charge now preferred against him.

With respect to the nature of the case, which will be proved on the present occasion, the evidence will probably commence as to transactions which took place on Sunday the 8th of June in the present year; you will find, however, from that evidence, that there can be no doubt in the mind of any reasonable person, that although the proof will only be of a meeting on the Sunday the 8th of June, yet that considerable preparations had been previously made to carry into effect the plan which was then finally digested and concluded upon. The prisoner at the bar, George Weightman, is a sawyer, residing at Pentridge, in this county; and it will appear to you, that on Sunday the 8th of June, at a public house in the town of Pentridge, known by the sign of the White Horse, a considerable number of persons were assembled, and a person of the name of Brandreth, and who also was called by the persons present the Nottingham captain, was one of those who were so assembled, and the prisoner, George Weightman, will also be proved to you to have been present during the greater part of the morning during which these persons were so met. The whole conversation, and all the deliberations of that morning, were upon a revolution, and an alteration in the Government, and how that was to be effected; and it will appear to you that their plan was, that a general rising should take place on the following night, Monday the 9th of June; that persons from Pentridge, from Southwingfield, from Ripley, and other places in that neighbourhood, should meet on that evening at some point, and proceed to Nottingham Forest, where it was held out to them they should meet a considerable body of men, also having the same object in view; and having united their forces at Nottingham Forest, they were to take possession of the town of Nottingham, and afterwards they should be enabled to prosecute their further designs with ease by going down the Trent, and I believe to London, and to attempt that, which they had in view, an alteration of the Government. You will hear that

Brandreth had a map before him, on which the places were marked from whence they expected bodies of men to join them; that it was stated upon that occasion, that not only would the persons in this neighbourhood, but persons from the North also join them on this common expedition; that they had no doubt of success, and that the following night, at nine or ten o'clock, should be the time at which they were to commence their operations.

Gentlemen, the prisoner, George Weightman, will be proved to you to have been present during the whole or the greatest part of these consultations; and you will judge not only from that circumstance, but from his subsequent conduct, how far he was a party acting and contributing towards the common design. At present it will be sufficient for me to state to you, that upon that Sunday their plan was conversed upon, that the means by which they should procure arms were also considered; and although it appears that pikes had been in preparation, and had been made by some of the persons at Southwingfield, yet that a Paper was then read, containing an account of the different houses at which arms would probably be found on the following night, and that they were to take those arms by force; and not only arms, but they were to compel all the persons they could to join them upon this expedition, and those who were not willing were to be forced to join their ranks, and march in a common body towards Nottingham.

I will not fatigue you, at this late hour of the day, by stating to you particularly all that passed at that meeting; you will hear it from the witnesses, from whom you will learn that upon that occasion verses were recited (which will be stated and commented on hereafter) directed and pointed to the common object and design, and to the means by which it was to be executed.

It was arranged that on the Monday night the Pentridge and Southwingfield people were to assemble, the latter at a place called Hunt's Barn; the prisoner at the bar lived at Pentridge, which is at some distance from Hunt's Barn; he, however, will be proved to have been present there at the original meeting, and Brandreth the leader, and Turner, who took a prominent part in the transactions, were there with him before they commenced their march on the expedition in question. George Weightman had been previously seen in the town of Pentridge that evening with Brandreth and William Turner; and it is important to attend to what passed at Pentridge at the time he was proceeding with these persons towards Hunt's Barn; for you will find by a conversation which took place there, that he was fully aware of the nature of the meeting, which indeed he must have been from having been at the public-house the day before; his expressions upon this occasion, however, confirm his knowledge of the plan, for he stated to a person, who will be called as a witness, that they expected that evening an engagement at the Butterley works. These are iron works in the neighbourhood of Pentridge, and it will appear in evidence that in anticipation of something of the sort which took place on Monday the 9th of June, preparations had been made at those works to prevent their getting arms, or forcing men out to join them.

From Hunt's Barn the party proceeded towards Topham's close, where they were to meet the general party from Pentridge. Weightman accompanies them; and in their way to Topham's close they begin that system which had been resolved on, namely, attacking houses and demanding arms, and compelling men to join them; he is present at one or two houses which were attacked in the way from Hunt's Barn to this close; and during the whole, or the greater part of that way he carried a quantity of bullets, which it was expected they might have occasion to use in the course of their march. Upon their arrival at Topham's close, they did not meet the Pentridge men as had been arranged, and therefore it was determined that George Weightman, who was a Pentridge man, with some others, should separate from the main body and go in the direction of Pentridge from whence they expected the Pentridge men, in order if he met them to stop their advance, and to take them round by another way to a place called Pentridge-lane-end, where they were to join the main body under Brandreth, who was to proceed in a straighter direction to that point.

Weightman and his party accordingly proceeded in the direction I have stated in order to meet the Pentridge people; and I believe it will be proved that in his way to Pentridge other houses were attacked and persons were compelled to join that party with which he was then associated, and arms also were taken; and I believe it will appear to you, that in the course of that march to Pentridge the prisoner took a very active part. I will not detail to you now the circumstances, because I think it better you should hear them from the witnesses than receive any possible prejudice from any statement I shall make; but it will be proved, that in their march to Pentridge, persons were forced to join them, and that Weightman took an active part in compelling them so to do.

The Pentridge party were to proceed, as I stated, to Pentridge-lane-end, where they were to meet the other party under Brandreth; it will appear to you, however, that Weightman went to the town of Pentridge, and there probably deposited the bullets at some house, because he afterwards joined them in their march from Pentridge without the bullets.

Brandreth's party proceeded in their course to a house occupied by a man of the name of Hall; from thence to the houses of persons of the names of Walker and Bestwick, to Samuel Hunt's, to Mary Hepworth's, and other places, and during their whole progress they were attacking the houses where they expected and where it appeared, from the accounts given the day before, they knew there were arms. You will find they demanded arms on one occasion at Mr. Fletcher's; he said he had no arms; they insisted he had, and compelled the production of a pistol; but what I wish to state is, that during their march they pursued the purpose of compelling the production of arms and forcing persons to join them, as agreed the night before; and although the prisoner was not present at that part of the transaction, yet I can state to you with confidence that if he shall be proved to be a party in the general common object, and was pursuing that object elsewhere (as he was in his way from Topham's close to Pentridge) he is equally answerable for the acts of Brandreth and his party as if he were present, and therefore it is most material for you to see in what manner these different parties were proceeding, whether Weightman was present at all the transactions or not.

Gentlemen, the party having by force and by most violent outrages, and most cruel acts, compelled the production of arms, and forced some persons to join them, proceeded towards Pentridge, where they were met by George Weightman, who had before carried the bullets thither, and had probably depofited them there. He then joined them, and they proceeded up Pentridge, pursuing the same course; assailing in the dead of night the peaceable inhabitants, rousing them from their rest, and compelling them to give up what arms they had; and in many instances forcing the inhabitants to join the party. Weightman is with them, and you will see what he does, as they proceed further in their expedition.

I stated to you, that it was expected by this party that they should meet a considerable body of persons at Nottingham Forest, at an early hour on the following day; it was therefore most important, finding as they must have done, that by the outrages which they committed, and the resistance they met with, they were delayed in their progress, to dispatch somebody from Pentridge to Nottingham, to see how matters were going on there, and also to intimate the cause of the delay in their arrival there. A poney is taken by the prisoner Weightman, belonging to a person of the name of Booth, at Pentridge town, and he was despatched to Nottingham, for the express purpose, as was stated at the time, of procuring tidings of what was going on there at that time; and he was to return, and meet the party at Langley mill, which is in the road from Pentridge to Nottingham.

He accordingly mounted the poney, and rode off in the direction of Nottingham; of course by this step he is absent during the proceedings which subsequently take place;

but, as I before stated to you, if you are satisfied that he was a party in the common design, and that he was lending all the aid and assistance he could to it, the acts which were done in his absence are evidence against him; and therefore let it not be said, that because he is absent, therefore the outrages which were done are not to affect him. In a transaction of this sort, in a scheme of this description, it must necessarily happen, that persons have different duties assigned to them. Some men are to command the forces, others are to procure intelligence, all of them however are to lend their best assistance to the common object; and, therefore, a man like Weightman, who is despatched in order to procure information to aid them in that which they have in view, is as culpable as the man who is left behind to head the party in his absence.

But his going to Nottingham, and what subsequently took place, form another feature in this transaction, because it shews his will, his mind, his intention on the present occasion; and therefore there can be no excuse for him, as there is for some who had arms forced on them, and were compelled to join this party; but he took a voluntary part, and did that which no force could compel him to do; because when mounted on the horse he might have left them; but he proceeded, and did that, which, if he is guilty, greatly enhances his guilt. He returned, and stated to them that which unquestionably was not true, which he must have known was utterly false, and which, therefore, could have been stated to them for no other object than to keep up their spirits, and induce them to continue in that scheme and plan which they had originally formed; for on his return you will find there was an anxiety displayed by many of the persons to know how things were going on at Nottingham, for Tuesday morning had then arrived, it was seven or eight o'clock; they were anxious therefore to know whether their expectations were to be fulfilled, and whether they were to meet this body at Nottingham; and you will find, that upon their enquiry he rides along the ranks, and tells them to keep up their spirits, and march forward; that Nottingham had been taken, the soldiers would not move from their barracks, that all was well, and therefore that they should press forward with as much expedition as they could. Gentlemen, all this was utterly false; Nottingham had not been taken, the soldiers were not afraid to proceed from their barracks. It was a compleat fiction, and could only be invented to keep up the spirits of the party, which at that time, after a march of many miles, during a wet and stormy night, were drooping, and to induce them to continue in the scheme they had formed. True it is that at two o'clock, in Nottingham Forest, a body of men assembled as had been expected; but it is true also, that before Weightman could have arrived they had dispersed.

Gentlemen, soon after his return, although many of the persons with Brandreth and Turner continued to march on their way to Nottingham; yet others became disheartened, fell off by degrees, till at last, on the appearance of some troops under Captain Philips from Nottingham, although there was an attempt by one man to form some of them in the road with an appearance of resistance, yet they dispersed in all directions, and threw away their arms, which were collected by the soldiers, and a great number of the party were taken prisoners in the course of that morning.

Having stated to you these facts, will they, if proved, leave any room for you to doubt about an insurrection upon that night? there can be none; it will be proved beyond all contradiction; their object will be proved with equal clearness; you will find it by their declarations, you will see it as strongly by their acts, you will learn by their declarations, that they intended, (wild as might be their scheme) to overturn the present government if they could; and, Gentlemen, you will recollect that you are not to consider upon the present occasion whether this was a wise and well-digested scheme on their part, whether it was probable they could effect their purpose, whether the number of the persons or of the arms was adequate to the intended effect,—that is not the question; but the question is, whether they had the intention imputed to them, and did they act upon that intention, and was George Weightman acting in concert with them in prosecution of their common design.

As to George Weightman, the unfortunate prisoner at the bar, you will find him at the meeting on Sunday, you will find him one of the first to assemble on Monday night at Hunt's barn with the captain and other persons; you will find him proceeding till it was convenient for their purpose to detach him from them; and on their arrival at Topham's close, his leaving them is not a voluntary act of his to remove himself from the party, but with a view to direct the Pentridge people in the way, and to join Brandreth again; and it is confirmed that he did not want to secede from them, since he joined them at Pentridge town, and attacked with them several houses, and afterwards performed that important office of going to Nottingham to procure information, and of returning to meet them in the way I have described to you.

Gentlemen, if these facts are proved, and I think they will be proved, the case I apprehend will be clearly made out against the prisoner at the bar; but as I before stated to you, your judgment is not to be swayed by any thing which I have had the honour of stating to you, but you are to draw your conclusion from the evidence; and if I state any thing which is not proved, dismiss it from your minds; if you think the inferences I have drawn from his acts are too strong, dismiss them also; but if when you come to a calm review of this case, you find the facts proved by satisfactory testimony, if you find the conduct of George Weightman to be such as I have depicted to you, then it will be for you to say whether there has not been an insurrection, whether the object of that insurrection was not the overthrow of the government, and whether George Weightman was not a participator and an actor in that scheme.

Gentlemen, I will not now fatigue you with any further observations upon this case, my only object I can assure you has been to state to you clearly and with precision the nature of the charge against the prisoner; to state, to you also, without embellishment and without any argument beyond that which the facts require, the nature of the evidence which will be adduced against the prisoner at the bar. It is in my apprehension a plain case; it will however be for you in the result to determine whether I am mistaken in that or not; you will judge when you have heard the evidence, whether that evidence does come up to the statement which I have made; if it does, and if it proves the charge against the prisoner on this indictment, then as I stated in the outset dismiss from your minds every thing that has passed on these trials; look neither backwards nor forwards beyond the verdict you are now to give; satisfy your minds and consciences in pronouncing that verdict; and if you do, I am perfectly confident you will satisfy the justice of the case.

EVIDENCE FOR THE CROWN.

Anthony Martin sworn.

Examined by Mr. Serjeant Vaughan.

Q. Were you in the service of Messrs. Jessop, at the Butterley works, in the month of June last?

A. Yes.

Q. Did you on Sunday morning, the 8th of June, go to Pentridge?

A. Yes.

Q. With whom?

A. John Cope.

Q. At what time of the day?

A. Between nine and ten o'clock.

Q. At what time did you arrive there?

A. About nine or ten o'clock.

Q. Where did you go to?

A. We went to Nanny Weightman's croft, and sat down there.

Q. Is that the mistress of the public-house, the White Horse?

A. Yes.

Q. That is behind the White Horse?

A. Yes.

Q. How came you to leave the croft?

A. There was a little girl came and spoke to us to go into the house.

Q. In consequence of a message you received, you went into the house?

A. Yes.

Q. When you went into the house, what room did you go into?

A. Through the house into the parlour.

Q. When you went into the parlour who did you find there; how many people were assembled at that time?

A. There were about six or seven people.

Q. Can you tell us the names of any of them?

A. There was Brandreth there.

Q. The Nottingham captain, as he is called ?

A. Yes.

Q. Who else?

A. Ormond Booth, and Joseph Weightman, and George Weightman.

Mr. Justice Holroyd. By George Weightman, do you mean the prisoner?

A. Yes.

Mr. Serjeant Vaughan. When you speak of him in future call him the prisoner. Any body else?

A. There was his brother Joseph; he lived there.

Q. Do you know whether George lived at the house or not?

A. I cannot say whether he did or not.

Q. Do you remember any other names?

A. No.

Q. What were they talking about; who was taking a lead in the conversation?

A. Brandreth.

Q. What did you hear him say?

A. He was talking about the revolution, and of overturning the Government.

Q. Mention, as nearly as you can, the expressions that were used; what did he say?

A. He was talking about which way they must proceed.

Q. Proceed to do what?

A. There was nothing could be done excepting by the overturn of the present Government.

Q. What further did he say?

A. He was delivering out some verses about the Government.

Q. Who was delivering out some verses?

A. Brandreth.

Q. When you say he was delivering out some verses about the Government, do you mean he was handing them about, or repeating them?

A. He repeated them, and gave them to different persons.

Q. Did he repeat them more than once?

A. Yes.

Q. Do you remember any of those verses?
A. Yes.
Q. Repeat them?
A. " Every man his skill must try,
He must turn out and not deny;
No bloody soldier must he dread,
He must turn out and fight for bread;
The time is come you plainly see,
That Government opposed must be."

Q. You say the conversation was about the Government and the revolution?
A. Yes.
Q. Was there any thing said as to the meeting, or what was to be done or not?
A. Yes, they were to meet on Monday night.
Q. Who said so?
A. Brandreth.
Q. Brandreth said they were to meet on the next night?
A. Yes.
Q. To meet where, and for what purpose?
A. To overturn the Government.
Q. Was there any thing said about arms or any thing
A. Yes.
Q. What was said about arms?
A. Turner brought a list.
Q. At what time did Turner come in?
A. Perhaps it might be one o'clock.
Q. Which Turner?
A. William Turner.

Mr. *Justice Holroyd.* Had the prisoner continued in the room all this time?
A. No, he was not in the room all the time.
Mr. *Serjeant Vaughan.* He was in and out?
A. Yes, he was out the greatest part of the time.
Q. Was he frequently in and frequently out?
A. He was in in the morning when I went in, but he went out soon afterwards and continued out for a considerable time, and then came in again.
Q. Was he there during any part of the time when

Brandreth was talking about a revolution and the Government, and what was to be done?

A. I cannot really say whether he was there or not when he was speaking those words.

Q. Do you remember whether he was there when Brandreth said any thing about the Government?

A. Yes, he was there when he was talking about it.

Q. Was any map or any thing produced?

A. Yes, Brandreth produced a map.

Q. Do you remember whether the prisoner was in the room at any time when that map was produced?

A. I cannot recollect whether he was or not.

Q. How often might he be in and out of the room during the time you were there?

A. He was in and out two or three times.

Q. Did he sit down when he was in the room?

A. Yes.

Q. What I want to know is, whether he came in to wait upon the company, or whether he was in there and sitting down with the company?

A. Part of the time he was waiting upon the company.

Q. What relation is he to Mrs. Weightman who keeps the house?

A. He is her son.

Q. You say he did wait upon the company, but he sat down at other times; who did he talk with when he was there?

A. He was talking with Ormond Booth in general; he went away with Ormond Booth just after dinner, and staid away the remainder part of the day while I was there.

Q. Do you know whether he had any conversation with Brandreth?

A. I cannot say that he had whilst I saw him.

Q. Whilst he was in the room was any thing said about Nottingham?

A. Yes.

Q. State to my Lord and the Jury what was said about Nottingham whilst the prisoner was in the room.

A. There was some money gathered for Joseph Weightman to go to Nottingham.

Q. Was it stated what he was to go to Nottingham for?

A. He was to go to Nottingham to see whether they were all ready there; whether all was right and ready.

Mr. Justice Holroyd. Was that said?

A. Yes.

Mr. Serjeant Vaughan. It was said that he was to go for that purpose to see whether they were all right and ready?

A. Yes.

Q. How were the expences of Joseph Weightman, who was to go, to be paid?

A. There was some little money gathered in the room to bear his expences.

Q. At the time that you are speaking of?

A. Yes.

Q. When was he to go?

A. He was to go on the Sunday, directly, and come back on that day and let them know.

Q. What was this map that was produced by Brandreth produced for?

A. He pointed out different places where they were to meet and to go to; I believe the places were pricked out on the map by crosses.

Q. Can you state any further conversation that took place about what they were to do; where were they to go to?

A. They were to go to Nottingham, and to take the town.

Q. What were they to do then?

A. They were to return back to the barracks which they had pointed out.

Q. Where were the barracks?

A. At Butterley.

Q. What was to be done at Butterley?

A. It was to be made a barracks of.

Q. Was any thing said about a rising, or who was to rise or expected to rise?

A. Yes, they talked of a regular thing throughout the country.

Q. Was there any thing said about who were coming?

A. They expected all the northern parts were coming that morning they said.

Q. And you say it was expected to be a regular thing throughout the country?

A. Yes.

Q. Was any thing said about success or failure, or what was to become of it?

A. Yes, they were to go and overturn the government.

Q. You say William Turner came in there; who came in with him?

A. Isaac Ludlam.

Q. Upon William Turner coming in with Ludlam, was there any thing said about arms?

A. Yes.

Q. What was done when Turner came into the room and spoke about arms?

A. He wanted to know where the list of the arms was belonging to Pentridge and Ripley.

Q. Who wanted to know that?

A. William Turner.

Q. What answer was made to him upon making that enquiry?

A. They said they had no pikes, but they had a few guns.

Q. Who said that?

A. Several of the company.

Q. Did they say where the pikes were?

A. Yes.

Q. Where?

A. They lay in a stone quarry.

Mr. Justice Holroyd. I thought he said they had no pikes.

A. They had no pikes in Ripley and Pentridge, but they had a few guns.

Mr. Serjeant Vaughan. What was said about Wingfield; did Turner produce any thing?

A. Yes, he produced a list of the spikes, and the swords and guns in Wingfield parish?

Q. When he produced this list, what did he do with it?

A. He gave it to Ludlam, and Ludlam read it.

Q. Isaac Ludlam the elder?

A. Yes.

Q. He read it to the company?

A. Yes.

Q. What was this that he read?

A. It stated where the guns were, and where they had to fetch them from the different people's houses.

Q. Did he state the number?

A. Yes, he stated the number, as well the number of guns at every house, where they had to fetch them from.

Q. Do you remember the names of any gentlemen's houses that were mentioned?

A. Yes, some of them; Master Stirley's for one.

Q. Stirley, or Stelly?

A. Stelley I believe.

Q. Any others?

A. George Godber's, Robin Brickshaw's.

Q. Was any thing said about vermin?

A. Yes.

Q. What did you hear said?

A. Turner said the Wingfield people had some vermin to kill in their own parish, and they must kill it before they went out of it.

Q. Was any name mentioned?

A. No; I cannot recollect there were any names mentioned, that I heard.

Q. Was any thing said about a badger?

A. Yes; he was talking of a plan about drawing the badger.

Q. Who was?

A. Turner.

Q. What was his plan of drawing the badger?

A. It was to lay a bundle of straw in the yard before the door, till the badger came out.

Q. What was to be done with the straw?

A. They were to set it on fire, and then they were to shoot the badger if he came out.

Q. Was any thing said about the Wingfield people, their preparations, or their more or less of forwardness?

A. Yes; Turner said, he thought the Wingfield people

were the forwardest of any people about, for they had even turned out to get pike shafts in the day-time.

Q. Was any thing said about Butterley?

A. Yes; Turner asked the Butterley people whether they would go and assist the Wingfield people.

Q. Assist them in what?

A. In killing the vermin; an objection was made that they should have enough to do with their own. Weightman was not there, when all this was mentioned?

Q. Was he there at intervals when part of the conversation took place; or do you mean that he only heard what you have already stated?

A. I cannot say that he heard any thing of what Turner said.

Q. What further conversation took place there?

A. I cannot exactly say.

Q. Was any thing said about the tide?

A. Yes; they said they might as well try to stop the tide, as try to stop their proceedings.

Q. That who might as well try to stop the tide?

A. Government.

Q. I believe you were a special constable?

A. Yes.

Q. How long were you sworn in a special constable before this Sunday?

A. The night before.

Q. For what purpose?

A. To defend my master's property.

Q. To defend the works at Butterley; Mr. Jessop's property?

A. Yes.

Q. Did you, whilst you were in the room, make any observations about their proceedings, or what they were talking about?

A. Yes; I told them to mind what they said; and they said they would cram me up the chimney if I said any thing about it.

Q. Do you remember who said that?

A. I cannot say exactly which it was said that.

Q. Was any thing else said to you besides cramming you up the chimney?

A. No.

Q. At what time did you leave the room?

A. Between three and four o'clock.

Q. Who was it that said he would cram you up the chimney?

A. I cannot say who it was.

Q. Was the prisoner in the room at that time?

A. I cannot say whether he was or not; they were talking about that in the morning; he was not gone out, I believe.

Q. You believe he was not gone out of the room when they were talking about that?

A. No.

Mr Justice Holroyd. Do you know whether he was or not?

A. He was not gone out, I am sure.

Mr. Serjeant Vaughan. Do you mean, then, that he was in the room?

A. Yes.

Mr. Justice Holroyd. You recollect now that he was in the room?

A. Yes, he was in the room.

Mr. Serjeant Vaughan. On Monday night were you alarmed during any part of the night at the Butterley works?

A. Yes.

Q. About what time on the night of the 9th, or the morning of the 10th?

A. Between three and four o'clock on the morning of the 10th.

Q. Were you gone to bed?

A. No.

Q. How came you to be up?

A. We were ordered on guard by Mr. Jessop.

Q. You told us you were sworn in on the Saturday night as a special constable?

A. Yes.

Q. How many of you were upon guard?

A. I cannot say how many.

Q. Were there many men?

A. Yes, I dare say thirty or forty, or more.

Q. Was Mr. Goodwin there?

A. Yes.

Q. Did you see any thing of the prisoner at the bar at Butterley?

A. No.

Cross-examined by Mr. Cross.

Q. His mother was the landlady of this public-house which you have spoken of?

A. Yes.

Q. And he occasionally acted there as waiter?

A. Yes, he used to fill some little liquor there.

Shirley Asbury sworn.
Examined by Mr Clarke.

Q. Do you live at Pentridge?

A. No, at Greenwich.

Q. Is that in the parish of Pentridge?

A. No, in the parish of Ripley.

Q. What is your employment?

A. Engineer.

Q. Where at?

A. At Mr. Jessop's works.

Q. At the Butterley works?

A. Yes.

Q. Do you recollect on Sunday the 8th of June, taking a walk with a person of the name of Elsden?

A. Yes.

Q. Do you know the White Horse at Pentridge?

A. I do now, but I did not before.

Q. In the course of your walk that morning, did you go into the White Horse at Pentridge?

A. Yes.

Q. At what time in the morning was it?

A. It was about twelve o'clock.

Q. Twelve at noon?

A. Yes.

Q. What did you go in there for?

A. We went in there to have a pint of ale.

Q. What room did you go into?

A. We went into the kitchen.

Q. How long did you continue in the kitchen?

A. It might be about half an hour.

Q. Did you then go into any other room?

A. Yes.

Q. What room?

A. The parlour.

Q. How came you to go out of the kitchen into the parlour?

A. Mrs. Weightman went into the parlour, and told them there were two Butterley chaps in the kitchen, and to know whether they had any objection to their coming in.

Q. She told the persons who were there?

A. Yes.

Q. What answer did you hear the people in the parlour give to that question of Mrs. Weightman's?

A. That they should have no objection; that there was nothing there as a secret.

Q. You heard them say that?

A. Yes.

Q. Did you go in?

A. Yes.

Q. You both went in?

A. Yes.

Q. How many persons do you think there were in the parlour, when you went in?

A. There might be about twenty.

Q. Was it nearly full?

A. Yes.

Q. Do you recollect the names of any of the persons that were in there, when you went in?

A. Yes.

Q. Tell me some of them?

A. There was Brandreth, Cope, Anthony Martin, Mac Kesswick, John Moore, and Edward Moore.

Q. Do you know the prisoner, George Weightman, by sight?

A. Yes.

Q. Did you see any thing of him in the room?

A. Yes.

Q. Was he there when you went in, or did he come in afterwards?

A. He was in when I went in.

Q. You say Brandreth was there?

A. Yes.

Q. What did they call Brandreth?

A. Captain.

Q. Was it said where he came from?

A. From Nottingham.

Q. Where was he sitting?

A. He was sitting just fronting the door, with his back towards the door.

Q. Had he a table near him?

A. Yes.

Q. Did you hear what they were talking about when you went in, or at any time when you were there?

A. They were talking about a revolution.

Q. What revolution?

A. That was to take place the next night.

Q. Do you recollect what they said about it; what they were to do?

A. They were to go to overthrow the Government.

Q. Who were to go to overthrow the Government?

A. No, they did not say who was.

Q. Was any body to come to assist them?

A. Yes.

Mr. *Denman.* He has not said who were to do it.

Mr. *Clarke.* I asked whether any persons were expected to come to join them?

A. They wanted the Butterley people to come to join them.

Q. Was any thing said about their meeting; where they were to meet?

A. No, I cannot recollect where they were to meet; they were to meet at ten o'clock the next night.

Q. Do you know who were to meet; what places were to meet the next night?

A. They wanted the Butterley people to meet them; and Cope told them they had enough to do at home, and could not meet them.

Q. Was any thing said about the Wingfield people?

A. Yes; the Wingfield people were to meet them.

Q. Do you recollect whether any Wingfield people came into the room whilst you were there?

A. Yes.

Q. Who were they from Wingfield that came in?

A. William Turner and Ludlam.

Q. What Ludlam?

A. Isaac Ludlam?

Q. Old Isaac Ludlam?

A. Yes.

Q. Did they either of them say any thing or do any thing?

A. They said they had no doubt they should succeed in what they were going to undertake.

Q. What was it they were going to undertake?

A. To overthrow the Government.

Q. Had Brandreth any thing before him?

A. He had a map.

Q. What did he do with that map?

A. He was pointing and pricking out places where they were to meet, and which they were to take.

Q. Did you hear of any place in particular which they were to go to take?

A. Nottingham.

Q. And what were they to do when they had taken Nottingham?

A. When they got to Nottingham they were to have plenty of rum and one hundred guineas each.

Q. What were they to do, supposing them to have taken Nottingham?

A. They were to go to London to overthrow the Government.

Q. Were they to go to any other place?

A. They were to go to Newark from Nottingham; they

said it would be like a journey of pleasure to Newark from Nottingham, down by the Trent boats.

Q. Did any body produce any paper?

A. Yes, William Turner.

Q. Had Turner made any enquiry about any arms before he produced that paper?

A. He wanted to know where their list was, the list of the Butterley chaps was.

Q. A list of what?

A. A list of their arms.

Q. You have said that William Turner produced a paper?

A. Yes.

Q. What was done with that paper?

A. He gave it to Ludlam.

Q. Did Ludlam read it?

A. Yes.

Q. Aloud?

A. He read it so as almost every one might hear it.

Q. What was it that he read?

A. It was concerning what guns such and such people had, and which they meant to have.

Q. What people were they?

A. I cannot recollect what people they were.

Q. Where did they live, did you understand?

A. I was a stranger there at that time.

Q. Was it said in what parish they lived?

A. I do not know where they were to have them from, but such and such people had them.

Q. Was it expressed what parish those arms were in?

A. No, I cannot recollect that it was.

Q. That was read by Ludlam out of the paper which he received from William Turner?

A. Yes.

Q. Did the Pentridge people produce any list of arms?

A. No, the Wingfield people produced that paper.

Mr. Justice Holroyd. Turner was a Wingfield man?

A. Yes.

Mr. Clarke. Was any thing said about any arms in Pentridge?

A. I did not hear that there were any arms in Pentridge; Turner said, there were a quantity of spikes in a stone quarry for men that volunteered.

Q. Do you know what number was mentioned?

A. About forty.

Q. Was there any thing said about killing vermin?

A. Yes.

Q. Who said that, and what was it?

A. It was Turner said that—he said they had vermin to kill, and every parish should kill its own vermin.

Q. Did you hear any thing said about a badger?

A. Yes, they said that they should draw the badger.

Q. Who said that?

A. William Turner.

Q. How?

A. They were to take a bundle of straw and set it on fire before his door, and when he came out they were to shoot him.

Q. Who was this they were to shoot?

A. Colonel Halton.

Q. Did you hear Isaac Ludlam say any thing about Nottingham?

A. No, I do not recollect hearing Isaac Ludlam saying anything about Nottingham.

Q. Do you recollect whether there was any poetry recited?

A. Yes.

Q. Who was it by?

A. Brandreth.

Q. Do you recollect what the verses were?

A. Yes.

Q. What were they?

A. " Every man his skill must try,
   He must turn out and not deny;
   No bloody soldier must he dread,
   He must turn out and fight for bread;
   The time is come you plainly see,
   That Government oppos'd must be."

Q. I think you said there were about twenty persons in the room?

A. Yes.

Q. Did the same persons continue there, or was there a change of persons?

A. Some came in and some went out.

Q. Was there any secret made of this conversation which they held in this place?

A. No.

Q. Do you remember a person of the name of Mac Kesswick coming in?

A. Yes.

Q. Can you tell me whether he knew the captain or not?

A. Yes, he knew him, he came part of the road with him from Nottingham.

Q. He said so there, did he?

A. Yes; when he first came in he said he thought there were too many there for that business.

Q. What sort of spirits were those persons in that were talking in this way?

A. They were in good spirits; they said they had no doubt they should succeed in what they were going to undertake.

Q. Do you recollect Joseph Weightman being there?

A. Yes.

Q. Was he to do any thing?

A. Yes, to go to Nottingham to see how they were getting on.

Q. Which Joseph Weightman was it?

A. It was not the brother, I understood afterwards.

Q. A person of the name of Joseph Weightman?

A. Yes.

Q. Was it an elderly man?

A. No.

Q. He was to go to Nottingham to see how they were going on?

A. Yes.

Q. When was he to go?

A. He was to go as that night.

Q. When was he to come back?

A. The same night, I suppose.

Q. Was any thing given or got from the company for him to go?

A. There was sixpence a-piece gathered round from every one who liked to give.

Q. Did you give a sixpence?

A. Yes; I did not know what I was giving it for.

Q. You were asked for sixpence which you gave, but you did not know what you were giving it for?

A. No.

Q. Did you understand afterwards what that sixpence was collected for?

A. Yes; to supply him with money to go to Nottingham.

Q. Did you hear any thing said about gunpowder?

A. Yes, there was a barrel of gunpowder that Brandreth wanted to produce, so that he might learn them how to make cartridges; as for lead, they could get plenty upon the road, off churches.

Cross examined by Mr. Denman.

Q. Was Martin gone when that was mentioned about the lead?

A. I cannot recollect whether he was gone or not.

Q. Just look at this young man, and tell me how soon he came into the room after you got there?

A. He was in when first I went.

Q. How long did he stay?

A. I cannot say how long he stopped after I went in, he went in and out to fetch drink.

Q. Was he there when the verses were spoken?

A. I cannot say that he was there at the time that the verses were spoken.

Q. Was he there when the talk was about the badger?

A. He went away in the afternoon.

Q. He did not go away in the morning?

A. He went away soon after he had had his dinner.

Q. He dined before he went, did he?

A. Yes, I believe he did.

Q. At what time did he dine; did he dine with the rest, or separately?

A. I cannot tell whether he dined with the rest, or not.

Q. You say, he went after dinner, and you saw him dine?

A. It was after my dinner time that he went.

Q. Did he dine with the rest, or did he not?

A. I did not see the rest dine.

Q. Did you see him dine?

A. George.

Q. Yes, George?

A. No, I did not see him dine.

Q. I thought you said, he went away, after dinner?

A. It was after my dinner.

Q. Did you dine?

A. Not there.

Q. Where did you dine?

A. Not any where.

Q. Was Cope talking about the badger?

A. Not that I heard.

Q. You did not hear him say any thing about that?

A. No.

Q. Nor about the vermin?

A. No.

Q. How were they to go from Newark to London?

A. I do not know how they were to go; they were to go from Newark to London, they did not say how.

Q. You are sure they were to take Newark?

A. Yes.

Q. Was there to be a parliament at Newark too?

A. I did not hear them mention any thing about a parliament at Newark.

Q. How were they to take that?

A. They were to take it by force.

Q. Be so good as to tell me what force they were to take to Newark?

A. I do not know how they were to take it.

Q. Who said they were to take Newark by force?

A. Brandreth.

Q. But he did not say what force was to be used?

A. No, I do not recollect what force was to be used.

Q. Did he say so?

A. Yes.

Q. What?

A. He said they were to take Newark.

Q. What reason will you give to-day, for not having mentioned this to a magistrate or your master before?

A. Because I was not asked it before you asked me.

Q. Asked what?

A. What I have told you.

Q. I ask what reason you will give to-day for not telling a magistrate or your master of this intended rising?

A. Because we told them there were constables in the room, and they must mind what they said; and they said they would cram us up the chimney, if we said any thing. I did not know I was to go to people's houses to hear what they had to say; I was not sworn in on that account, I was sworn to protect my master's place.

Q. So because you were not to go about to houses to hear what people had to say, having gone by accident to this house at Pentridge, and having heard all this business against the Government and your master, you did not think it your duty to mention any thing about it?

A. We dare not mention any thing about it.

Q. You did not know it was your business, you say; was it that you dare not mention it, or you did not think it was your business?

A. I dare not mention it.

Q. It was your business, but you were afraid to do it?

A. I was afraid from what they said.

Q. Did you think it was your duty to mention it or not.

A. Whether I thought it was my duty or not, I did not mention it.

Q. Did you think it was your duty to mention it, or did you not?

A. When they said what they did, I did not think it was my duty to mention it; when they said they would murder any body who said any thing about the concern.

Q. Who said they would murder?

A. Brandreth and Turner.

Q. At what time of the day?

A. I cannot exactly remember the time of the day.

Q. Was that before or after the dinner you have talked about?

A. After dinner; it was nearly dinner time when I went, it was twelve o'clock.

Q. This was generally known that there was to be such an attack at Butterley?

A. Yes, then it was; it was not known before that time, I suppose.

Q. Then if you suppose it was not known before that day, I suppose that you could not abstain from telling your master, because you thought he knew it?

A. I did not tell him.

Q. I ask about the reason?

A. The reason I did not tell was, because they said they would murder any body who said any thing about it.

Q. It was not because you thought he knew it originally?

A. The reason I did not mention it was, because they said they should murder any body who said any thing about it.

Q. Among other reasons was that one, that you thought your master knew it before, and that it was generally known?

A. I do not know that it was known before.

Mr. Justice Holroyd. He says it was known then, but he did not know that it was known before.

Mr. Denman. You knew nothing at all about it before?

A. No.

Q. I should have thought you had been glad to get rid of it as soon as you did know of it, but you kept it all to yourself?

A. Yes, I thought it the best way.

Q. I do not know whether my learned friend asked you, how the Government was to be overturned?

A. I do not know how it was to be overturned; it was to be overturned, as they talked.

Q. Was it not mentioned how?

A. By the *forcement* that was to go.

Q. What was the *forcement* to do to overturn the Government?

A. I do not know; that was the term that was mentioned.

Q. That they were to overturn the Government?

A. Yes.

Re-examined by Mr. Clarke.

Q. You were talking about dinner, am I to understand you to mean the actual dining, or the dinner hour?

A. The dinner hour.

James Shipman sworn.

Examined by Mr. Gurney.

Q. Do you live at Southwingfield?

A. Yes.

Q. Were you standing at the door of the house at which you lodge on the evening of Monday the 9th of June last?

A. Yes.

Q. At about what time?

A. At about half past eight.

Q. Did you see the prisoner at the bar, George Weightman?

A. Yes.

Q. Was he alone, or in company with any other person?

A. He was in company with a strange man.

Q. Who did that strange man afterwards turn out to be?

A. They called him Jeremiah Brandreth.

Q. Did either of them say any thing to you?

A. Yes.

Q. Which?

A. George Weightman says, come along.

Q. To you?

A. I cannot say whether it was to me he spoke that way.

Q. Upon his saying that, did you go near him?

A. I was taking a step towards him, and I asked them where they were going, and the strange man advanced towards me and began to tell me.

Q. Was George Weightman near him at the time?

A. George Weightman stood in the same position where I saw him at first.

Q. The strange man began telling you where they were going?

A. Yes.

Q. What did Brandreth then say?

A. He said they were going to an old barn, up in the fields; that there was a meeting there of the towns of Wingfield, Crich, Pentridge, and Alfreton.

Q. What more did he say?

A. He said there were arms and ammunition there for as many as went, and more would be taken on the way as they went to Nottingham; he said there would be a band of music meet them on their way to Nottingham; and he said there would be thousands of men to meet them on Nottingham Forest.

Q. Did you ask him any question upon that?

A. I asked him what they would do for provisions, for something to eat when so many thousands were got together.

Q. What answer did he give to that question?

A. He said there would be bread and beef, and half a pint of rum for every man.

Q. Did he say where they would have this beef, bread, and rum?

A. When they got to Nottingham Forest I understood.

Q. What did you say to him next; did you ask him any thing about the women?

A. I asked him what those poor women were to do; there were a vast number standing about; I asked him what the poor women and children were to do when the husbands were gone.

Q. What answer did he give you?

A. He said there would be a provisional government

formed at Nottingham, and they would be sent down to relieve the wives and children of those who were gone away.

Q. Did either of the women say any thing upon this?

A. There was an old woman stood near to Brandreth, as he is called, and tapped him on the shoulder and said, " my lad we have got a Justice of the Peace here."

Q. What did Brandreth say to that?

A. He says you will have a different one than that one, who will allow you plenty.

Q. Did he speak about any thing from the North?

A. Yes, he said that clouds of men would come down from the North and take all before them, and those that refused to go would be shot.

Q. Did he say any thing about guineas?

A. He said every man who would volunteer would have one hundred guineas.

Q. Where?

A. When they got to Nottingham Forest.

Q. After all this did Brandreth and George Weightman leave?

A. George Weightman was not near me, but Brandreth left me.

Q. How near was George Weightman to you?

A. He must be about fifty yards off.

Q. At last did George come towards Brandreth and you?

A. He shifted, I cannot say whether he came any nearer or not.

Q. Did he say any thing to Brandreth?

A. He said come along, we are now half an hour too late; that was all that I heard George say.

Q. Upon George Weightman saying that to Brandreth, did Brandreth say any thing more to you?

A. He told me to come along, and I should have a good gun.

Q. What answer did you make?

A. I cannot justly say.

Q. Did you go with him or refuse to go?

A. I told him as I did not like the proceedings, or something of that sort.

Q. After that did they both leave you?

A. They left me, and George Weightman was a little in front; I cannot say whether they went together.

Q. Did they go the same way?

A. Yes.

Q. And that you think was about half past eight?

A. Yes.

Q. Did they go in the direction towards Hunt's Barn?

A. They went along the passage that leads to the road that goes to Hunt's Barn.

Cross-examined by Mr. Cross.

Q. Was the prisoner near while Brandreth had that conversation with you?

A. He was not nigh when the conversation passed.

Q. Then you cannot in short take upon yourself to say that he heard that conversation?

A. No, I think he could not.

Thomas Turner sworn.

Examined by Mr. Gurney.

Q. In the month of June last did you live with your father, near Southwingfield?

A. Yes.

Q. I believe you have been taken up on this business, and have been in confinement from that time?

A. Yes.

Q. On the evening of Monday the 9th of June, at about what time did you leave your father's house?

A. Nine o'clock, or a little before it might be.

Q. In company with whom did you leave it?

A. Samuel Ludlam and John Walker.

Q. Did you go up the village?

A. Yes.

Q. How far?

A. Only as far as the Meeting-house, not into the village.

Q. That I believe is near Colonel Halton's gates?

A. Yes.

Q. Whom did you see there?
A. We saw George Weightman and William Turner.
Q. By George Weightman do you mean the prisoner?
A. Yes.
Q. And any other person?
A. Yes; but I did not know who it was.
Q. Do you now know that that other person was Brandreth?
A. Yes.
Q. What had they?
A. Guns.
Q. Each?
A. Yes.
Q. What was William Turner doing with his gun?
A. He was loading it.
Q. What with?
A. With the bullets.
Q. Did George Weightman say any thing to you?
A. Yes.
Q. What did he say?
A. He said, "Come, lads, I expect an engagement very soon."
Q. Where, did he say?
A. At Butterley.
Q. Did he say with whom?
A. Jessop's men.
Q. Did he say any more?
A. No.
Q. Were you told then any thing where they were going to?
A. Yes, William Turner told us we must go to this barn.
Q. By this barn, what barn do you mean?
A. Hunt's Barn.
Q. You say you did not then know who Brandreth was?
A. No.
Q. Did you ask any body who he was?
A. Yes.
Q. Who did you ask?
A. William Turner.

Q. What answer did he give you?

A. He said that is our captain from Nottingham.

Q. Where did the prisoner and Brandreth and Turner then go?

A. To the barn.

Q. Did you and your two companions follow them?

A. Yes.

Q. Did you find any persons assembled at the barn?

A. We did not go to the barn, but we could see them there.

Q. How many in number do you think?

A. There might be about a score or more.

Q. Were they armed or unarmed?

A. Armed.

Q. In what way?

A. Different ways; with pikes and guns and swords.

Q. Was William Barker one of them?

A. Yes.

Q. John Hill?

A. Yes.

Q. Was Robert Turner one?

A. Yes.

Q. Was Manchester Turner one?

A. Yes.

Q. And Charles Swaine another?

A. Yes.

Q. Were those all armed that you have named?

A. Yes; without it was Robert Turner, I cannot say as to him.

Q. Were there any more arms there than those men had in their hands?

A. Yes, there were a few by the hedge-side.

Q. What were they?

A. Pikes.

Q. Did Brandreth tell you where you were going to?

A. Yes; he said we were going to Nottingham Forest, where there would be a great quantity of people to meet us.

Q. How many do you think there were of you at that

time collected, with what you found at the barn, and you who went there besides?

A. Between twenty and thirty I think.

Q. Were you formed into rank?

A. Yes.

Q. By whom?

A. By Brandreth and William Turner.

Q. Did you receive any thing to carry?

A. Yes, a bag of bullets.

Q. From whom?

A. From George Bramley.

Q. What orders were then given you?

A. Brandreth ordered us to march.

Q. For what place?

A. For a field of Mr. Topham's.

Q. Is that Topham's close.

A. Yes.

Q. When you marched away, what was done with the pikes that you had that were more than the people wanted who were there?

A. I did not see them taken up, but I suppose they were taken away.

Q. Did you see any of them carrying more than one pike?

A. Yes, there were several that had two pikes.

Q. Did you see whether George Weightman carried any thing besides his gun?

A. No, I cannot say that I did.

Q. In your way to Topham's close were any houses attacked?

A. Yes.

Q. And arms taken?

A. Yes, I believe so; I did not see them taken.

Q. Whose house was the first attacked?

A. James Hardwicke's.

Mr. Gurney. I believe, according to the plan, it is Samuel Hardwicke's, my Lord.

A. It is father and son; the father's name is Samuel and the son's James.

Q. The first house was Hardwicke's?
A. Yes.
Q. Whose house was the second?
A. The company went away to Henry Tomlinson's; I did not go with them.
Q. And then did you march for Topham's close?
A. Yes.
Q. Who did you expect to meet there?
A. The Pentridge people.
Q. Who had told you they would meet you there?
A. George Weightman the prisoner.
Q. Did any more persons join you at Topham's close?
A. Yes.
Q. Who?
A. Isaac Ludlam and his two sons.
Q. Had they arms?
A. Yes.
Q. What?
A. Pikes.
Mr. Justice Holroyd. Had they all pikes?
A. Yes.
Mr. Gurney. Had the Pentridge people met you there as you expected?
A. No.
Q. In consequence of that, what was agreed to be done?
A. George Weightman took the bag of bullets.
Q. The bag of bullets which you had carried?
A. Yes; and said he would go by the wire-mill, and if he met the Pentridge people he would turn them to Pentridge-lane-end.
Q. Did he go then?
A. Yes.
Q. And any persons with him?
A. He and several others there left us.
Q. Were they all armed or mostly armed those that went with him?
A. I cannot say whether they were armed or not when they went with him.
Q. They were part of those who had marched with you?

A. Yes, Miles Bacon and Samuel Marriott were two of them.

Q. What had they?

A. Samuel Marriott had a gun when he went to the close; I do not know what he had when he went with them.

Q. To whose house did the party that you remained with go?

A. To Elijah Hall's.

Q. Brandreth commanded your party?

A. Yes.

Q. And Turner?

A. Yes.

Q. Was any gun taken from Mr. Hall?

A. Yes.

Q. Taken by force, or did he give it willingly?

A. It was demanded by Brandreth; he did not give it willingly.

Q. Did Brandreth do any thing, or threaten him?

A. Yes; he said he should break the door open, if he did not give it him.

Q. Was any person of his family forced to go with you?

A. Yes.

Q. Who was the person forced to go with you?

A. Elijah Hall's son.

Q. Was Manchester Turner one of your party there?

A. Yes.

Q. Robert Turner?

A. Yes.

Q. And Barker?

A. Yes.

Q. Isaac Ludlam the elder?

A. Yes.

Q. And his sons?

A. Yes.

Q. Swaine?

A. Yes.

Q. And many others?

A. Yes.

Q. Do you remember Barker's saying any thing?

A. Yes; he said to Elijah Hall, he had wished for that day to come long, but it had come at last.

Q. To whose house did you go next?

A. To Isaac Walker's.

Q. Were any arms taken there?

A. Yes.

Q. What?

A. A pistol.

Q. What kind of pistol?

A. A brass pistol.

Q. Who had that pistol for that night and morning?

A. Brandreth.

Q. To whose house did you go next?

A. Henry Bestwick's.

Q. What was done there?

A. I did not see what was done there.

Q. Did you hear?

A. Yes, I heard the windows broken.

Q. You heard the windows broken, but you were not so near as to see what they did?

A. No.

Q. To whose house did you go next?

A. To Samuel Hunt's.

Q. Were you entertained with any thing there?

A. Yes.

Q. With what?

A. Bread, and cheese, and beer.

Q. Did any persons go with you from that house?

A. Yes.

Q. Who?

A. Samuel Hunt, and his man.

Q. Is that Daniel?

A. I believe so.

Q. Did they take any arms with them?

A. I cannot say whether they did or not.

A. To whose house did you go next?

A. Mrs. Hepworth's.

Q. Was any violence used to get into that house?

A. Yes.

Q. By whom?

A. Brandreth; Brandreth went to the door, and began thundering.

Q. And by any other person?

A. Yes.

Q. Who?

A. Samuel Hunt.

Q. What did he do?

A. He threw a stone at the door.

Q. What sort of stone?

A. Apparently a coping stone.

Q. To break the door open?

A. Yes.

Q. Did Brandreth and the other demand anything to be given out of the house?

A. Yes.

Q. What?

A. The arms.

Q. Were the arms given out?

A. Yes.

Q. Were they given out at first?

A. No.

Q. Upon that, was the kitchen window broke in?

A. Yes.

Q. Did Brandreth fire into the house?

A. Yes.

Q. Did he kill any body?

A. Yes,

Q. Who?

A. Robert Walters.

Q. Mrs. Hepworth's servant?

A. Yes.

Q. Upon that were the arms given out?

A. Yes.

Q. To what place did your party next proceed?

A. Towards Pentridge-lane-end.

Q. Upon the road to Pentridge-lane-end, did you meet any other party to join you.

A. Yes; there was a party upon the road when we got there.

Q. Did that party join yours?

A. Yes; they joined us a little while after.

Q. Were they armed?

A. Yes.

Q. With guns and pikes?

A. Yes.

Q. Did any of your party leave the rest, and go to a farm called Buckland Hollow?

A. Yes.

Q. What did they do there?

A. I do not know; I heard a disturbance there.

Q. You could not see what they did; you did not go?

A. No.

Q. Were any other houses attacked?

A. Yes, several.

Q. Were their arms taken?

A. I did not see them taken.

Q. Did you hear them called for?

A. Yes; I heard them at folks's doors, calling them up.

Q. And calling for their arms?

A. Yes.

Q. To what place did you then march?

A. We then went a little higher into the lane, towards Pentridge, and we were then formed into rank, we and the others who had joined us.

Q. By whom were you formed into rank?

A. Brandreth and William Turner.

Q. Did Brandreth enquire for any description of persons there?

A. Yes.

Q. For whom?

A. He asked if there were men in the ranks who had been soldiers, or in the militia, or knew discipline.

Q. What did he say he wanted with them?

A. If there were, they must turn out, and keep the men in order.

Q. Upon that, did any men turn out?

A. Yes.

Q. Who?

A. Charles Swaine.

Q. Had he been in the militia?
A. I believe so.
Q. William Turner, I believe, had been a soldier?
A. Yes, many years, I believe.
Q. Did Brandreth, and Turner, and Swaine, form you into ranks like soldiers?
A. We were formed in when Swaine turned out.
Q. How were the men with guns placed?
A. First, two and two.
Q. And where were the pikes put?
A. They were put next.
Q. Were you then marched to Pentridge?
A. Yes.
Q. Did George Weightman, and his party there, join you?
A. I saw George Weightman again at Pentridge town-end.
Q. At Pentridge town-end were any more houses attacked?
A. Yes; there was Brandreth, and Turner, and them, were calling folks up.
Q. Who besides Brandreth and Turner; did Weighman join in it?
A. I did not see him in particular; I saw him in the street, but I did not see him at any body's house.
Q. Was he with the party when it was done?
A. Yes, he was in the street along with the party when it was done.
Q. Was Mr. William Booth's house one of those that were attacked?
A. Yes, I believe it was.
Q. Did you observe George Weightman do any thing with respect to any thing belonging to Mr. Booth?
A. I saw him with Mr. Booth's poney at his gate.
Q. What did he desire you to do with respect to that poney?
A. He asked me to give him a leg on, for a man of the name of Storer, who pretended to be sick.

Q. Was Storer a person who had been forced out of his house?

A. I understood so.

Q. Did you help Storer on?

A. Yes.

Q. Did he remain on, or fall off.

A. He fell off before he had gone far.

Q. I believe Storer was at last left behind?

A. Yes, I believe he was.

Q. Who had the poney then?

A. I do not know who had it then.

Q. To what place were you then marched?

A. To Butterley furnace.

Q. Did you observe George Weightman leave you before you went to Butterley furnace?

A. He was not with us at Butterley furnace, but I do not know when he parted from us.

Q. At Butterley furnace you saw Mr. Goodwin, I believe?

A. Yes.

Q. I shall not ask you what passed there; we shall learn that better from him;—were you then marched to Ripley?

A. Yes, to Ripley town-end.

Q. What did you do there?

A. Brandreth ordered us to halt, and to give three huzzas.

Q. For what purpose?

A. He did not say what purpose.

Q. Where were you marched to then?

A. To Codnor.

Q. At what house at Codnor did you stop?

A. The Glass House public-house.

Q. What refreshment had your party there?

A. Some ale.

Q. To what amount?

A. Eight and twenty shillings.

Q. Were any men forced out of a farm yard near Codnor, to join your party?

A. I believe there were.

Q. How many?
A. Three.
Q. Were you then marched on to Langley mill?
A. Yes.
Q. Whom did you meet at Langley mill?
A. George Weightman.
Q. Coming as from whence?
A. From Nottingham, I understood.
Q. Was he on Booth's poney?
A. He was on a poney.
Q. What did he say to you all?
A. Brandreth and some of the company surrounded him, and asked him how they were going on at Nottingham.
Q. What answer did he give?
A. He said the people had risen, the town was taken, and the soldiers were in their barracks.
Q. Did he say what you were to do with your party?
A. And we were to march forward.
Q. Were you marched forward?
A. Yes.
Q. And how far did you go with them?
A. Two or three miles beyond Eastwood.
Q. Towards Nottingham?
A. Yes.
Q. And then, I believe, you turned back and left them?
A. Yes.
Q. Had any accident happened to Robert Walters, before you left him?
A. Yes; I understood he was shot.
Q. By a gun going off by accident?
A. Yes.
Q. From the time George Weightman met you, till Robert Walters was wounded, had George Weightman accompanied your party?
A. No, I think not; I did not see him any more after we were there.

Cross-examined by Mr. Denman.

Q. The prisoner was with you at Hardwicke's and Tomlinson's?

A. I cannot say whether he was at Tomlinson's or not; he was at Hardwicke's.

Q. Then Hardwicke's was the only house you can state he was at, before you came to Pentridge-lane-end?

A. Yes.

Q. He was not at Hepworth's, and the other houses you have mentioned?

A. No.

Q. You say he was in the street of Pentridge, when they were knocking people up?

A. Yes.

Q. And there was something of the kind done at Pentridge-lane-end?

A. Yes, there was.

Q. It was from Pentridge-lane-end he went off to Nottingham?

A. I saw him in Pentridge.

Q. He went from Pentridge?

A. I do not know; he was not with us at Butterley.

Q. You do not know when he got on the horse to go?

A. No, I do not.

Q. Between Butterley and Pentridge you missed him?

A. Yes.

Q. And then he came back in the way you have stated?

A. Yes.

Q. After Langley mill, you did not see him at all?

A. No.

[*Adjourned to To-morrow morning, eight o'clock.*]

SPECIAL ASSIZE, DERBY.

Friday, 24th October, 1817.

George Weightman was set to the bar.

Henry Tomlinson, sworn.

Examined by Mr. Serjeant Copley.

Q. You are a farmer I believe, and live in Southwingfield Park?

A. Yes.

Q. Do you remember on Monday evening the 9th of June, any person coming to you from Hardwicke's house?

A. Yes.

Q. At what time in the evening was that?

A. When he came to our house it might be about a quarter past nine o'clock.

Q. In consequence of what he told you, what did you do?

A. I locked up the door and went out into the yard.

Q. Did you go alone into the yard, or did any person go with you?

A. My wife went with me into the yard.

Q. After you had got into the yard, did you perceive any persons coming towards the house?

A. Yes.

Q. About how many might there be?

A. There appeared to me to be between thirty and forty.

Q. Were they armed or unarmed?

A. They were armed.

Q. What with?

A. Some with spikes and some with guns.

Q. What did they first do?

A. They went up to my door and began for to rattle.

Q. What did you do upon that?

A. I went up to them, and asked them what they wanted.

Q. What did they say?

A. That they wanted me and my gun.

Q. What did you say to that?

A. I told them they must have neither.

Q. What did they say?

A. I told them that the gun was not at home, it was gone to Ashover to be mended.

Q. What did they say to that?

A. They said I must open the door, or they would break it; and I must find the gun, or they would search the house.

Q. What did you do upon that?

A. I opened the door and there were two men that followed me in, the captain and another man.

Q. When they were in the house what did they do or say?

A. They said they would have the gun, and I went into another room to fetch it out.

Q. Did you bring it to them?

A. Yes, I brought it into the house, and the captain demanded and took it.

Q. After they had taken the gun did they go out?

A. Yes, he went out of the door and took the gun with him; and I followed him to the door, and stood at the door.

Q. While you were standing at the door did they say any thing to you?

A. Yes; he said " come you must go and all."

Q. Who said that?

A. The captain.

Q. What answer did you make to that?

A. I told him I would not; he said " You had better go while to-night than stop till the morning," that there was a great gang coming from Sheffield, and a great cloud out of the North that would sweep all before them.

Q. What did you say to that?

A. I told him I would not go; he presented his gun and swore he would shoot me if I would not go; I told him I would go a little way, but it should not be far.

Q. Was any thing said about Nottingham?
A. Yes.
Q. What?
A. He said they were going to Nottingham, and they should be at Nottingham by half-past eight or nine o'clock, I am not sure which.

Q. Was any thing said about London?
A. Yes; he said they should not need to go further than Nottingham, for London would be taken by the time they got thither.

Q. Did they force you to go with them?
A. Yes, they did.

Q. Were any arms put into your hands?
A. Yes.

Q. What?
A. They gave me a spike.

Q. On their giving you a spike what did they do?
A. I asked them to let me have my own gun and they would not, they said they would make me carry a spike.

[*Several pikes were produced and laid upon the table.*]

Q. By a spike, what kind of instrument do you mean?
A. Like that. (*pointing out one of the pikes.*)

Q. Was the prisoner George Weightman among the party?
A. When we went down from the door, he was in the yard.

Q. Had you known him before?
A. Yes.

Q. Which way did the party proceed?
A. They went as if they were going for Nottingham, I suppose.

Q. When you say you suppose, I want to know whether they went in the direction towards Nottingham?
A. Why it is not a direct turnpike road to Nottingham.

Q. Would it lead to Nottingham, going in that way?
A. Yes, it would.

Q. Did you go on the same way.
A. Yes.

Q. After you had gone on some little way, did you speak to George Weightman?

A. Yes; I spoke to him before I went out of the yard.

Q. What did you say to him?

A. I lit upon him in the yard, and asked him, "Are you one?" and he said "Yes."

Q. Upon his saying "yes," what did you say to him?

A. I told him, I thought it was a very hard case to take me, and leave my wife by herself in such a lonely spot.

Q. What further did you say?

A. He said it was a hard case; I must go a little bit, and I might turn again.

Q. How far did you go?

A. About three hundred yards, as near as I could guess.

Q. When you had got three hundred yards, what then happened?

A. He gave me a bit of a nudge, took my spike, and bid me to turn again.

Q. Did you do so?

A. Yes; Weightman was a friend of mine that night, or else I should have fared worse.

Q. Had you known him for some time?

A. Yes.

Q. You went home then?

A. Yes.

Cross-examined by Mr. Cross.

Q. How long have you known him?

A. I should think I have known him for these ten or a dozen years. I have no great acquaintance with him, you know.

Q. You have known him from a child?

A. No.

Q. About what age was he when you first knew him?

A. I cannot justly say.

Q. He was a boy at that time, was not he?

A. He was grown up a man when I knew him.

Q. How far did he live from you?

A. About three miles.

Q. I am told you have had an opportunity of knowing his general character for some time past?

A. Why yes; I never heard any thing particular against the man while this broke out; the man always seemed a very civil and decent character, for any thing I heard.

Q. Was he a quiet and peaceable man?

A. Yes; he always appeared a very civil man; a man always very civil when he came to me.

Mr. Henry Bestwick sworn.

Examined by Mr. Gurney.

Q. I believe you are a farmer residing at Southwingfield Park?

A. Yes.

A. On the night of Monday the 9th of June, was your house attacked by any party of people?

A. Yes.

Q. At about what hour?

A. About half past eleven o'clock.

Q. Was your house broken open?

A. Yes.

Q. Were any arms taken?

A. Yes.

Q. What?

A. A gun.

Q. Had you before that time heard any thing from the prisoner of what was to happen?

A. Yes, we had had a conversation upon the subject.

Q. The prisoner and his brother Joseph are, I believe, by trade sawyers.

A. Yes.

Q. On the Saturday before that Monday, were they doing work for you as sawyers?

A. Yes, they were.

Q. State what passed between you?

A. I had been much alarmed from the conversation that had been regularly spoken of for some days before.

Q. In consequence of that alarm, did you say any thing to the prisoner and his brother?

A. Yes; he and his brother were sawing timber for me; it was intended for the roofing of a building that I had.

Q. And you said what?

A. I said to Weightman, there was such a report of a revolution taking place.

Q. Give it us in the first person; there is such a report of a revolution taking place?

Mr. Denman. Did he say this to both of them?

Mr. Gurney. You said it to both of them?

A. Yes.

Q. They were both working; one above, and the other below?

A. Yes.

Q. You said, "there is such a report of a revolution taking place;" what further?

A. "That it is of no signification talking of building, or of going on with any other business."

Q. What answer did the prisoner give to this?

A. He said, he believed the day and the hour were fixed when the whole nation was expected to rise; and before the middle of the week, he believed there would be hundreds of thousands in arms; and he said there were men appointed all over the nation, or the country, I cannot say which word he used.

Q. To do what?

A. To take command of such and such companies of men; and he said he did not think there was a house within fifty miles but what it was known what fire arms they had in it, and he believed they would be called for.

Q. Did he say any thing about the Peak?

A. That conversation was spoken; but I think if I recollect right, it was from his brother.

Q. Was he present?

A. Yes, he was.

Q. What did his brother say in his presence?

A. He said that they would be coming out of the Peak like clouds.

Q. Any thing more?

A. That is the greatest part that I recollect.

Q. Do you remember Joseph Weightman saying any thing about blankets?

A. Yes; he said this would not prove like the blanket business at Manchester.

Q. Any thing more?

A. I do not recollect.

Cross-examined by Mr. Denman.

Q. Did this young man often work for you?

A. No.

Q. Did you know him?

A. I did know him, but that was about all I could say.

Q. Was this the first time he ever worked for you?

A. Never in his life before these two days.

Q. Perhaps you have had no opportunity of knowing what his general character has been?

A. I never knew much about him in my life, except that I knew him if I met him on the road.

Q. You used to speak to him if you met him?

A. Exactly so.

Q. How far did you live from him?

A. Hardly two miles.

Henry Taylor sworn.

Examined by Mr. Reader.

Q. I believe you are a butcher at Southwingfield?

A. Yes.

Q. Were you and any body with you, your son, and William Smith, about to go to the house of John Wilkinson on the night of Monday the 9th of June?

A. Yes.

Q. At what time did you leave your own house?

A. At nearly ten o'clock.

Q. Yourself, your son Samuel, and William Smith?

A. Yes.

Q. Did you met any persons as you were going there?

A. No.

Q. Did you see the prisoner, George Weightman?

A. Yes, he met us.

Q. Between your house and Wilkinson's?

A. Yes.

Q. Was any body else with him?

A. Several.

Q. Who were they?

A. There was James Taylor, and Benjamin Taylor, and Joseph Taylor, and Joseph Wilkinson.

Q. The person to whose house you were going?

A. Yes.

Mr. Justice Holroyd. I thought you said you were going to the house of John Wilkinson?

A. His father's.

Mr. Reader. Those persons you knew?

A. Yes.

Q. Were there any others besides, whom you did not know?

A. Yes, several.

Q. Had they any thing with them?

A. Yes, they had spikes; James and Joseph and Benjamin Taylor, all had spikes.

Q. By spikes do you mean these sort of things?

A. Yes.

Q. Had any body else spikes besides them?

A. I cannot recollect that there were any others.

Q. Were the handles peeled or not peeled?

A. Yes, I believe they were peeled.

Q. Had the prisoner, George Weightman, any thing with him?

A. I cannot recollect that he had at first, but he took up a bag of bullets at the same time.

Q. Was that soon after you joined them?

A. Directly upon the same spot.

Q. Did any of them say any thing to you?

A. Yes.

Q. What did they say?

A. They demanded my son first to go.

Q. To go with them?

A. Yes.

Q. Your son Samuel?

A. Yes, and George.

Q. Whom do you mean by George, the prisoner?

A. Yes, he got hold of my son's collar and pulled him on to the turnpike-road.

Q. Did he say any thing to him?

A. He insisted upon his going along with them.

Q. Did you say they insisted, or George Weightman insisted?

A. George Weightman insisted.

Q. What else did he do?

A. Nothing particular that I recollect.

Q. Did he give him any thing?

A. Either he or James Taylor gave him a spike.

Q. Such a kind of thing as one of those?

A. Yes.

Q. Did they do any thing to you?

A. Yes, then they insisted upon my taking one.

Q. A pike you mean?

A. Yes.

Q. What did you say or do?

A. I told them I had rather not; they insisted upon my going; I said very well, I can go without a spike; James Taylor gave me one, and would insist upon my taking it; he said it was easier for me to carry one, than for them to carry so many a piece.

Q. Had any of them more than one a piece?

A. Them three had three or four a-piece, the Taylor's.

Q. They were carrying three or four a-piece?

A. Yes.

Q. Did you take the spike or not?

A. Yes, I took the spike.

Q. Where did you go?

A. We went right to the wire-mill.

Q. You have spoken of William Smith, did he go with you?

A. Yes, he did.

Q. Did he go willingly?

A. He was not willing; but he see'd we were forced to go.

Q. Then you say you proceeded towards the wire-mill?

A. Yes.

Vol. II.   D d

Q. You say you were going from your house to John Wilkinson's?

A. Yes.

Q. And in your road you met those persons?

A. Yes.

Q. Did you go on to John Wilkinson's?

A. No.

Q. They turned you towards the wire-mill?

A. Yes.

Q. Which way were the prisoner and the party with him coming from when you met them?

A. From towards Wilkinson's.

Q. Did you all proceed to the wire-mill?

A. Yes.

Q. Who carried the bullets?

A. George Weightman.

Q. Quite on to the wire-mill?

A. I think so; to the best of my knowledge.

Q. What was done when you got to Marriott's, the wire-mill?

A. There were two or three went up to the door, and insisted upon his gun, and Marriott's son to go along with them.

Q. Did they appear to be in bed?

A. Yes.

Q. Did they make any noise at the door, or about the house?

A. They rattled the door.

Q. What answer was made?

A. Young Marriott said the gun was out of repair; and as for himself, he should not go.

Q. What was said to that?

A. They said, out of repair or in, they would insist upon having the gun; and if he would deliver the gun, they would excuse him.

Q. Was the gun delivered?

A. Yes.

Q. By whom?

A. Young Marriott delivered it.

Q. Out of the window?
A. Yes.
Q. Did you then go away?
A. Yes, very shortly after.
Q. Were you joined before you left Marriott's, by any other party?
A. Yes, there was a party came into the yard from old Pentridge, and joined us there.
Q. In the yard.
A. Yes.
Q. Then you went away?
A. Yes.
Q. Who carried the bullets?
A. I think George Weightman carried the bullets half way up to the turnpike road.
Q. The turnpike road from Chesterfield to Derby, do you mean?
A. Yes; and then he delivered them to another man.
Q. Do you know who that other man was?
A. No.
Q. Where did the other party then go to?
A. Up to the turnpike road; and then the biggest part of them went to Mr. Lister's.
Q. What became of the rest?
A. The others went to Pentridge.
Q. Down the road?
A. Up the hill.
Q. Do you know what the party were to go to Lister's for?
A. It was not mentioned further than that they were going to fetch two guns, which they said Lister had.
Q. Did you go with that party, or the other?
A. I went to Pentridge.
Q. Which did Weightman, the prisoner, go with?
A. To Pentridge.
Q. You went with his party?
A. Yes.
Q. Where did you go to in Pentridge?
A. To old Mrs. Weightman's there, at first.

Q. Did the prisoner Weightman go with you?
A. Yes.
Q. Who had got the bullets then?
A. George Weightman.
Q. He had got them again then?
A. Yes.
Q. Did you hear any thing of any other bullets?
A. Yes; we went up just above the wire mill; as we were going towards the road, James Taylor said there were another bag of bullets or two, that were gone up the park.
Q. Through Southwingfield park?
A. Yes.
Q. Where did you and the prisoner go from Mrs. Weightman's?
A. I went no further; the prisoner said that he would go to his brother William's, with the bullets; and he went, and a man or two with him, I think.
Q. Did you see him go to William's?
A. I saw him go through William's gate, into the yard.
Q. What became of you after that?
A. I returned home.
Q. You got away, and returned home?
A. Yes, I did.
Q. Do you know Topham's close?
A. No, I cannot say that I do.
Q. Do you know Topham?
A. Yes.
Q. There is a close near his house?
A. There are two Topham's.
Q. It is near Frichley-lane?
A. They are both near Frichley-lane.
Q. How far is that from Wilkinson's?
A. One of them is within three hundred yards of Wilkinson's house?
Q. How far is the other from Wilkinson's house?
A. As far again, I dare say.
Q. Then the other is about six hundred yards from Wilkinson's?
A. Yes.

Samuel Taylor sworn.

Examined by Mr. Reynolds.

Q. Are you the son of Henry Taylor?
A. Yes.

Q. On the 9th of June last, did you live with your father at Southwingfield park?
A. Yes.

Q. Were you and William Smith and your father, going towards Wilkinson's on that night of the 9th of June?
A. Yes.

Q. At what hour?
A. About ten o'clock, or between ten and eleven.

Q. In going there, were you met by any number of persons?
A. Yes.

Q. How many?
A. I cannot say, I am sure; about half a score perhaps.

Q. Was George Weightman, the prisoner, with them?
A. Yes.

Q. Did he say any thing to you?
A. Yes.

Q. What?
A. He came to me, and insisted upon my going with him?

Q. Did you say any thing to him?
A. No, I said nothing to him; I refused going with him.

Q. Did he then do any thing to you?
A. Yes, he collared me, and insisted on my going with him.

Q. Where were you; where did he take you when he collared you?
A. I was on the side of the road, and he pushed me into the middle of it.

Q. Was any thing given to you?
A. Yes, George Weightman gave me a pike.

Q. Was it like one of those?

A. Yes.

Q. Do you know the Taylor's?

A. Yes.

Q. James Taylor?

A. Yes.

Q. And Benjamin Taylor?

A. Yes.

Q. And Joseph Taylor?

A. Yes.

Q. Were they there?

A. Yes.

Q. Had they any thing with them?

A. Yes, they all carried three or four pikes.

Q. Was there a person of the name of Samuel Marriott there?

A. Yes.

Q. Had he any thing with him?

A. Yes, he had a bag, which I expected were bullets.

Q. What do you mean by " I expected were bullets;" did you hear any thing said about what they were?

A. Yes.

Q. Did you hear it mentioned what was in the bag?

A. Yes, I heard some of the party mention that they were bullets.

Q. Was that bag given by Marriott to anybody?

A. Yes.

Q. To whom?

A. To George Weightman.

Q. To the prisoner?

A. Yes.

Q. You have told us you were going to Wilkinson's; which way did the party go, to or from Wilkinson's, when you joined the party?

A. They were coming down Boden-lane when I met them, and went towards Marriott's?

Q. Is that the wire-mill?

A. Yes.

Q. If the party had come from Topham's close, would

they have come that way they were going when you met them?

A. I do not know I am sure.

Q. The wire mill was a different way from Wilkinson's?

A. Yes, it was the way leading on to Pentridge.

Q. You say you went to John Marriott's at the wire mill?

A. Yes.

Q. When you were there, did any other persons join you?

A. Yes, a party joined us.

Q. What was done at Marriott's the wire mill?

A. They insisted upon Mr. Marriott's gun, and also one of his sons to go with them.

Q. What was said to this demand?

A. They refused to give them the gun.

Q. What was said about his son's going?

A. And also his son's going with them.

Q. What further passed?

A. Some of the party said, if they would give them the gun, they would excuse his son going with them?

Q. Was the gun then given?

A. Yes.

Q. Did they then go on towards Pentridge?

A. Yes.

Q. Where did you afterwards go; did you go to Mr. Lister's?

A. Yes.

Q. Was the prisoner with you when you went to Mr. Lister's?

A. No, he was not.

Q. What had become of him?

A. He went up towards Pentridge.

Q. Did a party go with him?

A. I do not know I am sure.

Q. What was done at Lister's?

A. They went to the window and demanded a gun.

Q. Did they get the gun?

A. Yes; I did not see it given to them.

Q. How do you know they got the gun?
A. Some of the party said they had got the gun.
Q. Did you then go to Mr. Sellars's house?
A. Yes.
Q. That is near Pentridge mill, is not it?
A. Yes.
Q. What was done at Sellars's?
A. They rattled at the door.
Q. What did they demand there?
A. They demanded Mr. Sellars.
Q. Did Mr. Sellars go with them?
A. Yes.
Q. Did you go on to Mr. Samuel Fletcher's?
A. Yes.
Q. Was a gun and a man taken from Fletcher's?
A. Yes.
Q. The man's name was Shipman, was not it?
A. Yes.
Q. Where did you go next?
A. To Mr. Storer's.
Q. What was done at Storer's?
A. They rattled at the door, and insisted on one of Mr. Storer's sons, and also his gun.
Q. What did you get from Storer's, did you get any thing?
A. Yes; one of his sons and a gun.
Q. Where did you go to next?
A. No where till we got to the Glass House.
Q. Did you make any endeavour to get away; do you know Isaac Ludlam?
A. Yes.
Q. Did you endeavour to get away anywhere?
A. When I got to the Glass House I stopped at the door to get away.
Q. Who prevented you, or what prevented you?

Mr. Denman. It is not right to press any thing against Ludlam.

Mr. Gurney. It is our duty to prove the general conduct and language of the different conspirators.

Mr. Denman. It appears to me something more than general conduct.

Mr. Gurney. It is all indicative of the general plan.

Mr. Reynolds. Was any thing done or said to prevent you at that time?

A. I expected he stopped at the door to keep garrison.

Q. Did you go to Butterley?

A. Yes.

Q. I believe you went on through Langley mill to Eastwood, did not you?

A. Yes.

Q. And then I believe you made your escape. did not you?

A. Yes, beyond Eastwood.

Cross-examined by Mr. Denman.

Q. How many hours do you think you might be with the party altogether?

A. I am sure I cannot say.

Q. The prisoner was not there all the time, nor even the greatest part of the time?

A. No.

Q. You did not make much resistance, I believe you knew it would be unavailing.

A. I should have been glad to get off.

Q. But you knew in the first instance, when they insisted upon your going, that there was no possibility of your resisting, was not that so; did not you know that it was impossible for you to resist, if they carried you along with the tide of their numbers, did not you know that, when first they took you with them?

A. Yes, I were like to go with them.

Q. You could not help yourself? well I will not press the question.

Re-examined by Mr. Reynolds.

Q. Will you allow me to ask another question; which does not arise out of this? Did you see George Weightman?

Mr. Denman. I must object to this.

Mr. Reynolds. Then I would beg the Court to ask whether he saw George Weightman, on his return, at Langley mill? If the Court have the least doubt about putting it, we will not press it.

Mr. Justice Holroyd. Did you see the prisoner at the bar afterwards at Langley mill?

A. Yes, I did.

William Smith sworn.
Examined by Mr. Richardson.

Q. Where do you live?
A. At Wingfield park.

Q. Do you know the three Taylors—Benjamin, James, and Joseph Taylor?
A. Yes.

Q. On the 9th of June last did you see them at any time in the afternoon or evening?
A. Yes.

Q. About what time?
A. About five o'clock.

Q. In the afternoon?
A. Yes.

Q. Was anybody with them?
A. Isaac Ludlam.

Q. And Isaac Ludlam, junior?
A. Yes.

Q. Had they any thing with them?
A. Some poles.

Q. How many?
A. Three or four apiece?

Q. They were carrying them?
A. Yes, they were.

Q. Look at those poles upon the table, and tell me whether they bore any resemblance to them?
A. Yes, they resembled them.

Q. Which way were they going?
A. Down the Park lane, towards James Taylor's.

Q. That evening did you see any of the Ludlams come out, or go any where?
A. I saw them go from home.

Q. Which of them?

A. Old Isaac, young Isaac, and William.

Q. Isaac's two sons.

A. Yes; and Samuel Briddon.

Q. From whence did they go?

A. From Isaac Ludlam's.

Q. From old Isaac's?

A. Yes.

Q. Which way?

A. They went down the lane towards Boden-lane.

Q. Is that in the direction towards Topham's close?

A. Yes, Boden-lane is.

Q. Were they armed?

A. Yes.

Q. How armed?

A. They were armed with poles, a pole apiece.

Q. Were those such poles as you had seen before that day?

A. They appeared to be such as I had seen before that day.

Mr. *Justice Holroyd.* Do you mean similar to those you had seen before on that day, or before that day?

Mr. *Richardson.* Do you mean similar to those you had seen in the hands of the Taylors that day?

A. Yes.

Q. That evening did you go with the last witness Samuel Taylor and anybody else?

A. Henry Taylor.

Q. Toward's Wilkinson's?

A. Yes.

Q. In your way there did you meet any party of men?

A. I met a party of men in Boden-lane.

Q. Were they armed?

A. Yes.

Q. How?

A. With poles.

Q. Had the poles any thing at the end of them?

A. Yes, spikes at the end of them.

Q. When you speak of poles, do you mean poles with spikes?
A. Yes.

Q. Was the prisoner at the bar, George Weightman, with them?
A. Yes.

Q. Way anything said to you by any of them?
A. Yes, they demanded us to go.

Q. You and the persons who were with you?
A. Yes.

Q. Were you obliged to go with them?
A. James Taylor gave me a pike, and demanded me to go down the lane with them; we went down to Boden-lane-end.

Q. Willingly or not?
A. We refused.

Q. What then?
A. We must go, they told us.

Q. Was anything done to you?
A. No.

Q. They told you you must go?
A. Yes.

Q. Did you go?
A. Yes.

Q. Did you go with them to Marriott's, at the wire-mill?
A. Yes.

Q. They got a gun there?
A. Yes.

Q. I will not go into the detail of these proceedings; did you go from thence to the Chesterfield road?
A. We went up Pentridge common, and so on to the Derby road.

Q. Did some of them there go off over the heath towards Pentridge?
A. Yes.

Q. The others went down the turnpike road?
A. Towards William Lister's.

Q. Did George Weightman go with the party towards Pentridge?
A. Yes.

Q. And you went with the other party towards Lister's?
A. Yes.
Q. You got a gun there, did not you?
A. Yes.
Q. Did you go to Sellars's?
A. Yes.
Q. And to Samuel Fletcher's?
A. Yes.
Q. And to James Turner's?
A. Yes.
Q. And to Storer's?
A. No, I did not go there; I do not know any thing about that.
Q. Did you get guns and men at either of those places?
A. At James Turner's.
Q. What did you get at James Turner's?
A. James Turner.
Q. To join the party?
A. Yes.
Q. Were you at Pentridge with them, or Pentridge-lane-end?
A. Yes, Pentridge-lane-end.
Q. Did you go to any houses there?
A. No.
Q. Where did you remain?
A. On the road.
Q. While you remained on the road, did you bear any of the party rattling or knocking at any of the houses there?
A. I heard them rattling at the doors.
Q. I believe you went with the party to Butterley, did not you?
A. Yes.
Q. To Codnor?
A. Yes.
Q. And as far as Eastwood?
A. Yes.
Q. Did you endeavour to escape from them?
A. At Codnor.

Q. Could you?

A. No.

Q. At Eastwood you did escape?

A. Yes.

Q. Did you see anything more of George Weightman, from the time when you parted with him, he going towards Pentridge?

A. I saw him going up Pentridge common.

Q. Where did you see him at that time; what was he doing?

A. He was carrying a bag of bullets; they were supposed to be bullets.

Q. What do you mean by saying, " they were supposed to be bullets?"

A. I did not see them.

Q. Was anything said about the bag?

A. Yes, some of the party said they were bullets.

Q. Did you see him after that, before you quitted the party at Eastwood?

A. I saw him again at Pentridge.

Q. What was he doing then?

A. He had a horse then.

Q. What was he doing with the horse; was he leading it or riding it?

A. He was leading it then.

Q. Was that Booth's poney?

A. I do not know whose poney it was.

Q. It was a poney?

A. Yes, it was a poney or a horse; I did not take particular notice.

Q. Did you see him go off with that?

A. No, I saw him in Pentridge with it; I did not see him go off with it.

Q. Did you see him again, before you quitted the party at Eastwood?

A. Yes, I saw him on a bridge; Langley bridge, I think they call it.

Q. On horseback?

A. Yes.

Q. Which way was he coming?

A. He was upon the bridge when I saw him.

Q. Was that in the way to Nottingham?

A. Yes.

Q. Did you meet him there?

A. I do not know whether we met him there, but I saw him there.

Q. Did you hear him say any thing?

A. No.

Q. Did you see anything more of him after that, before you quitted the party at Eastwood?

A. No.

Samuel Marriott sworn.

Examined by Mr. Balguy.

Q. You are the son of Mr. John Marriott?

A. Yes.

Q. He lives at the wire-mill?

A. Yes.

Q. In the parish of Southwingfield?

A. Yes.

Q. Were you at home with your father, on the night of the 9th of June?

A. Yes.

Q. Were you disturbed at any time that night?

A. Yes.

Q. About what time?

A. About eleven o'clock.

Q. Were you all gone to bed at that time?

A. Yes.

Q. What were you disturbed by?

A. By a quantity of men making a noise at the door.

Q. In consequence of this, did you get out of bed?

A. Yes, and went to the window.

Q. Did you throw the window open?

A. Yes, I threw the window open, and asked them what they wanted.

Q. What answer did you receive?

A. They said I must come out, and go along with them.

Q. Did they say anything else?

A. I denied, and they said, I must come out; and then they said I must give them the gun and all.

Q. Upon their asking for your gun, what did you say?

A. I told them we had not one.

Q. What did they say to that?

A. They said they were all our neighbours, and knew that we had one.

Q. Did they say any thing else?

A. They did; they were determined to have the gun; I told them it would do them no good, there was no lock on it; to which they said, lock or no lock, they must have the gun, and if I would not go down and give it them, they would break open the door; I refused, and then they said something about the pike men.

Q. This conversation took place between you and the party, the men who were just under your window?

A. Yes.

Q. Did you afterwards see another party of men?

A. Yes, there was a party of men came down our yard, who met them just before our house.

Q. Was it after they had said something about the pikemen, that you saw the other body of men approach?

A. Yes.

Q. What had they got?

A. I cannot very well say what they had got; the first party that came to us had five or six pikes when they advanced towards the door; I went down and gave them the gun at the parlour window.

Q. Was it the first body or the second body that advanced towards the door?

A. The first body.

Q. How many did you see in all, do you suppose?

A. I cannot tell; between thirty and forty, I suppose, by the appearance of them.

Q. Did you know any of them?

A. I knew the prisoner, George Weightman.

Q. He was there, was he?

A. Yes, he was one of them.

Mr. Elijah Hall, the elder, sworn.

Examined by Mr. Solicitor General.

Q. I believe you are a farmer and miller living in Southwingfield Park?

A. Yes.

Q. Do you remember your house being attacked on the night of Monday, the 9th of June?

A. I do.

Q. A few days before that, had you seen the prisoner, George Weightman, any where?

A. I had.

Q. How many days before, do you think?

A. I do not exactly recollect.

Q. About how many?

A. Perhaps three or four days before.

Q. Where was it that you saw him?

A. I saw him at a saw-pit in a field of mine.

Q. Was one of his brothers with him?

A. There was.

Q. At work with him?

A. Yes.

Q. Do you know the name of his brother?

A. I do not.

Q. Were they sawing timber at that time, for Mr. Bestwick?

A. They were.

Q. Did any conversation take place between you and the prisoner, George Weightman?

A. I believe there did.

Q. Relate, as accurately as you can, what it was that he said to you?

A. I recollect very little of it.

Q. But what you do recollect of it——

Mr. Denman. He does not seem to be certain that there was any.

Mr. Solicitor General. Was there a conversation between you and him?

A. There was.

Q. State, as well as you can recollect, what it was that passed?

A. George Weightman said, in a few days I should see something that I little expected; that it was well known what arms there were in the country, in the neighbourhood; and that there was a gentleman in the neighbourhood who had proffered two barrels of gunpowder.

Q. Did he state what the gunpowder was for?

A. I understood, by his discourse, there was to be a general rising, and that it was for that purpose.

Q. Did he state, or did you learn from him, what the rising was to be for?

A. I do not recollect any more?

Q. I asked you just now, if, on the night of the 9th, your house was attacked, about what hour was that?

A. About eleven o'clock.

Q. Who was it that attacked your house; what persons?

A. The persons that I know were Jeremiah Brandreth, William Barker, William Turner, Manchester Turner, I would say Robert Turner.

Q. How many others when first you saw them?

A. I think there might be nearly thirty.

Q. Were they armed?

A. They were.

Q. In what manner?

A. With pikes and guns.

Q. Pikes such as those.

A. Similar to those; and Manchester Turner had a sword.

Q. What did they demand when they came to your house?

A. They demanded my fire arms.

Q. Did you refuse?

A. I did.

Q. You at first refused?

A. Yes.

Q. What did any of them say upon your refusal?

A. They said, they knew I had both guns and pistols, and they would have them.

Q. Were there any threats used by them?

A. Yes, there were; they threatened to fire the house.

Q. Where were you when first they came?

A. I was in the yard.

Q. Your door was locked, I believe.

A. Yes, it was.

Q. After those threats, I believe, the door was opened?

A. Yes.

Q. Some of them went into your house?

A. They did.

Q. Did any of them go up stairs?

A. They did.

Q. For what purpose?

A. To fetch my sons out of bed; the captain had previously threatened to blow my brains out if I did not fetch them out myself.

Q. Did they bring your son down stairs?

A. They did.

Q. Elijah Hall the younger?

A. Yes.

Q. Did they force him to go with them?

A. They did.

Q. Did they procure any arms at your house?

A. They did.

Q. What arms?

A. They took a gun, and they searched the house over for more; I had another gun and a brace of pistols in the house, but they did not find them.

Q. Did you ask them where they were going?

A. I did.

Q. Which of them?

A. The captain.

Q. That is Brandreth?

A. Yes.

Q. What did he tell you?

A. He said they were going to Nottingham.

Q. For what purpose did you learn?

A. He said there was a general rising throughout the country; he believed at that moment that the country was all up in arms, that Nottingham would be given up before they got there, if it was not by that time; he believed it was then.

Q. Was anything more said, by any of them, as to their purpose in going to Nottingham?

A. Yes, there was; they said they should proceed from Nottingham to London, and wipe off the National Debt, and begin again afresh. I then asked them if they knew the consequence of what they were doing, if they did not acccomplish their design.

Q. What was the answer?

A. That they well knew that what they had done already would hang them; they could but be hanged, and they were determined to go on.

Q. Do you remember any other expressions used by them?

A. On leaving, the captain said, "I doubt I have hurt you by pushing my gun, if I have I am sorry for it; but let me tell you, if I had heard one disrespectful word of your character I should have blown your brains out."

Q. Did they then go away?
A. They did.
Q. They took your son with them?
A. They did.

Cross-examined by Mr. Denman.

Q. George Weightman was not at your house that night?
A. I did not see him.
Q. You have no reason to believe he was there?
A. I have not.
Q. How long have you known him?
A. I have known him many years.
Q. He is a married man?
A. I suppose he is; I believe he is.
Q. You know he has a wife and three children?
A. I know he has a wife; I do not know how many children.

Do you know enough of his character, as a sober and peaceable man, to be able to give any account of it?

A. I do; his character is that of a sober peaceable man, for any thing that ever I heard.

Q. You were surprised when you heard him in the saw-pit talking about this rising?

A. I was.

Q. Did you remonstrate with him against the part he appeared to be taking?

A. I did not; the reason was, I considered it as an idle tale.

Q. Then with that impression upon your mind, you made no communication to anybody of what he had been stating; you did not tell the magistrate, any thing of that sort?

A. I did not.

Elijah Hall, the younger, sworn.
Examined by Mr. Solicitor General.

Q. You live with your father at Southwingfield park?
A. I do.
Q. Do you remember on Monday night, the 9th of June, being disturbed in your bed?
A. Yes.
Q. About what hour?
A. Between eleven and twelve.
Q. What was it disturbed you?
A. A disturbance at the door of a number of people.
Q. Did any persons come up into your bed-room?
A. Yes.
Q. How many?
A. Perhaps half a dozen.
Q. Was Brandreth the captain, one of them?
A. No, he was not.
Q. He was not one of those who came up into your room?
A. No.
Q. What did the persons say who came into your room?
A. They demanded me to get up and go along with them.

Q. Were they armed?
A. Yes.
Q. Did they use any threats to you?
A. They did.
Q. What sort of threats?
A. They threatened to shoot me if I did not go along with them.
Q. In consequence of those threats, and the number of persons who were there, did you go with them?
A. I did.
Q. Did you dress yourself?
A. I did.
Q. Did they give you any arms?
A. Yes.
Q. What arms?
A. They gave me a pike.
Q. When you got down stairs and were with them, did you see Brandreth the captain?
A. Yes, I did.
Q. And many others?
A. And several others.
Q. Where did you go to from your father's house?
A. I went from there to Isaac Walker's.
Q. What was done at Isaac Walker's?
A. There was a great disturbance made at the door.
Q. By the party you were with?
A. Yes, by the party I was with.
Q. Did they get any arms at Walker's?
A. Yes.
Q. What?
A. They got a gun and a pistol at Walker's.
Q. Where did you go to from Walker's?
A. To Henry Bestwick's.
Q. Did you get any arms there?
A. We got a gun there.
Q. By force?
A. They broke into the house there.
Q. From Bestwick's did you go to Samuel Hunt's?
A. Yes.

Q. I believe there you staid some time?
A. Yes.
Q. From Samuel Hunt's where did you go?
A. To Mary Hepworth's.
Q. Were arms demanded at Mary Hepworth's?
A. They were.
Q. At first were they given or were they refused?
A. They were refused.
Q. Was any thing done there after that refusal?
A. Yes.
Q. What?
A. There was a great disturbance made at the door.
Q. And at the kitchen window I believe?
A. Yes, and at the ktichen window too.
Q. Did the captain fire into the kitchen?
A. Yes, he did.
Q. I believe Robert Walters, Mrs. Hepworth's servant, was shot upon that occasion, and died?
A. He was.
Q. He was shot by the captain, Brandreth?
A. Yes, he was.
Q. After that, did they procure arms at Mary Hepworth's?
A. Yes.
Q. Where did you go to from Mary Hepworth's?
A. We went from there to Pentridge-lane-end.
Q. Did you meet any other party at Pentridge-lane-end?
A. Yes.
Q. Were they armed in the same way with pikes and guns?
A. They were.
Q. The party having joined there, which way did they go?
A. They went along with the others.
Q. Which way?
A. Towards Pentridge.
Q. Did you know any of the persons who joined you there?
A. No; I cannot say that I did.

Q. Were they Pentridge people, do you know, or did you observe them or not?

A. I do not know.

Q. At Pentridge did they knock at many houses?

A. They did.

Q. In the same way as they had done before?

A. They did.

Q. And broke into several houses there?

A. They did.

Q. Did they procure arms?

A. I did not see them.

Q. Did you march in order up to Pentridge, or how?

A. Yes, in order.

Q. Where were you formed in ranks?

A. In Pentridge-lane.

Q. By the captain, I believe?

A. Yes.

Q. In Pentridge you contrived to get away from them, and returned to your father's?

A. Yes, I did.

Q. Whilst you were with them, did you hear any of them say where they were going, or what they were about to do?

A. I did.

Q. Where was it they said they were going?

A. They said they were going to Nottingham.

Q. To do what?

A. To show themselves upon the race course.

Q. What did they say they were going to do.

A. To meet many other parties there.

Q. What did they say they were then going to do?

A. I do not recollect any thing particular.

Q. Did they say any thing about the parliament?

A. Yes; they said they were going to pull down the parliament house, and to break the laws.

Cross-examined by Mr. Cross.

Q. You did not see any thing of the prisoner at the bar, during any of the time you have been speaking of?

A. Yes; I saw him just before I made my escape.

Q. But till that moment you had seen nothing of him, either at your house, or at Hepworth's?
A. I had not.

Re-examined by Mr. Solicitor General.

Q. Where was it you saw him?
A. In Pentridge town.

Mr. Isaac Walker sworn.
Examined by Mr. Serjeant Vaughan.

Q. I believe you are a farmer in Southwingfield park?
A. Yes.
Q. Were you disturbed about eleven o'clock on Monday night the 9th of June?
A. About half-past eleven.
Q. Were your family gone to bed?
A. Yes.
Q. What happened to you, what disturbed you?
A. The dog barking.
Q. Did you get up?
A. Yes.
Q. What did you observe on getting up?
A. I put my head out of the window, and saw a number of men coming into the yard.
Q. What number do you think?
A. About forty.
Q. Did you observe whether they were armed or not?
A. Yes, they were all armed apparently.
Q. What did they do or demand?
A. They demanded the door opening first.
Q. What further?
A. They demanded a gun and a brace of pistols.
Q. Did they say what they wanted them for, or where they were going?
A. They said they were going to Nottingham.
Q. Did they say what they were going to Nottingham for?
A. I asked them what for; they said that was no business of mine, that they were determined to have my arms.

Q. Did you give them your arms?

A. I told them I had a gun, but no pistols.

Q. What remark was made upon that by any of the mob?

A. They said they knew we had pistols.

Q. Did they say what quantity of pistols?

A. A brace of pistols.

Q. What did you say to that?

A. I told them I had not; when they had got the gun they went away.

Q. After going away, how soon did any of them return?

A. In a few minutes.

Q. Upon their return, what did they demand of you?

A. They said they knew I had one pistol, if I had not two, and they were determined to have it.

Q. Did you give them the pistol?

A. Yes; I was forced to do it.

Q. Do you remember who took the pistol?

A. Jeremiah Brandreth, I believe, the man whom they called their captain.

Q. What did he do with it?

A. He fired it off; I do not know what he did with it afterwards.

Q. It was loaded when you gave it them?

A. Yes.

Q. Did they ask you whether it was loaded?

A. Yes, they did.

Q. Then they left you?

A. Yes.

Cross-examined by Mr. Denman.

Q. The prisoner was not there?

A. I did not see him.

Q. How long have you known this prisoner, George Weightman.

A. Some years; I cannot exactly say how long.

Q. You knew him a boy?

A. No; perhaps two or three years.

Q. Have you known enough of him to be able to tell us what his general character has been?

A. No, I cannot say.

Q. How far do you live from him?

A. Three miles and a half perhaps.

Mrs. Mary Hepworth sworn.

Examined by Mr. Serjeant Vaughan.

Q. You are the widow of a farmer in Southwingfield Park?

A. Yes.

Q. Were you disturbed at any time on the night of the 9th of June?

A. Yes.

Q. At what time on the night of the 9th of June was your family disturbed?

A. Between eleven and twelve.

Q. What disturbed you?

A. A loud noise at the door; a man calling out for men and guns.

Q. I believe you were in bed?

A. I was in bed and asleep.

Q. Did you get up and go down stairs?

A. Immediately.

Q. Whom did you find in the kitchen when you went down stairs?

A. Robert Fox, William Hepworth my son, and Robert Walters.

Q. Fox and Walters were your servants?

A. They were.

Q. What happened in the kitchen?

A. They say said if we did not deliver the men and guns they would blow our brains out immediately.

Q. What was done upon that?

A. We told them we should not.

Q. What was done upon your giving them that answer?

A. They immediately broke the window, and forced the shutters into the room, and fired immediately and shot Robert Walters.

Q. How soon did he die in consequence of that shooting?

A. Perhaps ten minutes; but I cannot be certain.

Q. What was done after they had shot Robert Walters?

A. They still kept making noises; they were a great many stones thrown.

Q. Did you deliver them any arms?

A. The gun; they still demanded a man; I told them we could not let them have a man; that I thought killing one man was sufficient.

Q. What did they say to that?

A. I went up stairs; there was a party in the garden; I told them the same, that they must go away.

Q. What did they do with the gun?

A. We gave them the gun, with the but end towards them.

Q. How came you to give it them with the but end towards them?

A. They desired to have that given towards them; I went up stairs to tell them to go away; they told me if we did not retire from the window, they would serve us the same.

Q. What was Walters doing at the time he was shot?

A. He was stooping down, as if he was putting his boots on.

Q. He was not offering resistance?

A. No; he never spoke from the time he came down stairs.

Cross-examined by Mr. Cross.

Q. You could not see any thing of the prisoner at the bar at your house that night?

A. I saw nobody; it was very dark; we could just discern the men in the yard.

Samuel Levers sworn.

Examined by Mr. Clarke.

Q. Did you in June last live with Messrs. Wheatcrofts, at Buckland Hollow?

A. Yes.

Q. In what parish is Buckland Hollow?
A. I do not know.
Q. How far from Pentridge?
A. About a mile.
Q. Do you remember on the night of Monday the 9th of June being disturbed, after you were in bed?
A. Yes.
Q. About what hour?
A. About one o'clock in the morning.
Q. What were you disturbed by?
A. Mr. Wheatcroft's farming man called me up.
Q. When you got up what did you see?
A. I went part of the way down stairs, and when I got part of the way down stairs, there were some people in the house.
Q. Do you know any of them?
A. No; I turned back to my room.
Q. What happened then when you went back to the room?
A. A man came up with one eye that carried a sword.
Q. Did he come into your room?
A. Yes; up into the garret.
Q. Have you seen that man since?
A. No, I have not.
Q. What did he do when he came up?
A. He said, "Come, come, you must get up and go along with us."
Q. What else did he say?
A. He did not say any more; I got up.
Q. What did you do when you got up?
A. I put part of my clothes on, and they would not let me stop to put on the rest; I went down stairs.
Q. What did they do with you?
A. I went down to the second landing.
Q. How came you to go down to the second landing?
A. There was a man with a gun and a pistol; they said they had shot one man, and they would serve me the same.

Q. Who was that man do you know?

A. He was afterwards called the Nottingham captain.

Q. Brandreth?

A. I do not know his name.

Q. Did you come down stairs.

A. Yes, I came down to the second landing; and the man with one eye said, they had been men of great property, and were very sorry to do it; but there were men from Sheffield, and that part of the country, coming to meet them.

Q. Did you go down stairs then?

A. Yes.

Q. Whom did you find down stairs?

A. There were several people in the house, I did not know them.

Q. Were they armed?

A. Yes.

Q. How?

A. Some with guns and some with spikes.

Q. Did you hear any of them say where they were going to?

A. Yes; they said they were going to Nottingham.

Q. Had your master any gun in the house?

A. Yes.

Q. What became of that?

A. Mr. Wheatcroft's farming man, John Dexter, asked if he might carry the gun, and they permitted him.

Q. Did they take the gun?

A. No, I believe he took it out of the house himself.

Q. Were you and Dexter compelled to go with those persons?

A. Yes.

Q. When you got out of the house into the yard, did you find any more persons there?

A. Yes, several more persons there.

Q. Were they armed?

A. Yes.

Q. With what?

A. Some with guns and some with spikes.

Q. Do you know any of them?

A. No.

Q. You say there was a man there who was afterwards called the Nottingham captain, did he put you into any order?

A. Why they insisted upon us going on with them; we went to Pentridge-lane-end, and they formed us into a rank there.

Q. Was there any body appointed to make you keep in order?

A. Between Pentridge and Pentridge-lane-end he halted, and called out for any men who had served as soldiers.

Q. Did any body quit the ranks to fall out upon that?

A. Yes; they called one man captain Turner.

Q. Did you hear that captain Turner say any thing?

A. There was a few of the inhabitants that refused to open their doors, and he called out for the iron crow.

Q. Did they go to any doors after that?

A. Yes, a few in Pentridge.

Q. Were there any houses in Pentridge broken open?

A. There were several, I believe.

Q. Was any thing taken away from them?

A. I cannot say.

Q. Did you happen to go near Mr. William Booth's?

A. Yes.

Q. Was his poney fetched out?

A. Yes, I believe it was.

Q. Did you see it?

A. I saw it come out of the yard.

Q. Do you know the prisoner, George Weightman, by sight?

A. I cannot say that I positively know him.

Q. Did you see him that night?

A. I saw a man in a large round hat, a fustian slop, and a pair of fustian trowsers.

Q. What is a slop?

A. A jacket; but I cannot swear to him: I afterwards knew his name was George Weightman; but I am a stranger to that part of the country.

Q. I do not ask you what his name was, but whether the man who stands there is the man whom you saw?

A. I am sure I cannot swear to him.

Q. What did you see that man do?

A He afterwards went down the lane.

Q. How did he go; was any thing done with Booth's pony?

A. Yes, he got on it.

Q. Did he take any thing with him?

A. I saw a bag of something.

Q. What were they?

A. They said they were bullets.

Q. The men said they were bullets?

A. Yes.

Q. Where was this man that mounted this pony going to?

A. They said he was going to Nottingham, to see how they were going on there.

Q. Which way did he go with the pony?

A. He went down a lane that goes to Butterley works.

Q. Does that go down the lane?

A. I am sure I cannot say; we followed him down the same place.

Q. You say the people said he was going to Nottingham?

A. Yes.

Q. How far did you go with those persons?

A. I went to the other side of Eastwood.

Q. Did you go as far as Langley mill?

A. Yes.

Q. At Langley mill did you see any thing of the man that went off upon the pony?

A. Yes, he met us at Langley mill.

Q. Upon the pony?

A. Yes.

Q. Did you hear him say any thing?

A. No, I did not hear him say any thing; he called the Nottingham captain to him, and the Nottingham captain told us, this man said, that things were all going on very well at Nottingham, and that the soldiers were all made up in the barracks, and there was a number of people on the forest to meet them.

William Booth sworn.

Examined by Mr. Gurney.

Q. I believe you live at Pentridge, do you not?
A. Yes.
Q. On the night of Monday, the 9th of June, were you alarmed by any number of persons coming to your house?
A. Yes.
Q. At about what hour?
A. Between twelve and one.
Q. Did you look out?
A. Yes, I got up to the window.
Q. Looking out, what did you see?
A. I saw a great number of men standing at the door, round the door.
Q. Were they armed?
A. Yes.
Q. How?
A. Some with guns and some with spikes.
Q. By spikes, do you mean such things as those lying upon the table?
A. Yes.
Q. What did those men tell you they wanted?
A. They called out " halloo!" I got up and asked them what they wanted? they said, " I want you and your gun."
Q. What did you say?
A. I said, I had no gun.
Q. What was then said to you?
A. He said, we must then come down and open the door; I said, " I cannot go with you."
Q. Did you say why?
A. I said, I was ballotted for the militia, and had to come to Derby that very day.
Q. What reply was made to that?
A. They said, " we will free you from the militia, come down stairs and open the door, or I will blow your brains out."

Vol. II.   F f

Q. Did you at last come down stairs?
A. Yes.
Q. Whom did you find?
A. When I came down stairs and drawed the bolt, the door fell into the house.
Q. The door had been roughly used, and it broke off from the hinges?
A. Yes.
Q. Had they been trying at the door before you came down?
A. Yes, they kept beating the door all the time I was talking with them.
Q. When you came down what was said to you?
A. There was a quantity of men rushed into the house.
Q. Where they armed?
A. Yes, some of them.
Q. Was Brandreth one?
A. Yes.
Q. Was William Turner another?
A. Yes.
Q. What did Brandreth then say to you?
A. He says, " where are your clothes?" I said they were up stairs.
Q. You had come down without your clothes?
A. Yes; he said, " go and put them on immediately;" I went up stairs as quick as I could, but before I had put one stocking on and tied it, they followed me up with a candle.
Q. Was that Brandreth?
A. One of them was.
Q. What did he say to you?
A. He said, " what have you been doing as you are not dressed?" I said I would make what haste I could, I could not find my clothes; he said, " look quickly or else I will shoot you."
Q. Were you forced down stairs?
A. Yes.
Q. Before you were quite dressed?
A. Yes.

Q. Were your boots laced?
A. No.
Q. Did you offer to lace them?
A. Yes.
Q. Upon your offering to lace them, what did Brandreth say?
A. He said, " if you stop to lace your boots, I will shoot you."
Q. Did they then force you out into the ranks?
A. Yes, they forced me out of the house before them.
Q. Did they put you into the rank?
A. Yes.
Q. How was the rank formed; how many deep?
A. Two deep.
Q. How were they armed?
A. Some with guns, and some with spikes.
Q. What weapon was given you?
A. They did not give me any; they asked me as they took me out if I had a gun; and I said as I was not possessed of one.
Q. Upon that, what did they say?
A. They told me that I must take a fork; I said I could not find any, and did not take any.
Q. Did those men attack many other houses besides yours?
A. Yes.
Q. And take arms and men?
A. Yes.
Q. Among others, did they attack Mr. Storer's
A. Yes.
Q. Did they take him and his gun?
A. Yes.
Q. While you were at or near Mr. Storer's, do you remember seeing the prisoner and a party coming towards you?
A. No, I cannot say that I did.
Q. Did you see him?
A. Yes.

Q. Where did you see him first?

A. At Pentridge.

Q. How far is that from Mr. Storer's?

A. About half a mile, as nearly as I can tell.

Q. Who came with him?

A. I did not see who came with him.

Q. Do you remember after you were in Pentridge, Brandreth ordering any gun to be fired?

A. Yes.

Q. Did he say for what purpose?

A. To alarm them at Butterley, that they might get in readiness.

Q. Was the gun fired?

A. Yes.

Q. Was Mr. William Booth's house attacked?

A. Yes.

Q. I do not mean your house, I mean another William Booth's?

A. Yes.

Q. Was his pony taken out of the stable?

A. His pony was brought out of the yard.

Q. By whom!

A. By George Weightman.

Q. Did you afterwards see Mr. Storer put upon that pony?

A. No, I did not.

Q. Did you after that hear Brandreth give the prisoner Weightman any directions about that pony?

A. Yes.

Q. What did he say to him?

A. He told him he must take that pony and go to Nottingham, and bring tidings, and come again to Langley mill, and meet them at Langley mill.

Q. What more did he say?

A. I did not hear him say any thing more.

Q. Did he say any thing about what time they were to be at Nottingham?

A. As they were going up Pentridge, Brandreth said Pentridge does not appear to be in readiness at all;

I thought it would have been the readiest place.

Q. Did he say at what time they ought to have been at Nottingham?

A. At three o'clock.

Q. After Brandreth had told the prisoner to take the pony and go to Nottingham, did he mount the pony and go off?

A. Yes.

Q. Towards Nottingham?

A. Yes.

Q. Were you then marched to Butterley?

A. Yes.

Q. In rank?

A. Yes.

Q. Did you there see Mr. Goodwin?

A. Yes.

Q. Were you halted opposite the office?

A. Yes.

Q. Did Mr. Goodwin speak to Brandreth and your men?

A. Yes, he spoke to Brandreth, and said, "what do you want?"

Q. What answer was given?

A. He said, we want your men.

Q. Did Brandreth say that?

A. Yes.

Q. What did Mr. Goodwin say?

A. He said, "you are too many already, without you were going for a better purpose; dismiss your men, and let them all go to their homes, you will all get hanged."

Q. Were you then marched to Ripley town-end?

A. Yes, over the coke hearths.

Q. Were you halted there?

A. Yes.

Q. What did Brandreth then direct you to do?

A. He halted us, and told the men to give three huzzas.

Q. For what purpose?

A. To alarm Ripley.

Q. Why to alarm Ripley?

A. For them to go along with them, as I expect.

Q. Were you then marched to Codnor?
A. Yes.

Q. Did you knock up the man who kept the Glass House public-house.
A. Yes.

Q. Was a quantity of beer given to the party?
A. Yes.

Q. Did any men join you at Codnor, who had left you for a short time?
A. Yes; there were some came up whilst we were in the house.

Q. Who led them?
A. I do not know justly.

Q. Who were they?
A. Samuel Hunt was one.

Q. While you were there, did you ask William Turner any question?
A. Yes.

Q. What was it?
A. I asked him where they began? he said at ten o'clock last night at Wingfield.

Q. You, I believe, are in the service of Mr. Pearson, of Wingfield?
A. Yes.

Q. Did you ask Turner any question about Pearson?
A. Yes; I asked him if they had called at Mr. Pearson's, and he said no.

Q. What more did he say?
A. He said, " we mean to call on that beggar when we come back."

Q. Were you then marched on?
A. Yes, very soon after.

Q. In going out of Codnor, were you halted near the house of a Mr. Stirland?
A. Yes.

Q. Did any of your party go and search his premises, for men and arms?
A. Yes; there were some of the party went into the yard.

Q. Who where they?

A. William Turner was one, and Samuel Hunt was another which I knew; there was not any other that I knew.

Q. How many men did they take away?

A. Three or four.

Q. Any arms?

A. They brought some forks?

Q. Some pitch forks?

A. Yes.

Q. Did you then march on to Mr. Raynor's?

A. Yes.

Q. Was Mr. Raynor threatened if he would not go?

A. Yes.

Q. Were you then marched to Langley mill?

A. Yes.

Q. At Langley mill, did you meet the prisoner?

A. Yes.

Q. On Mr. Booth's pony?

A. Yes.

Q. Was he coming as if from Nottingham?

A. Yes; he seemed as if he was coming that way.

Q. What did he say to you, what news did he bring?

A. Somebody asked him how they were going on.

Q. Where?

A. At Nottingham; he said, " the soldiers are all in the barracks; they are doing well; march on my lads as fast as you can."

Q. Were you then ordered to march on, and did you march on?

A. Yes.

Q. How far did you go with them?

A. I went beyond Eastwood with them.

Q. Did you then get away?

A. Yes.

Q. You left them marching on towards Nottingham?

A. Yes.

Q. Was John Bacon one of them?

A. Yes, I saw John Bacon.

Q. Was Thomas Weightman another?
A. Yes.
Q. Joseph Weightman, junior?
A. Yes.
Q. Samuel Walters?
A. Yes.
Q. Old Isaac Ludlam?
A. Yes.
Q. And his two sons?
A. Yes.
Q. William Turner?
A. Yes.
Q. Manchester Turner?
A. Yes.
Q. Edward Turner?
A. Yes.
Q. Joseph Topham?
A. Yes.
Q. Samuel Hunt?
A. Yes.
Q. John Onion?
A. Yes.
Q. Joseph Savage?
A. Yes.
Q. James Taylor?
A. Yes.
Q. Joseph Taylor?
A. Yes.
Q. Benjamin Taylor?
A. Yes.
Q. German Buxton?
A. Yes.
Q. James Barnes?
A. Yes.
Q. William Barker?
A. Yes.
Q. Edward Haslam?
A. Yes.

Q. John Horsley?
A. Yes.

Q. Were those all armed?
A. Why I cannot say justly whether they were all armed or not.

Q. Were most of them armed?
A. Yes, most of them were.

Q. After you had quitted them and turned back, did you meet with any person following them?
A. Yes.

Q. Who was that?
A. Joseph Weightman and Nathaniel Walters.

Q. What Joseph Weightman is that?
A. He is of another family.

Q. Did they stop you?
A. No, they did not stop us.

Q. They went on after the other party?
A. Yes.

Henry Hole sworn.

Examined by Mr. Serjeant Copley.

Q. Do you live at Pentridge-lane-end?
A. Yes.

Q. Do you remember on the evening of Sunday the 8th of June, seeing Samuel Hunt?
A. Yes; I saw Samuel Hunt and eight or ten others stand before George Turner's smithy door.

Q. At what hour?
A. About nine o'clock, or it might be turned.

Q. What had you in your hand?
A. I was coming along the turnpike-road with a jug of milk, and he said, " thou art fetching that for these men to night."

Q. What did you say to that?
A. I said, " what men?"

Q. What answer did he make?
A. He said," these revolutioners who will come to night or to-morrow night."

Q. What answer did you give?

A. I said, " I believe not; and he offered to lay me a wager of five shillings of it."

Q. After that, I believe you parted?

A. Yes.

Q. On the following night, about twelve o'clock, were you alarmed?

A. About twenty minutes before twelve o'clock, I and my wife were alarmed by some blows coming upon the door.

Q. What did you do?

A. I got up to the window and said, " halloo, who is there, what do you want!"

Q. What answer was given?

A. They said we want you to volunteer yourself to go with us, or else we will break the door down and murder you.

Q. What did you do upon that?

A. I went down and opened the door.

Q. Whom did you find at the door?

A. I found four men, two that I knew, and two that I knew not.

Q. Were they armed?

A. They were armed with pikes.

Q. Who were the men that you knew?

A. Joseph Weightman and Joseph Topham.

Q. What passed when you got down to the door?

A. I asked where they were going; they said they were going to Nottingham; I told them I could not pretend to go with them, that I had no money to take me there, nor nobody to take care of my family while I was gone.

Q. What answer was given to that?

A. They said I wanted no money, they should keep me on roast beef and ale; and there was people fixed to take care of every body's family that went, who would come in two days or under.

Q. What further did they say?

A. I dressed me and went out, and a pike was forced upon me.

Q. Did they say any thing about Yorkshire?

A. They said I had better go that night than stop till morning, for they would come in the morning out of Yorkshire like a cloud, and would take all before them.

Q. Did they say what would happen to those that did go?

A. That those who did not go would all be shot.

Q. After this conversation, what did they do?

A. I dressed myself and went out, and a pike was forced upon me.

Q. Did this conversation you have been speaking of, pass before you were dressed, or when you were dressing?

A. Before I was dressed; I had only my breeches on.

Q. You have said there were four men with pikes at the door, did you go with them?

A. Yes, I did.

Q. How far did you go before you saw some others?

A. I went about thirty or forty yards along the turnpike road, and then I saw some others.

Q. Where were they; near what house?

A. Near John Sellars's.

Q. Were they armed or unarmed?

A. They appeared to be armed; some with guns and some with spikes, and some with other weapons.

Q. What were they doing at Sellars's house?

A. I saw John Sellars come out of his door; I suppose they were stopping for his dressing.

Q. While you were there, did you hear a gun go off?

A. Yes, a little before I got there I did.

Q. Was that in the direction of Mrs. Hepworth's house?

A. Yes, I supposed it to be there.

Q. Did you afterwards see another party come across the meadows, as if from Mrs. Hepworth's house?

A. I heard of one, I did not see the party.

Q. Did they join the party at Sellars's?

A. No, they joined the party going into Mr. Fletcher's yard.

Q. Was that the same party that had been at Sellars's?

A. They joined the party that went to Mr. Sellars's.

Q. And there they joined the party that came across the fields from Mrs. Hepworth's?

A. Yes, I supposed it to be the same party.

Q. Did they attack Mr. Fletcher's house?

A. Yes.

Q. What did they get from Mr. Fletcher's?

A. They got a gun and a man.

Q. What was the man's name?

A. William Shipman.

Q. Was he a serving man of Mr. Fletcher's?

A. Yes.

Q. After they had got the man and the gun, was any order given by any body?

A. The captain gave orders to march.

Q. Which way did they then go?

A. We went along the turnpike a little way, and we were there then divided into two companies.

Q. Did the captain head one of the companies?

A. The captain headed the biggest part of the men that went towards the row of houses.

Q. Who headed the other?

A. There was Samuel Hunt and eight or ten others went towards Samuel Booth's.

Q. Was any attack made upon Samuel Booth's?

A. Yes, Mr. Hunt knocked at the door.

Q. What did he knock at the door with?

A. With his pike end?

Q. What did he demand?

A. Mr. Booth appeared at the window, and he demanded his son.

Q. What did Mr. Booth say?

A. He begged, as he was a neighbour, that he would go off from the house without him.

Q. Hunt lived near that place I believe.

A. Yes, he did.

Q. What did Hunt say?

A. He said, " nay, we must have him, the captain is coming, and I am sure he will not go without him."

Q. Did he say any thing more?

A. Yes; he said he had better go that night than stop till morning, for he said they would come out of Sheffield in the morning, and out of Yorkshire, and would take all before them.

Q. In the mean time did the captain come up?

A. In the mean time the captain came up before we left the house.

Q. What took place afterwards?

A. We marched towards Mr. Wheatcroft's at Buckland Hollow.

Q. Who headed that party?

A. The captain.

Q. Did you all go?

A. All that were at Mr. Booth's.

Q. Did you make an attack upon Wheatcroft's house?

A. Yes; Brandreth knocked with the but end of his gun at the door.

Q. Without going into the particulars, tell me whether you attacked the house and obtained any thing from it?

A. The door was forced open, and they brought away three men and a gun.

Q. After you had attacked the house and obtained the three men and a gun, did you return to Pentridge-lane-end?

A. We returned to Pentridge-lane-end, and joined the other party.

Q. After you had joined the other party, were you formed in any way?

A. We were formed into ranks three deep.

Q. By whom?

A. By Brandreth the captain.

Q. Did any body assist him?

A. I saw William Turner assisting him in the first part of it; but I did not see him in the last part of it.

Q. How were you placed with reference to the arms you had?

A. The biggest part of the muskets were in front, the pikes in the middle, and a few muskets behind.

Q. Did you then proceed to Storer's house?

A. We proceeded then along the road as far as Storer's.

Q. Was John Storer forced from the house?

A. He was brought and put into the rank; he was from the house at the time I first saw him.

Q. Was any body set over him to guard him?

A. There was a guard fixed over him.

Q. Armed, how?

A. Armed with a musket.

Q. Did you go from thence to Pentridge?

A. Yes.

Q. Did you attack houses in Pentridge?

A. Yes, they attacked a good many houses, and got some men and guns.

Q. When you were in Pentridge, did you see the prisoner, George Weightman?

A. Yes, I saw him.

Q. Was he on foot, or on horseback?

A. First when I saw him he was on horseback.

Q. On a pony?

A. Yes.

Q. Had he any conversation with Brandreth?

A. I saw him and Brandreth stand a little aside the men, but I do not know what conversation they had.

Q. Were they conversing together?

A. They appeared to be; I did not hear the words that passed.

Q. What was the colour of the pony?

A. Brown.

Q. How was George Weightman dressed?

A. He was dressed apparently in a short slop, that went round him a little below his waist.

Q. After this conversation that he had with Brandreth, what did he do?

A. He rode off towards Nottingham.

Q. Where did the party go to from Pentridge?

A. They went along the road to Butterley.

Q. When they arrived at Butterley works, were they drawn up?

A. They were, in ranks.

Q. Did any body knock at the gates?

A. William Turner and Brandreth knocked at the gates with the but ends of their guns.

Q. Did Mr. Goodwin, the manager, come out?

A. Mr. Goodwin came out at the office door, and said, what do you want?

Q. You need not tell us all that passed in the way of conversation; but Mr. Goodwin came out and addressed them?

A. Yes.

Q. After that, was the order given to march?

A. Yes, an order was given to march, and we went over the coke hearths to Ripley.

Q. When you arrived at Ripley was any order given to halt?

A. There was order given to halt.

Q. By whom?

A. By Brandreth; he said, " there must be three cheers given here, to let the Ripley men know that we are going."

Q. After this did they march on to Codnor?

A. Yes, they marched on to Codnor, to the Glass House.

Q. The Glass House is a public house?

A. Yes.

Q. Did all the party go to the Glass House, or some part of them to another public house?

A. That party all went to the Glass House.

Q. Did you get any drink at the Glass House?

A. Yes.

Q. Was John Bacon one of that party?

A. Yes, he was.

Q. Do you remember his saying any thing in the Glass House?

A. I remember hearing him make a speech in the back kitchen; I did not hear it all; he was making it when I went in; I had been at the front door.

Q. What did you hear him say?

A. The first I can recollect is, that the Government had robbed and plundered them of all that ever they had; that

that was the last shift that ever they could make; they must either fight or starve.

Q. While you were there, do you remember Hunt coming up with another party?

A. Yes, I saw Hunt, and a man whom they called Manchester Turner, come up with the party.

Q. Was a bill called for?

A. Yes, there was a bill called for, of the liquor.

Q. Did the landlord give it?

A. Yes, the landlord gave it either to Brandreth or to John Bacon, I do not know to which.

Q. Upon the bill being given, what was said to the landlord?

A. They said it would be paid in a fortnight, when the job was over.

Q. When you left the public house, which way did you march?

A. We marched towards Langley mill.

Q. Were you joined by any of the other party?

A. We were joined by a party that came from Hartsay, and a party that came from Swanwick, from the two other public houses.

Q. The two other public houses at Codnor?

A. Yes.

Q. Was an attack made upon Mr. Raynor's house in the way?

A. Yes.

Q. What was done?

A. William Turner first went in, he ordered young Mr. Raynor to turn out, and take his man and his gun.

Q. Did they threaten Mr. Raynor?

A. Yes; I heard them threaten to shoot Mr. Raynor three or four different times, but I could not hear all that was said, I was not nigh enough to the house.

Q. They did not succeed in getting young Mr. Raynor?

A. They got his servant man, a gun, and a pitching fork.

Q. Do you remember after you had left Mr. Raynor's house, meeting any man on the road with cows?

A. Yes, they took the man.

Q. Did they force him to join them?

A. Yes.

Q. When you were near Langley mill, did you see the prisoner at the bar?

A. Yes, I saw him coming back from Nottingham, on the horse upon which I had seen him ride out of Pentridge before.

Q. That was just before you got to Langley mill?

A. No, just after we got past Mr. Bowles's.

Q. Before he came up to you, or spoke to you, had he any conversation with the captain?

A. I saw him stand a little on one side the men with the captain.

Q. Speaking to him?

A. I was not near enough to hear what they said.

Q. Were you near enough to see whether they were speaking?

A. Yes, apparently they were.

Q. After this conversation, did he ride along the ranks?

A. Yes.

Q. What did he say to the men, as he rode along the ranks?

A. I heard him say, " you have nothing to do but to march on; they bombarded Nottingham at two o'clock this morning, and it is given up to them."

Q. Did they march on?

A. Yes, they marched on.

Q. Did they pick up any more men before they got to Eastwood?

A. They took one or two about Langley mill, but I do not know how far they went.

Q. Was James Barnes one of the party?

A. Yes.

Q. Do you remember having any conversation with him at Eastwood?

A. I asked him what he was going to do when he got to Nottingham; he said, they had fixed up a new government at Nottingham, and they were going there to defend it, until other counties came into their terms.

Vol. II.   G g

Q. What more did he say?

A. He said, it would be soon all over; for by a letter which he had seen from London yesterday, the keys of the Tower would be given up to the Hampden club party, if they were not already.

Q. Was that all he said?

A. He said, he had never been set down more than five minutes at once, since four o'clock yesterday morning.

Q. Did you ask him what he had been doing?

A. Yes, I asked him; and he said he had been providing guns, spikes, and ammunition.

Q. When you first got into Eastwood, were you marching regularly, or had you got into disorder?

A. When we got into Eastwood we were broken out of rank, and in no order; the men appeared disorderly.

Q. Were you again formed into rank there?

A. We were formed into rank there again?

Q. By the captain?

A. By the captain, William Turner assisting.

Q. After you had been formed into rank, did you turn out?

A. Yes; I turned out after I had been in a little while, and stood a little distance from the men.

Q. Did Brandreth come up to you?

A. Brandreth came up to me, and ordered me into rank again.

Q. What did he say to you?

A. I said, I should not go in for him, or for any other man.

Q. What did he say?

A. He said, if I did not go in again, he would shoot me immediately.

Q. Had he a gun at that time in his hand?

A. He had a gun, and I perceived that he had cocked the gun; I stepped up to him with a stack paring knife I had in my hand.

Q. Having this stack paring knife in your hand, and stepping up to him, what did you say?

A. I swore, that if he offered to level the gun, I would

hack his head off.

Q. What did he do upon that?

A. He stood a little while, and then turned off.

Q. What did you do upon that?

A. I marched off towards Langley mill.

Q. That was back again?

A. Yes.

Q. After you had got a short distance, thirty or forty yards, did you hear any thing?

A. I heard a cry of, " Do not shoot."

Q. Did you, in consequence of that, turn round?

A. I turned round, and saw Brandreth with a gun at his shoulder pointed towards me.

Q. Who was standing near him?

A. Thomas Turner took hold of the gun, and turned him off.

Q. Upon that, did you continue to go back?

A. I went back a little further.

Q. Did Joseph Savage come up to you?

A. A man of the name of Savage, I do not know his christian name.

Q. Was he one of the party?

A. Yes.

Q. What had he?

A. A short pistol; it appeared to me about a foot long?

Q. Did he say any thing as he came up to you?

A. He said, if I did not turn back, he would blow a bullet through me.

Q. What did you say to that?

A. I said, if he did, that he must do it before he got too nigh me, or I should have a hack at him with that which I had in my hand.

Q. Upon that did he leave you?

A. He said, he should be sorry to shoot me or any other man; and then he turned back.

Q. Did you continue your return homewards?

A. I returned homewards;—no, I did not go directly homewards; I followed the men a little way to see how they went on; I watched them a little way, and I could see them breaking up in every direction; I could here and there see a few go.

Q. Deserting?
A. Yes, at every gate.
Q. Did you afterwards return home?
A. I afterwards returned homewards.
Q. While you were going homewards, did you see any other party?
A. I saw a party of about fifty the first.
Q. Which way were they going?
A. They were going along the turnpike road towards Nottingham.
Q. Were they going in the same direction, following the other party?
A. Yes.
Q. Did you see any other party?
A. I saw another party at Langley mill, against Mr. Bowles's.
Q. Were they also going in the same direction?
A. They stood still when I first saw them; afterwards they appeared to move, but I was not nigh them.
Q. How many might that party consist of?
A. I thought about sixty.
Q. Besides those two parties, did you see any other persons going in the same direction?
A. No, I cannot say that I did.
Q. You got home?
A. Yes.

Charles Walters sworn.

Examined by Mr. Reader.

Q. I believe that you lived with Mr. George Argile, of Hartsay, in June last?
A. Yes.
Q. He is a farmer at Hartsay?
A. Yes.
Q. In what parish is Hartsay?
A. In Pentridge parish.

Q. After you were in bed, were you alarmed on the night of the 9th of June?
A. Yes.
Q. About what time?
A. About a quarter before three o'clock, on the morning of the 10th?
Q. What were you alarmed with?
A. Five or six men.
Q. Where were the men?
A. At the door.
Q. Were they making a noise?
A. Yes.
Q. What kind of noise?
A. Rattling and shaking at the door.
Q. Did they ask for any thing?
A. Yes.
Q. What?
A. They demanded men and arms.
Q. Did you get out of bed?
A. Yes; my master first.
Q. Was your master in the room with you?
A. No; but my master spoke to them first.
Q. What did you do?
A. I did not at first; I concealed myself in a bacon chest in a room adjoining.
Q. Did any body come into that room?
A. Yes.
Q. And found you?
A. Yes.
Q. They opened the chest and found you?
A. Yes.
Q. Were they armed?
A. Yes.
Q. What with?
A. One had a sword.
Q. There were more than one?
A. Yes.
Q. How many were there?
A. Four.
Q. Was that man a one-eyed man?
A. Yes.
Q. Was it Manchester Turner?
A. Yes.

Q. Did they force you out of the chest?
A. Yes.
Q. What did he threaten to do?
A. He threatened to run his sword through me, if I did not get up.
"Q. Who were the other three persons in the room?
A. The one was Edward Turner, the other Samuel Hunt, and the other a young lad from Swanwick.
Q. In consequence of those threats did you get up?
A. Yes.
Q. Did you ask what they wanted?
A. Yes.
Q. What did they answer?
A. They demanded, that I should go along with them?
Q. Did you ask them where they were going?
A. Yes.
Q. What did they say?
A. They said they were going to do well.
Q. Who said that?
A. I cannot positively recollect who it was.
Q. Did they say where they were going to?
A. No, they did not say where they were going to; Samuel Hunt said, " Do not be against going; there is better men than you going; I am going myself."
Q. Did you go?
A. Yes.
Q. Did they take any other person from the house but you?
A. No.
Q. Any arms?
A. A gun.
Q. Whose gun was that?
A. The property of my master.
Q. Mr. Argile's property?
A. Yes.
Q. Did he deliver it up voluntarily, or did they force it from him?
A. They forced it from him.
Q. Where did you go?
A. To John Bonsall's.

Q. Did they get any thing there?
A. His man and his gun.
Q. How far did he live from Mr. Argile's?
A. Perhaps a hundred yards.
Q. Where did they go next?
A. To Peter Cope's.
Q. Did they take any thing from thence?
A. They demanded a man and arms, and they took a gun.
Q. Did you go to many other houses?
A. No.
Q. Did you go to Butterley?
A. Yes, we went to Butterley.
Q. I will not stop to ask what passed there; there you were halted?
A. Yes.
Q. From thence you went to Ripley?
A. To Greenwich.
Q. And so on to Ripley?
A. Yes.
Q. Then to Codnor?
A. Yes.
Q. Did any other persons join you, before you got to Codnor?
A. No.
Q. Where did that party join you?
A. At Codnor.
Q. Where did that party come from?
A. From Swanwick, I suppose.
Q. What house did your party go to at Codnor?
A. Mr. Clark's.
Q. What was the sign?
A. I do not know.
Q. That is not the Glass House, I believe?
A. No.
Q. Did you afterwards go to Langley mill?
A. Yes.
Q. Were you halted there?
A. Yes.

Q. Did you see any thing of the prisoner, George Weightman?

A. Yes.

Q. Was he on foot or on horseback?

A. On horseback.

Q. Which road had he come?

A. He had come from towards Nottingham.

Q. Were you in rank at the time he came?

A. Yes.

Q. Did you hear him say any thing?

A. Yes.

Q. What did you hear him say?

A. He said, " All is well at Nottingham; rush on, rush on my lads, they are at it now at Nottingham, and the job is nearly done."

Q. After he had said this, where did he go?

A. He went into the yard of the public house.

Q. With whom?

A. I did not see.

Q. Did you see Brandreth the captain?

A. I cannot say as to him.

Q. Was any thing said, by any body, as to what they were doing at Nottingham, after he had gone into the yard?

A. No.

Q. You then marched on with them?

A. Yes.

Q. Where did you march to?

A. To Eastwood.

Q. At Eastwood you took an opportunity of escaping?

A. No, I offered to do so.

Q. Could you do it?

A. No.

Q. When did you escape?

A. I escaped the other side of Eastwood common.

Hugh Booth sworn.

Examined by Mr. Reynolds.

Q. Are you a wheelwright?

A. Yes.

Q. On the 9th of June did you live at Pentridge-lane-end with your father?
A. Yes.
Q. About what hour?
A. Between twelve and one.
Q. What disturbed you?
A. A party of men.
Q. What did they do?
A. They came and knocked at the door.
Q. Did you get up?
A. Yes.
Q. Did you go down stairs?
A. Yes.
Q. When you got down stairs, who was the first man you saw?
A. Samuel Hunt.
Q. Was he armed with any thing?
A. Yes.
Q. What with?
A. With a pike.
Q. Whom else did you see?
A. I saw Joseph Topham.
Q. Was Joseph Topham armed?
A. Yes.
Q. Whom else did you see?
A. There were many others that I did not know.
Q. Were you forced to go with them?
A. Yes.
Q. Did you go to John Turner's in Pentridge-lane?
A. Yes.
A. Did you hear any body say any thing there?
A. Yes.
Q. Whom?
A. Joseph Topham.
Q. What did he say?
A. He asked John Turner to get up.
Q. Did they get Turner away?
A. No, they did not.

Q. Did you go on to Anthony Storer's?
A. Yes.
Q. Did you see John Storer?
A. I saw him in the ranks.
Q. In going into the village of Pentridge, did you hear any of the party say any thing?
A. Yes.
Q. Who was it?
A. Isaac Ludlam.
Q. What did you hear him say?
A. "It is brought to a head at last; we are going to Nottingham, there will be a parliament formed there."
Q. Did he say any thing else?
A. He said they were going to guard it.
Q. Did they go to Nathaniel Walter's afterwards?
A. Yes.
Q. Was he fetched out?
A. No.
Q. Did they go up to John White's?
A. Yes.
Q. Did you go with them there?
A. No.
Q. Did you make any further enquiry of Isaac Ludlam?
A. I asked him where we were going.
Q. Did he make any further answer?
A. He said that they were going to Nottingham.
Q. Do you know Manchester Turner?
A. No.
Q. Did you see a person with one eye?
A. I did not see him; I saw a person with a blue coat and blue trowsers, who carried a sword.
Q. Did he say any thing?
A. Yes.
Q. What did he say?
A. He said they were going to Nottingham to unload the burthen England had so long undergone.
Q. Were you put into the ranks?
A. Yes.
Q. Did you go on to Pentridge?
A. Yes.

Q. Do you know Ann Viton?
A. Yes.
Q. She lives at Pentridge?
A. Yes.
Q. Did you stop there?
A. Yes.
Q. Did you hear any thing said there?
A. I heard Joseph Topham say, here are John Bacon and George, we will have both them out.
Q. Did any of the party go up to Viton's?
A. Yes.
Q. Who?
A. The Nottingham captain.
Q. Brandreth?
A. Yes; William Turner and Joseph Topham, went towards Viton's door.
Q. Did you see whether they went in or not?
A. No, I did not.
Q. Did you see any body standing at her door?
A. No.
Q. Where was Samuel Hunt?
A. I do not know.
Q. When you were at Benjamin Topham's, did you hear any thing said about the engine?
A. Yes.
Q. What was said about the engine?
A. I heard one of the party say, here is our master's foreman down at the engine, we will go and fetch him up.
Q. Did you hear any of the party say any thing to that?
A. Samuel Hunt said, I will go with you.
Q. Did you go on to old Joseph Weightman's?
A. Yes.
Q. Did you go to James Booth's?
A. Yes.
Q. You mean you and the others?
A. Yes.
Q. At James Booth's was any thing taken away?
A. I did not see any thing.

Q. Did you go to George Topham's?
A. Yes.
Q. Did you stop there?
A. Yes.
Q. Was any thing done there?
A. The captain said, bring me a ringer, and take in Ben here.
Q. The Nottingham captain, Brandreth?
A. Yes.
Q. What is a ringer?
A. An iron bar.
Q. Was any thing done there?
A. I did not see any thing.
Q. You went afterwards to William Booth's?
A. Yes.
Q. To any other places?
A. No.
Q. Did you see any thing of George Weightman?
A. Yes.
Q. Where did you first see him?
A. I saw him at William Booth's, against William Booth's gate.
Q. Was he walking, or what?
A. He was leading a pony.
Q. Did you hear the party say any thing about him or his pony?
A. No; John Storer was upon the pony.
Q. Did you afterwards see any body else upon the pony?
A. I saw George Weightman afterwards upon the pony.
Q. Did he go away?
A. Yes.
Q. Was any thing said by the party as to where he was gone?
A. I did not hear any thing.
Q. You went on to the Butterley works?
A. Yes.
Q. After you had gone from Butterley, did any other

persons join you?

A. I went no further than Butterley.

Q. You got into the office?

A. Yes, I did.

Q. Besides those you have mentioned, whom else did you see there; did you see William Ludlam?

A. Yes.

Q. Joseph Savage?

A. Yes.

Q. Whom else did you see, Joseph Taylor?

A. Yes.

Q. Benjamin Taylor?

A. Yes.

Q. James Taylor?

A. Yes.

Q. Alexander Johnson?

A. Yes.

Q. You have mentioned George Weightman, any other Weightman?

A. Joseph Weightman, William Weightman, and Thomas Weightman.

Q. Do you know a person of the name of Samuel Walters, or Dudley?

A. Yes; I saw him.

Q. He was of the party?

A. Yes, he was.

Q. Were those persons armed?

A. Yes.

Q. All.

A. Yes.

Mr. John Storer sworn.

Examined by Mr. Richardson.

Q. I believe you are a farmer at Pentridge-lane-end?

A. Yes.

Q. The son of Anthony Storer?

A. Yes.

Q. Were you disturbed at any time on the night of the 9th of June, and by what?

A. By a body of armed men.

Q. Doing what; how did they disturb you?

A. They presented guns at me.

Q. Did you hear any noise first of all?

A. Yes, a violent knocking at the door.

Q. Did they say any thing?

A. Yes.

Q. What did they say?

A. They said, " damn your eyes, come and go with us, or we will shoot you."

Q. Did you go to the window to look out?

A. Yes, I did.

Q. Did you see any number of armed men when you looked out of the window?

A. Yes, I saw twelve or fifteen.

Q. Did they do or say any thing to you at that time?

A. They said, they would shoot me if I would not go with them.

Q. Did they or you say any thing more?

A. I asked them if there was no excuse; they said, no.

Q. What was further said?

A. They said, the captain had shot Hepworth's man, and all must go, or be shot.

Q. In consequence of the threats used to you, did you come down and join them?

A. Yes, I did.

Q. Did they demand your arms?

A. Yes; they demanded my gun, or they would shoot me, and all in the house.

Q. Was any thing said about ammunition?

A. They asked me if the gun was loaded? I told them not; they asked me if I had any shot and powder? I told them I had a little shot; they said, it did not *mean*, they should soon have plenty of ammunition.

Q. Did you bring your gun with you when you went out?

A. Yes, I took an old gun with me.

Q. I believe you pretended to be sick?

A. I told them I had been very unwell the day before, and was not fit to go with them, and could not carry the gun; they said, it must go by the baggage.

Q. What did you say to that?

A. I asked them where the baggage was.

Q. What answer did they make?

A. That they had not any, but soon should have.

Q. Did you ask any question about what their object was, or where they were going to?

A. I asked them where they were going to.

Q. What answer was given?

A. They said, to Nottingham; that there was a general rising; that twenty-five or thirty thousand were coming from Sheffield; that several hundred thousand would be assembled that day; that liberty would be gained; and an end of slavery.

Q. Did you go with them into Pentridge-lane?

A. Yes, I did.

Q. Was the body there formed into ranks?

A. No; they waited for the captain and the main body coming from the lane end.

Q. Did the captain and the main body come and join them?

A. Yes, they came up.

Q. What was then done?

A. The captain ordered them to fall in three deep.

Q. Was that done?

A. Yes.

Q. What else was done?

A. He asked if there were any men who could do their duty, or who had been in the militia; if there was, they must fall out.

Q. Did any fall out in consequence of that?

A. I believe some did.

Q. Was the body formed three deep?

A. It was.

Q. Were there any persons who acted as officers?

A. Yes.

Q. Was there any rear guard?

A. There was an advance and rear guard appointed.

Q. Being formed, did you, by the captain's order, march to Pentridge?

A. We did.

Q. Were houses attacked there?

A. Different houses were broken open, and men and guns taken out.

Q. Who were the active persons employed?

A. Jeremiah Brandreth.

Q. Any others?

A. A young man he called Manchester Turner, William Turner, Isaac Ludlam; George Weightman the prisoner appeared very active.

Q. Any other in particular?

A. Yes, several more; Samuel Hunt and others.

Q. Active in what you have been mentioning; attacking the houses, and taking the guns and the men.

A. Yes.

Q. At Pentridge you contrived to effect your escape?

A. Yes, I feigned myself ill.

Q. After being threatened very hard, you were permitted to make your escape?

A. Yes.

Q. Did this body of armed men march away from Pentridge soon after?

A. They did.

Q. Soon after they were gone, did you go to William Weightman's house?

A. Yes, I did.

Q. You went in company with William Booth, I believe?

A. Yes.

Q. Did you find any thing there?

A. There was a bag of bullets.

Q. Of what size or weight?

A. Of different sizes; I thought about four or five stone weight.

Q. Did William Weightman say any thing to you about them?

A. He said he must follow with the bullets.

Q. Follow whom?

A. Follow the armed men.

Q. What did William Booth and yourself do, in consequence?

A. We advised him not, but to hide them and himself too; he said he must take them, or he should be shot.

Q. Did you go for a constable?

A. Yes, I went with Booth to Edmund Clarke, a constable.

Q. To fetch him?

A. Yes.

Q. In order to prevent his carrying the bullets?

A. Yes, to take them away.

Q. Did you return with the constable to William Weightman's house?

A. Yes.

Q. Where you had seen the bullets?

A. Yes.

Q. Could you get into it?

A. We did not go in; his wife stood at the door, and held it in her hand.

Q. Could you find either William Weightman or the bullets?

A. No; she said the bullets were gone.

Q. You did not see them, or William Weightman?

A. No.

Q. How long might you have been absent in going for the constable and returning?

A. Not more than ten minutes.

Cross-examined by Mr. Denman.

Q. You pretended to be ill, you say?

A. Yes.

Q. In consequence of your appearing to be ill, did some of those persons hold you upon the pony?

A. Yes.

Q. Do you recollect who did that?
A. George Weightman was one.

William Shipman sworn.

Examined by Mr. J. Balguy.

Q. Were you in the service of Mr. Samuel Fletcher, in the month of June last?
A. Yes.
Q. He lives at Pentridge-lane-end?
A. Yes.
Q. Do you remember being disturbed on the night of the 9th of June?
A. Yes.
Q. What disturbed you?
A. A knocking at the door.
Q. What time of the night?
A. About twelve o'clock.
Q. Did you get up?
A. Yes.
Q. Whom did you find there?
A. Joseph Topham.
Q. Did you find many persons there?
A. Yes.
Q. Armed or unarmed?
A. They were armed.
Q. What did they want?
A. They wanted a man and a gun.
Q. Did they take a gun?
A. Yes; I gave it them through the window.
Q. Did they force you to join them?
A. Yes.
Q. When you joined them, how many persons did you find in that body?
A. I can hardly answer; there were twelve or thirteen.
Q. When you got into the lane, how many were there, thirty or forty?
A. Yes, I dare say there were.
Q. Did you go with them to Pentridge town?
A. Yes.

Q. When you got to Pentridge town, do you remember seeing the prisoner, George Weightman?

A. Yes.

Q. Had he marched with you to Pentridge town, or did he join you there?

A. I did not see him till we got to the bottom of Pentridge town?

Q. Were you in ranks at the time?

A. Yes.

Q. Where did you see the prisoner?

A. The first that I saw of him was at the bottom of Pentridge.

Q. Were you marching on, or were you halting at the time?

A. We were halted.

Q. Was he in the ranks himself, or standing by the side of the ranks?

A. He was by the side of the ranks when I saw him.

Q. Do you remember a person of the name of Tapleton coming up to the prisoner, and speaking to him?

A. Yes.

Q. What did he say to him?

A. He told him there were two barrels of gunpowder in Mr. Harvey's warehouse at Heage, but they had not strength enough to get it out.

Q. Did the prisoner say any thing to him?

A. I did not hear him.

Q. Do you remember going on to James Walters's?

A. No.

Q. In Pentridge?

A. No, I went near to James Walters's.

Q. When you were near to James Walters's, did you see the prisoner?

A. Yes.

Q. Did you hear him say any thing at that time?

A. Yes, he came into the house I was in, to light a candle.

Q. What house was that?

A. Thomas Shipman's.

Q. How far was that from Walters's house?
A. About twenty yards.
Q. What did he say when he came to light the candle?
A. He said, 'well, lads, we are going to draw the badger?'
Q. Had they before been talking of going to Walters's house, and taking Walters out of it?
A. I had not heard that.
Q. I believe you went with this party as far as Langley mill?
A. Yes, to Kimberley.
Q. Do you remember after you had en the prisoner in Shipman's house, seeing the prisoner again?
A. Yes.
Q. Where was that?
A. At Mr. Booth's in Pentridge.
Q. Did you see him take Booth's pony?
A. No.
Q. Did you see him on the pony?
A. Yes.
Q. Did he ride away from you on the pony?
A. Yes, he rode down towards Butterley.
Q. Is that in the road towards Nottingham?
A. Yes.
Q. I think you say you contined with those persons to Kimberley?
A. Yes.
Q. How far is that from Nottingham?
A. I do not know, about five miles, I think.
Q. When was the next time that you saw the prisoner?
A. At Langley mill.
Q. Was he on horseback at that time?
A. Yes.
Q. Which way was he riding?
A. Towards us.
Q. You were marching towards Nottingham, and he was riding as from Nottingham, and met you?
A. Yes.
Q. Were you marching in ranks at that time?
A. Yes; some of us, not all.
Q. Did you hear the the prisoner say any thing?
A. Yes.

Q. What did you hear him say?
A. They *axed* how they were going on?
Q. How they were going on, where?
A. At Nottingham.
Q. What did he say to that?
A. He said, well, the soldiers were in the barracks, the town was taken, we should march forwards, and we should have nothing to do when we got there.

Samuel Clifton sworn.

Examined by Mr. Solicitor General.

Q. I believe you live near Kimberley?
A. Yes.
Q. Does your house adjoin the turnpike road?
A. It is close by the turnpike road.
Q. How far is that from Nottingham?
A. Six miles; a trifle above six miles.
Q. Is that the road from Pentridge and Ripley to Nottingham?
A. It is the road from Ripley.
Q. Do you know Langley mill?
A. Yes.
Q. It is the road leading from Langley mill to Nottingham?
A. Yes.
Q. Early on Tuesday the 10th of June, do you recollect seeing any person going along the road on a pony?
A. To the best of my knowledge about five o'clock in the morning, it was a wet morning; I had no clock in the house.
Q. Were you getting up at the time?
A. I was just turning out to open my window shutters.
Q. What sort of a person was it upon the pony?
A. A stout well-built man.
Q. How was he dressed?
A. In a kind of a slop dress with trowsers.
Q. Which way was he going?
A. Towards Nottingham.
Q. Did he say any thing to you?
A. He asked me if I had seen a body of men go by.

Q. What answer did you make to that?

A. I told him no, that I was but just got up.

Q. What did he say to that?

A. He told me I should soon see them coming by.

Q. What did you say to him then?

A. I asked him what was amiss; and he told me he supposed Nottingham was taken by that time;—in the next place, I asked him where he was going; he said he was going to Nottingham for orders to know if he was to bring the men up.

Q. What more did you say to him?

A. I asked him the sense of it, and he said, "liberty," and rode off.

Q. Which way did he ride off?

A. Towards Nottingham.

Q. Did you see the same man again in the course of that morning?

A. I went and reported the circumstance.

Q. You went and reported the circumstance to somebody; I must not ask you the particulars of that: did you see the same man again in the course of that morning?

A. In the course of an hour and a half, I met the same man on his return; I had no watch in my pocket, but I suppose it was about that time.

Q. Where were you?

A. Near the tan yard.

Q. Near Kimberley?

A. About a quarter of a mile from our house.

Q. Nearer Nottingham?

A. Nearer Ripley road.

Q. Did you ask him any thing on his return?

A. I asked him how they were getting on in Nottingham; he told me they had been at it all night, but no lives lost. I asked him if the soldiers were out of the barracks, he said they durst not come out.

Q. Did he say any thing more?

A. I will repeat the whole: I asked him if he was a servant or a neighbour; he said, no; he came from Pentridge, he had orders to bring his men up, and he rode off towards Ripley.

Mr. George Goodwin sworn.

Examined by Mr. Serjeant Vaughan.

Q. I believe you were the managing clerk at the Butterley works, in the month of June last?

A. I was.

Q. Tell me on what day preceding the 9th of June, you swore in any special constables?

A. On the 7th, the Saturday preceding?

Q. How many did you swear in?

A. About a hundred and fifteen, or a hundred and sixteen.

Q. On the evening of the 9th or the morning of the 10th, did you see any persons assembled.

A. On the morning of the 10th, a little after three o'clock, I saw the prisoner Weightman.

Q. Did you know him before that time?

A. I did.

Q. What was he doing, on foot or on horseback?

A. He was on horseback, riding from Pentridge towards Nottingham, past the Butterley works.

Q. Did you speak to him?

A. I did; I called to him to stop.

Q. Did he make you any answer?

A. He did not; he merely turned his head round and rode off.

Q. In what direction?

A. In the direction of Nottingham.

Q. How soon after he had rode off, did you see any body of persons coming towards your works?

A. Very soon afterwards; almost immediately afterwards; in the course of a few minutes.

Q. What did you see?

A. A body of men marching on the road from Pentridge.

Q. Were they armed?

A. They were armed; the greater part with guns, and some with pikes, and there were a few that had no arms.

Q. Were they marching orderly?

A. They were marching in regular military order, like a body of soldiers.

Q. When they came to your works did they stop?

A. They marched up to the gates of the iron works, which were closed, and there the captain halted and fronted.

Q. Who gave the order?

A. The captain, Brandreth; "Halt! to the right face, front!"

Q. Upon that being done, what followed?

A. I said, "What do you want; what is your object here;" he said, "We want your men."

Q. The captain said that?

A. Yes; I said, you shall not have one of them; you are too many already, except you were going for a better purpose; I bid them disperse, and told them them the law would be too strong for them, that they were going with halters about their necks, and would all be hanged.

Q. What became of them, after some further conversation?

A. The captain gave them the word "March!" and they went away.

Q. After they were gone, were they followed by any other body of persons?

A. There was another body came in about a quarter of an hour.

Q. How many?

A. About forty, I should think; but I was not very near them; they did not come so far as the office.

Q. Was that body armed?

A. They were, as far as I could see.

Q. After that body had passed, were they followed by any other individual that you knew?

A. They were; in about half an hour William Weightman, the brother of the prisoner, and a young man of the name of Taylor, came; Joseph Weightman was on horseback.

Q. Did you stop Weightman, and take any thing from

him?

A. I stopped him, and took from him a bag of bullets.

Q. Is that the bag?

A. That is the bag.

Q. Do you know what weight of bullets there were?

A. About eighty-four pounds weight.

Q. Of different sizes?

A. Yes, there are a great variety of sizes, for various bores.

Q. Did you find any thing besides bullets?

A. There are moulds for making cartridges, and paper.

Q. Was there any smaller bag within the bag?

A. There was a smaller bag within the larger bag; a stocking foot, or something of that kind—this is it. *(producing it.)*

Q. What did that contain?

A. There were bullets in that.

Q. Do you know how many rounds of ball there are?

A. I think there may be from fifteen hundred to two thousand balls of different sizes; I cannot say exactly, but that is my guess.

Q. You have told us before, you had sworn in special constables; had you made any preparations before hand for defending your works?

A. We had on the Monday afternoon; we had caused a few pikes to be made; we expected from the appearances there would be a disturbance.

Cross-examined by Mr. Denman.

Q. How long have you known this young man?

A. Several years.

Q. As many as ten?

A. Not so many as ten, I should think.

Q. Do you know what character he has borne, as a peaceable, sober, quiet man?

A. I do not know much of his character; he was in our service for some time; he then behaved properly.

Q. You do not know what his general character has been since that?

A. I do not know further, than his character while he was with us.

William Roper sworn.

Examined by Mr. Clarke.

Q. Where do you live?

A. At the race stand on Nottingham Forest.

Q. Were you coming home from Nottingham to your own house on Monday night, the 9th of June?

A. Yes.

Q. About what time?

A. About half past eleven o'clock.

Q. Did you see any persons upon the Forest as you came along?

A. Yes.

Q. Many?

A. I saw two men first on the race course, and two afterwards; after that considerably more.

Q. Did you afterwards see any other men?

A. Yes.

Q. How many do you think?

A. I should suppose about a hundred.

Q. How were they when you first saw them; standing still, or going on?

A. Standing still.

Q. Drawn up in line?

A. Yes.

Q. Had any of them any thing with them?

A. Yes.

Q. What was it?

A. Long poles in their hands; those to the right of the line, not all of them.

Q. How many might there be with poles of those you saw?

A. About a dozen.

Q. Were they such sort of poles as those upon the table?

A. Yes.

Q. Did you go into your own house?

A. Yes.

Q. Did you see any thing more of those men;

A. Yes.

Q. Where?

A. Under the piazzas in front of the stand.

Q. Under the piazzas in front of your house?

A. Yes.

Q. Did they say any thing to you?

A. I went out of the house, and saw the people come; and after that I went in, and locked the door; about one o'clock there was a violent knocking at the door; I went to the door, and asked them what they wanted; they asked me if I had got any fire-arms in the house; I told them, yes, I had; they told me I must deliver them up to them; I told them I would not; they said, if I would not, they should be under the necessity of breaking the door open, and taking them by force.

Q. What did you say to that?

A. I told them, if they did, I would blow the first man's brains out that entered.

Q. Did you hear them say any thing upon that?

A. Yes; they said, would I? I said, yes; they then called the men with the fire-arms.

Q. What did they say?

A. A man at the door said, " the men with the fire-arms come forward!" The place is paved with flag stones; I heard a bustle upon the floor, and then I heard one come forward, who asked how many arms I had; I told them I had two, a rifle piece and a fusee. They asked me if I would give them to them; I told them, no; they asked me, if I would sell them; I told them, no, I would neither sell them nor give them, I would not part with them.

Q. Did they ask any other questions?

A. No, I do not recollect any others.

Q. What became of them?

A. They asked me if I had not more; I told them, no, I had not; and then they told me, they understood there were some arms lodged there; I told them there were no arms there but my own; but if they disputed my word, if they would draw back, and select one of their party, he should come into the house, but I told them if a second came in, that I would run him through, that I was prepared for them.

Q. About what o'clock was it when they left the piazzas.
A. About two.
Q. You saw no more of them?
A. No.
Q. Did you find that they left any thing behind them?
A. I went out at three o'clock in the morning, and found a pole at the door.
Q. That sort of pole?
A. Not so good as one of those.

Captain Frederick Charles Philips sworn.

Examined by Mr. Gurney.

Q. I believe you are a Captain in the 15th Hussars?
A. I am.
Q. On Monday the 9th of June last, were you stationed at Nottingham barracks?
A. I was.
Q. In the evening of that day, was Nottingham in a state of quiet, or of commotion?
A. I understood it was in a state of commotion; there were troops sent for from the barracks, by the Magistrate.
Q. When your troops arrived, I believe the mob had dispersed?
A. They had dispersed; we were kept there about half an hour.
Q. You went into the town with the troops, and found the tumult had subsided?
A. Yes; and we then returned to the barracks.
Q. In consequence of symptoms that appeared, was there a Magistrate in the barracks all night?
A. Yes, Mr. Kirkby staid there all night.
Q. At an early hour in the morning did any alarm reach the barracks, as to what was going on elsewhere?

A. I was ordered out at half-past six in the morning to go with Mr. Rolleston and Mr. Mundy, who were Magistrates.

Q. Besides your cavalry, was there a body of infantry?

A. Not at that time; there was at night.

Q. Did you go on the road towards Eastwood?

A. Yes.

Q. As you approached Eastwood, did you observe some men in a state of dispersion?

A. I observed some men making their escape to the left of the road, armed with pikes.

Q. Some of them were pursued, and then you proceeded straight forwards?

A. Some were; and then we proceeded on through Eastwood.

Q. Did you find any body in the road beyond Eastwood?

A. Between Langley mill and Eastwood, there was a party consisting of about sixty.

Q. Was that party armed?

A. Chiefly, I think.

Q. Did it appear to have a leader?

A. There did; there appeared to be a man, whom I took to be their leader, attempting to form them upon the road.

Q. Do you mean, to form them to receive the charge of your cavalry?

A. It appeared so to me.

Q. Did they wait to receive the charge of your cavalry?

A. No, they dispersed; they paid no attention to this man, and they ran across the fields.

Q. Did you and the Magistrates and the soldiers pursue, and take all the prisoners you could?

A. We did; we took about six and thirty.

Q. As those persons fled, did many of them throw away their arms?

A. Most of them threw away their arms; five or six of the men were taken with arms in their hands; the rest of them threw them away?

Q. Did your men pick up a considerable number of muskets and pikes?

A. Yes, they did.

Q. Those are part of them, I believe?

A. Yes, those are part of them.

Q. There are a great many more in the adjoining room, I believe?

A. Yes, there are.

Q. The guns were loaded, I believe?

A. Yes, they were; at least I saw three or four of them that were.

Mr. Attorney General. That, my Lord, is the case of the Crown.

Mr. CROSS.

May it please your Lordships.

Gentlemen,

YOU are the fourth Jury who, in the course of ten days, have been impanelled, after more than an hundred challenges on the part of the Accused, to try the truth of the allegations contained in this Indictment; and although you have been properly cautioned, by the Solicitor General, to forget the former verdicts, it is impossible for me to forget, that the three Juries who have preceded you, have successively, with the unanimous concurrence of the learned Judges, found the allegations in the Indictment to be proved; that there has been an Insurrection, which had for its object nothing less than the overthrow of the Constitution and Government of the Realm, and that Treason has been committed;—what then remains to his Counsel for discussion, but the question, whether the individual now upon his trial, took a voluntary and active part in the commission of that treason;—alas! Gentlemen, that he did so, has been proved by at least a dozen witnesses, and we have none to contradict them, nor can we refute their testimony. Gentlemen, under these painful circumstances, I trust my learned friend, and myself, will not be suspected of any dereliction of our duty, when we forbear to controvert those facts which have been so repeatedly found to be proved. I trust, Gentlemen, that we have fully and faithfully discharged that duty, which the Court, at the request of all the prisoners, has been pleased to assign to us; we have endeavoured to bring into their service, all the means that nature, education, or experience, have supplied to us; we have, I trust, left nothing undone, that it was in our power to do in their behalf;—for myself, I beg leave to say, this has been the most arduous and the most anxious labour of my life. Deeply have I commiserated the condition of these misguided men; I am persuaded, and I am confident every one who has heard these trials, is persuaded, that they are not the authors of this Treason;—it originated not with them,—they are the ignorant and deluded instruments of Traitors, more wicked, but more wary, than themselves; but, Gentlemen, if the sword of justice must fall somewhere, and somewhere I fear it must, may the blood of the unhappy victims lie heavy on the heads of those, by whom, in a season of adversity and discontent, they have been seduced from their allegiance.

Gentlemen, with regard to the wretched man who stands before you at the bar, we can only implore for him the mercy of the Crown;—we can only implore the recommendation of those, whose recommendation perhaps, on such an occasion, may be listened to, and may be of effect;—we hope there are circumstances, in his case, which may lead to some distinction in his favour; his was but a subordinate part in these outrages; and you will not fail to recollect with what generosity of heart he assisted the escape of one, who was forced against his will to take a part in them; his appearance and demeanour you yourselves have had an opportunity of judging of; he is the parent of an infant family, now with their anxious mother, waiting, with throbbing hearts, the event of your decision; he is but at an early period of life, he might yet learn a salutary lesson from these proceedings, and yet become an useful and industrious, and a loyal member of the community;—such, these unhappy transactions found him, and such, he would still have been, if he had not been thus basely seduced from his allegiance. To those seductions, which have misled so many loyal people from their duty, I have on a former occasion alluded; I shall do no more than allude to them at present;—my unfortunate client casts himself, with all humility and contrition, for mercy, at the foot of that Throne he has assaulted, where mercy, on just occasions, is never sought in vain; for mercy alone I can ask, and that mercy, I confidently hope, may be extended to him.

Gentlemen, this day brings to a close, another year of the long and glorious reign of our venerable and gracious Sovereign; would to God it might close these unhappy proceedings! may the next year commence a new era of domestic peace and civil union!—may this great Nation henceforth enjoy a long continuance of that prosperity, which nothing but civil discord can prevent!—A salutary lesson has, I am sure, been given to the Public, by these proceedings; and I trust all, who have witnessed them, will retire in admiration, of the inflexible integrity, the wisdom, the supremacy, and the majesty of the Law of England, to which the prince and the people owe equal homage and subjection.

EVIDENCE FOR THE PRISONER.

Samuel Curzon, sworn.

Examined by Mr. Denman.

Q. How long have you known the prisoner George Weightman?

A. Three years and better; he has lodged at my house at different times for three years; not three years together, but at different times.

Q. Have you had an opportunity of knowing what his character has been?

A. Oh yes; he always behaved very well at my house, and paid his way like a man.

Q. Was he always considered a peaceable and quiet man?

A. For any thing I have known.

Q. And you have had an opportunity of knowing?

A. Yes, he has been at my house a deal.

John Smith, sworn.

Examined by Mr. Denman.

Q. How long have you known the prisoner?

A. Something better than ten years; he has worked with me about six years at intervals.

Q. What has his character been?

A. I never saw any thing against him; but he has appeared to be an honourable upright man.

Q. Did you consider him a peaceable, and sober and well conducted man?

A. Yes, I never saw any thing to the contrary.

Edward Clark, sworn.

Examined by Mr. Denman.

Q. I believe you are the constable of Pentridge?

A. Yes.

Q. How long have you known George Weightman?

A. Upwards of twenty years; ever since he was a little boy.

Q. What character has he borne?

A. I never knew any thing against him till this unfortunate affair.

Q. Did he bear a good character as a peaceable and quiet man?

A. Yes, I never heard the contrary; not till this happened.

Mr. DENMAN.

May it please your Lordships,

Gentlemen of the Jury,

I THINK you will agree with me, that it is quite impossible for any counsel, or any man who is concerned in the defence of this unfortunate prisoner, to have an opportunity of addressing the Jury, upon the subject, without exercising that privilege; yet I do feel, after what has been already said to you, by my learned friend, with so much feeling, sense, and truth, that I should be doing something worse than wasting your time, if I were to attempt to add any thing to the impression, which not only his address, but the whole circumstances of this case must have made upon your minds. The cause is over; we do not make the show of an unavailing resistance;—we have cast away our arms;—we cry for mercy! It will be for you to say, when those circumstances are detailed to you by the learned Judge, which have been already proved in evidence, but upon which I really am not competent to observe, whether you do not think that the conduct and character of this unfortunate individual are such, as to entitle him at your hands to that recommendation, which I am sure the Crown would be happy to attend to, if you, under all the circumstances, thought yourselves privileged to give it. I will not detain you longer, Gentlemen, from hearing the evidence: which, I trust, will convince you that you ought to bestow that assistance and that succour, which alone an unfortunate and misguided man is capable of receiving at your hands.

Mr. JUSTICE HOLROYD,

Prisoner at the bar: Now is the time for you to say any thing which you may wish to say in your own defence. You are entitled, if there is any thing you wish to say to the Jury, to say it, although your Counsel have urged what they thought fit. Do you wish to say any thing?

Prisoner. I leave it to my counsel, my Lord.

REPLY.

MR. ATTORNEY GENERAL.

Gentlemen of the Jury,

AFTER what has been said, by both my learned friends, standing as Counsel for the prisoner at the bar, it is impossible that it can be necessary for me to take up many moments of your time, in the few observations that I have to address to you. My learned friend, Mr. Cross, has truly stated to you, that the nature and character of this transaction, generally speaking of it, have been most thoroughly, most anxiously investigated, by the learned Judges and by three former Juries; that the nature and character of the transaction, as constituting the offence of High Treason in somebody, have, after that investigation, been decided, and been decided in a manner, against which no human being, with a reasonable mind, can lift up his voice. Gentlemen, let me do justice, however, to my learned friends, in saying this, that whilst it was possible that argument could be kept up, for the advantage of those for whom they have been counsel, every thing that learning and research—every thing that ingenuity and talent—every thing that eloquence and forcible appeal to the understanding, or passions, of those who were to decide, could be brought into the field, for the advantage of those for whom they have been concerned, has by them been done. I am quite sure that they, when they shall retire ultimately from this place, may go home and lay their hands upon their hearts and say, we have done our duty; for they have done it well.

Gentlemen, as has been truly stated by my learned friend, Mr. Cross, if the character of the transaction itself is decided (and about that there can be no doubt) namely, that these acts, committed with the intentions with which they were committed, amount to the crime of High Treason, the only other question that can remain in the individual case is, whether the particular person standing before you is implicated in those acts, cognizant of the intentions with which they were committed, and a party, and an assistant, and an active partizan, in the commission of those acts. Gentlemen, a body of evidence has been brought before you, which my learned friends have truly stated they can have no means of contradicting, because it is perfectly true, and it is impossible to contradict it, which does bring home to the prisoner at the bar, beyond a doubt, that he was concerned in this transaction; that he was cognizant of the intent of those who were acting at the times about which we have given evidence; that hi mind went along with them, and that he applied all the energy, if I may use the phrase, of which he was capable at the time, in carrying on, as an active partizan, this unfortunate and nefarious transaction.—If that be so (about which no human being can doubt) you have, as Jurymen, to exercise and to perform only your duty of pronouncing, according to the evidence you have heard, that verdict, which can alone be supported by the evidence, namely, that he is Guilty.

Gentlemen, with respect to that forcible appeal, that has been made by my learned friend, to mercy, I, and those who stand here, are not the dispensers of that most excellent quality, when properly exercised, which belongs to man; that must be left to others. My learned friends have introduced one branch, or one species of evidence which, as addressed in one point of view, has been wisely done, and properly done, as in another point of view it can have no effect—I mean, the evidence to this man's character. As applying to the facts of the case, upon which you are to exercise your judgment, it has no weight; and I will tell you why:—In cases in which it is doubtful whether crimes are committed; where there is reasonable doubt or balance of testimony, character may be introduced to shew or to endeavour to shew, the improbability of a person, who has that character, committing the offence;—but when the facts are proved beyond all doubt and dispute; when there is no contradiction in the testimony; when, if what the witnesses have proved, is true, the guilt of the prisoner is apparent, however one may lament that a man, previously of good character, may have committed such a crime; if the crime has been committed, and that is proved, the verdict must follow in consequence of that proof.

Gentlemen, with respect to that which has been addressed to you, upon the subject of recommendation, I have not one word to say upon the subject; that must be matter for your own consideration; that must be matter which must be weighed entirely by others. I will not say one word upon that subject; because whatever I might think about it, as applied to the particular case, unless I were called upon by my duty to step between any human being and mercy, I certainly should abstain from doing it; if I were called upon, I must then perform my duty; but all the duty I have here, is to bring the case against the prisoner at the bar, fairly before your judgment, that, upon that case you may exercise your honest understandings, and pronounce that, which you are bound to do by your general duty as men, and which as jurymen you have bound yourselves to do by the solemn obligation of an oath; pronounce a Verdict according to the Evidence.

SUMMING UP.

Mr. JUSTICE HOLROYD.

Gentlemen of the Jury,

After the very long and patient investigation, which every one must be satisfied has been given, both to the present case, and likewise to those which have preceded it, the judgment of the learned Counsel upon the part of the prisoners, has felt, that it is impossible they can stand against such a body of evidence as has been given against the prisoner at the bar in the present case; for that the facts which are given in evidence, supposing them to be true, and of that no doubt appears to be entertained, but of that, it is your province to judge; that strong body of evidence which has been given, supposing it to be true, is sufficient most clearly and indisputably to establish the crime of High Treason against the prisoner at the bar.

There is not, in law, certainly, any doubt that an insurrection for general public purposes, that is, a rising of a considerable body of people for those purposes, and the attempting to carry them into effect by force of arms, is a levying of war, and is High Treason; and there cannot be the smallest possible doubt that that design which has been spoken of by the different witnesses, supposing it to be true, and you see by how many witnesses it has been confirmed, upon the testimony of the greatest part of whom there does not appear to be the smallest impeachment; supposing the design to exist, there cannot be the least doubt but that such a design, to subvert the Constitution and to depose the Government, is unquestionably High

Treason; no Judge has ever doubted it, either before the revolution of 1688, or since; upon all occasions it has been acted upon, and never questioned by any of them.

Gentlemen, most unquestionably it is my own opinion, and I speak the opinion, I believe, of the rest of the Court, when I say this, respecting the learned Counsel for the prisoner, that no learning, ability, or ingenuity, has been wanting, on their part, or the most strenuous exertions; and that, if any thing more could have been done, with the smallest hope of success, consistently with their duty to you and to the Public, it would have been done; there have been in the preceding cases the most strenuous exertions on the part of the prisoners by their counsel; here they have acted wisely, in endeavouring to put the case upon the mercy of the Crown; for as to mercy, that is the prerogative of the Crown. It is your province, and it is the province of the Court, in stating to you the points of law, and in guiding your decision rightly to the points of fact, to confine ourselves to the law as we find it laid down, and to the facts as they are proved; those alone are the duties of the Court; the only question you have to decide is, whether the prisoner is guilty, or not?

Gentlemen, if you wish it, I will go through the evidence, and state the different points of law, and likewise the different observations upon the facts, how they bear upon the prisoner; in case you are not satisfied, that the charge is proved against him; or if any one of you has a doubt about it;—but if no one of you has the least doubt, it would be an unnecessary waste of your time, and the time of the Country, to be proceeding to recapitulate the evidence, and to make observations upon it If it be in any degree wished for by any one of you, and you think justice will be better executed by you in consequence of my so doing, I am most ready to proceed.

The Jury consulted together.

Lord Chief Baron Richards. Gentlemen, if you have any desire to withdraw, in order to consider whether you wish to have the evidence stated to you, there is not the least objection to it. The learned Judge is very desirous of doing, whatever is considered by you most useful.

Foreman of the Jury. The Gentlemen wish to retire, to consider of their verdict.

Lord Chief Baron Richards, If you wish to retire, to consider of your verdict, perhaps it would be better that you should hear the evidence first.

Foreman of the Jury.—No, my lord, we are all satisfied with the evidence; we have heard the evidence, and would not wish to hinder the Court in hearing it again.

Lord Chief Baron Richards.—Let us understand each other, upon this very important subject; the learned Judge has stated to you, his readiness to read to you all the evidence that has been taken by him; if you have any doubt at all upon the subject of the evidence, it is very fit that you should hear it; if you have no doubt upon the subject of the evidence, then to be sure you need not be troubled with it. Will you have the goodness to consider, whether you wish to hear the evidence or not? You can tell without going out, I should conceive, whether you wish to hear the evidence; you must not go and consider of your verdict out of doors, without knowing what the evidence is.

A Juryman.—We have no doubt upon the evidence.

Lord Chief Baron Richards.—Then if you have no doubt, you may bring in your verdict.

The Jury consulted together.

Foreman of the Jury.—My lord, the Jury seem to wish the evidence to be proceeded in, and commented upon.

A Juryman.—My lord, the Jury are all satisfied; they do not wish to hear the evidence.

Lord Chief Baron Richards.—Are you all of the same opinion, Gentlemen?

The Jury consulted together.

Foreman of the Jury.—We are satisfied, my Lord; we say, that the prisoner is Guilty; but we strongly recommend him to mercy, in consideration of his former character.

The Verdict was recorded, That the Jury found the prisoner GUILTY; that he had no lands, &c. to their knowledge; and that they strongly recommended him to Mercy, in consideration of his former character.

Adjourned to to-morrow morning, nine o'clock.

SPECIAL ASSIZE, DERBY:

Saturday, 25th October, 1817.

Thomas Bacon, John Bacon, Samuel Hunt, Joseph Turner, otherwise called Manchester Turner, Edward Turner, John Onion the elder, John Mac Kesswick, German Buxton, and Josiah Godber, were set to the bar.

MR. DENMAN.

My Lord,

I AM now to make an humble application to the Court, which I trust will meet with attention; it is simply this, that these persons, who have been called up, and pleaded Not Guilty, may be permitted to withdraw that plea, and plead Guilty; and throw themselves upon the merciful consideration of those in whose hands their case is.

Mr. Attorney General. I can make no objection, of course, to what is proposed.

The Prisoners severally pleaded Guilty.

John Moore, Edward Moore, Charles Swaine, John Hill, Joseph Rawson, otherwise Joseph Thorpe, George Brassington, William Hardwick, William Weightman, Alexander Johnson, and Thomas Betterson, were set to the bar.

Mr. Denman. On behalf of these prisoners, I beg leave to submit the like motion, that they may be also permitted to withdraw their plea of Not Guilty, and plead Guilty.

The Prisoners severally pleaded Guilty.

Isaac Ludlam the younger, Samuel Ludlam, William Ludlam, Robert Turner, Joseph Weightman the younger, James Weightman, Thomas Weightman, William Adams, John Wright, Joseph Topham, Thomas Ensor, and Joseph Savage, were set to the bar.

The panel was called; and the first twelve Gentlemen who appeared, were sworn.

THE JURY:

William White.	Thomas Robotham.
Thomas Borough.	Robert Frost.
William Morley.	John Tempest.
William Wilkes.	Thomas Archer.
John Stretton.	Thomas Orme.
Robert Beard.	William Bailey.

The Jury were charged with the prisoners, in the usual form.

MR. ATTORNEY GENERAL.

May it please your Lordship,

Gentlemen of the Jury,

I THINK I see collected in that box, some Gentlemen who have served upon former juries during the trials which have taken place under the commission under which their Lordships are sitting; others, I believe, are in that box, who have not been impanelled upon the former juries, but who probably have heard that, which has been passing during the former trials.

Gentlemen, you who have officiated before, during the existence of this commission, have had a most important, a most anxious, and most painful duty to perform: important, as it affected the community at large, and the prisoners, whose conduct has hitherto been the subject of investigation; anxious, as it related to yourselves, that you might duly, and well, and faithfully exercise that important duty; and painful in the extreme when you came to its ultimate fulfilment and performance, in consequence of your having found yourselves obliged, in the sacred execution of that function, to pronounce some of your fellow subjects guilty of the crimes with which they were charged. To relieve your minds in some degree at the present moment, I will tell you in the outset, of what I have to address to you, which will be very short, that from the exercise of the painful part of your duty, you will upon the present occasion be relieved. Gentlemen, it has been truly said, by a most able writer upon the subject of the criminal law of England, that one of the ends, and final causes of human punishment, is to deter, by the example of the convicted, others from offending in such like cases. I think I cite the very words of that great and eminent writer, Mr. Justice Blackstone. When many persons are engaged together in committing crimes of a public nature, it is absolutely necessary, for the purpose of attaining that end, and final cause, to bring some, and often many of them, to the bar of a criminal court of justice; but when once the period arrives, at which one may hope—may almost confidently hope, that the examples which have been made by conviction, may attain that end; there can be nothing so gratifying as at that time to sheath the sword of justice, and extend the hand of mercy, towards the remainder of the criminals.

Gentlemen, you observe that amongst those unfortunate men who stand at the bar, many are in a very early stage of life; that they are very young; from that which has appeared hitherto, and from the names which have been read to you, you will have discovered, that many of them are connected by ties of relationship to others, who have appeared to be guilty of the offence with which they have been charged; some of them are cousins, others are brothers, others are the nephews of those who have appeared to be most active in this most nefarious scheme; and with respect to two, they are the sons of one of the convicted persons. I am willing to suppose, that without due consideration, which, young as they are, still it was their bounden duty to pay to the obedience of the laws of their country, they have been induced to follow the bad example of others, to whom they would naturally have looked up as patterns of every thing that was good, by way of example, and therefore, have been misled by their examples, in pursuing that course which is charged upon them. Gentlemen, it is for this reason that I have brought them before you this morning; not for the purpose of offering Evidence against them, in order that you may convict, but for the purpose of stating to you, that I will offer no Evidence, in order that you may pronounce a verdict of Acquittal; hoping and trusting, that, so far from this having any improper effect upon their minds, it will restore them back to the bosoms of the families to which they belong, to the friends who may hitherto have had affection and regard for them, and that, being so restored, they may profit by the example, which, from these proceedings, has been set, and become that, which I hope, up to the time when they engaged and embarked in this dangerous and dreadful concern, they were; honest, sober, industrious, religious members of society; and that, from this moment, they will, by their industry, their honesty, and their integrity, endeavour faithfully to perform their duties, in the several stations of life, into which it has pleased God to call them; this I most fervently hope!— And if, hereafter, I should hear that they have done so, that they have become valuable members of society, and that, if it pleases God to prolong their lives, they have, as they advanced in age, given examples to others of steadiness, of sobriety, and of integrity, if I shall hear this, which I hope I shall, I declare I shall derive more gratification from that, which I am doing at this moment, than almost from any previous action of my life.

I have endeavoured, through the course of this proceeding, to perform my duty, as well as my poor talents would enable me, with justice to the Country, and with justice to all who have been brought before you; I can have no object but the welfare of the community; I hope, and I am willing to believe, that the step which I am at present taking, will operate as much to restore the minds of men to a due sense of their obligation to the laws of their country, as any previous step, that in the course of these proceedings, has taken place. I ought to apologize to their Lordships, and to you, for having stated that which I have done, but I have thought it right to state my reasons for the conduct I am pursuing; I may err, for aught I know, in my judgment, but it is the result of serious consideration in my mind, and I think I have come to the right conclusion.

Lord Chief Baron Richards.—Gentlemen of the Jury The Attorney General having, with that humanity which belongs to him, and, I may say, to those whom he represents, here declined to offer any Evidence against the unfortunate Prisoners at the bar, your only duty is, to find them, not guilty.

The Jury, immediately, found the Prisoners, NOT GUILTY.

Clerk of Arraigns. Did the Prisoners, or any of them, fly for it?

Foreman. Not to our knowledge.

Lord Chief Baron Richards. Prisoners: The Jury, because there has been no evidence offered against you on the part of the Crown, have acquitted you. I hope, that you, and every one in Court, heard every word which was addressed by the learned Attorney General to the Jury, and that every word has made its due impression: let me beseech you never to forget the danger which you have now escaped, or the tenderness which enables you to avoid death; for I, who have before me the depositions which have been taken before the magistrates, know, and it is my duty to tell you, that I must have pronounced the sentence of death upon you, if the King's Attorney General had chosen to proceed against you. He has taken compassion upon your youth; he has trusted, that you have been misled by others, to whom you gave improper confidence, and he flatters himself, as I flatter myself, that you will lead more correct and better lives in future. Take warning by what has passed; go home, and thank your God for the mercy which you have received; endeavour to lead sober and religious lives, and strive, day and night, to reform yourselves, and that conduct will render you once more a credit to society, and will enable you to lead happy lives here, and a happy eternity hereafter: Go home and thank God.

Mr. Solicitor General. There has been an Inquisition returned before your Lordships, charging, that some person unknown fired at, and killed Robert Walters, and charging Isaac Ludlam the elder, William Ludlam, William Barker, William Turner, Manchester Turner, and Robert Turner, as principals in the second degree. The first objection to the Inquisition, which I apprehend is fatal to it, is, that there is no proper venue to the allegation of the offence. In the margin there is, " Liberty of the Hundred of Scarsdale, in the county of Derby;" then it goes on, " An Inquisition taken, (and so forth,) within the hundred and county aforesaid, before His Majesty's Coroner for the liberty and hundred aforesaid, on the oaths of twelve persons, who do upon their oaths say, that some person or persons unknown, with force and arms, *at the parish aforesaid*, in the county aforesaid," no parish having been named; I apprehend that is a decisive objection.

Mr. Justice Abbott. No doubt of it.

Mr. Denman. Then, I apprehend, that disposes of all the records before the Court; and I think it may be proper for me to say, from the part I have taken in these Proceedings, that no man can wish more than I do, that all which has fallen from my learned friend should have its due effect on the individuals he has so mercifully discharged; and I trust, if any spirit of disaffection and discontent has pervaded the country, which has produced on their minds something like a perverted allegiance—something like a notion that their neighbours, and those to whom they looked up, had been justified in the proceedings they adopted, it will be destroyed by seeing such a mode of administering the laws, and such a disposition to apply mercy wherever it can be properly applied.

The Prisoners who had been convicted, and those who had pleaded Guilty, were put to the bar, and severally asked by the Clerk of the Arraigns, " What have you to say for yourself, why the Court should not pass sentence of Death upon you, according to law;"—when the following made answers:

Jeremiah Brandreth. I would ask for mercy if mercy can be extended towards me; and I would address you in the words of our Saviour, " if it be possible, let this cup pass from me; but not my will, but your will."

Isaac Ludlam. May it please your Lordships, if you can shew mercy, do, for the sake of my wife and family, whom, I hope, your Lordships will take into consideration, and shew mercy unto me. I hope the Court will in pity remember me, and spare my life; it shall be a life corresponding to the will of God and man; I shall take it as one of the greatest favours my God can grant me.

John Bacon. I hope you will have mercy upon me.

Samuel Hunt. I hope, my Lord will have mercy on me.

Edward Turner. I hope your Lordships will have mercy upon me.

John Onion the elder. I have borne a good character before, and I beg pardon for my offence.

John Mac Kesswick. I earnestly beg their Lordships will extend mercy towards me.

German Buxton. I hope I shall be treated with mercy,

Josiah Godber. I am a poor ignorant man, and I hope your Lordships will have mercy upon me.

John Moore. I hope your Lordships will have mercy upon me.

Edward Moore. I beg that I may be remembered in mercy.

Charles Swaine. Do, my Lord, have mercy upon me.

John Hill. I hope my Lords will shew mercy.

Joseph Rawson. I hope my Lord will have mercy upon me.

George Brassington. I humbly beg their Lordships will extend their mercy towards me.

William Hardwick. I trust I shall have mercy.

William Weightman. Please my Lord to have mercy upon me.

Alexander Johnson. I hope your Lordships will extend mercy to me, for the sake of my parents.

Thomas Bettison. I hope for mercy.

Sentence.

LORD CHIEF BARON RICHARDS.

PRISONERS at the bar: To see so many persons, especially of your description, standing in the miserable condition in which you stand now before me, is indeed most melancholy; and you exhibit to the Public, a spectacle, as afflicting as it is uncommon. I thank God it is very uncommon. It must be most satisfactory to the world, and I hope administer some consolation to you, that you have had every assistance and every advantage that any man labouring under any charge could have wished for. You have been defended by Counsel of your own selection, who, without any the least interruption from any quarter, used every exertion in your favour, which their experience, their learning, and their great abilities could suggest to them;—I am speaking of such of you as persisted in their plea of Not Guilty. You who were tried at all, were tried by several Juries, of as great respectability, as patient, and as attentive, as ever appeared in a British court of justice. During the whole of the investigation which has taken place upon this important and solemn occasion, every attention has been paid by every side, to every thing that belonged to your defence. Those Juries were compelled, by the clearest and most irresistible evidence, to find the four they tried, guilty of High Treason. Those of you who were not tried by the Juries, desired to be at liberty to withdraw your plea of Not Guilty;—you knew that your cases being the same, had been decided by the other cases; and that you were concluded by the verdicts which were given, and the rectitude of which you were obliged to admit;—you were conscious of your guilt, and pleaded Guilty: You are, therefore, all of you, guilty of High Treason, which the indictment charged against you; the highest and greatest offence known to the Law; it indeed in a manner includes every other. Your insurrection, I thank God, did not last long; but whilst it continued, it was marked with violent outrages, and by the murder of a young man, who did not offer even the least appearance of provocation to you; that conduct showed the ferocity of your purpose. Your object was, to wade through the blood of your Countrymen, to extinguish the Law and the Constitution of your Country, and to sacrifice the property, the liberties, and the lives of your fellow subjects, to confusion and anarchy, and the most complete tyranny. God be praised, your purpose failed.

It is not my intention to dwell upon this dreadful picture, which you exhibit; but I trust I may be allowed to express my sincere hope, and my earnest wishes, that the example which you furnish on this important day, may deter others from yielding to the wild and frantic delusions of a rebellious spirit, and frighten others, if there be such, from being instruments in the hands of hellish agitators, if there are any behind, who, to gratify their own malignity, provoke and excite them, and plunge them into ruin in this world, and it is to be feared, in the next also! Let me beseech you to weigh well your conditions; your lives are become forfeit to the violated Laws of your Country; make the most of the small remnant of those lives that you shall enjoy; endeavour to make some compensation to the society which you have injured, and pray God fervently for his forgiveness. I have nothing more to say upon this melancholy occasion, except that I must repeat my sincere wishes, that your example may serve as a great lesson to others; and that the excellent advice which some of you received from Mr. Goodwin, may never be forgotten by others, " That the law is too strong for rebels, and that they always carry the halter about their necks." I hope others, by remembering what passes to-day, may avoid the dreadful situation in which you are placed.

I cannot trust myself with speaking more upon the

subject, but I hasten to pronounce upon you the last and awful sentence of the law; That you, and each of you, be taken from hence to the gaol from whence you came, and from thence be drawn on a hurdle to the place of execution, and be there severally hanged by the neck until you be dead—and that afterwards, your heads shall be severed from your bodies, and your bodies divided into four quarters, shall be disposed of as His Majesty shall direct; and may the Lord God of All Mercies have compassion upon you!

Isaac Ludlam. I hope your Lordships will have mercy upon me.

Lord Chief Baron Richards. Gentlemen of the Jury: Your labours are over; and I think I should not be doing justice to the Jurymen of this County, if I did not, in my own name, and in the name of the learned Judges who surround me, render our thanks to you for your great attention and care. I may venture to say, that I never saw Jurors, to whom I am more obliged to pay every kind of respect and gratitude, than the Juries who have assembled here on this occasion.

On Friday the 7th of November, *Jeremiah Brandreth, William Turner,* and *Isaac Ludlam* the elder, were drawn on a hurdle to a platform erected in front of the County Gaol of *Derby,* where they were hanged until they were dead; when they were cut down, and their heads were severed from their bodies:—His Royal Highness the Prince Regent, acting in the name and on the behalf of His Majesty, having graciously remitted the remainder of their Sentence.

George Weightman, Thomas Bacon, John Bacon, Samuel Hunt, Joseph Turner, otherwise called *Manchester Turner, Edward Turner, John Onion* the elder, *John Mac Kesswick,*

German Buxton, John Hill, and *George Brassington,* received His Majesty's Pardon, upon condition of being transported for life.

Josiah Godber, Joseph Rawson otherwise called *Joseph Thorpe,* and *Thomas Bettison,* received His Majesty's Pardon, upon condition of being transported for fourteen years.

John Moore, received His Majesty's Pardon, upon condition of being imprisoned for two years.

Edward Moore, and *William Weightman,* received His Majesty's Pardon upon condition of being imprisoned for one year.

Charles Swaine, William Hardwick, and *Alexander Johnson,* received His Majesty's Pardon upon condition of being imprisoned for six months.

TABLE of CONTENTS.

VOLUME THE FIRST.

	Page.
PROCEEDINGS on the 26th of July, 1817 The Indictment	3

Wednesday, 15th October.

The JUDGES	15
The Counsel for the Crown and for the Prisoners	ibid.
The Grand Jury	16
THE LORD CHIEF BARON's Address to the Grand Jury	ibid.
The Arraignment of the Prisoners	18

TRIAL OF JEREMIAH BRANDRETH.

Thursday, 16th October.

The Panel of the Petit Jurors, with the Challenges	20
Objection to a Juryman being challenged after the Oath was begun to be administered; and argument thereon	23
The Jury sworn	34
Mr. ATTORNEY GENERAL's Speech in opening the Case	35
Anthony Martin's Examination	59
Shirley Asbury's Examination	73
James Shipman's Examination	85
Henry Tomlinson's Examination	106
Mr. Elijah Hall, senior's Examination	110
Elijah Hall, junior's Examination	116
Isaac Walker's Examination	120

Friday, 17th October.

	Page.
Mrs. Mary Hepworth's Examination	122
Mr. Samuel Fletcher's Examination	125
William Shipman's Examination	127
Henry Hole's Examination	137
William Booth's Examination	150
Mr. George Goodwin's Examination	151
Objection to the admissibility of declarations in the absence of the Prisoner, and Argument thereon	158
Mr. Goodwin's Examination—continued	160
William Roper's Examination	161
Objection to Evidence of Declarations; and Argument thereon	165
William Roper's Examination continued	175
Launcelot Rolleston, Esq's Examination	176
Captain F. C. Philips's Examination	179
Mr. Cross's Speech	182
John Hazard's Examination	210
Mr. Denman's Speech	211
Mr. Solicitor General's Reply	245

Saturday, 18th October.

The Lord Chief Baron's Summing up	270

TRIAL of WILLIAM TURNER.

Monday, 20th October.

Discussion respecting the Publication of the Proceedings in Newspapers	313
The Panel of the Petit Jurors, with the Challenges	319
The Jury sworn	322
Mr. Solicitor General's Speech in opening the Case	ibid.
Anthony Martin's Examination	338
Shirley Asbury's Examination	357
Thomas Turner's Examination	371
Henry Tomlinson's Examination	388

CONTENTS OF VOL. I. 505

Page.

Mr. Elijah Hall, senior's Examination	392
Elijah Hall, junior's Examination	398
Mr. Isaac Walker's Examination	404
Mrs. Mary Hepworth's Examination	407
Joseph Wilkinson's Examination	409
Mr. Samuel Fletcher's Examination	414
William Shipman's Examination	416
Henry Hole's Examination	422
William Booth's Examination	433
Mr. John Storer's Examination	443
Mr. George Goodwin's Examination	451
Mr. George Raynor's Examination	457
William Roper's Examination	462
Captain F. C. Philips's Examination	466
Thomas Hallowes, Esq's Examination	468

Tuesday, 21st October.

Mr. Cross's Speech	470
William Taylor's Examination	486
John Burton's Examination	487
John Armstrong's Examination	ibid.
Mr. Denman's Speech	488

VOLUME THE SECOND.

Trial of WILLIAM TURNER—(continued).

Tuesday, 21st October 1817—(continued.)

Mr. Attorney General's Reply	3
Mr. Justice Dallas's Summing Up	29

CONTENTS OF VOL. II.

Trial of Isaac Ludlam the Elder.

Wednesday, 22d October.

	Page.
The Panel of the Petit Jurors, with the Challenges	75
The Jury sworn	77
Mr. Attorney General's Speech in opening the Case	ibid
Anthony Martin's Examination	95
Shirley Asbury's Examination	110
William Smith's Examination	127
Thomas Turner's Examination	137
Henry Tomlinson's Examination	150
Mr. Elijah Hall, senior's Examination	153
Elijah Hall the Younger's Examination	159
Mr. Isaac Walker's Examination	163
Mrs. Mary Hepworth's Examination	166
Henry Hole's Examination	168
John Dexter's Examination	178
Objection to the Examination of the Witness, as not properly described in the List delivered to the Prisoner, and Argument thereon	179
John Dexter's Examination, continued	182
William Booth's Examination	188
Hugh Booth's Examination	194
Mr. George Goodwin's Examination	200
Mr. John Storer's Examination	206
William Roper's Examination	213
Captain F. C. Philips's Examination	215

Thursday, 23d October.

Mr. Cross's Speech	219
Mr. William Eaton's Examination	231
Mr. Denman's Speech	ibid
Mr. Solicitor General's Reply	270
Mr. Justice Abbott's Summing Up	295

CONTENTS OF VOL. II.

Trial of George Weightman.

	Page.
The Panel of the Petit Jurors with the Challenges	344
The Jury sworn	345
Mr. Solicitor General's Speech, in opening the Case	346
Anthony Martin's Examination	357
Shirley Asbury's Examination	366
James Shipman's Examination	377
Thomas Turner's Examination	380

Friday 24th October.

Henry Tomlinson's Examination	393
Mr. Henry Bestwick's Examination	397
Henry Taylor's Examination	399
Samuel Taylor's Examination	405
William Smith's Examination	410
Samuel Marriott's Examination	415
Mr. Elijah Hall the Elder's Examination	417
Elijah Hall the Younger's Examination	421
Mr. Isaac Walker's Examination	425
Mrs. Mary Hepworth's Examination	427
Samuel Lever's Examination	428
William Booth's Examination	433
Henry Hole's Examination	441
Charles Walter's Examination	452
Hugh Booth's Examination	456
Mr. John Storer's Examination	461
William Shipman's Examination	466
Samuel Clifton's Examination	469
Mr. George Goodwin's Examination	471
William Roper's Examination	474
Captain F. C. Philips's Examination	476
Mr. Cross's Speech	479
Samuel Curzon's Examination	481
John Smith's Examination	ibid
Edward Clark's Examination	482
Mr. Denman's Speech	ibid
Mr. Attorney General's Reply	484
Mr. Justice Holroyd's Summing Up	487

Lightning Source UK Ltd.
Milton Keynes UK
UKOW041050031011

179677UK00004B/24/P